THE NOBEL PRIZE WINNERS

Physics

THE NOBEL PRIZE WINNERS

Physics

Volume 2
1938 – 1967

Edited by
FRANK N. MAGILL

SALEM PRESS
Pasadena, California   Englewood Cliffs, New Jersey

03779506

PHYSICS

Library of Congress Cataloging-in-Publication Data
The Nobel Prize winners.
Includes bibliographies and indexes.
Contents: v. 1. 1901-1937 — v. 2. 1938-1967 — v. 3. 1968-
1988.
1. Physicists-Biography. 2. Nobel prizes.
[1. Physicists-Biography. 2. Nobel prizes]
I. Magill, Frank Northen, 1907-
QC15.N63   1989   530'.092'2-dc19   89-6409
[B]
[920]
ISBN 0-89356-557-1 (set)
ISBN 0-89356-559-8 (volume 2)

PRINTED IN THE UNITED STATES OF AMERICA

CONTENTS

page

Alphabetical List of Nobel Prize Winners................................ xxv
Enrico Fermi 471
Ernest Orlando Lawrence 483
Otto Stern 495
Isidor Isaac Rabi 505
Wolfgang Pauli 517
Percy Williams Bridgman 527
Sir Edward Victor Appleton 537
Patrick M. S. Blackett 549
Hideki Yukawa 561
Cecil Frank Powell... 571
Sir John Douglas Cockcroft... 579
Ernest Thomas Sinton Walton 591
Felix Bloch 601
Edward Mills Purcell... 611
Frits Zernike 621
Max Born.. 629
Walther Bothe 643
Willis Eugene Lamb, Jr. 653
Polykarp Kusch 663
William Shockley 673
John Bardeen 683
Walter H. Brattain 695
Chen Ning Yang 705
Tsung-Dao Lee 715
Pavel Alekseyevich Cherenkov 727
Ilya Mikhailovich Frank 735
Igor Yevgenyevich Tamm.. 745
Emilio Gino Segrè 755
Owen Chamberlain 767
Donald A. Glaser 777
Robert Hofstadter 787
Rudolf Ludwig Mössbauer 797
Lev Davidovich Landau.. 809
Eugene Paul Wigner 819
Maria Goeppert Mayer 829
J. Hans D. Jensen.. 841
Charles Hard Townes 851

NOBEL PRIZE

	page
Nikolay Gennadiyevich Basov	859
Aleksandr Mikhailovich Prokhorov	869
Shin'ichirō Tomonaga	881
Julian Seymour Schwinger	891
Richard P. Feynman	901
Alfred Kastler	911
Hans Albrecht Bethe	923

ALPHABETICAL LIST OF PRIZE WINNERS

page

Alfvén, Hannes (1970) III-953
Alvarez, Luis W. (1968) III-935
Anderson, Carl David (1936)..................................... I-437
Anderson, Philip W. (1977)...................................... III-1131
Appleton, Sir Edward Victor (1947).............................. II-537

Bardeen, John (1956 *and* 1972) II-683, III-985
Barkla, Charles Glover (1917) I-215
Basov, Nikolay Gennadiyevich (1964) II-859
Becquerel, Antoine-Henri (1903) I-53
Bednorz, J. Georg (1987) III-1333
Bethe, Hans Albrecht (1967) II-923
Binnig, Gerd (1986) III-1323
Blackett, Patrick M. S. (1948) II-549
Bloch, Felix (1952) II-601
Bloembergen, Nicolaas (1981) III-1219
Bohr, Aage (1975) III-1061
Bohr, Niels (1922) I-263
Born, Max (1954) II-629
Bothe, Walther (1954)... II-643
Bragg, Sir Lawrence (1915) I-201
Bragg, Sir William Henry (1915) I-201
Brattain, Walter H. (1956) II-695
Braun, Karl Ferdinand (1909) I-137
Bridgman, Percy Williams (1946) II-527
Broglie, Louis de (1929) I-361

Chadwick, Sir James (1935)...................................... I-415
Chamberlain, Owen (1959) II-767
Chandrasekhar, Subrahmanyan (1983) III-1261
Cherenkov, Pavel Alekseyevich (1958)............................ II-727
Cockcroft, Sir John Douglas (1951).............................. II-579
Compton, Arthur Holly (1927) I-325
Cooper, Leon N (1972) III-997
Cronin, James W. (1980)... III-1203
Curie, Marie (1903)... I-65
Curie, Pierre (1903).. I-65
Dalén, Nils Gustaf (1912) I-167

NOBEL PRIZE

page

Davisson, Clinton Joseph (1937) I-449
Dirac, Paul Adrien Maurice (1933) I-403

Einstein, Albert (1921) I-253
Esaki, Leo (1973) III-1017

Fermi, Enrico (1938) II-471
Feynman, Richard P. (1965) II-901
Fitch, Val L. (1980) III-1211
Fowler, William A. (1983) III-1271
Franck, James (1925) I-295
Frank, Ilya Mikhailovich (1958) II-735

Gabor, Dennis (1971) III-973
Gell-Mann, Murray (1969) III-945
Giaever, Ivar (1973) III-1027
Glaser, Donald A. (1960) II-777
Glashow, Sheldon L. (1979) III-1171
Guillaume, Charles-Édouard (1920) I-243

Heisenberg, Werner (1932) I-381
Hertz, Gustav (1925) I-305
Hess, Victor Franz (1936) I-427
Hewish, Antony (1974) III-1053
Hofstadter, Robert (1961) II-787

Jensen, J. Hans D. (1963) II-841
Josephson, Brian D. (1973) III-1037

Kamerlingh Onnes, Heike (1913) I-177
Kapitsa, Pyotr Leonidovich (1978) III-1143
Kastler, Alfred (1966) II-911
Klitzing, Klaus von (1985) III-1301
Kusch, Polykarp (1955) II-663

Lamb, Willis Eugene, Jr. (1955) II-653
Landau, Lev Davidovich (1962) II-809
Laue, Max von (1914) I-189
Lawrence, Ernest Orlando (1939) II-483
Lederman, Leon M. (1988) III-1349
Lee, Tsung-Dao (1957) II-715
Lenard, Philipp (1905) I-87

NOBEL PRIZE

page

Lippmann, Gabriel (1908) I-117
Lorentz, Hendrik Antoon (1902) I-33

Marconi, Guglielmo (1909) I-127
Mayer, Maria Goeppert (1963) II-829
Michelson, Albert Abraham (1907) I-107
Millikan, Robert Andrews (1923) I-273
Mössbauer, Rudolf Ludwig (1961) II-797
Mott, Sir Nevill (1977) III-1119
Mottelson, Ben R. (1975) III-1071
Müller, Karl Alexander (1987) III-1333

Néel, Louis-Eugène-Félix (1970) III-963

Pauli, Wolfgang (1945) II-517
Penzias, Arno A. (1978) III-1155
Perrin, Jean-Baptiste (1926) I-315
Planck, Max (1918) I-223
Powell, Cecil Frank (1950) II-571
Prokhorov, Aleksandr Mikhailovich (1964) II-869
Purcell, Edward Mills (1952) II-611

Rabi, Isidor Isaac (1944) II-505
Rainwater, L. James (1975) III-1079
Raman, Sir Chandrasekhara Venkata (1930) I-371
Rayleigh, Lord (1904) I-79
Richardson, Sir Owen Willans (1928) I-349
Richter, Burton (1976) III-1089
Rohrer, Heinrich (1986) III-1323
Röntgen, Wilhelm Conrad (1901) I-21
Rubbia, Carlo (1984) III-1281
Ruska, Ernst (1986) III-1313
Ryle, Sir Martin (1974) III-1045

Salam, Abdus (1979) III-1181
Schawlow, Arthur L. (1981) III-1229
Schrieffer, John Robert (1972) III-1009
Schrödinger, Erwin (1933) I-391
Schwartz, Melvin (1988) III-1349
Schwinger, Julian Seymour (1965) II-891
Segrè, Emilio Gino (1959) II-755
Shockley, William (1956) II-673

page

Siegbahn, Kai M. (1981) III-1241
Siegbahn, Karl Manne Georg (1924) I-283
Stark, Johannes (1919) I-233
Steinberger, Jack (1988) III-1349
Stern, Otto (1943) II-495

Tamm, Igor Yevgenyevich (1958) II-745
Thomson, Sir George Paget (1937) I-461
Thomson, Sir Joseph John (1906) I-97
Ting, Samuel C. C. (1976) III-1099
Tomonaga, Shin'ichirō (1965) II-881
Townes, Charles Hard (1964) II-851

van der Meer, Simon (1984) III-1291
Van Vleck, John H. (1977) III-1107

Waals, Johannes Diderik van der (1910) I-147
Walton, Ernest Thomas Sinton (1951) II-591
Weinberg, Steven (1979) III-1193
Wien, Wilhelm (1911) I-157
Wigner, Eugene Paul (1963) II-819
Wilson, Charles Thomson Rees (1927) I-337
Wilson, Kenneth G. (1982) III-1253
Wilson, Robert W. (1978) III-1163

Yang, Chen Ning (1957) II-705
Yukawa, Hideki (1949) II-561

Zeeman, Pieter (1902) I-43
Zernike, Frits (1953) II-621

THE NOBEL PRIZE WINNERS

Physics

1938

Physics
Enrico Fermi, Italy

Chemistry
Richard Kuhn, Germany

Physiology or Medicine
Corneille Heymans, Belgium

Literature
Pearl S. Buck, United States

Peace
Nansen International Office for Refugees

ENRICO FERMI
1938

Born: Rome, Italy; September 29, 1901
Died: Chicago, Illinois; November 29, 1954
Nationality: Italian
Areas of concentration: Radioactivity and nuclear reactions

Fermi's discovery of the statistical laws governing the movement of atomic particles, joined with his subsequent researches into electrodynamic spectroscopy, led to his demonstrating that neutron bombardment causes transformation in the nuclear structure of nearly every element, thus permitting synthetically created elements beyond the ninety-two natural elements of the periodic table

The Award

Presentation

Professor H. Pleijel, Chairman of the Nobel Committee for Physics, presented the Nobel Prize in Physics to Enrico Fermi on December 10, 1938, on behalf of the Royal Swedish Academy of Sciences and King Gustav V, from whom Fermi accepted the prize. Pleijel's presentation, delivered in Italian, surveyed the way in which element structure has historically been perceived. He noted that the dream of medieval alchemy was essentially to change atomic structure by transforming base elements into gold, but that until the dawn of the twentieth century the chemical elements were considered essentially immutable. A series of individuals, all of the modern era, paved the way for Fermi's research: Antoine-Henri Becquerel (1852-1908), who discovered radioactivity in uranium; Marie (née Skłodowska) Curie (1867-1934), who discovered and produced polonium and radium; Ernest Rutherford (1871-1937), who postulated the atom as analogous to the solar system, with electrons revolving about a small central positive nucleus which constitutes nearly the entire mass of the atom; and Frédéric Joliot (1900-1958) and his wife, Irène Joliot-Curie (1897-1956), who investigated the radioactive properties of disintegrating isotopes. Fermi made use of the findings of these scientists and his own early work on the nature of atomic particle movement, employing neutrons (uncharged elementary particles of atoms) to shatter the atomic structure of elements. He then discovered that heavy substances bombarded by neutrons assumed distinctive and unusual characteristics. This procedure took on special significance when applied to uranium, until then the heaviest and most unstable element of the periodic table. Fermi used his method to produce two new elements, numbers 93 and 94, which he named "ausenium" and "hesperium."

Nobel lecture

Fermi's Nobel lecture, titled "Artificial Radioactivity Produced by Neutron Bombardment," is a brilliant summary of his own research and what inspired it. It shows why Fermi was in great demand as a popular speaker and college lecturer during the last third of his career, since he explains in comprehensible language, though without patronizing, exactly what impelled his work, the nature of his research, and its potential significance. Fermi acknowledged first the work of Rutherford, who had demonstrated in 1919 that when the nucleus of a light element is struck by a fast alpha particle (one that is positively charged and emitted by certain radioactive substances), a certain disintegration occurs within the struck nucleus; moreover, the alpha particle remains captured within the nucleus and a proton is emitted in its place, thus altering the original configuration of the nucleus. He also credited the work of Frédéric Joliot and Irène Joliot-Curie, who, in 1933, had charted the time lag in emission of electrons that follows the nearly instantaneous disintegration attending alpha particle bombardment.

Fermi subsequently decided that neutrons could be used instead of alpha particles as bombarding projectiles, their drawback of scarcity compensated by their increased ability, because uncharged, to invade the nuclei of all atoms. His first experiments, in essence controlled nuclear reactions, used small amounts of radon and beryllium powder to produce relatively large numbers of neutrons (2×10^7 per second). With the help of his associates, Fermi proved that he could activate even the heaviest, most inert elements by neutron bombardment. He was subsequently able to postulate three equations which demonstrate the different results when neutrons are directed against light and heavy elements and to accelerate the speed of the reactions by using paraffin, or water for hydrogen-based elements, as catalytic agents.

Fermi continued the lecture, noting the thermal (heat-producing) properties of controlled neutron bombardment. Temperature increases by the degree to which neutrons are retained in diffusion with the paraffin; it decreases as they escape or are captured by some nucleus. The neutrons themselves move at different speeds, their activity determined by induced temperature changes. Considerable increases in activation occur when the paraffin, which slows neutron movement, is cooled from room temperature to that of liquid oxygen. A significant number of neutrons then actually reach the point of thermal agitation; more important, the diffusion process continues within the paraffin for a relatively long period.

By setting two radiation detectors at equal distances from a neutron source (the edge of a rotating wheel spun at high velocity within a hollowed-out paraffin block), Fermi discovered that the detector behind the source became considerably more active than the one in front. He was, accordingly, able to calculate the speed of neutron escape and, concomitantly, the amount of time the neutrons remained within the paraffin—in this case, 10^{-4} seconds. The probability of a neutron being captured by a nucleus, Fermi concluded, is large when slow neutrons move through an activated like element.

The final section of Fermi's address contained characteristically generous praise, not only for his Italian colleagues but also for others working in related areas in various countries.

Critical reception

Immediate reaction to the Royal Swedish Academy's choice of Fermi as the 1938 Nobel physics laureate was surprisingly temperate in both the free and the Fascist press. Few outside the scientific community grasped the military applications of Fermi's work, though almost at the moment Fermi was receiving the prize, Germany was about to announce the discovery of nuclear fission, which depended upon the very work for which he was being recognized. Fermi had discouraged press fanfare, primarily because he intended to use his trip to Sweden as a means of emigrating to the United States without returning to Italy and was afraid that excessive publicity might result in scrutiny of the "4D" immigration visa he had quietly obtained from U.S. authorities. There was also a real possibility that the Fascist Italian government might intervene to seize the prize money, which Fermi needed to establish himself, his wife, and their children, Nella and Giulio, in the United States.

As a result of these peculiar circumstances, the initial reaction was subdued. In Italy, *Popolo d'Italia*, the official government organ, on November 11 buried an announcement of Fermi's award beneath a list of new laws regulating minorities: Jews, Gypsies, homosexuals, and unmarried men. *Corriere della sera*, as opposed to Benito Mussolini as it could legitimately be and still remain in publication, was forced to run the same simple notice. Fermi had been under increasing indirect attack in Fascist newspapers in the weeks preceding the Stockholm announcement for having appointed several Jewish scientists to the institute of the University of Rome, or, as *Popolo d'Italia* had characterized it on October 10, for "having transformed the physics institute into a synagogue."

In the early fall of 1938, Fermi's friend Niels Bohr, the Danish physicist, had discreetly asked Fermi at a Copenhagen physics conference what his reaction would be should he be offered the prize. This unorthodox question had been sanctioned by the Nobel Committee, which was all too aware that the award could cause problems for Fermi in Italy, as it had for German pacifist writer Carl von Ossietzky, who had been given the 1935 peace prize. Fermi determined to emigrate at this time, and Bohr was instrumental in securing the subdued factual coverage which appeared in the free world's press.

The New York Times ran several small articles, one on European reactions to those being considered (November 8), a larger, factual piece on Fermi once the award had been announced (November 11), a feature story with a photograph in its Sunday edition (November 12), and a transcription of the proceedings (December 11). On December 24, the Fermis boarded the *Franconia* at Southampton, England, and arrived in New York on January 2, 1939. Two days before their arrival, at last safe from reprisals, *The New York Times* announced Fermi's intention to join the Columbia University physics faculty.

Biography

Enrico Fermi was born in Rome, Italy, on September 29, 1901, the son of Alberto and Ida de Gattis Fermi. His father, a senior civil servant, held the post of chief inspector in the Ministry of Communications. Fortunately, the elder Fermi quickly recognized his son's talent for mathematics. His position in the Ministry of Communications allowed him to seek the counsel of Italy's best mathematicians on the boy's early schooling. It took little time for young Fermi's teachers at the local *liceo* (academic grammar and preparatory school) to recognize the boy's gifts, and in 1918, armed with a fellowship, he entered Pisa's prestigious Scuola Normale Superiore for his undergraduate training. By 1922, Fermi had obtained his doctorate in physics from the University of Pisa.

Postgraduate honors followed one upon the next. In 1923, Fermi won a national scholarship from the Italian government which allowed him to study quantum mechanics with physicist Max Born (1882-1970) at the University of Göttingen, Germany. (Born, also a refugee from Fascism, would win the 1954 Nobel Prize in Physics, sharing the honor with German physicist Walther Bothe.) The Rockefeller Foundation granted Fermi a fellowship in 1924, and this allowed him to continue his studies at the University of Leiden in the Netherlands.

During these early years, Fermi was primarily interested in mechanical physics, the most mathematical branch of the discipline, and so it follows that his first academic post was that of lecturer in mathematical physics and mechanics at the University of Florence. Having returned to his native Italy, he set to work on what would be known as the "Fermi statistics," mathematical formulas which govern the movement and behavior of atomic particles. He succeeded during his years at Florence (1924-1926) in describing the movement of those subatomic particles, subsequently called "fermions," which obey the exclusion principle postulated by Austrian physicist Wolfgang Pauli—essentially, that no two electrons can occupy the same orbit in the electron structure of an atom. By 1927, Fermi had been elected full professor of theoretical physics at the University of Rome, the institution at which he would do the research recognized in 1938 by the Royal Swedish Academy.

Scientific Career

Had Fermi done nothing further than the early work of his postgraduate years, his place in the history of quantum physics would have been assured. Not yet twenty-seven, he held one of the most desirable academic posts in Italy, had his own staff of researchers, and received regular and generous government grants with which to continue his work. Ironically, his principal benefactor during these important early years was Italy's new Fascist government, in power since 1922 and led by Benito Mussolini. Mussolini had set advancement of the sciences as a mandate for his new Italy, and he poured funds into scientific research, even though there is little evidence (and certainly none in 1927) that he recognized the military applications of Fermi's work. Thus the stage was set at the beginning of Fermi's career: a dictator bent on reestablishing Italian glory at whatever cost, and a young scientist, who loathed all that Fascism represented, setting to work in an area whose destructive potential was at least as great as its constructive applications and dependent for his work's continuation on the very individuals he despised.

In effect, then, Fermi had to exercise diplomatic as well as scientific skills during these important years. On the whole he succeeded, for although the government perceived that Fermi was no friend of Fascism, it recognized, unlike Germany, the importance of its gifted scientists. Fermi's marriage in 1928, one year after his Rome appointment, to Laura Capon, who was Jewish, certainly did not pass unnoticed among the Fascist authorities. Clearly, her religion was an important factor in the couple's dramatic departure from Sweden to the United States immediately after Fermi received the Nobel Prize. By 1938, war in Europe was imminent, Mussolini had signed an alliance with Germany, and Adolf Hitler had visited Italy and was pressuring Mussolini to establish programs similar to those already under way in Germany for the elimination of Jews.

Amazingly, Fermi was able to carry out some of his most productive work during the tense years from 1927 to 1938. He became deeply involved in theoretical investigations of various spectroscopic phenomena, and this, along with his earlier work on atomic particle movement, brought his attention to the nucleus itself. By 1934, he had postulated the beta decay theory, which concerned radioactive disintegration of a nucleus with the accompanying emission of a beta particle. He discovered, in essence, that the residual nucleus has one more unit of positive charge after electron emission and one less after positron emission. His work here stemmed directly from his studies with Pauli on the neutrino (a neutral particle, difficult to detect, with little or no mass, no charge, and almost no interaction with matter). Also in 1934, after the discovery of artificial radioactivity by Irène Joliot-Curie and her husband, Fermi showed that neutron bombardment can alter the nuclear structure of nearly every element, the heavy as well as the light. This finding led to his discovery of "slow neutrons" and made possible the discovery of nuclear fission by German physicists Otto Hahn and Fritz Strassmann in early 1939, coinciding almost to the week with Fermi's arrival in the United States.

Events in Fermi's life, and in the world, moved with dramatic swiftness beginning in 1939. The Fermis had left Europe at precisely the right moment. Aside from Fermi's understandable concern about how his wife would be received in Italy in view of the Italian-German alliance, he was certainly aware, even as he delivered his Nobel lecture, of an imminent German breakthrough in fission research. That Fermi would have been assigned to work with Hahn and Strassmann is almost certain. His decision to emigrate to the United States, which seems either fortuitous or prescient if considered apart from these external events, was actually quite carefully calculated. It may also have altered the course of history; it certainly altered that of atomic research.

On arriving in the United States in January, 1939, Fermi assumed his professorship in physics at Columbia University, New York. By March, he had joined with a prominent international group of physicists, including Leo Szilard, Edward Teller, Eugene Paul Wigner, and Bohr, in a voluntary agreement which by June, 1940, would involve hundreds of physicists throughout the free world: to suspend publication of the results of their work. Fermi's ad hoc committee simultaneously attempted to warn U.S. military authorities of the possible threat of German fission research, but this attempt came to naught. Fortunately, Szilard and Wigner persevered, contacting Albert Einstein, their senior colleague at the Institute for Advanced Study, Princeton, New Jersey. These three reached Einstein's acquaintance, economist Alexander Sachs, a personal friend of President Franklin D. Roosevelt, and it was Sachs who hand-delivered Einstein's badly typed but ultimately history-making letter which set forth all too clearly the devastating potential of the atomic research then well under way in Germany.

Enough was known by the publication blackout date of mid-1940 for either side to follow the series of logical steps that would produce the atom bomb. The United States was fortunate on two counts: It had not yet entered the war and had a wealth of European scientists in residence, Fermi most notable among them. Thus began, at Roosevelt's order and without the knowledge of even the highest officials of government, the Manhattan Project (so called because it was under nominal control of the Manhattan District Corps of Engineers). Its mission: to develop an atom bomb.

So it was that after only eighteen months in the United States, Fermi became a primary figure in American atomic research. Columbia University, with no questions asked, allowed Fermi to continue his work with others at the University of Chicago, and it was in that city, on a squash court beneath the west stands of Stagg Field, the university's stadium, that Fermi supervised construction of the first atomic pile. He engineered the first self-sustaining chain reaction there on December 2, 1942, and immediately thereafter worked with American physicist J. Robert Oppenheimer at remote Los Alamos, New Mexico, on the bomb's construction and detonation. Much to his delight, Fermi received an early granting of U.S. citizenship in 1944, and after the war, on November 29, 1954, he assumed the Charles H. Swift professorship in physics at the University of Chicago.

Fermi chose not to remain part of the team of scientists that stayed at Los Alamos after the war. Though there had been some professional friction between him and Oppenheimer, the director of the research team, Fermi from the first was appalled by the devastation and suffering which had followed indirectly from his life's work. (In later years, Oppenheimer would share Fermi's feelings and himself become an advocate of the peaceful uses of atomic energy.) Fermi had always considered himself a theoretical physicist and a teacher, rather than a research scientist with programs fixed by external directors and subject to political whims. As he assessed his career in the postwar years, he was quietly distressed that so much of his life had been subjected to such external pressures. In the years of his professorship in Rome, he had had to deal with a Fascist government he loathed merely to do what he loved, which was to pursue the study of physics for its own sake. Fermi remained an apolitical man in the years following his naturalization as a U.S. citizen. Though his loyalty to his new country could never be questioned, he was disturbed by the climate of fear that arose during the postwar years. Leaving Los Alamos on good terms and resuming his professorship at the University of

Chicago gave him, in his final years, the autonomy he had never enjoyed before.

By the early 1950's, Fermi had become increasingly concerned that the peaceful applications of his life's work be emphasized. He pointedly did not wish to be known as the developer of the atom bomb—one reason that the formation of the Atomic Energy Commission in 1950, of which he was a founding member, pleased him greatly. As originally constituted, the commission would act as a supervisory board to minimize the chances of accidental war or atomic catastrophe. It would also serve to encourage the work of scientists in the peaceful uses of the atom. Fermi considered these boundless and wished them to be his legacy. Had he lived longer, he certainly would have become more outspoken on these issues. As it happened, his wife, a gifted writer and speaker, carried on effectively in his place. She became a regular representative at the International Conference on the Peaceful Uses of Atomic Energy throughout the late 1950's, and her books on atomic research and on the intellectual history of the prewar years have become classics. In the best tradition of theoretical physics, Fermi remained both a visionary and an optimist. He was convinced that as long as sanity prevailed, the world would be infinitely better for his work. Cynicism may lead one to question his judgment, but not his sincerity.

The last years of Fermi's life were filled with honors and a wealth of publications impossible during the war years. He continued in an advisory capacity at Los Alamos and assisted in the development of the hydrogen bomb. The Atomic Energy Commission named him to receive its first special award, worth $25,000, shortly before his death. Despite the hiatus in his publishing caused by the war, Fermi wrote prolifically on his areas of interest, in English as well as in Italian and German and for a general as well as a scholarly audience. A complete list of his writings, including unpublished works, appears in *The Collected Works of Enrico Fermi* (1962-1965).

Those unable to read technical, scholarly Italian or German will find it difficult to trace the development of Fermi's works through his writings; nevertheless, a sufficient number of items in English, including textbooks and transcriptions of courses Fermi taught at the University of Chicago, make it possible for the interested lay reader to obtain a good grasp of Fermi's work as it stood in the period just before his Nobel award and as it developed in the postwar years until his death. The textbook *Thermodynamics* (1937) is outdated, but it was a standard, and it remains of historical interest. Fermi wrote it in English while still in Italy, and it remained untranslated until after his death, when it was published in Italy with the title *Thermodinamica* (1958). An earlier, related book, *Molecole e cristalli* (1934; *Molecules, Crystals, and Quantum Statistics,* 1966) underwent the more conventional translation process and holds similar historical interest.

More worthwhile, because it incorporates the results of research conducted during the war, is Fermi's *Elementary Particles* (1951), intended for the undergraduate student and based on the Mrs. Hepsa Ely Silliman Lectures delivered at Yale University in 1950. Three reproductions of lecture notes prepared for advanced courses at the University of Chicago are *Nuclear Physics* (1949), *Notes on Quantum Mechanics* (1961), and *Notes on Thermodynamics and Statistics* (1966).

Bibliography

Primary

PHYSICS: *Introduzione alla fisica atomica*, 1928; *Fisica ad uso dei Licei*, 1929; *Molecole e cristalli*, 1934 (*Molecules, Crystals, and Quantum Statistics*, 1966); *Thermodynamics*, 1937 (*Thermodinamica*, 1958); *Fisica per le Scuole Medie Superiori*, 1938; *Nuclear Physics*, 1949; *Conferenze di fisica atomica*, 1950; *Elementary Particles*, 1951 (*Particelle elementari*, 1952); *Notes on Quantum Mechanics*, 1961; *The Collected Works of Enrico Fermi*, 1962-1965; *Notes on Thermodynamics and Statistics*, 1966.

Secondary

Fermi, Laura. *Atoms for the World*. Chicago: University of Chicago Press, 1957. This book is a serious study by Fermi's wife, a prolific science writer for popular audiences, on the role of the United States in assuring the peaceful uses of atomic energy. It grew out of her participation in the International Conference on the Peaceful Uses of Atomic Energy and her own and her husband's conviction that his work should never again be applied to destructive purposes. Several of its conclusions, particularly on problem-free nuclear power generation, may seem naïve, but the book is sincerely written, given the period in which it appeared. Fermi here includes her husband's role in atomic research only as part of international research then under way.

_____. *Atoms in the Family: My Life with Enrico Fermi*. Chicago: University of Chicago Press, 1954. Fermi's wife relates the story of her life with her husband, dramatically and with great flair, in this volume. In addition to the expected factual information, she provides lucid accounts designed for the general reader of Fermi's work as it progressed. The author planned this volume as a memorial to her husband to accompany the intended publication of his collected works. The book includes a selected bibliography of Fermi's works.

_____. *Industrious Immigrants: The Intellectual Migration from Europe, 1930-1941*. Chicago: University of Chicago Press, 1968. This volume is an imposing study of the huge numbers of gifted scholars forced to flee the advance of Fascism. It concentrates primarily on scientists known to the Fermis and is written with feeling for the drama of the period. It also considers how world history might have been changed had these individuals been either allowed or forced to continue research in their native countries.

_____. *Mussolini*. Chicago: University of Chicago Press, 1966. A curiously interesting and unsurprisingly hostile biography of Italy's prime minister and dictator, this book describes the relationship between intellectuals and Fascist Italy. It also makes interesting observations about how Mussolini's own background and his desire to restore Italy's grandeur led him to make vast expenditures of borrowed money for unreferred grants to often-dubious projects and how this caused financial difficulties in Italy once Mussolini had determined to emulate Hitler's policies of military conquest.

Segrè, Emilio. *Enrico Fermi: Physicist*. Chicago: University of Chicago Press, 1970. This biography has become a standard source of information on Fermi's life. It was written by a former student, later a colleague and personal friend of the scientist. It contains more on Fermi's intellectual history and methods than previously available and does so in straightforward language, even in its discussion of technical scientific matters. It also includes photographs, notes, and a bibliography.

Wilson, Jane, ed. *All in Our Time: The Reminiscences of Twelve Nuclear Pioneers*. Chicago: Bulletin of the Atomic Scientists, 1975. In this collection, a dozen physicists connected with the beginnings of nuclear research recall the beginnings and high points in their careers. In addition to chapters by Herbert L. Anderson and Albert Wattenberg, both of whom were present at the first chain reaction experiment, there are chapters by Nobel physics laureate Luis W. Alvarez on Berkeley in the 1930's, J. H. Manley on organizing the wartime laboratory, and R. R. Wilson on recruiting for Los Alamos.

Ziman, J. M. *Electrons in Metals: A Short Guide to the Fermi Surface*. New York: Barnes and Noble, 1970. This is a good undergraduate's introduction to what is known as the Fermi surface—that is, the electron configuration in real metals—and how this may be measured. A thin book organized as a student's guide, it contains many illustrations and a brief list of references. It covers the topics of electron gas, bands and zones, Bloch electrons, band structure and calculation, and measurement of Fermi surfaces.

Robert J. Forman

1939

Physics
Ernest Orlando Lawrence, United States

Chemistry
Adolf Butenandt, Germany
Leopold Ruzicka, Switzerland

Physiology or Medicine
Gerhard Domagk, Germany

Literature
Frans Eemil Sillanpää, Finland

Peace
no award

ERNEST ORLANDO LAWRENCE
1939

Born: Canton, South Dakota; August 8, 1901
Died: Palo Alto, California; August 27, 1958
Nationality: American
Area of concentration: Nuclear physics

Lawrence invented the cyclotron and was a major contributor to the development of the atom bomb during World War II. In his later years, he studied the properties of the electrical spark and became interested in applying the cyclotron to biology and medicine

The Award

Presentation

Ernest Orlando Lawrence's reluctance to travel to Sweden at the start of World War II in Europe and his desire not to leave his work brought about an unprecedented situation. The presentation and acceptance speech for the 1939 Nobel Prize in Physics were made in Wheeler Hall auditorium on the campus of the University of California at Berkeley on February 29, 1940, more than two months after the originally scheduled presentation in Stockholm. The ceremonies were quite long. Raymond T. Birge, head of the physics department, began the events by announcing the discovery of element number 85 by two Berkeley physicists and the successful production, in the several preceding days, of a new radioactive carbon. Both these announcements all but overshadowed the original purpose of the ceremonies: to present the Nobel Prize to Lawrence.

The actual presentation was made by C. E. Wallerstadt, the Swedish consul general, who bestowed the honor on behalf of the Royal Swedish Academy of Sciences and King Gustav V for Lawrence's invention of the cyclotron, which would become one of the basic machines of experimental physics. The speech, delivered in English, covered the development of the cyclotron and the contributions it had brought about in the growing science of nuclear physics. Wallerstadt commented on the development of the cyclotron and the fact that it had permitted and encouraged research on artificial radioactive elements, which were destined to revise scientific thinking about the structure of matter and of the universe itself. He noted the fears of Europeans at the opening of a major war, in which Sweden found itself in a difficult geographical position, and expressed hope that science would be able to do something to quell the rising tide of pessimism about the war's outcome.

Nobel lecture

Lawrence's response to the Nobel award was rather short, not so much a lecture as a listing of facts which, although perhaps astounding to his audience, were straightforward enough to him. He commented on the "new frontier of the atom" and spoke dispassionately about what had enabled him to build the cyclotron and what its potential was. He predicted that a four-thousand-ton cyclotron would be the major instrument in finding the key to the nearly limitless reserves of energy stored in the atom. Lawrence gave considerable credit to coworkers who had toiled long and hard to accomplish the breakthroughs that the cyclotron had made possible and said that he was receiving the prize as a representative of his associates, both past and present, who had shared in the development of the invention. "No individual," he said, "is responsible for a single stepping stone along the path of progress"; he went on to assert that where the path is smooth, progress is most possible, citing his own work as an example.

Lawrence spoke of a new field of atomic research requiring bombardment guns capable of delivering energies of more than a hundred million volts. With optimism, he explained that the design for a four-thousand-ton cyclotron had already been completed and that the obstacles to success were not technical but financial. He went on to say that with instruments such as the cyclotron, it might be possible to duplicate energy similar to cosmic rays, or even similar to the energies of the stars. Lawrence was not a dreamer, but rather a very pragmatic seeker of concrete answers in the midst of all of his researches. He had a clear concept of what he wanted to achieve and was able to convey the idea of that future goal to his audience.

The official Nobel lecture, delivered years later on December 11, 1951, was an explanation of Lawrence's creation of the cyclotron and its development over the years from a simple invention to an increasingly powerful tool of physics. Lawrence used slides to illustrate successive stages in the developmental process. Studying the diagrams of a Norwegian engineer, Lawrence had begun to wonder whether, instead of using a long line of cylindrical electrodes, it would be possible to accelerate positive ions by using two electrodes over and over again, sending the ions back and forth through the electrodes by some sort of magnetic field arrangement. At the same time, Lawrence pointed to Professor G. Ising as the developer of methods of multiple acceleration, beginning in 1924.

The cyclotron grew from a device with a diameter of less than 12 inches to a 184-inch machine, the synchrotron, capable of accelerating ions to energies of several billion electron volts. A cyclotron built at Brookhaven was called the "cosmotron," and another at Berkeley was called the "bevatron." Lawrence explained that it was possible to achieve even high-energy projectiles by using heavier ions and that the only barrier to reaching for such higher energies was the availability of money to build the machinery.

Critical reception

By the time the Nobel Prize was actually awarded to Lawrence, the world was engulfed in a savage war in which the Germans had launched an attack on the Low Countries and were driving toward Paris. American newspapers were crammed with two-page spreads of maps, diagrams, and quotations from conferences held in

Europe. Americans were moved to help their longtime European allies; everywhere there were collections of food and clothing for citizens of bombed cities and for refugees. These events overshadowed the achievements of science and certainly detracted from the invention of the cyclotron and Lawrence's Nobel award.

In addition, the simultaneous announcement at the Nobel presentation of the discovery at Berkeley of a new carbon element, number 85 in the periodic table of elements, was inevitably the focus of attention. *The New York Times* of March 1, 1940 (the day following the ceremony), ran an article on the front page about the discovery; the Nobel Prize presentation simply happened at the same time and in the same place. The headline read, "New Element and a Carbon Germ Tracer Credited to Dr. E. O. Lawrence's Cyclotron." Of eleven paragraphs, only one mentioned Lawrence's receiving the Nobel Prize.

The *St. Louis Post Dispatch* for March 1, 1940, carried a two-column report of the events at Berkeley on an inside page, but the headline read, "New Element, Carbon Germ Tracer, Credited to California Cyclotron." The subheadline added, "Discoveries Announced When Nobel Physics Prize of $40,000 Is Given to Dr. E. O. Lawrence." The reporter of the news item covered Lawrence's acceptance speech in some detail, more than appeared in most other publications. In *The New York Times* of December 10, 1939—the day when Lawrence would have received the Prize in Europe—columnist Alma Luise Olson, reporting from Stockholm, commented sharply, "Now that transmutation figures indirectly in the news through the award of the Nobel Prize in physics to Professor Ernest O. Lawrence of the University of California, it is interesting to recall that Strindberg in his day tried to find the secret of making gold."

Lawrence often sought publicity, not for himself but for the Berkeley Radiation Laboratory. He viewed publicity as necessary for keeping the reputation of the laboratory before the public, especially before those who held the purse strings of grants and funding. He seldom shied away from reporters, although he rather disliked having to deal with them and by all accounts disliked having to talk about himself.

With the official announcement of the 1939 physics prize came news about the Ohio and Nebraska primary elections, government wire-tapping scares, concern over the Soviet invasions in Finland, Nazi air bombardments of the Netherlands, and pleas for American relief for the people of Finland. In an uneasy world where science had been put to work building war weapons and engineering the deaths of thousands, Lawrence's achievement seemed lost in the shadows of the many insecurities of everyday life.

Biography

Ernest Orlando Lawrence was born August 8, 1901, in Canton, South Dakota, the son of Carl Gustavus and Gunda Jacobson Lawrence, staunch Lutherans. Ernest was graduated from the University of South Dakota in 1922 with a bachelor's degree; in 1923, he received a master of arts degreee from the University of Minnesota. Ernest's father was a teacher at a Lutheran Academy in Canton and had a reputation for being progressive. As a young engineering student at the University of South Dakota, Ernest followed his father's example and studied hard enough to earn his degree with high honors. His academic prowess guaranteed him entrance into graduate school; he received a doctorate from Yale University in 1925. He worked and researched at Yale until 1928, then moving to the University of California at Berkeley to continue research into nuclear physics. He published several seminal papers on the subject and began his work on particle acceleration. It was at Berkeley that he built his first cyclotron, in 1929, and by 1932 he had used it successfully. He became the youngest full professor at Berkeley at the age of twenty-nine, and in 1936 he became the director of the Berkeley Radiation Laboratory.

In 1937, Lawrence received the Elliott Cresson Medal of the Franklin Institute in Philadelphia, the Comstock Prize of the United States National Academy of Sciences, and the Hughes Medal of the Royal Society, London. These awards were followed in 1939 by the Nobel Prize in Physics, the Duddell Medal of the Royal Physical Society in 1940, the Faraday Medal in 1952, the American Cancer Society Medal in 1954, the Enrico Fermi Award in 1957, and, in the year of his death, the Sylvanus Thayer Award. He was also decorated with the Medal for Merit and made an officer of the Legion of Honor.

Lawrence was a dedicated writer and researcher who opened doorways to many new advances in nuclear physics. His work on the atom bomb project during World War II was crucial to the success of the program. After the war, he became active in attempts to suspend atom bomb testing. Later contributions to knowledge of the ionization potentials of metals, the measurement of small time intervals, and the measurement of the electron's energy-mass ratio continued to bring him the highest respect of colleagues throughout the world and to earn for him the many prizes mentioned here.

Lawrence and his wife, Mary Kimberly Blumer, had six children: two boys and four girls. Lawrence died in 1958 in Palo Alto, California, after a rich and rewarding lifetime of invention and vital breakthroughs in the field he loved. At the time he became ill, he was a member of an American delegation to the 1958 Geneva Conference for the suspension of atom bomb testing.

Scientific Career

Lawrence's distinguished career began in 1925, when he earned a Ph.D. in engineering from Yale University. It was here that he began to acquire a national reputation for the kind of intense inventiveness that later would bring him international fame. He stayed at Yale for three years as a professor, moving in 1928 to the fledgling physics department at the University of California at Berkeley. Accepting this position was a critical factor in his ultimate success. One evening in the library at Berkeley, browsing through a Norwegian engineer's report written in German, Lawrence suddenly realized a way to improve considerably the acceleration of charged particles without electrical breakdown of equipment. Unable to read German, he studied the diagrams carefully. It is reported that the next afternoon, a colleague's wife met him hurrying across the campus; he exclaimed to her, "I'm going to be famous!"

The key to Lawrence's success in inventing the cyclotron was his realization that a charged particle could be kept in motion simply if it were hurried along in an endless circular path and continually pushed faster and faster by the jolts of a magnetic field. Each successive pass around the circle would be met by another kick from the electrical charge, and the particles would be accelerated to higher and higher velocities. Other physicists had failed in this task because they had thought only in terms of linear acceleration.

Previous researchers had built a proton accelerator which took up a huge amount of floor space. They were able to achieve 125,000 volts of electricity with makeshift equipment, but Lawrence was bent on reaching at least 1 million volts with his tiny cyclotron. In the spring of 1932, a campus shack in some disrepair was turned over to him as a facility in which to conduct his experiments. Lawrence immediately named it the Radiation Laboratory and went to work to raise money for his research. In 1932, he achieved his early goal of generating a million volts in order to bombard atomic nuclei with particle beams. With a circular cyclotron less than a foot in diameter, built with the help of M. Stanley Livingston, he was able to accelerate protons to about 5 percent of the speed of light. (In comparison, the proton synchrotron at Batavia, Illinois, has a 2-kilometer diameter and can accelerate protons to 0.999998 times the speed of light.)

A cyclotron consists of a large cylindrical box placed between the poles of an electromagnet. The box is pumped free of air until a very high vacuum exists inside. Charged particles, such as protons or deuterons, are fed into the center of the box. Inside the box are two hollow D-shaped electrodes, called "dees," which are connected to a source of high-voltage electricity. In operation, the electrical charge on the dees is reversed very rapidly by an oscillator. The action of the field of the electromagnet causes the charged particles inside the cylindrical box to move in a semicircle in a fixed period of time. The potential applied to the dees is adjusted to reverse itself in the same time period. At each crossing of the gap between the dees, the ions gain energy from the electric field. They move faster and faster as they approach the outside of the box. When they reach the outer rim of a circular box, they are then deflected toward the target, an atom, at a tremendous speed.

In 1932, attention was being focused on nuclear physics and especially on quantum mechanics, a field of physics that already could explain almost all the properties of matter outside the nucleus of the atom. Since physics was an intensely competitive field at this time, most scientists suddenly turned their attention away from the electron shell of the atom and began working on nuclear physics. Lawrence, meanwhile, continued his researches and brought together at Berkeley one of the strongest teams of scientists working in nuclear physics, especially in the acceleration and bombardment of atoms.

Lawrence's invention changed the focus of nuclear physics research and allowed scientists to discover a large number of new active isotopes and analyze their relations to the stable elements. The cyclotron also made possible new research in radioactivity, which had been all but disregarded, because the naturally radioactive elements had already been thoroughly investigated by nearly everyone with an interest in the subject. In 1939, Lawrence was summoned by the Nobel Committee to receive the Nobel Prize in Physics, which was awarded to him for "the invention of the cyclotron, its development and results obtained with it, especially relating to artificial radioactive elements." A number of scientists who followed Lawrence, such as Melvin Calvin (winner of the Nobel Prize in Chemistry for 1961) and the team of John Cockcroft and Ernest Walton (the physics laureates for 1951), made use of Lawrence's cyclotron in their own researches with further success.

Worried about wartime travel and about the month the trip would take away from his work, Lawrence arranged to have the Nobel presentation made at Berkeley by the Swedish consul general. It was an unprecedented action that nevertheless took place, on February 29, 1940, at Wheeler Hall auditorium on the Berkeley campus. Lawrence's acceptance speech was short and directed mostly at the prospects for building a hundred-million-volt cyclotron, which, he claimed, was not a technical or scientific problem but rather a money problem best handled by college presidents. Amid the growing tensions of German and Japanese aggressions, Lawrence wished to get on with the business of building the device, and he applied to the Rockefeller Foundation for a $1.15 billion grant at a time when all the cyclotrons in the world were worth only $2 million. Despite considerable debate over the role of science in an age of "science gone to war," the Rockefeller Foundation approved Lawrence's request.

Just before the outbeak of World War II, word came from Europe that Otto Hahn and Lise Meitner had split the atom, releasing a large amount of energy in the process. The two scientists had discovered that it was possible to cause uranium atoms to fission when struck by neutrons. In New York City, Nobel Prize laureate Enrico Fermi believed that such a process, if properly controlled, could result in a chain reaction and an enormous explosion—a sudden release of massive amounts of energy. At Berkeley, Lawrence had already begun working on the problem. His original motivation for becoming involved in the atom bomb project was a desire to help the British and the United States' other allies caught up in the war in Europe. Before Pearl Harbor, he had never believed that the war would involve the United States; by September of 1941, however, he had come to realize his own necessary place in the development of the atom bomb and also the criticality of the race with the Germans. He made his entire staff at the Berkeley Radiation Laboratory available for the project and was later appointed to the high position of program chief for electromagnetic separation in the Manhattan Project, the code name for the atom bomb project. Three other program chiefs were also named: Nobel laureates Harold Urey and Arthur Holly Compton and physicist Eger Murphree.

Lawrence knew that identically charged ions of different weights, moving in a magnetic field, followed different trajectories. If uranium ions were sent through the magnetic field of his cyclotron, the ions of the isotope uranium 235 would be separated from the ions of uranium 238, and they then could easily be collected. In 1941, physicist Glenn T. Seaborg discovered that uranium 238, after bombardment with neutrons, transformed itself into a new element, number 94 in the periodic table; he called this new element "plutonium" after the planet Pluto. If the nonfissioning uranium 238 could be put into a chain-reacting pile, it would immediately produce an atomic explosion. Slowly, the stage was being set for the creation of the atom bomb, and Lawrence's contribution to that development was to prove essential.

It was his association with the bomb program that brought him into closer contact with J. Robert Oppenheimer (1904-1967) and began a lifelong relationship. Lawrence and Oppenheimer did not agree on many aspects of physics. Oppenheimer, it is reported, had little tact and was impatient with Lawrence's dream of a hundred-million-volt cyclotron. For Lawrence, the cyclotron was all-important, and he resented the other man's attitude toward his work. Nevertheless, the two remained close friends.

The atom bomb project was officially approved in December, 1942, under the code name "Manhattan Engineering District," after the successful creation of a critical mass of uranium was announced by Fermi and Compton at the University of Chicago. The jobs of building an electromagnetic separation device and of carrying out detailed studies of plutonium fell to Lawrence and his Berkeley colleagues. The amounts of scarce metals needed were staggering; the magnet coil windings alone, for example, required 28 million pounds of silver, worth some $400 million.

The atom bomb's devastating results weighed somewhat on Lawrence's mind, and he later entered a period of personal resistance to the further use of the weapon under any circumstances. It became apparent that the U.S. government intended to continue testing nuclear explosive devices, a practice which Lawrence directly opposed, and he made innumerable statements protesting such tests. A weapon with such unprecedented destructive power must have been a bitter conclusion to the pure research that had won for him the Nobel Prize and other honors in the past. Perhaps it was the realization that his lifework had contributed to widespread suffering and carried the threat of yielding even greater destruction that caused Lawrence to turn to research into the medical uses of radiation and related areas of physics. This work brought him more honors in the final years of his life. His work with his brother James, a physician, in the treatment of cancer, for example, earned for him the 1954 American Cancer Society Medal.

The cyclotron's importance lies in the influence it has had on the production of artificially radioactive substances and the ability to produce active isotopes in large amounts. The cyclotron opened new fields, especially in medicine and biology. At the time of the Nobel award, the cyclotron was the most complex and extensive apparatus to be conceived in the physics community. Finally, Lawrence himself had a great talent for leadership and was able to gather around him and encourage others who themselves carried out brilliant work in this new field. After the war, he achieved enormous prestige and made the Berkeley Radiation Laboratory the world center for high-energy physics. He became an adviser to the Atomic Energy Commission and the Department of Defense, promoting the development of the hydrogen bomb and helping to establish weapons research at Livermore, California.

In his lifetime, Lawrence met and often worked closely with the best scientists the United States could produce. In project after project, he always seemed to be in the forefront of major breakthroughs and discoveries, most of them the result of his basic achievements as a younger man and his invention of the cyclotron. He never left the Berkeley complex and was never seriously tempted to join another university. That early decision in 1928, which sent him to the barest beginnings of a physics department at Berkeley, had a profound influence on the entire course of his life. The Berkeley Laboratory spawned at least five additional Nobel Prize winners, and it was there that the transuranium element 103 was discovered and named "lawrencium."

Toward the end of his life, Lawrence began to speak out for dismantling the foundations of the nuclear arms proliferation. To this end, he joined an American delegation that was to meet with Soviet counterparts in Geneva, Switzerland. While there, he suddenly became violently ill. He was flown immediately back to Palo Alto to be rushed into surgery, but he never recovered; he died on August 27, 1958. In his life, he had received far more recognition for his achievements than is usually accorded most men of science, and certainly more than any other physicist of his time. His goal-oriented energies, the scope of his grasp of the physics of his time, and the intensity of his work ethic made him unusual in many respects, and certainly one of the most outstanding men of his age.

Bibliography

Primary

PHYSICS: "On the Production of High Speed Protons," *Science*, vol. 72, 1930 (with N. E. Edlefsen); "Disintegration of Lithium by Swiftly Moving Protons," *Physical Review*, vol. 42, 1932 (with M. Stanley Livingston and Milton G. White); "An Improved Cyclotron," *Science*, vol. 86, 1937 (with Donald Cooksey); "High Energy Physics," *American Scientist*, vol. 36, 1948; "High Current Accelerators," *Science*, vol. 122, 1955.

Secondary

Davis, Nuel Pharr. *Lawrence and Oppenheimer*. New York: Simon & Schuster, 1968. This fascinating account of the entwined careers of two of America's outstanding scientific figures is more than a review of their professional relationship. It is, at once, a description of the blossoming of physics as a leading American scientific field, an unusual biographical look at the real personalities of these two intriguing figures, and a major statement about academic science in its most brilliant age. It is interesting to see how World War II drove the two men apart, finally separating them altogether, philosophically and occupationally. Lawrence is seen as a man almost obsessively driven to hold onto his position of power in the scientific community of his age, while quickly coming at odds with the humanist theoretician who once had been one of his closest friends.

Groves, Leslie R. *Now It Can Be Told: The Story of the Manhattan Project.* New York: Harper and Brothers, 1962. The creation of the atom bomb is more than simply the story of one of the most secretive and most incredible accomplishments of the modern age. In a greater sense, it represents the science of pure physics as practiced by the world's most influential scientists, including Ernest O. Lawrence. Written by one of wartime America's most controversial figures, the man in charge of it all, this book is an in-depth account of the personalities of the men who made it all possible and their struggles against time and each other. The role of Ernest Lawrence in the project was pivotal in the race against the Germans and is ably described by Groves. Lawrence was probably the one scientist in the project with whom Groves had close contact.

Kevles, Daniel J. *The Physicists: The History of a Scientific Community in Modern America.* New York: Alfred A. Knopf, 1977. This far-reaching account of the major scientific contributors of the age of nuclear physics goes beyond the recounting of primary events and the description of personalities. It is the clear and lucid story of the creation of the American community of brilliant scientific thinkers, theoreticians, and experimenters. The cult of personality, the competition for fame and fortune among jealous universities, and the sudden burst of major tools of science are all remembered.

Schück, H., et al. *Nobel: The Man and His Prizes.* Norman: University of Oklahoma Press, 1950. One cannot understand the significance of the Nobel award without first understanding how it came to exist. This excellent if lengthy volume traces everything the reader could possibly want to learn about the prizes and the man who created them. Ernest Lawrence is mentioned, along with other important physicists of the past eighty years.

Weart, Spencer R. *Scientists in Power.* Cambridge, Mass.: Harvard University Press, 1979. The author has woven together the forces of politics, sociology, and technology to tell the story of the inventors and physicists who propelled the United States to a position of high leadership among the nations of the world. In the midst of this melee of professional jealousies, wartime threats, and the scramble for public attention stands the figure of Ernest Lawrence, the creator of the basic tool of nuclear physics.

Thomas W. Becker

1943

Physics
Otto Stern, United States

Chemistry
no award

Physiology or Medicine
no award

Literature
no award

Peace
no award

OTTO STERN
1943

Born: Sohrau, Upper Silesia, Germany; February 17, 1888
Died: Berkeley, California; August 17, 1969
Nationality: American
Area of concentration: Quantum physics

Stern's contributions to the development of the molecular ray method of determining the magnetic moment of subatomic particles led to the discovery of the proton magnetic moment and to the further confirmation of the theory of quantum mechanics

The Award

Presentation

Professor E. Hulthén's presentation speech was broadcast on December 10, 1944, from Stockholm. He commented on the works of both Otto Stern and Isidor Isaac Rabi, the 1944 physics award winner, who was a student of Stern. Hulthén began the speech with a comparison of electric and magnetic properties; he reviewed first the similarities, then the contrasts. He then described the famous experiment that Stern and Walther Gerlach had performed in Frankfurt in 1920. In the experiment, a gas was heated electrically in a small furnace and allowed to pass through a small aperture into another, larger container. The second container was constantly being evacuated, so that a high vacuum was produced. This procedure would prevent the collision of the gaseous particles with air molecules and allow them to maintain a straight path. An inhomogeneous magnetic force (the magnet's force varied from end to end) was exerted on the molecules, producing a mechanical angle of diversion, which was then measured on the container wall on the side opposite to the aperture. Classical physics predicted a diffuse beam; but the result was a number of clear-cut beams. This result offered further proof that the new space quantization theory was correct. The experiment also made possible the actual calculation of the magnetic moment of the electron, which proved to approximate closely the universal magnetic moment, "Bohr's magneton" (named for Niels Bohr).

In 1923, Hulthén said, Stern had begun directing his own research, and, through further experimentation and the development of the molecular ray, he had later made other discoveries. In 1933, he proved that a particle's magnetic moment was not inversely proportional to its mass. Hulthén concluded the presentation speech with a short description of the further advances made by Rabi.

Nobel lecture

Stern's Nobel lecture, "The Method of Molecular Rays," was delivered on December 12, 1946, in English. He stated at the beginning of his speech that he intended to clarify the distinguishing features of his molecular ray method of experimentation. He stressed that "directness and simplicity" were the chief characteristics of the method. He then used his experiments to illustrate his point.

Stern first described the group of experiments that had proved the fundamental assumptions concerning kinetic motion, the motion of bodies in relation to forces exerted on them. In the molecular ray apparatus, an elementary assumption was used: Gaseous molecules travel in a straight line until they are deflected by another molecule, such as an air molecule. It was proved, in 1911, that gas particles actually do travel in straight lines, like rays of light. (Deposits of sodium condensed from a beam reflected a straight line of transmission. This experiment resulted in the term "molecular ray," or "molecular beam.") In the experiment, an oven electrically heated the gas or vapor, which was then allowed to escape through a hole. A larger container, surrounding the oven, was connected to a vacuum pump through the floor. The constant evacuation of the air was necessary to prevent collision of the gas particles with air particles. A partial wall, containing another hole termed a "collimating slit," was located directly across from the oven hole. Only a portion of the molecules would pass through the slit.

Stern's next two experiments concerned the measurement of the velocity of particles. The first one used two toothed wheels, one set in calculated motion. It was possible to calculate the velocity of particles by figuring the number of rotations per second required to allow a particle to pass through the openings of both wheels. Although not very accurate, the method allowed the production of molecules with almost uniform velocity.

The second experiment, conducted in Pittsburgh, Pennsylvania, by Stern and two other scientists, used molecular free-fall to measure velocity. The same molecular beam apparatus was used, and measurements were taken at the point of impact to determine the amount of downward deviation. The faster particles fell a shorter distance than the slower ones.

In his lecture, Stern went on to stress the sensitivity and power that his apparatus had shown in other experiments, including those of Rabi, who gave no lecture. His conclusion reiterated the "simplicity and directness" of his procedure. "It enables us," he said, "to make measurements on isolated neutral atoms or molecules with macroscopic tools. For this reason it is especially valuable for testing and demonstrating directly fundamental assumptions of the theory."

Critical reception

Stern was living in Pittsburgh at the time that he delivered his Nobel lecture. He had left Germany when Adolf Hitler came to power, in 1933. The newspapers of the period reported little that was not related to World War II. There were only four Nobel Prizes awarded for 1943; two of the winners were American, one was Hungarian, and one was Danish. For 1944, when Rabi was chosen as the physics winner, there were six; three were American, and the International Red Cross received the coveted Peace Prize. Stern did not deliver an acceptance speech until 1946, after the war had ended.

In December, 1944, when Stern's award was announced, the war was being vigorously waged on all fronts. The Soviet Union was setting up a provisional government on Hungarian soil. American bombers were pounding Tokyo. The Battle of the Bulge was under way in the Ardennes region, and the United States was retaking the Philippines. Consequently, the headlines of the day were full of the advances or retreats of the participants.

World War II was truly a universal war. The civilians in the countries where fighting was occurring were busy trying to survive, and even the American people were occupied with heavy production and rationing. The hometown death reports took precedence over awards, the value of which was undoubtedly questioned to a certain extent because of the strong animosities among the nations.

Stern's accomplishments were a breakthrough in the quantization of subatomic particles; they laid the way for the "atomic age." Before his experiments, there were two possible avenues toward further development in theoretical physics: classical theory and quantum theory. Stern's solid, unique proof of aspects of the quantization theory and his sound procedures, with their broad applications, enabled scientists to make a united effort in their investigation of the world of the atomic particle.

Biography

Otto Stern was born in Sohrau, Upper Silesia, Germany (modern Zory, Poland), on February 17, 1888. His father was a well-to-do grain merchant of Jewish descent. When Stern was four years old, his family moved to Breslau, where he attended school. He began his study of physical chemistry at the age of eighteen and earned his doctorate from the University of Breslau six years later, in 1912. With his newly won degree in hand, he joined Albert Einstein's staff at the University of Prague and later followed him to the University of Zurich. While there, Stern became a *Privatdozent* at the Swiss Federal Institute of Technology (FIT). Altogether, he worked with Einstein for two years.

Stern had just accepted his first professorship of theoretical physics at the University of Frankfurt am Main, in 1914, when he was called to World War I military duty. After the war, he spent a short time at the University of Berlin, in 1918, then returned to Frankfurt, where he remained until 1921. It was in Frankfurt that Stern turned from theoretical physics to experimentation. In 1920 he began the experiments which would later lead to the Nobel Prize in Physics. Stern was an associate professor of theoretical physics at the University of Rostock in 1921 and 1922. He then left to become a professor of physical chemistry at the University of Hamburg. He was also the director of the laboratory there until 1933, when he fled from Nazi anti-Semitic persecution and emigrated to the United States.

Stern became a research professor of physics at the Carnegie Institute of Technology in Pittsburgh and remained there until his retirement in 1945. In that same year, he was elected to the National Academy of Sciences, and in 1946, he delivered his acceptance speech for the 1943 Nobel physics prize. He died in Berkeley, California, on August 17, 1969, at the age of eighty-one.

Scientific Career

After obtaining a solid theoretical background in physics from his graduate studies and from his association with Albert Einstein, Stern branched out into experimental physics. His theoretical work centered on statistical thermodynamics and the quantum theory. To understand the unique approach of Stern's experimentation, a simple understanding of the quantum theory is important. The quantum theory attempted to explain the unusual behavior of atomic particles, behavior which deviated from the "classic" theory, which puts all physical relationships under a common rule. A good example of the classic theory is the idea that something as large as a planetary system and something as small as an atom will function in the same manner, and the same mathematical formulas will govern their properties. When scientific experimentation became more advanced, however, and the functions and properties of subatomic particles were explored, a theory was proposed to explain certain deviations: the quantum theory, or the theory of space quantization. It inaugurated an entirely new system of thought for dealing with molecules and the very basis of matter. It was with this theory that Stern concerned himself. In 1920 he began working with his molecular ray apparatus, and continued his work, collaborating with Walther Gerlach, at Rostock. He perfected his procedures while at Hamburg.

The apparatus he invented was ingenious in its simplicity. Stern utilized one of the basic assumptions about the behavior of gases: Gaseous particles travel in a straight line, unless they collide with one another or with another particle, such as an air molecule. With this assumption in mind, Stern devised an electrically powered oven to heat gas or vapor. A slot in the side of the oven allowed particles to escape into an outer, larger container. A vacuum pump continually pumped out the air, producing a high vacuum. Into this larger container, a partition was placed directly in line with the oven slit. The partition also had an opening: the "collimating slit." This aperture admitted only the central portion of the diffuse spray of gas particles coming from the oven slit. The cross section of gas particles leaving the collimating slit could be calculated with simple geometry, since the dimensions of the slit and the distance involved were known.

The narrow beam, called a molecular ray or beam, was then subjected to a special magnet, one in which the power varied along the length. The goal of this experiment was to determine the magnetic behavior of the particles. The magnetic moment of a particle, very simply stated, is the magnetic strength of one of the poles of the electrically charged atom multiplied by the length of its axis. With a homogeneous magnet, one in which the force is the same along the length of the magnet, the atom's axis will be aligned parallel to the magnet, and no change in the directional flow will be observed. With Stern's device (which was knife-shaped at one end and grooved at the other), however, an uneven force was exerted on the particles. The particles were subjected to magnetic force from every possible direction, and they were unable to align themselves with the fluctuating pull; they traveled a cone-shaped path around the directional pull of the magnet. That resulted in a change in the atoms' forward movement, and they would strike the far wall of the container, forming a pattern. The fact that there were distinct beam patterns and not a simple broadening of the ribbon-shaped beam of atoms allowed to pass through the collimating slit was cause for great interest.

Stern was not content to continue proving theories valid which already were fairly well accepted. The classic theory was valid for many studies, but it failed when it was applied to molecular problems. The two theories in existence at the time predicted two different impact patterns. The classic theory stated that there were many values possible for the angle of deflection in such a situation. Such a situation would result in the broadening of the beam. The quantum theory, however, said that only certain values were possible. When the distinct beam patterns appeared, the quantum theory was further justified as the correct avenue for future research.

Stern believed that the macroscopic capabilities of his molecular ray apparatus made it valuable. James Franck (1882-1964) and Gustav Hertz (1887-1975) had first found direct support for the basic quantum-theory hypothesis in experimentation with electron bombardment. In their famous experiment, they found that when an atom was bombarded with electrons, the energy increases in the atom were of a finite nature. They had used an atomic technique in their work, however, whereas Stern used an almost mechanical method. The same method could be used for determining the magnetic moment of a magnet or of something as small as an atom. When the progressively smaller results were compiled, they clearly illustrated the shift to quantum mechanics. Stern's methods also used neutral particles; the atomic methods used ions, in which the energy exchanges could complicate the interpretation of the results.

Stern used the same "mechanical" procedures for a group of experiments which addressed the wave nature of molecular beams. Experimental proof of the wave nature had already been found, in 1927, but Stern went on to perform his own proof, with helium gas. He used the velocity test with the toothed wheels; the helium struck lithium fluoride, and the angle of diffraction was measured. Because the lattice constant of the lithium fluoride was known, it was possible to calculate the beam's wavelength. The results agreed with theory within 2 percent. The "direct, primitive" experiment was remarkable in its yielding of the same results gained by complex atomic testing.

Stern found, too, that with the molecular ray method of experimentation, a longer period in which to measure the magnetic moments was available. The minimum amount of time used to measure all the particles should be the same. In Stern's experiment, the particles were in their natural state, which had an unlimited life span; in atomic experiments, the atoms were in an excited state and would produce flashes of energy to regain their normal configuration. The time allowed for measurement was only the life span of an excited atom, or ion, which is approximately 10^{-8} seconds. Stern had about twice the time, or 10^{-4} seconds.

The results of these tests were, again, extremely interesting. Theory had stated that the magnetic moment of a particle is inversely proportional to the mass. Since the proton of the hydrogen molecule is about two thousand times more massive than the electron, the magnetic moment of the proton should have been two thousand times smaller than that of the electron. The magnetic moment of the proton, however, was measured to be approximately two and a half times larger than the theory predicted.

The unique nature of Stern's experimental method highlighted the shift from classic theory to quantum theory as the materials decreased in size. The simplicity and versatility of his apparatus made possible a wide variety of tests in the area of quantum mechanics, further supporting the quantum theory and helping to pave the way for the "atomic age."

Bibliography

Primary
PHYSICS: *Der geschichtliche Ursprung der sachsischen Leibzucht*, 1896; *Der Zitterlaut R. Nebst angabe von Winken und Hilfsmitteln zur Entwicklung des R*, 1907; *Zur kinetischen Theorie des osmotischen Druckes konzentrierter Lösungen und über die Gültigkeit des Henryschen Gesetzes für konzentrierte Lösungen von Kohlendioxyd in organischen Lösungsmitteln bei tiefen Temperaturen*, 1912; *Der Taubstummenlehrerberuf*, 1912.

Secondary
Bohm, David. *Quantum Theory*. Englewood Cliffs, N.J.: Prentice-Hall, 1951. A college-level text which delves into the complexities of quantum theory without inflicting innumerable formulas on the reader. It can be quite complex, however, and a basic understanding of physics is necessary.
Glasstone, Samuel. *Sourcebook on Atomic Energy*. 2d ed. Princeton, N.J.: Van Nostrand, 1958. This book is considered to be the basic source for scientists, laymen, and teachers on the history of the field of atomic energy. It is not extremely complex, but a high school background in physics is valuable.
Heisenberg, Werner. *The Physical Principles of the Quantum Theory*. Chicago: University of Chicago Press, 1930. This source provides a fairly complex discussion of early experimentation and discoveries in the field of quantum physics. There have been many developments in the area, however, since the book appeared.
Humphreys, Richard F., and Robert Beringer. *First Principles of Atomic Physics*. New York: Harper & Brothers, 1950. A basic, high school-level text, with clear explanations and comparisons. Stern is not specifically mentioned; however, the results of his experimentation are explained quite well. Most physics texts do not refer to Stern, except for the Stern-Gerlach experiment, because of the confirming nature of many of his results.
Richtmyer, Floyd K., E. H. Kennard, and T. Lauritsen. *Introduction to Modern Physics*. 5th ed. New York: McGraw-Hill, 1955. A good place for the less advanced researcher to begin reading.

Rojansky, Vladimir. *Introductory Quantum Mechanics*. New York: Prentice-Hall, 1938. This text would be easier for the beginner than David Bohm's book. Quantum mechanics is never easy, however, without an advanced mathematics and physics background.

Ellen F. Mitchum

1944

Physics
Isidor Isaac Rabi, United States

Chemistry
Otto Hahn, Germany

Physiology or Medicine
Joseph Erlanger, United States
Herbert S. Gasser, United States

Literature
Johannes V. Jensen, Denmark

Peace
International Red Cross Committee

ISIDOR ISAAC RABI
1944

Born: Rymanow, Austria-Hungary; July 29, 1898
Died: New York, New York; January 11, 1988
Nationality: American
Area of concentration: Nuclear physics

Rabi devised the resonance method of magnetic moment measurement, which became the central technique in all modern molecular- and atomic-beam experiments

The Award

Presentation

Professor E. Hulthén of Stockholm delivered a broadcast as a substitution for the traditional award ceremony, since it was not possible to convene the Nobel Committee and its honorees in Sweden in 1944. His lecture took place on December 10, 1944, and was broadcast on shortwave radio. A separate and precedent-shattering ceremony took place in the Waldorf-Astoria Hotel in New York City on December 11, 1944, when the Swedish Minister to the United States, Wollmar F. Bostroem, acting as the personal representative of King Gustav V of Sweden, presented Nobel awards to six residents of the United States—five Americans and a Dane— including Isidor Isaac Rabi's mentor from Hamburg, Otto Stern (1888-1969), who won the award for 1943. Rabi did not actually receive his Nobel medallion until a later ceremony at Columbia University, where Nicholas Murray Butler, the president of Columbia, presented it to him.

Professor Hulthén's account of Stern's and Rabi's work began with a recollection of how the French scientist André-Marie Ampère (1775-1836), a pioneer in the charting of magnetic fields, had tried to locate the origins of magnetic fields in rotary currents of electricity in particles of matter. Although Ampère's hypothesis was essentially accurate, Hulthén pointed out, his successors in the field of electrotechnics were unable to account for the influence of a magnetic field on the movement of an electron, even with the instruments of spectroscopy available in the latter part of the nineteenth century. In 1920, Otto Stern and Walther Gerlach (1889-1979) directed a thin line of molecules into a magnetic field, where it was divided into several sharply defined beams, the number corresponding to the angular momentum (or directional positions) of the atoms in relation to the field. Stern eventually determined that the atomic nucleus itself possessed a rotational direction, or spin, and with the molecular beam method, he was able to determine the magnetic factor of the nucleus in relation to that of the electron in a hydrogen atom.

Rabi had worked with Stern in the late 1920's, and with Stern's encouragement, he approached the problem of how the atom reacts to a magnetic field. According to a theorem formulated by the English mathematician Sir Joseph Larmor (1857-1942), the effect of the magnetic field on the atom develops from the rotation of the electron and the atomic nucleus around the direction of the field, a phenomenon likened by Hulthén to the gyroscopic, or spinning, movement of a top. If the strength of the magnetic field is known, the magnetic factor, or moment, of the electron and of the atomic nucleus can be estimated, provided that the rotation can be observed and measured.

Calling Rabi's solution both simple and brilliant, Hulthén described how Rabi had inserted a strand of wire into the magnetic field and then ran an oscillating current of variable frequency through the wire. When the atom beam passed through the magnetic field, it was influenced by the current, which controlled the rotation, or spin, of the nucleus. When the current was at a certain frequency, Rabi discovered, the atom would make a "quantum jump" from one state of angular rotation to another; that is, its position in the field was radically altered. The crucial part of the experiment was that Rabi could detect and measure the frequency, or resonance, at which the jump took place with remarkable accuracy. With this method, Hulthén concluded, Rabi had "established radio relations with the most subtle particles of matter, with the world of the electron and of the atomic nucleus." The determination of the magnetic moment of various atoms (Rabi worked primarily with sodium) would follow.

Nobel lecture

Wartime conditions prevented Rabi from delivering the traditional lecture, but on January 21, 1945, Rabi presented the fourth Richtmyer Lecture, a series in honor of F. K. Richtmyer sponsored by the American Association of Physics Teachers. In his tribute to the former Cornell University physicist, he offered "a straight scientific talk" on one of his specialties, radiofrequency spectroscopy—another designation for the resonance method—and noted four directions for future research. The third possibility was an idea for an atomic clock which he based on the experiments he and his colleagues had done on radiofrequency variations and their effects on the nucleus. The thrust of his discussion was that there might be specific applications for the discoveries he had been making, which indicates the cast of his mind at the time when he won the Nobel Prize. On the other hand, considering the importance of the Prize, Rabi might have reached in a different direction in his Nobel lecture and talked about the relationship of the study of physics to the gradual development of human understanding of the universe itself. Rabi reserved his philosophical reflections for his later years, but he might have believed that the worldwide audience for a Nobel lecture warranted his most serious thinking. His comments on the new physics suggest the direction such a lecture might have taken:

Physics will never have an end. The novelty of nature is such that its variety will be infinite—not just in changing forms but in the profundity of insight and the newness of ideas that will be necessary to find some sort of clarity or order in it. I think the only thing you can compare it to is the mystical idea of God with infinite attributes.

Critical reception

Because of all-consuming interest in the events of World War II as the Allies drove deep into the German heartland at the close of 1944, the selection of I. I. Rabi for the Nobel Prize in Physics was not given much attention outside the scientific community. Because of wartime conditions, no prizes were awarded from 1940 to 1943, and Rabi's award was also the first one given outside Sweden, in what *The New York Times* described as a "precedent shattering ceremony." The affair had been arranged by the American-Scandinavian Foundation, and this was the first time since the inception of the award that the prizes had been presented by anyone other than the King of Sweden.

Rabi, in his wryly self-deprecating fashion, referred to the occasion as an "ersatz ceremony," but it was attended by many members of the Scandinavian nobility, who undoubtedly regarded it as an important show of unity among the Allied forces, symbolizing the cooperation of Americans and Europeans. Crown Prince Gustav Adolf of Sweden addressed the gathering by shortwave radio, and then Harold Willis Dodds, the president of Princeton University, delivered the principal address, remarking that "the world needs leaders such as are symbolized by the whole pattern of Nobel prizes." Rabi was listed among other participants at a forum following the fourth annual American Nobel anniversary dinner, and his picture appeared on page 34 of *The New York Times* with those of the other winners.

The popular press, preoccupied with the war, largely ignored the awards (*Newsweek* did not have a regular feature devoted to science in 1944), with the exception of *Time* magazine, which, in an article that included a picture of "Columbia's Rabi," concisely stated that the Nobel Prizes had gone to three men "who have been studying atoms." The article described Rabi as a "tousle-haired Columbia professor, born in Austria and raised in New York City," and attempted to explain his molecular-beam method by comparing it to the action of the atom-smashing machine, or synchro-cyclotron, that Rabi had likened to "studying the Taj Mahal by dynamiting it and considering its fragments." As an example of Rabi's contribution, *Time* pointed out that Rabi had learned that the deuteron, the simplest known nucleus, revolves "like a football spinning end over end"—a somewhat clumsy analogy but one typical of attempts to give a graphic, comprehensible picture of the properties and behavior of subatomic particles. The picture of the tumbling football stands in vivid contrast to the images of destruction used in the following summer to capture the awesome, lethal forces unleashed by the process of nuclear fission. Before the advent of the postwar atomic age, however, physics never really caught the public's imagination.

Within the scientific community, a kind of quiet jubilation marked the announcement of the award. Physicists from the Radiation Laboratory at the Massachusetts Institute of Technology and from the Radio Research Laboratory at Harvard attended a party for Rabi in Cambridge, Massachusetts, and Lee DuBridge recalls, "There was general rejoicing in the Radiation Lab." Two of Rabi's colleagues in Cambridge, George Uhlenbeck and Felix Bloch, composed a song with the refrain

"Twinkle, twinkle Otto Stern;/ How did Rabi so much learn?" The award was not unexpected, since, as Polykarp Kusch, a Nobel winner in 1955, observed, "It seemed to be inevitable. It was a brand new mold of spectroscopy and you can learn all kinds of things about molecules, atoms and nuclei. We knew this. We didn't underestimate our papers." That did not lessen the satisfaction, however, and Rabi remembers that the award was "an excuse for many parties in different parts of the country." Although Rabi's life was permanently changed by his celebrity so that he became more of an organizer of others' work and a spokesman for science after the award, his ability to keep celebrity in perspective was assisted by Nicholas Murray Butler, president of Columbia since Rabi had begun working there, who called him "Fermi" when he made a few comments at the Columbia presentation.

Biography

Israel Isaac Rabi was born in Rymanow, a small town then part of Austria-Hungary, now in Poland, on July 29, 1898. Shortly after his birth, his father, David, emigrated to the United States alone in search of economic opportunity, and within a year had accumulated sufficient funds to send for his wife Sheindel and their infant son. The Rabis lived on the Lower East Side of Manhattan, a neighborhood populated by Yiddish-speaking Jews, and when young Rabi was enrolled in school, his mother told the registrar that his name was "Izzy," a diminutive of Israel, which was recorded as, and thus changed officially to, Isidor. The Rabis moved to Brownsville, in Brooklyn, when Rabi was ten, and he decided to attend Manual Training High School, three miles away, instead of the more esteemed Boys High School, because he wanted to explore a non-Jewish environment. Similarly, he chose Cornell University to become part of a broader American experience, but when he received his bachelor of science degree in chemistry in 1919, he found that there was no place in industry for anyone of Jewish background. He spent three years back in New York City, working at menial jobs and amusing himself. He entered graduate school in chemistry at Cornell in 1922, and when he was rejected for a fellowship in physics, he transferred to Columbia University, where he received his doctorate in 1927.

With Helen Newmark, his bride of one year, he moved to Europe to study with the greatest physicists of the twentieth century—men such as Otto Stern, Werner Heisenberg, Wolfgang Pauli, and Niels Bohr. In August, 1929, with a strong recommendation from his mentors in Europe, he began a thirty-eight-year career as a teacher at Columbia University, beginning as a lecturer in theoretical physics and eventually becoming the first university professor at Columbia, in 1964. At Columbia, assisted by brilliant colleagues and students, he began the series of experiments on the magnetic properties of atomic nuclei that culminated in his resonance method for determining the rotational states of atoms and molecules. This work was carried out through the 1930's and led to his winning the Nobel Prize in 1944.

In 1940, with the beginning of World War II, Rabi, very much aware of the Nazi threat from his contacts with the eminent European physicists forced to flee to the

United States, joined the Radiation Laboratory at the Massachusetts Institute of Technology; there, he was instrumental in developing radar systems for weapons. In 1942, while still ostensibly employed at the "Rad Lab," Rabi became an adviser to J. Robert Oppenheimer, who was directing the Manhattan Project (the atom bomb project) at Los Alamos. After the war, he worked to create the Brookhaven, Long Island, National Laboratory for Atomic Research to explore the peaceful uses of atomic energy.

Rabi accepted the chairmanship of the physics department at Columbia in 1945, but he found that his fame enabled him to become a civilian spokesman for American scientific endeavors and resigned the chair in 1949 to work as an adviser in the newly established Atomic Energy Commission. He held this position from 1952 to 1956 and served as a member of the American delegation to the International Conference on the Peaceful Uses of Atomic Energy, held in Geneva in 1955. He retired from teaching in 1969 but continued to work with universities and the government to support the scientific inquiry to which he had dedicated his life.

Scientific Career

Rabi was born at the dawn of the modern age of physics, when original scientific experimentation in the United States was almost nonexistent. By the time he won the Nobel Prize, American physics had developed to the point that Rabi and his colleagues were about to complete the experiments that enabled the Allies to develop an atom bomb before the vaunted scientists of Adolf Hitler's Third Reich could successfully manufacture one. By the time he was appointed university professor at Columbia, his students had already won or shared four Nobel awards, and the new disciplines of particle physics and radio astronomy had revealed facts concerning the tiniest components of matter and the farthest reaches of the universe hardly dreamed of by even the most imaginative scientists at the end of the nineteenth century. For Rabi, however, a man of unusual imagination and extraordinary curiosity, none of the great discoveries of the twentieth century was very surprising; he believed that the power of human intelligence could carry science beyond the limits of any mystery—that true scientific inquiry could reveal the outlines of the divine.

Rabi's childhood in a family of devout, orthodox, even fundamentalist Jews immersed him in an ethos of wonder and reverence, but the singularly analytic nature of his own intellect led him to an interpretation of the awesome phenomena of existence distinctly different from the one propounded by his parents' faith. Before the age of ten, he had independently discovered a description of the Copernican universe in his local library and returned home to dismay his parents by proclaiming, "It's all very simple. Who needs God?" At first reluctant to participate in the ritual declaration of manhood of the Bar Mitzvah service at thirteen, Rabi eventually agreed to a ceremony in which he delivered an address, not from the Torah (the sacred Jewish text), but one of his own composition, entitled "How the Electric Light Works." This fierce independence of mind, combined with an ability to work within the context of a system about which he was not particularly enthusiastic, enabled Rabi to move comfortably in almost any milieu and to recognize the elements of crucial convergences in fields that, by the standards of the scientific establishment, were unrelated.

Rabi's senior thesis succeeded in locating previously suspected but never-isolated forms of manganese oxidation states, although the data went unnoticed until rediscovered by a British chemist and published in the *Journal of the Faraday Society*. Rabi had already sensed that the branch of chemistry in which he was interested was called "physics," and he entered Columbia University as a graduate student in physics in 1925, supporting himself by tutoring students at the City College of New York. There was no one at Columbia who could teach him more than he had learned from reading European journals and discussing them with fellow graduate students, and his doctoral project was conducted entirely on his own, because "the last thing in the world I wanted . . . was for someone to help me."

For his dissertation topic, Rabi decided to test the magnetic susceptibility of various complicated crystalline salts, such as nickel ammonium sulphate hydrate. He found the job of cutting and grinding physical specimens tedious and routine, contrary to his nature and his growing sense of the kind of physics he wanted to practice. In a characteristic stroke of brilliance, he solved the problem by inventing a new and much more efficient approach to the process. He recalls that one day he happened to be reading, for sheer pleasure, James Clerk Maxwell's *Treatise on Electricity and Magnetism* (1873), and he recognized that Maxwell's explanation of how a nonuniform magnetic field (a field with different strengths in different regions) could alter the magnetic susceptibility of a body within it. From this insight, Rabi was able to get the data he needed. First, he produced a solution that would not dissolve his crystals. Then, he placed the crystal, attached to a glass fiber to supply an electric current, into the solution. By varying the solution through the addition of a standard magnetic salt until the magnetic susceptibility of the crystal vanished—that is, until all observable motion ceased—he could determine the precise amount of fluid needed to cancel magnetic susceptibility. When the weight of the fluid was compared with the weight of an identical tube of water for which magnetic susceptibility was known, it was possible to calculate the susceptibility of the crystal itself, since the weights were in the same ratio as the magnetic susceptibility. As John Rigden, Rabi's biographer, points out, "The old method was crude, a brute-force approach. Rabi's method had style."

During the time that Rabi was working on his dissertation, the new quantum physics was being invented by Werner Heisenberg, Erwin Schrödinger, and others in Europe. Rabi believed that he could learn only from the masters themselves, and with no letters of introduction, he and his wife departed for Europe. As Rabi put it, "We knew the libretto, but we had to learn the music." He moved rapidly from Copenhagen, where he worked with Niels Bohr, to Hamburg, to study with Otto Stern, and eventually to Leipzig in 1929, to listen to Heisenberg himself, before going on to Zurich and Wolfgang Pauli's laboratory. In the two years he spent in Europe (with other Americans, such as J. Robert Oppenheimer and Edward Teller), he observed first-rate minds at work and came to the conclusion that American physics needed leaders. He was clearly equal in ability to the younger European scientists he met. On his return to the United States, he began the work which would make him one of the preeminent leaders of American science, choosing as his twin themes of exploration during the 1930's a challenge to the principles of quantum mechanics, to see how well they explained the intricacies of molecular motion, and an attempt to measure as precisely as possible the properties and characteristics of the still-mysterious atomic nucleus.

He had begun to work on molecular-beam experiments with Otto Stern, experiments which appealed to him because, as Rigden puts it, "they had the elegance of simplicity plus the allure of power." In 1931, he formed a molecular-beam laboratory at Columbia and began to gather about him some of the most prominent American physicists of the next three decades. His teaching, while a bit chaotic, was considered tremendously exciting (he won the Ørsted Medal, the highest award of the American Association of Physics Teachers, in 1981), "an open window in a stuffy room." As Leon Lederman says, "How bad Rabi's lectures were but how successful his teaching was. There was a sort of electricity in the air." Working with the young men he had inspired, Rabi refined the molecular-beam apparatus so that he could measure the spin, or rotation, of the sodium nucleus in 1933; measure the magnetic moment of the proton and neutron of the heavy isotope of hydrogen in 1934; refine the beam by the "T-method," in which the magnetic field itself could be made to rotate to determine signs (positive and negative) within the field; and in 1937, begin the development of the method of magnetic resonance that led to his Nobel Prize-winning experiments. As Hans Bethe observed, there were three key events in the formative years of nuclear physics, one of them being the discovery of the quadropole moment of the deuteron. Without Rabi's development of the magnetic resonance method to a state of considerable precision, this discovery would not have been possible.

During the late 1930's, Rabi had been aware of the rise of Fascism in Europe through contacts with his friends and fellow scientists, and in addition to his feelings as a Jew (he had begun in the 1920's to include his middle name, Isaac, in his signature in defiance of anti-Semitism), he felt deep concern over what he regarded as the threat to the principles of civilization that he believed the spirit of free scientific inquiry embodied. "I took the war personally," he recalled. When President Franklin D. Roosevelt organized the National Defense Research Committee in June, 1940, Rabi knew many men in the organization and maintained informal contact with them about the ways in which the scientific community could aid the war effort. When the NDRC established the Radiation Laboratory at the Massachusetts Institute of Technology, Rabi "wanted to be in on it," and he left New York City for Cambridge. The "Rad Lab" was instrumental in developing the somewhat primitive British radar technique into an effective weapon, and Rabi was especially active, not only in the technical development of the system but in negotiations with the armed services. His straightfoward but relaxed approach and his lack of any need for glory won the confidence of military men suspicious of freewheeling theoretical physicists. As Rabi remarked, "When we got to know one another, when they learned we were trying to help them and that we respected them, when they discovered we didn't want any of glory, we came to be friends with great mutual respect."

Once the radar project was successfully initiated (it enabled the Allies to detect German U-boats and end that menace and to knock down 85 percent of the V-1 rockets launched toward England), Rabi joined his old friend, the mercurial J. Robert Oppenheimer, at Los Alamos in 1942 to help organize the top-secret Manhattan Project. All the leading scientists there knew that the Germans were capable of discovering and applying the secrets of nuclear fission, and they found themselves in a race with no sense of the position of their formidable opponent. Rabi was uncertain about the ethics of bombing and was unsure whether the atom bomb was even a practical possibility, but his anxiety about the Nazis' getting the weapon first drove him to use his best scientific and organizational abilities to advance the project. Its eventual success both pleased and troubled Rabi, for, like many other scientists there, he knew immediately and profoundly just how destructive the new weapon was.

When the war ended, Rabi oversaw the publication of a twenty-eight-volume edition of the findings of the Rad Lab, thus forming the basis for the flourishing postwar American electronics industry. He saw in the structural arrangements of the Manhattan Project a basis for further advancement of American science, in that younger men had learned directly from the greats of the field in a kind of brotherhood of physics. Rabi returned to Columbia to chair its department of physics and to further this brotherhood, but he found himself in competition with the University of California at Berkeley and the University of Chicago for the best young scientists. He had hoped to return to his prewar work as well, but his Nobel-laureate celebrity and changing conditions caused him to shift his focus so that he was never fully involved in the actual procedures of experimental work again.

He resigned from the chairmanship in 1949 so that he could devote more time to national priorities, including the development of a nine-school consortium into the Brookhaven National Laboratory, one of the most advanced American facilities for the study of nuclear physics. He worked with other scientists to establish a national authority on atomic research (the Atomic Energy Commission, established in 1946), with a presidential advisory board, of which he was a member. He expressed his doubts about the efficacy of building a hydrogen bomb and was concerned after its development that the scientists had turned the weapon over to persons "who do not respect the human spirit." Determined to make the best of the situation, he supported a 1955 UNESCO conference in Geneva on the international control of nuclear weapons, which eventually led to the first nuclear test-ban treaty, and also testified at a hearing to determine whether Oppenheimer was a threat to the security of the United States. Under no illusions about Oppenheimer's eccentricity, Rabi stood by his principles and supported Oppenheimer by forcing the inquisitors on the committee to go beyond a narrow view of patriotism and national security. Rabi's cool demeanor and quiet strength impressed even his adversaries, who noted his fairness and powers of reason.

Rabi had known and admired Dwight D. Eisenhower from Eisenhower's days as president of Columbia and was able to convince Eisenhower to appoint a trusted, unbiased, and candid person as his first science adviser: James Killian, the president of the Massachusetts Institute of Technology, was the first to fill the job, in 1957. This position permitted the scientific community to keep in touch with the powers in Washington until Richard Nixon, who seemed to regard scientists as adversaries, abolished it in 1973. During its existence, it led directly to the formation of the National Aeronautics and Space Administration and to federal programs to fund science education. Eisenhower remarked the year before he died that Rabi and his associates were among the few men who came to Washington to serve their country, not themselves. Rabi continued to offer advice and counsel to the government, including suggestions to build bigger satellites and a warning to Secretary of Defense Robert McNamara not to use nuclear weapons in Vietnam in 1968.

Through the 1970's and 1980's, Rabi continued his life as a kind of elder statesman of science, receiving awards for his work, serving on committees, and lecturing on the place of the scientist in a decent and humane world. He had become, by acknowledgment, the dean of American physics. He had lived to see his dreams of a world-leading American physics community realized and to see many of his students in positions of prominence throughout the United States. As Lee DuBridge put it when Rabi retired from Columbia in 1968, "Rabi has been a key figure in lifting American physics and other areas of American science from the primitive role they occupied during his student days to the position of international leadership which American science occupies today." On the same occasion, Jerrold Zacharias, Rabi's associate through the 1930's, displayed what had been referred to as the "Rabi Tree," a schematic diagram in the form of a tree with roots and trunks, still growing, that was originally designed by the U.S. Navy to illustrate the importance of basic research. To make its case, the Navy chose a scientist, Rabi, whose work had been crucial to the progress of physics and built a structure illustrating his influence on basic research. The "tree" and an accompanying illustrative key, plus commentary, appear in John Rigden's biography of Rabi. As Rigden concluded, "the tree still lives. Nourishment still flows freely and vigorously from the trunk through the major branches. New branches continue to sprout, and the tree grows outward and upward."

Bibliography

Primary
PHYSICS: *My Life and Times as a Physicist*, 1960; *Science and Public Policy*, 1963; *Science: The Center of Culture*, 1970.

Secondary

Bernstein, Jeremy. "Profiles: Physicist." *The New Yorker* 51 (October 13-20, 1975): 47-50, 47-50. Bernstein, an accomplished scientist himself, interviewed Rabi at length. He places Rabi's comments in the context of his work as an experimental physicist and a member of the American scientific community. The writing is lucid, with what are probably the most understandable explanations of Rabi's experiments available for the layman. Rabi himself emerges as an engaging and brilliant man.

Kevles, Daniel J. *The Physicists: The History of a Scientific Community in Modern America*. New York: Alfred A. Knopf, 1977. As Kevles explains in his preface, Rabi himself suggested this book, since his generation of physicists "changed the world." Kevles covers the development of American physics through the twentieth century, placing scientific work in relation to national and international events. His book is thorough, detailed, and clearly written. In addition to solid annotation, it has an essay on the sources Kevles used, which would provide useful information for further study of any aspect of the field.

Motz, Lloyd, ed. *A Festschrift for I. I. Rabi*. New York: New York Academy of Sciences, 1977. These firsthand accounts by Rabi's students and colleagues are affectionate reminiscences which help to give some sense of what it was like to know and work with Rabi.

Newman, James R., ed. *What Is Science?* New York: Simon & Schuster, 1955. A landmark collection of essays on the subject of science and the scientific outlook. Twelve eminent scientists and philosophers, including Bertrand Russell and Julian Huxley, explain their fields of expertise to the layperson. This volume is an excellent place to start if one seeks an overview of modern scientific thought and its implications for society.

Rigden, John S. *Rabi: Scientist and Citizen*. New York: Basic Books, 1987. An extremely good biography of Rabi and the most complete source for information about the scientist and his work. Rigden covers both the man and his career, providing a full-scale portrait of Rabi and a solid explanation of his life and work. There is an epilogue by Rabi offering ideas developed late in his life. Includes two appendices, plus an illustration of the famous "Rabi Tree," with an explanatory note.

Segrè, Emilio. *From X-Rays to Quarks: Modern Physicists and Their Discoveries*. San Francisco: W. H. Freeman, 1980. Described by the author as an "impressionistic view of the events as they appeared to me during my scientific career which started about 1927," this volume is a very well-organized and factual account of the development of physics from the end of the nineteenth century to the last decades of the twentieth. It has some technical material that might be difficult for the layperson to grasp, but it includes many photographs and illustrations and is written clearly, with a sense of style. Ten mathematically rigorous appendices cover crucial discoveries and offer some interesting speculation on the implications of the discoveries described.

Leon Lewis

1945

Physics
Wolfgang Pauli, Austria and United States

Chemistry
Artturi Virtanen, Finland

Physiology or Medicine
Sir A. Fleming, Great Britain
Ernst Boris Chain, Great Britain
Lord Florey, Australia

Literature
Gabriela Mistral, Chile

Peace
Cordell Hull, United States

WOLFGANG PAULI
1945

Born: Vienna, Austria; April 25, 1900
Died: Zurich, Switzerland; December 15, 1958
Nationality: Austrian; after 1946, American
Area of concentration: Quantum mechanics

The discovery of the exclusion principle enabled Pauli to explain the structure of the periodic table of the elements and to formulate fundamental theories of electrical conductivity in metals and the magnetic properties of matter

The Award

Presentation

In ceremonies held December 10, 1945, eight Nobel awards for achievements in physics, chemistry, medicine, and literature for 1944 and 1945 were presented. Each of the laureates stepped forward to the flourish of trumpets and was saluted by Gustav V, the eighty-seven-year-old King of Sweden. Since Wolfgang Pauli could not be present, the United States *chargé d'affaires*, Christian M. Ravndal, received the physics prize diploma and a $30,000 check on Pauli's behalf.

Professor I. Waller, a member of the Nobel Committee for Physics, delivered the presentation speech. He explained that Niels Bohr (1885-1962) had proposed a model of the atom in which electrons could only be in certain atomic orbits. The energy and two other properties of the orbit were to be specified by whole numbers called "quantum numbers." Pauli showed that, in fact, four quantum numbers were required to specify an electron's orbit. He then stated his exclusion principle: Only one electron can have a given set of quantum numbers. Every electron must have a different set of quantum numbers.

Pauli was able to use his principle, coupled with Bohr's theory, to explain the periods that occur in the periodic table of the elements. Later, the exclusion principle was indispensable for Pauli's theories of electrical conductivity in metals and of the magnetic properties of matter. Professor Waller stated that the Nobel Prize was awarded to Pauli for these and many other important contributions to atomic and nuclear physics.

Nobel lecture

Pauli delivered his lecture before the Nobel Committee on December 13, 1946, the year after his receipt of the award. The speech was titled, "Exclusion Principle and Quantum Mechanics." He began by recalling how, in the early 1920's, research on Bohr's atomic theory had been vigorously pursued. The theory had both successes and failures. One of its obvious failures was its inability to predict the regularities of the periodic table of elements. When arranged by atomic weight from the lightest to the heaviest, the elements fell naturally into groups of 2, 8, 18, or 32. Their properties changed in a fairly regular way from the beginning to the ending of each group. Bohr suggested that the electrons were arranged in "shells" around the nucleus and that the first shell was completed with the two electrons of the helium atom. He had no explanation, however, for why atoms with more electrons did not put those electrons in the lowest energy state, the innermost shell.

Another problem of the time was the "anomalous Zeeman effect." It arises in the following fashion: When gas atoms are heated until they glow, and then the light they emit is passed first through a slit and then through a prism, it produces a spectrum. Such a spectrum is similar to a rainbow, but it usually has only certain spectral lines, instead of all the rainbow's colors. If the gas is now subjected to a magnetic field, the spectral lines may split into triplets. This splitting is called the Zeeman effect, named for Pieter Zeeman (1865-1943), its discoverer. It could be understood in terms of the Bohr theory as the expected interaction of an orbital electron with the magnetic field. Some spectral lines split into more than three lines, and this result is the anomalous Zeeman effect. Bohr's theory provided no explanation for it.

Pauli eventually found the solution. There had to be another quantum number associated with the electron, and this number would assume one of only two possible values. Later, George Uhlenbeck (born 1900) and Samuel Goudsmit (1902-1978) associated this new quantum number with electron spin (loosely speaking, the electron can spin like a top, either clockwise or counterclockwise). Pauli then formed his exclusion principle: Only one electron at a time could have a given set of the four quantum numbers. The exclusion principle can be seen as an extension of the idea that two bodies may not occupy the same physical space at the same time. The effect of the exclusion principle is to say that if two electrons are close in physical space—if, for example, they orbit the same atom—then they are excluded from occupying the same "energy space," the same "momentum space," and the same "electron-spin space." At least one of the quantum numbers describing energy, momentum, or spin must be different for any two electrons in an atom.

For that reason, no more than two electrons could be present in the innermost atomic state: Two electrons filled the state, and all other electrons were excluded. When the more advanced quantum theories of Werner Heisenberg (1901-1976) and Erwin Schrödinger (1887-1961) replaced Bohr's theory, the exclusion principle was retained. It was then possible to show that various atomic electron shells could hold only 2, 8, 18, or 32 electrons and thereby to explain the structure of the periodic table. Once the atomic states were correctly described (including the electron-spin quantum number), the anomalous Zeeman effect was easily explained.

Pauli concluded his paper with a survey of applications of the exclusion principle. He pointed out that it applied to neutrons and protons, as well as to electrons, and hence governed the structure of the atomic nucleus. He also related it to the general symmetry of mathematical functions.

Critical reception

In general, the public paid little attention to Pauli's prize; theoretical atomic physics was not the strong suit of the man on the street. To most people of the day, "atomic physics" meant only "atomic bomb." Hence, *The New York Times* made only a brief announcement of the award. *Science News Letter* of December 1, 1945, ran an article headlined "Atom Bomb Nobelists," in which it announced the prizewinners for chemistry and physics, Otto Hahn (1879-1968) and Pauli. Pauli, however, was never directly involved with the bomb. The article did go on to describe Pauli's exclusion principle in rather charming terms. It noted that electrons were very uniform and standard fellows, except when forced together in an atom. There, they insist on their rugged individuality, each demanding its own unique set of quantum numbers.

Since circumstances prevented Pauli from attending the Nobel ceremonies in Sweden, he was honored by his colleagues at a dinner on December 10, 1945, at Princeton University. Hermann Weyl (1885-1955) delivered an encomium. Ironically, Weyl had been among the first to have his theories pruned by the young Pauli. *Science* of February 22, 1946, reported that Weyl praised Pauli as the conscience and criterion of truth for theoretical physicists the world over and said that they were unanimous in applauding the Nobel Committee's decision to recognize Pauli. Stating that it was a bold conception and essential to an understanding of the periodic system of the elements, Weyl lauded the exclusion principle as a lasting achievement which would not be affected by future changes in theories. (It had already survived the change from the Bohr theory to the new quantum theory of Heisenberg and Schrödinger.) Weyl congratulated Pauli for several other accomplishments and then, ironically, expressed doubt about Pauli's prediction of the existence of a neutrino—an elementary particle that would, according to Pauli's predictions, be detected, less than a decade later.

Biography

Wolfgang Pauli was born on April 25, 1900, in Vienna, Austria. He was the son of Wolfgang Joseph Pauli and Bertha Schutz. Pauli's mother was a writer and had many contacts in the theater world and in the press. His father was a physician who became one of the founders of the field of colloidal chemistry. He eventually became a full professor and director of the Institute of Medical Colloid Chemistry at the University of Vienna. The Pauli family was close-knit, and consequently, Pauli was greatly influenced by his father. He was also influenced by a friend of his father, Ernst Mach (1838-1916), who was both a physicist and a philosopher. Appointed Pauli's godfather, Mach took his duties seriously enough to advise him concerning his education and to send various books for him to study.

Such high-powered help, along with Pauli's natural aptitude, eventually surpassed the school's offerings. Bored during high school classes, Pauli surreptitiously read works on advanced mathematics and Albert Einstein's general theory of relativity. After finishing high school, Pauli determined to study under Arnold Sommerfeld (1868-1951) at the University of Munich. Sommerfeld was one of the most highly regarded theoretical physicists of that time.

Obtaining his doctorate in 1921, Pauli spent a year at the University of Göttingen with Max Born (1882-1970), followed by a year at Copenhagen with Bohr—two of the greatest theoretical physicists of the day. Pauli was a lecturer at the University of Hamburg from 1922 to 1925, when he was appointed professor of theoretical physics at the Federal Institute of Technology in Zurich. He retained the post for the rest of his life, although he spent the war years at the Institute for Advanced Study in Princeton, New Jersey. He also spent brief periods at other universities in the United States.

Pauli enjoyed the theater and was quite proud of his sister Hertha, an actress. Kate Deppner, also an actress, became Pauli's wife in the late 1920's. After a divorce, Pauli married Franciska Bertram in April, 1934. Pauli was also interested in psychology. He corresponded with Carl Gustav Jung and wrote several articles on psychological subjects.

Pauli was awarded the Lorentz Medal in 1930, the Nobel Prize in Physics in 1945, the Franklin Medal in 1952, and the Max Planck Medal in 1958. He was a foreign member of the Royal Society of London and a member of the Swiss Physical Society, the American Physical Society, and the American Association for the Advancement of Science.

Scientific Career

Pauli began his professional career when he entered the University of Munich. The eighteen-year-old brought with him a paper on the general theory of relativity which was published a few months later. He aroused the interest of Albert Einstein (1879-1955) and of Hermann Weyl. Weyl was attempting to extend Einstein's theory by including electrical effects. With Weyl's encouragement, Pauli soon published two papers about Weyl's theories, including some serious criticisms.

Sommerfeld asked Pauli to assist him in writing an article reviewing relativity theory for inclusion in the 1921 edition of the *Mathematical Encyclopedia*. On seeing Pauli's first draft, Sommerfeld was so impressed that he turned the entire project over to the twenty-one-year-old Pauli. Pauli wrote a 237-page article which summarized all the important work done on the special and general theories of relativity up to that time. It has been described as an exposition of unsurpassed beauty, precision, depth, and completeness. Einstein praised it for the profound physical insight manifested and for the lucid, systematic presentation. Born's pithy remark was, "The little chap is not only clever but industrious as well." (Pauli was short and stocky.)

Pauli published two more significant papers as a graduate student. In them, he applied quantum principles in calculating magnetic and electrical properties of matter. Pauli's doctoral thesis, completed in 1921, on the hydrogen molecule ion was the most extensive application of the Bohr-Sommerfeld theory. The theoretical predictions did not match the experimental measurements, but this was not seen as very significant at the time. It was supposed that future experiments would yield values more in line with those predicted. A few years later, however, this lack of agreement would be taken as evidence that the Bohr-Sommerfeld theory was incorrect.

After receiving his doctorate, Pauli went to Göttingen to become Max Born's assistant. Pauli was a night person; as Born described it, "Pauli's neighbors were worried to watch him sitting at his desk, rocking slowly like a praying Buddha, until the small hours of the morning." Born reassured them that Pauli was quite normal, but a genius. This rocking became such a trademark that if a speaker saw Pauli rocking in the audience, they knew he was paying attention and all was well.

When Pauli went to Copenhagen to work with Bohr, he focused on the Zeeman effect. The intensity with which he applied himself is evident from a story which Pauli told. He said that he was strolling aimlessly along the beautiful streets of Copenhagen when he came across a colleague. The colleague remarked that Pauli looked very unhappy. Pauli's fierce reply was, "How can one look happy when he is thinking about the anomalous Zeeman effect?"

For most of his life, Pauli was employed as a teacher, but his greatest teaching was not done in the classroom. There, he had the tendency to mumble, to ramble, and to interrupt himself with thoughts about his subject. Nevertheless, his students were fascinated with his ideas, however awkwardly presented. Pauli's most effective teaching occurred spontaneously in small discussion groups or with individuals. He would not tolerate ideas which he thought were wrong, nor would he tolerate ideas which were not carefully thought through. His denigration of what he considered to be error was caustic and devastating. His bulldozing behavior did lead some to see him as an unkind man who tried to hurt weaker colleagues, but those who penetrated his gruff manner found him to be warm and patient. Pauli was regarded with great affection by all who knew him well.

As Pauli's reputation grew, so did the stories told about him. It seemed that whenever he entered a laboratory, some piece of equipment would break or cease to function. This mysterious occurrence became known as the "Pauli effect." Knowing that Pauli enjoyed a good joke, the organizers of a scientific conference once arranged for a chandelier to crash to the floor as Pauli entered the room. Pauli entered, and the rope holding the chandelier was released, but they had not counted on the Pauli effect: The apparatus failed to work as the rope jammed in the pulley.

Pauli enunciated his exclusion principle in 1925, along with his hypothesis of an additional quantum number for the electron. Ralph de Laer Kronig (born 1904), an American scientist, thought that this new quantum number could be identified with electron spin and asked for Pauli's opinion. Pauli convinced Kronig that the idea was without merit by showing him that it was contrary to experimental data. George Uhlenbeck and Samuel Goudsmit had had the same idea as Kronig and had already submitted a paper about it for publication when they heard of Pauli's critique. So great was the fame of the twenty-five-year-old Pauli that they prepared to withdraw their paper from publication. Paul Ehrenfest (1880-1933), however, convinced them to go ahead and publish, because they were yet young enough to survive an unsound paper. Pauli later accepted the concept of electron spin when it was shown that he had neglected a "subtle relativistic effect." Theory and experiment did concur, and

Uhlenbeck and Goudsmit were credited with the discovery of electron spin.

Pauli and others would soon show that half a unit of spin, or angular momentum, was to be associated with the electron, proton, and neutron, and a full unit was to be associated with the photon (a "particle" of light). The spin one-half particles might also align in such a fashion that their spins would either add together to give a full unit or subtract to give a zero unit, as is the case with the helium 4 nucleus.

Spin one-half particles must obey the exclusion principle and a kind of mathematics called "Fermi statistics." Conduction of electrons in a metal is an example of a system which obeys Fermi statistics. Particles with a net integer spin (zero or one) do not obey the exclusion principle. Instead, they obey a kind of mathematics called "Bose-Einstein statistics." All the nuclei in a sample of liquid helium 4 can be in the same low-energy state. It is this property which allows it (and not helium 3, which has a net spin of one-half) to become a superfluid. The exclusion principle is fundamental to the scientific understanding of many phenomena.

During 1925 and for the next several years, Pauli was deeply involved in helping Heisenberg and Schrödinger formulate and refine the new quantum mechanics. While the old Bohr-Sommerfeld theory could claim many successes, they often lacked strong logical support. For example, in explaining the Zeeman effect, one had to replace the square of a number (such as 5^2) with the number times itself plus one (5×6). The only reason for doing so was that it made the theory agree with experiment. The new quantum mechanics began with principles such as the dual wave-particle nature of electrons and proceeded logically from there. Its great advantage was that it did not require the previous artificial practices.

During the early 1930's, Pauli worked on beta decay, a process in which the nucleus emits a beta particle (an electron). Pauli concluded that for the energy and momentum of the system to be conserved (to be the same both before and after the emission), there must be another particle involved. The particle must be neutral (have no electric charge), have no mass, and have spin one-half. Finally, the particle must interact only very weakly with other matter. It was a bold hypothesis. Enrico Fermi (1901-1954) took up the beta decay problem, and it was he who named Pauli's particle the "neutrino." Finally, twenty-five years later, in 1956, neutrinos were actually detected in an experiment performed by Frederick Reines (born 1918) and Clyde L. Cowan (born 1919).

In spite of his eccentricities, Pauli's insight was so keen that whenever it was unclear if a new idea should be taken seriously, the question that naturally sprang to mind was "What does Pauli say about it?" After his death, he was greatly missed by the scientific community. The great scope, depth, and elegance of Pauli's work may be best appreciated by reading his classic *Handbook* and *Encyclopedia* articles: "Relativitätstheorie" (1921; *Theory of Relativity*, 1958), "Quantentheorie" (1926; quantum theory), and "Die allgemeinen Prinzipien der Wellenmechanik" (1933; the general principles of wave mechanics). In the United States, during the first half of the 1940's, he worked primarily on meson theory. This work is summarized in *Meson Theory of Nuclear Forces* (1946). His work just prior to his death concerned the neutrino. In a 1957 article titled "On the Conservation of the Lepton Charge," Pauli discusses the lack of conservation of parity in beta decay (there is a difference in observing the reaction from the right-hand side and from the left-hand side) and also the fact that there must be two different kinds of neutrinos.

Bibliography

Primary

PHYSICS: "Relativitätstheorie," *Encyklopädie der Mathematischen Wissenschaften*, vol. 5, 1921 (*Theory of Relativity*, 1958); "Quantentheorie," *Handbuch der Physik*, vol. 23, 1926; "Allgemeine Grundlagen der Quantentheorie des Atombaues," *Müller-Pouillets Lehrbuch*, vol. 2, 1929; "Die allgemeinen Prinzipien der Wellenmechanik," *Handbuch der Physik*, vol. 24, 1933; "The Connection Between Spin and Statistics," *Physical Review*, vol. 58, 1940; *Meson Theory of Nuclear Forces*, 1946; "On the Conservation of the Lepton Charge," *Nuovo cimento*, vol. 6, 1957.

Secondary

Born, Max. *My Life: Recollections of a Nobel Laureate*. New York: Charles Scribner's Sons, 1975. Born was Pauli's supervisor at the University of Göttingen. Born admires Pauli's genius but also points out where he might have been more helpful. Clearly written.

Fierz, Marcus, and V. F. Weisskopf, eds. *Theoretical Physics in the Twentieth Century: A Memorial Volume to Wolfgang Pauli*. New York: Interscience Publishers, 1960. A technical work in which fourteen authors recount personal memories of Pauli as they relate their scientific work to his. Three of the articles are in German; the others are in English. Included is a complete bibliography of Pauli's works, prepared by E. P. Enz.

Mehra, Jadish, and Helmut Rechenberg. *The Historical Development of Quantum Theory*. 5 vols. New York: Springer-Verlag, 1982. This five-book set covers the rise of quantum mechanics from 1900 to 1926. Although it is a technical work, the nonexpert will find much in it of value. A considerable amount of history is included between the technical points. There are numerous references to Pauli in each volume, and part of volume 2 is devoted to Pauli's life and works up to 1921.

Peierls, R. E. "Wolfgang Pauli." *Biographical Memoirs of Fellows of the Royal Society* 5 (1959): 175-192. This article may be the most accessible source for the layman. It is widely available and easy to read. Includes a nearly complete bibliography of more than 120 works by Pauli.

Segrè, Emilio. *From X-Rays to Quarks: Modern Physicists and Their Discoveries*. San Francisco: W. H. Freeman, 1980. A largely descriptive book that is easy to read. Segrè makes many references to Pauli and includes some interesting descriptions of how Pauli was perceived.

Weisskopf, Victor F. "Personal Memories of Pauli." *Physics Today* 38 (December, 1985): 36-41. This short article must be included here. Weisskopf was a student of Pauli's; he treats his subject with great affection and reveals more about the personality of the mature Pauli than does any other author.

Charles W. Rogers

1946

Physics
Percy Williams Bridgman, United States

Chemistry
James Sumner, United States
John Northrop, United States
Wendell Stanley, United States

Physiology or Medicine
Hermann J. Muller, United States

Literature
Hermann Hesse, Switzerland

Peace
Emily Greene Balch, United States
John R. Mott, United States

PERCY WILLIAMS BRIDGMAN
1946

Born: Cambridge, Massachusetts; April 21, 1882
Died: Randolph, New Hampshire; August 20, 1961
Nationality: American
Area of concentration: High-pressure physics

Bridgman's research into the effects of increasingly high pressures on materials led him to discover properties that were of great importance both theoretically and practically

The Award

Presentation

Professor A. E. Lindh, member of the Nobel Committee for Physics, presented the Nobel Prize in Physics to Percy Williams Bridgman on December 10, 1946, on behalf of the Royal Swedish Academy of Sciences and King Gustav V, from whom Bridgman accepted the prize. In Lindh's presentation speech, he noted that studies of the effects on materials subjected to high pressure dated back to the seventeenth century but were very limited because of the extremely primitive apparatus then available. Further high-pressure study was undertaken in the nineteenth century by French physicists using better equipment, with which they extended the range of materials and phenomena investigated. There was, however, a practical limit to the pressure attainable at that time of about 3,000 atmospheres, because of the strength of the materials available for construction of apparatus and the problem of leakage of the seals involved. (The atmosphere that surrounds Earth exerts a pressure of about 14.7 pounds per square inch at sea level. Thus, a pressure of 3,000 atmospheres corresponds to about 45,000 pounds per square inch.)

Higher pressures were attainable only after 1905, when, according to Bridgman, he accidentally discovered a way to solve the leakage problem by devising a sealing mechanism which became stronger with increasing pressure. With this new device, he was able to reach significantly higher pressures. His research was also aided by the availability of new materials, such as an extremely hard alloy called "carboloy," with which to construct his apparatus.

Bridgman was soon able to reach pressures of about 12,000 atmospheres, more than four times the previous pressure limit. Gradually, he increased the limit to 100,000 atmospheres. On occasion, he attained pressures of 400,000 atmospheres. He applied these high pressures to a variety of gases, solids, and liquids, studying, in particular, the effect of pressure on viscosity, heat conduction, electrical resistance, and crystal structure. His study of solid water, both ordinary and heavy, in which deuterium replaces hydrogen in the molecules, showed that seven modifications of ice are possible. Working in a field little studied by his fellow scientists at the time, Bridgman, an ingenious and indefatigable investigator, did pioneering work of immense scientific and technical importance.

Nobel lecture

In his address to the Royal Swedish Academy of Sciences, titled "General Survey of Certain Results in the Field of High-Pressure Physics," Bridgman presented a technical survey of his work with high pressures, which had spanned some four decades. Three aspects of this work were considered: the production of increasingly high pressures, the quantitative determination of the magnitude of the pressures successively attained, and the observed effects on a variety of materials under pressure.

The first essential component of Bridgman's apparatus was the leakproof sealing mechanism he had invented. Once this had been devised, the next challenge was to find a very strong material for the construction of the surrounding chamber. He found that a new material, carboloy—a combination of tungsten carbide and cobalt—proved most satisfactory. Determining the best shape and volume for the pressure chamber, together with a suitable mounting for it, were the next problems Bridgman faced and successfully solved. Determining the magnitude of the pressures attained required the correlation of specific data, and Bridgman was able to do this with remarkable accuracy (about 98 percent), depending on the range of pressures being studied. Over the years, Bridgman was able to achieve pressures from 12,000 atmospheres to about 100,000 atmospheres.

Once his apparatus was readied, Bridgman set out to measure the thermodynamic properties (specifically, the changes in volume as a function of pressure at various temperatures) of liquids and solids primarily, since all gases soon condensed under high pressure to their liquid or solid state, even at relatively high temperatures. In particular, he studied the variation in the melting-point temperature of substances as a function of pressure.

Bridgman's studies of the behavior of crystalline solids under pressure led to the recognition that the normal crystal lattice structure, such as that found at atmospheric pressure and room temperature, was deformed under high pressure, with the component atoms rearranging themselves to accommodate the new, higher pressure. Ultimately, when the pressure is high enough, the crystal structure collapses entirely. Bridgman also investigated other properties of matter, such as electrical resistance, thermal conductivity, and liquid viscosity, as they changed under pressure. He summarized his findings in graphs, which exhibited remarkably smooth contours for the most part. Occasional breaks, or discontinuities, required explanation of the mechanisms involved.

Bridgman, an experimenter first and foremost, was interested in the attempts of theoreticians to explain the results he had obtained. He noted in his address that wave mechanics, which had first been introduced into theoretical physics in the mid-1920's, seemed to be quite successful when applied to his data on crystals with a simple cubic lattice structure. He noted, however, that as of 1946, no satisfactory theory had been devised to explain most of his results.

Critical reception

The awarding of the Nobel Prize in Physics to Bridgman did not come as a surprise to the physics community. For many years, especially since the publication in 1931 of his book *The Physics of High Pressure*, he had been regarded as a truly pioneering figure in physical research at high pressures and the leading international authority in that field. There had been rumors for some time that he would be honored with the Nobel Prize for his work of several decades, despite the usual criterion that Nobel Prizes be awarded for work done in a few years immediately preceding the award. When, after the announcement in Stockholm of his award, he was telephoned by a reporter from *The New York Times* and asked for his reaction, Bridgman answered, "I am not saying anything until I receive official word from the Academy of Sciences. I was misinformed once before."

The same year that Bridgman won his award in physics, the award in chemistry was shared by three American chemists, and a European-born American scientist won the award in physiology or medicine. Publications such as *Time* magazine (November 25) and *Science Newsletter* (November 23) stressed this American sweep of the Nobel awards in their coverage almost as much as the details of the work for which the awards had been given.

In an editorial of November 16, *The New York Times* commented on all the Nobel Prizes awarded in 1946, stressing the importance of the recipients' achievements. Discussing the physics and chemistry laureates, the editor remarked that their work was recognizably for the benefit of mankind (a Nobel Prize prerequisite) no less than the work of the winners in peace or literature. He then went on to say,

> It is no criticism of the awards that the public does not know them as it knew Einstein, Marie Curie, Niels Bohr, R. A. Millikan and a few other earlier prize winners. Scientific research is a stern and lonely discipline, of which public acclaim is usually a purely accidental by-product.

When, on December 6, Bridgman and the Nobel Prize-winning chemists were about to board an airplane to fly to Stockholm for the presentation ceremonies, *The New York Times* sent a reporter and a photographer to record their departure. When Bridgman was asked to comment, he did not mention the prize or the ceremony he was about to attend. Instead, he voiced his concern about the role of scientists in peacetime; he feared domination of science by the military. He urged that American and Soviet scientists be free to communicate and work together freely. That, he believed, would be more conducive to a lasting peace than pouring huge amounts of money into secret laboratories. It is not surprising that in 1946, soon after the end of World War II, the press would emphasize the American sweep of the scientific Nobel Prizes and that a recipient, such as Bridgman, would be so concerned with what lay ahead for mankind in general and for science in particular.

Within the community of fellow physicists, there were many who offered their congratulations to Bridgman on his award by way of telegrams, telephone calls, and handshakes. He was the first Harvard physicist to win a Nobel Prize; the university considered that he had brought honor to the whole institution. In January, after Bridgman's return from Stockholm, a formal dinner, attended by the president of the university, James B. Conant, other administrators, and fellow physicists from Harvard and other institutions, was held to honor the new Nobel laureate.

Biography

Percy Williams Bridgman was born on April 21, 1882, in Cambridge, Massachusetts, the only child of Ann Maria Williams Bridgman and Raymond Landon Bridgman, a professional journalist who wrote on social and political matters. During his school years, the family lived in Newton, Massachusetts, a suburb of Boston, where young "Perce" attended public schools. He was a good student, rather shy but interested in sports and games. He excelled as a chess player.

He entered Harvard College in 1900 and was graduated summa cum laude in 1904. He continued at Harvard as a graduate student in physics, receiving his master's degree in 1905 and his doctorate in 1908. By that time, he was already drawn to studying the behavior of materials subjected to high pressure. The title of his doctoral thesis was "Mercury Resistance as a Pressure Gauge." On completion of his doctoral studies, Bridgman was appointed first as a Research Fellow and then as an instructor in physics at Harvard. He subsequently rose through the professional ranks, leaving Harvard only for brief periods of war-related work or for sabbaticals. To his colleagues, he became known as "Peter."

Bridgman was a dedicated experimental physicist who worked alone, save for two technical assistants, during the normal academic year. His summers were spent with his wife and two children in Randolph, New Hampshire, where he indulged his interests in gardening, mountain climbing, and photography and where he devoted considerable time to organizing his ideas and writing on philosophical as well as technical and scientific topics. He remained physically and intellectually active until shortly before his death, by his own hand, on August 20, 1961, at the age of seventy-nine, the victim of a crippling form of bone cancer.

Scientific Career

During the half century of Bridgman's career, he devoted himself unstintingly to his high-pressure studies and dominated that field of physics. His success was the result of a combination of ingenuity in designing his equipment, skill in manipulating it, and long hours of dedicated investigation of its capabilities. During the academic year, he regularly arrived, by bicycle, at his laboratory by 8:00 A.M., six days a week.

Although he held a regular professorial position at Harvard University, he had negotiated an unusual arrangement with the administration: His research would take precedence over all other faculty duties. He taught no undergraduate courses and only a limited number of graduate courses. He supervised very few doctoral dissertations. He did not attend faculty meetings or serve on committees, save one. When it became clear that his high-pressure studies cast significant light on geological phenomena, he did participate in a committee on experimental geology and geophysics that was formed in the 1930's. (The pressures he reached in his laboratory corresponded to pressures several hundred miles below Earth's surface.)

His output of publications was phenomenal. He wrote thirteen books and more than 260 papers. He lived long enough to see his high-pressure studies attract the attention of solid-state physicists and his techniques become routinely used for the production of synthetic materials, such as artificial diamonds and high-quality quartz crystals.

Bridgman brought to all of his activities a ruthlessly critical scrutiny and the same attention to detail that characterized his laboratory work. In connection with his own investigations and as part of his preparation for courses he was teaching, he began a critical examination of the concepts of physics as they were used within the profession and taught to students. His first book, *Dimensional Analysis*, published in 1922, focused on the dimensions associated with each physical concept and the relations among various concepts used by physicists. (Physicists consider mass, length, time, and electric charge to be the fundamental concepts from which the multitude of useful physical concepts are built. For example, speed is a combination of length and time; momentum involves mass, length, and time; force consists of mass, length, and time taken twice.)

In another book, *The Logic of Modern Physics*, published in 1927, Bridgman continued his close examination of physicists' concerns. He was stimulated, at least in part, by the relativity theory and quantum theory that had invaded physics in the early decades of the twentieth century. His own work on high pressures had little to do with either of these developments, but he eagerly sought to understand them. In *The Logic of Modern Physics*, he introduced operational analysis, a way of looking at concepts as meaningful only if the operations involved in their measurements can be specified. Indeed, he believed that a concept is defined by its corresponding set of operations. He included in such definitions mental operations (those done with pencil and paper) as well as physical, or mechanical, operations. He was especially eager to rid physics of all metaphysical notions. He considered meaningless those concepts that could not be given operational definitions. His was a philosophical approach in the tradition of Ernst Mach and the early Albert Einstein. Bridgman completed the writing of his book during a sabbatical of one semester. Its publication in 1927 was especially timely, coming, as it did, so soon after the advent of quantum mechanics. It was widely read and proved very helpful to many of his fellow scientists, who were searching for a way to grasp the new theoretical physics that was evolving around them.

Bridgman's operational analysis was widely discussed and debated by philosophers, who called it "operationalism," a term that Bridgman rejected as connoting something too dogmatic. He considered his view to be straightforward, rational thinking. He believed, furthermore, that his approach could be useful beyond the realm of physics and the other sciences. At one time, in the 1950's, he even gave a course on the application of operational analysis to social problems. His book *The Intelligent Individual and Society* (1938) concerns the application of operational thinking to everyday life.

Bridgman was a man of high personal integrity and social responsibility, passionately devoted to the ideal of personal freedom for the individual. During World War I, he left Cambridge for New London, Connecticut, where he was involved in developing effective submarine detection devices. In World War II, he served his country by conducting tests on the plastic flow of steel under pressure and by measuring the compressibility of uranium and plutonium, essential ingredients of the atom bomb.

With the rise of totalitarianism in the 1930's in Germany, Italy, the Soviet Union, and Japan, Bridgman became increasingly concerned about the cause of individual freedom. He issued a "manifesto" denying access to his laboratory to anyone from a dictatorship nation. A copy of his document was posted on the door of his laboratory, and his action was publicized in *Reader's Digest* of March, 1939. The article was reprinted in *Reflections of a Physicist* (1950), a collection of Bridgman's nontechnical essays. His purpose in barring persons from such nations was to demonstrate his aversion to their governments, not to punish the individual, who, he realized, might be quite blameless. In fact, as the situation in Europe deteriorated toward war, Bridgman became increasingly active in seeking to provide places of refuge in the United States for the victims of oppression in their homelands.

For the most part, Bridgman was a solitary individual, little given to joining organizations. He made an exception, however, in becoming an active member of the British Society for Freedom in Science, since the aims of that organization seemed so close to his own. He was especially worried about the intrusion of government into the activity and funding of science.

Bridgman was highly respected internationally and the recipient of many honors during his lifetime. In 1924, at a time when few American scientists were in the international mainstream of physics, he was invited to participate in the very prestigious Solvay Congress held in Brussels and convened to discuss the electric conductivity of metals. In addition to the Nobel Prize, Bridgman received medals from learned scientific societies, honorary degrees from academic institutions, and memberships in foreign academies of science. He was elected president of the American Physical Society.

In 1982, twenty years after his death, a celebration of the one hundredth anniversary of Bridgman's birth was held in Cambridge, Massachusetts. This took the form of a two-day interdisciplinary symposium, Reflections on P. W. Bridgman. Participants included former colleagues who, as young men, had come under the influence of Bridgman's work and personality, along with young persons from the history and philosophy of science community who had come to know and respect Bridgman only through his writings.

Bibliography

Primary

PHYSICS: *Dimensional Analysis*, 1922; *A Condensed Collection of Thermodynamic Formulas*, 1925; *The Logic of Modern Physics*, 1927; *The Physics of High Pres-*

sure, 1931; *The Thermodynamics of Electrical Phenomena in Metals*, 1934; *The Nature of Physical Theory*, 1936; *The Nature of Thermodynamics*, 1941; *The Nature of Some of Our Physical Concepts*, 1952; *Studies in Large Plastic Flow and Fracture, with Special Emphasis on the Effects of Hydrostatic Pressure*, 1952; *The Way Things Are*, 1959; *A Sophisticate's Primer of Relativity*, 1962; *Collected Experimental Papers*, 1964.

OTHER NONFICTION: *The Intelligent Individual and Society*, 1938; *Reflections of a Physicist*, 1950; *Philosophical Writings of Percy Williams Bridgman*, 1980.

Secondary

Birch, Francis, and Edwin Kemble. "Percy Williams Bridgman, April 21, 1882-August 20, 1961." *Biographical Memoirs, National Academy of Sciences* 41 (1970). This memoir was written by two of Bridgman's longtime colleagues at Harvard University. It contains a detailed assessment of Bridgman's scientific achievements and personal recollections of his personality.

Frank, Philipp. *The Validation of Scientific Theories*. Boston: Beacon Press, 1956. A collection of essays by philosophers of science that were originally delivered as addresses during the December, 1953, Boston meeting of the American Association for the Advancement of Science. The lectures constituted a symposium sponsored jointly by the Institute for the Unity of Science, the Philosophy of Science Association, and the section of AAAS devoted to the history and philosophy of science. Chapter 2 of this work, titled "The Present State of Operationalism," consists of seven commentaries, including one by Bridgman himself, on the role of operational analysis in scientific thought.

Newitt, D. M. "Percy Williams Bridgman, 1882-1961." *Biographical Memoirs of Fellows of the Royal Society* 8 (1962): 27-40. This memoir, prepared by Newitt for his recently deceased colleague among the Fellows, presents the information usually found in such obituaries but also includes an autographed portrait of Bridgman in his later years and a chronological listing of all Bridgman's published papers and books.

Katherine R. Sopka

1947

Physics
Sir Edward Victor Appleton, Great Britain

Chemistry
Sir Robert Robinson, Great Britain

Physiology or Medicine
Carl F. Cori, United States
Gerty T. Cori, United States
Bernardo Houssay, Argentina

Literature
André Gide, France

Peace
American Friends Service Committee, United States
Friends Service Council, Great Britain

SIR EDWARD VICTOR APPLETON
1947

Born: Bradford, England; September 6, 1892
Died: Edinburgh, Scotland; April 21, 1965
Nationality: British
Areas of concentration: Radio and atmospheric physics

Appleton's measurements of the height of the ionosphere and his analysis of its properties demonstrated the existence of the Heaviside layer and resulted in his discovery of what came to be known as the Appleton layer

The Award

Presentation

Professor E. Hulthén, member of the Nobel Committee for Physics, presented the Nobel Prize in Physics to Sir Edward Victor Appleton in December of 1947, on behalf of the Royal Swedish Academy of Sciences. Hulthén's presentation speech reviewed the first propagation of radio waves across the Atlantic, achieved by Guglielmo Marconi (1874-1937) in 1901, and questions about how such waves could follow the contour of Earth. In 1902, Oliver Heaviside (1850-1925) in England and Arthur Kennelly (1861-1939) in the United States proposed that Earth is surrounded by an electrically conducting layer that reflects radio waves.

According to Hulthén, Appleton had developed a brilliant method to compare ground waves with reflected waves by observing their interference effects (the cancellation of wave crests by the troughs of other waves) when the frequency was varied. Using this method, he was able to detect the Heaviside layer in 1924 and to measure its height of about 100 kilometers. His theoretical analysis made it possible to determine the amount of ionization (the separation of electrons from atoms) at different heights from the critical frequency that would allow the waves to penetrate the layer. This information was especially valuable in guiding choices of frequency for radio communications.

In 1927, Appleton discovered a second reflecting layer beyond the first and measured its height of about 230 kilometers. He showed that this so-called Appleton layer divides into two components during the day and merges into one during the night, with little variation for most of the night. He assumed that this effect was caused by the greater rarefaction at the highest level, which retards the recombination of ions with electrons. Variations in the Heaviside layer were shown to be closely correlated with the sunspot minimum of 1934 and sunspot maximum of 1937 and the corresponding variations in ultraviolet radiation from the Sun. Thus, Appleton's radio methods could be used to determine actual solar radiation much more accurately than measurements made at ground level.

Appleton's methods proved especially valuable in the development of radar and in its applications to meteorology. He also pioneered the detection of distant lightning discharges by their radio disturbances. In opening up the new field of atmospheric physics and the study of the ionosphere, he contributed to developments in other sciences, such as astronomy, geophysics, and meteorology.

Nobel lecture

Appleton's Nobel lecture, entitled "The Ionosphere," described his research on the upper atmosphere, a region beyond the realm of human experience at the time. He reviewed the earlier theoretical ideas about this region, beginning with those of Balfour Stewart (1828-1887), who had proposed that electrical currents flowing high in the atmosphere could explain the small daily changes in Earth's magnetic field. These variations would result from tidal movements in the surrounding "sea of air" caused by solar and lunar gravitational influences. Appleton also described the unsuccessful attempts to explain Marconi's long-distance radio transmissions in terms of wave diffraction (the spreading of waves) around Earth's curvature. These failures led to the theories of Kennelly and Heaviside in 1902, who independently postulated the existence of an electrical conductor in the upper atmosphere that would guide radio waves by reflection between this conducting shell and Earth's surface.

Appleton explained how his interest in this problem had developed during World War I when he noticed the fading of radio signals. On his return to Cambridge, he began to develop more accurate methods of measuring radio signals. When commercial broadcasting began from London, he noticed that fading of the signal intensity occurred in Cambridge at night. He suggested that this effect was caused by interference between direct waves along the ground and reflected waves from the upper atmosphere. He subsequently performed experiments in which variations in the frequency (and therefore the wavelength) of the transmitter's signal resulted in a sequence of maxima and minima in the intensity of the received signals. A simple relationship between the initial and final wavelengths and the corresponding number of maxima or minima made it possible to measure the height from which reflections would produce the observed interference effects. Thus, the existence of the Kennelly-Heaviside layer, or E layer, was established, and its height was measured as about 90 kilometers above the ground.

Continuing his research, Appleton found that he could penetrate the Heaviside layer before dawn. He drew the conclusion that reflections were the result of ionization, caused by the Sun, which was reduced enough at night by the recombination of electrons and ions (charged atoms) to permit penetration by radio waves. Then, in 1927, he discovered reflection from a higher layer, which had an altitude of about 230 kilometers and is now called the Appleton layer, or F layer. Further research led to the discovery of a critical frequency for the penetration of any layer which could be related theoretically to the electron density of each layer at any given time. The theory also gave the value of the magnetic field, which proved to be about 10 percent less at an altitude of 300 kilometers than on the ground. Magnetic variations in the upper atmosphere have shown the validity of Stewart's tidal theory.

Continuous measurements of electron densities in the ionosphere began in 1931, leading to a worldwide network of more than fifty stations using the critical-frequency method during World War II. These measurements soon revealed increases in ionization with increased sunspot activity. Since ionization is caused by ultraviolet light from the Sun, this radiation, little of which reaches Earth, could be measured by its ionizing effects. Large increases in solar ultraviolet radiation were discovered during sunspot activity, although little variation was observed at ground level. The sunspot cycle thus made it possible to forecast ionospheric weather and to determine the most suitable frequencies for future radio transmissions.

Critical reception

The announcement by the Royal Swedish Academy of Sciences that Sir Edward Appleton had been awarded the 1947 Nobel Prize in Physics was greeted with brief but positive responses by the press. *The Times* of London, on November 14, 1947, devoted only one paragraph to the announcement, perhaps because Appleton was so well-known and highly respected in England. It was noted that Appleton had become famous as a young man through his researches and that his name had become even more widely known thanks to his discovery of the Appleton layer. It was also noted that his work had been fundamental to the development of radar, a point that was greatly appreciated in Great Britain because of the importance of radar in the Allies' ultimate victory in World War II.

The New York Times of November 14 observed that both the physics and chemistry Nobel Prizes for the year had gone to Great Britain. It predicted "general approval of the awards," noting that "Sir Edward is England's leading authority on the ionosphere" and that he had distinguished himself by experimental skill and by brilliant and imaginative inferences from his discoveries. The article went on to review the puzzle of Marconi's transmissions over Earth's curvature and the postulated Kennelly-Heaviside layer. Appleton's discovery of several such layers was identified as the beginning of radar, and it was noted that he was one of the first to discover radio reflections from airplanes.

The British journal *Nature*, on November 22, provided a more detailed account of Appleton's life and work. It also predicted that the announcement of the award would be received with great satisfaction, especially by scientists and others concerned with pure and applied physics. It mentioned his contributions in two areas, either of which would have established his fame: He was the most active radio physics researcher in a quarter of a century, and as secretary of the Department of Scientific and Industrial Research, he was the leading government scientist in Great Britain. The article went on to summarize his discoveries in the ionosphere and his later work on meteors and sunspots. It also noted his heavy administrative burden during World War II, which had included advising the British government on the development of nuclear energy and establishing the special research section for the British contribution to the atom bomb.

Biography

Edward Victor Appleton was born on September 6, 1892, in Bradford, Yorkshire,

England, the eldest child of Peter Appleton and Mary Wilcock. As a boy, he had special interests in music and cricket and was an outstanding student, winning scholarships to Hanson Secondary School and then to St. John's College at Cambridge University. He studied natural science at Cambridge under teachers that included Sir Joseph John Thomson (1856-1940) and Ernest Rutherford (1871-1937), completing a first-class honors degree in physics in 1914. He then began graduate study in crystallography under William Lawrence Bragg (1890-1971), but when World War I began he joined the Royal Engineers and became a signals officer, which led to his lifelong interest in radio. In 1915 he wed Jesse Longson; they were to have two daughters.

After the war Appleton returned to Cambridge, where he was elected a Fellow of St. John's College in 1919 and an assistant demonstrator in physics at the Cavendish Laboratory in 1920. He began to study vacuum tubes and then turned to research on radio propagation. In 1924 he became Wheatstone Professor of Physics at King's College of the University of London, where his most important work on the ionosphere was done. His discovery and measurement of the Heaviside layer was honored by his election as a Fellow of the Royal Society in 1927, the same year he discovered the Appleton layer. In 1932 he held an expedition to northern Norway for radio research on the aurora borealis and was also elected vice president of the American Institute of Radio Engineers. He served as president of the International Union of Scientific Radio from 1934 to 1952.

Appleton returned to Cambridge as Jacksonian Professor of Natural Philosophy in 1936, but three years later he was appointed secretary of the Department of Scientific and Industrial Research. In 1941 he was knighted, and he served on the Scientific Advisory Committee of the War Cabinet, advising the government on the feasibility of atomic weapons and later assuming administrative control of British atom bomb research. In 1947, he was awarded the United States Medal of Merit as well as the Nobel Prize. He was appointed principal and vice-chancellor of the University of Edinburgh in 1949, where he remained until his death in 1965. There, he founded the *Journal of Atmospheric and Terrestrial Research* and served as its editor in chief for the rest of his life. He was instrumental in organizing the first International Geophysical Year (July, 1957, to December, 1958), which took place during a period of maximal sunspot activity. In 1964 his wife died, and a month before his own death he married his private secretary of thirteen years, Mrs. Helen F. Allison.

Scientific Career

Edward Appleton's scientific career began at Cambridge University, where he had completed his undergraduate studies. His first research assignment, in 1914, was with William Lawrence (later Sir Lawrence) Bragg, who with his father Sir William Henry Bragg (1862-1942) had shared the 1915 Nobel Prize in Physics for determining the wavelengths of X rays by crystal diffraction methods (the scattering of X rays from crystals). Appleton helped in working out the structure of one or two metallic crystals for a few months before his departure for military service. His duties as a signals officer in the Royal Engineers during World War I introduced him to problems in radio communications which he decided to investigate after the war.

On his return to Cambridge, Appleton began to study the action of vacuum tubes, one of which he had recovered from German equipment during the war. Between 1918 and 1924, he published more than a dozen scientific papers on this topic. He was joined in some of this work by Balthazar van der Pol, who had come to the Cavendish Laboratory from Holland to do research under J. J. Thomson. Later he wrote a textbook on the subject, titled *Thermionic Vacuum Tubes and Their Applications* (1931). He also published a paper in 1923 in the *Proceedings of the Royal Society* (vol. 103), jointly with the British radar pioneer Sir Robert A. Watson-Watt, titled "On the Nature of Atmospherics," which reported on their investigation of radio disturbance from lightning discharges.

During this time, he began to measure the strength of radio signals received at Cambridge from the new British Broadcasting Company station in London. He was assisted in this work by Miles A. F. Barnett, his first graduate student, who had come to Cambridge from New Zealand. They began to suspect that variations in the signals might be caused by reflections of radio waves from charged particles in the upper atmosphere, as had been postulated by Heaviside and Kennelly in 1902 to explain Marconi's transatlantic radio transmission the previous year.

Shortly after Appleton took up his new position as Wheatstone Professor of Physics at the University of London in 1924, he and Barnett performed a crucial experiment which marked the beginning of his extensive researches on the ionosphere. They arranged to use the new British Broadcasting Company transmitter at Bournemouth after midnight when broadcasting ended, with their receiving apparatus in the electrical laboratory at Oxford. By continuously varying the transmitter frequency, and therefore wavelength, they hoped to detect a changing intensity at the receiver produced by interference between the direct waves (along the ground) and the reflected waves (from the sky).

On December 11, 1924, they performed the experiment and duly observed the regular fading in and out of the signal. From the lowest and highest wavelengths of the transmitter and the corresponding number of oscillations in the intensity at the receiver between those wavelengths, they calculated that the reflection was from a height of about 100 kilometers. They published these results in 1925 in *Nature* (vol. 115), under the title "Local Reflection of Wireless Waves from the Upper Atmosphere," thereby establishing the existence and location of the Heaviside layer of the ionosphere. These results were confirmed with measurements of the angle of incidence of the reflected waves on the ground achieved by comparing the simultaneous signal variations on two receivers with different antenna orientations. Appleton published several additional papers with Barnett on these measurements.

Appleton continued his experiments, with a transmitter at the National Physical Laboratory and a receiving station at Peterborough, using an improved technique of rapid frequency changes so that variations in signal strength could be distinguished more easily from natural fading. In the winter of 1926, he found that before dawn the ionization of the Heaviside layer (E layer) was reduced sufficiently by recombination of electrons and ions to allow penetration by radio waves. Reflection was still observed from a higher layer, however, where the air was too thin for efficient recombination, and the lower boundary of what is now called the Appleton layer (F layer) was measured at about 230 kilometers above Earth. This result was published in 1927 in *Nature* (vol. 120) under the title "The Existence of More than One Ionized Layer in the Upper Atmosphere." A solar eclipse in 1927 made it possible to observe that the height of the Heaviside layer changed when the eclipse began, showing that ionization was caused by solar radiation.

The pulse, or radar, technique, which had been introduced in the United States by Merle Tuve (born 1901) and Gregory Breit (born 1899), was also developed at this time for measuring the ionosphere. In this method, a transmitted radio pulse resulted in two received pulses, one from the ground wave and one from the reflected wave, both of which could be recorded and compared on a cathode-ray oscillograph. The pulsed transmitter was located at East London College and the receiver at King's College of the University of London. This technique led to the discovery of the splitting of echoes, a result of the influence of Earth's magnetic field on the ionosphere, which separates a radio wave into two parts by double refraction (the bending of waves into two different components as they pass from one medium to another).

In developing his "magneto-ionic" theory to explain this result, Appleton showed that free electrons rather that ions caused the reflection of radio waves. The magneto-ionic theory was later modified by D. R. Hartree. Although this modification was later shown to be unnecessary, the result is still called the "Appleton-Hartree equation." The theory showed that the electron density and the magnetic field at any layer in the ionosphere can be determined by measuring the critical frequency for penetrating that layer. Systematic experiments on the variation of electron densities in the ionosphere were begun in 1931, and it was found that E-layer densities increased as the Sun was rising and decreased after noon. Ionization remained low at night, except for sporadic increases possibly caused by meteoric dust. A weak region of ionization was discovered below the E layer and designated as the D layer. Appleton first used the letter E to stand for the "electric field" in the Heaviside layer. He later used the letter F for the "field" in the Appleton layer. In using D for the lower level, he left earlier letters in the alphabet for the possible discovery of even lower levels. It was also found that the upper F layer splits into two parts under summer daytime conditions. Noon ionization levels were found to increase with sunspot activity between the sunspot minimum of 1934 and sunspot maximum of 1937, suggesting that sunspots increase the ultraviolet radiation that produces electrons even though little of this radiation reaches ground level.

In 1932, Appleton organized a scientific expedition to study the ionosphere in northern Norway as part of an international effort to study the polar region. There, he studied variations in the ionosphere under different auroral and magnetic storm conditions. He recorded the first example of a polar radio blackout caused by charged particles projected into the atmosphere from the Sun. He recognized the importance of worldwide investigations of the ionosphere, and by World War II, his methods were being used in more than fifty stations around the world to monitor ionospheric conditions. He also provided international leadership by serving as president of the International Union of Scientific Radio from 1934 to 1952.

When Appleton was appointed to the Jacksonian Chair of Natural Philosophy at Cambridge in 1936, he brought several of his research students with him and persuaded the university to build a new field laboratory for further study of the ionosphere. He also initiated work on ionized gases at the Cavendish Laboratory and served as acting director of the Laboratory after the sudden death of Lord Rutherford in 1937. That same year, he delivered the Bakerian lecture to the Royal Society on the topic of "Regularities and Irregularities in the Ionosphere," giving special attention to the relation between the ionosphere and variations in Earth's magnetic field. He showed that variations in the conductivity of the ionosphere during the sunspot cycle could account for observed geomagnetic changes. Some of these changes in the magnetic field seemed to correspond to tidal effects, and further research in 1937 and 1938 revealed a lunar tidal variation in the height of the E layer by as much as 2 kilometers at full moon. This work was done at Slough with K. Weekes and was published jointly in several articles under the title "Tides in the Upper Atmosphere."

In 1939, Appleton began a ten-year assignment as secretary of the government's Department of Scientific and Industrial Research. His duties became largely administrative, but he managed to pursue some research interests and published a few papers each year, except during the war years. His first task was to shift the department to wartime activities, including the development of radar, other defense-related studies, and secret work on the atom bomb. In connection with the latter, he was given the responsibility in 1941 of establishing and managing the "Directorate of Tube Alloys," which was the front for the British atomic research program. Much of his earlier work contributed directly to the development of radar, which, according to Sir Robert Watson-Watt, was an essential factor in its availability in time for the Battle of Britain. Many of his former research workers also became leaders in radar development. After the war he collaborated with J. S. Hey, who had discovered solar radio waves, in describing the nature of radio emissions from sunspots, and with R. Naismith on radar detection of meteor trails.

After Appleton returned to academic work as principal and vice-chancellor of Edinburgh University in 1949, he kept apprised of research on the ionosphere by working on the *Journal of Atmospheric and Terrestrial Research* and by employing assistants to analyze research results from observatories around the world. From a study of records of the F region, he discovered that noontime ionization peaked at two points on either side of the equator and dipped in between at the geomagnetic, rather than the geographical, equator. In this way, he showed that the structure of the F region is controlled by Earth's magnetic field. During this time, he also published several papers on ionospheric storms. In 1950 he chaired the special committee established by the Council of the Royal Astronomical Society that recommended construction of the giant, 250-foot radio telescope at Jodrell Bank near Manchester, England. Appleton's last major contribution was his leadership in helping to organize the first International Geophysical Year in 1957, a period of maximal sunspot activity.

Bibliography

Primary

PHYSICS: "On the Nature of Atmospherics," *Proceedings of the Royal Society*, vol. 103, 1923 (with Robert Watson-Watt); "Local Reflection of Wireless Waves from the Upper Atmosphere," *Nature*, vol. 115, 1925 (with Miles Barnett); "The Existence of More than One Ionized Layer in the Upper Atmosphere," *Nature*, vol. 120, 1927; *Thermionic Vacuum Tubes and Their Applications*, 1931; *Scientific Progress*, 1936.

OTHER NONFICTION: *Science, Government and Industry*, 1947; *The Practical Importance of Fundamental Research*, 1948; *Science and the Nation*, 1957.

Secondary

Craig, Richard A. *The Edge of Space: Exploring the Upper Atmosphere*. Garden City, N.Y.: Doubleday, 1968. This small book is part of the Science Study Series, which was written for secondary students and the lay public. It has a good chapter on the ionosphere, including historical background, and a clear introduction to many topics pioneered by Appleton and his students.

Hey, James S. *The Evolution of Radio Astronomy*. New York: Science History Publications, 1973. This history of radio astronomy describes some of Appleton's contributions to radio astronomy in his later years, especially his backing for the giant radio telescope at Jodrell Bank. Hey discovered radio emissions from the Sun and carried on some collaboration with Appleton regarding them, but he complains about Appleton's interference in continuing research efforts.

Mitra, S. K. *The Upper Atmosphere*. Calcutta: Asiatic Society, 1952. This book, dedicated to Sir Edward Appleton, is an exhaustive and highly technical treatment of the physics of the upper atmosphere. Chapter 6 concerns the ionosphere and includes a brief historical introduction and an extended discussion of the magneto-ionic theory. Appendix 1 discusses the effect of solar radiation on the upper atmosphere, and appendix 4 provides a derivation of the Appleton-Hartree formula. An extensive bibliography contains nearly three hundred references for chapter 6 alone.

Ratcliffe, John A. "Edward Victor Appleton." *Biographical Memoirs of Fellows of the Royal Society* 12 (1966): 1-21. This obituary article by one of Appleton's longtime associates is both a personal and a scientific biography, with reminiscences as well. It contains a list of Appleton's honors, decorations, and medals and of his most important papers, which total 140.

—————————. *Sun, Earth and Radio*. New York: McGraw-Hill, 1970. A very readable introduction to the history of ionospheric research. It uses no mathematics but provides an authoritative account with many graphs and illustrations. An appendix gives background on the nature of electromagnetic waves, and a short bibliography lists other books on the ionosphere and publications which illustrate the state of ionospheric knowledge at different times in the past.

—————————, ed. *Physics of the Upper Atmosphere*. New York: Academic Press, 1960. A dozen contributors to this highly technical book include several former students and associates of Appleton, each a specialist in his field. Chapter 9, on the ionosphere, describes much of the work originally pioneered by Appleton. The bibliography for this chapter contains more than three hundred references. Chapter 12 reviews the main discoveries of the International Geophysical Year of 1957-1958.

Joseph L. Spradley

1948

Physics
Patrick M. S. Blackett, Great Britain

Chemistry
Arne Tiselius, Sweden

Physiology or Medicine
Paul Müller, Switzerland

Literature
T. S. Eliot, Great Britain

Peace
no award

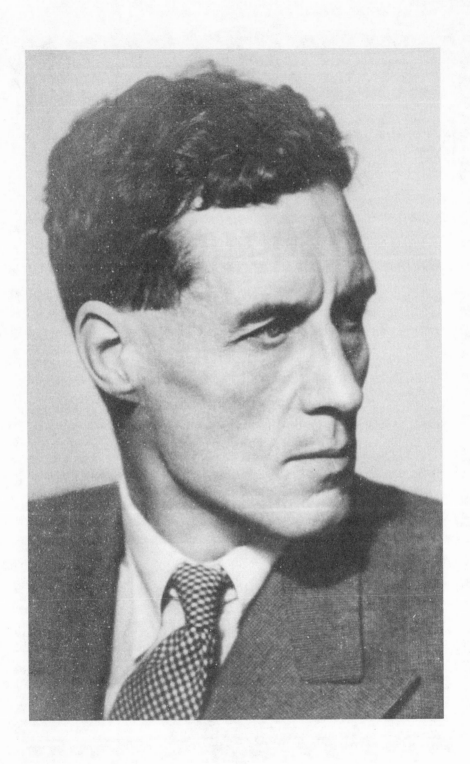

PATRICK M. S. BLACKETT
1948

Born: London, England; November 18, 1897
Died: London, England; July 13, 1974
Nationality: British
Areas of concentration: Nuclear physics and cosmic radiation

Blackett's improvements of the cloud chamber made possible a series of fundamental discoveries concerning cosmic rays and subatomic particles in the 1930's and 1940's. With it, he confirmed the existence of the positron and established the occurrence of pair creation

The Award

Presentation

On behalf of the Royal Swedish Academy of Sciences, Professor G. Ising, member of the Nobel Committee for Physics, presented the Nobel Prize in Physics to Patrick Maynard Stuart Blackett in December of 1948. Ising emphasized in his presentation that this award was for both discovery and invention, the two grounds for the Nobel Prize in Physics. Blackett's discoveries in cosmic radiation and nuclear physics had been possible only because of his invention of an improved cloud chamber. His apparatus combined two devices for the study of subatomic particles: the Geiger counter and the cloud chamber of Charles Thomson Rees Wilson (1869-1959). The former detects the passage of a charged particle; the latter shows its path. In the 1920's, Blackett used the cloud chamber to study heavy particles produced by radioactive decay. In 1925 he became the first person to photograph a nuclear disintegration.

Blackett's attention shifted to cosmic rays in 1932. He and Giuseppe Occhialini combined two Geiger counters with a cloud chamber. Cosmic rays entering this device activated the mechanism and photographed themselves, greatly increasing the efficiency of the method. Soon to follow were groundbreaking observations of pair creation (a negative and a positive electron, or a positron, created from gamma radiation) and of "showers" of electrons and positrons. This work confirmed the existence of positrons and illuminated the relation of matter and energy. Blackett's researches in the late 1930's depended on progressively more refined techniques and produced useful data on cosmic rays.

Nobel lecture

Blackett opened his lecture, "Cloud Chamber Researches in Nuclear Physics and Cosmic Radiation," by giving credit to Wilson for his cloud chamber and to Ernest Rutherford (1871-1937), who had pioneered the study of the atomic nucleus. Rutherford discovered in 1919 that when alpha particles (doubly ionized helium nuclei) emitted by radioactive material strike the nucleus of an ordinary nitrogen atom, the latter gives off a proton (the main component of all atomic nuclei). Events on the smallest level, however, were hidden from his observational technique.

To penetrate this mystery, Blackett related, Rutherford assigned him in 1921 to apply Wilson's cloud chamber to the problem. Charged particles traveling through the chamber separated the nitrogen in it into positive and negative parts, or ions, around which water vapor, with which the gas was saturated, formed droplets. Trails of droplets thus indicated the passage of a charged particle.

Blackett discussed his automatic cloud chamber and first major project: investigation of the details of nuclear transformation. During 1924, he photographed 400,000 tracks of charged particles. All but eight evidenced ordinary collisions between two objects. These collisions resulted in forked tracks. Rutherford's proton was shown leaving the collision site, but what of the alpha particle that collided with the nitrogen nucleus to start the process? It was not seen again; it was absorbed by the nitrogen nucleus. Since the identities of chemical elements are determined by the numbers of protons in their nuclei, a fundamental change had taken place. From helium (the alpha particle) and nitrogen, Blackett had produced hydrogen (the proton) and oxygen (the compounded nucleus that remained after the collision)—a new kind of oxygen, with one extra neutron. Blackett also noted that some of the energy of collision was converted into extra matter.

Throughout the 1920's, Blackett and his colleagues refined this technique, studying other nuclear reactions. In 1931, he and Occhialini applied the chamber to a new phenomenon: cosmic rays. Blackett stated that these rays from space had been discovered by Victor Franz Hess (1883-1964) in 1912 during a balloon flight. Blackett listed six scientists who had contributed to their study, but he gave pride of place to Carl David Anderson (born 1905). Anderson, a former student of Robert Andrews Millikan (1868-1953), had surrounded a cloud chamber with a magnetic field to study the energy of particles associated with cosmic rays. He found that the straighter were their paths in the field, the higher were their energies. He also discovered the positron.

Blackett and Occhialini in 1934 combined this advanced chamber with an automatic mechanism to obtain more photographs of cosmic rays than had been possible before. They readily confirmed Anderson's discovery of the positron. More important, they showed that positrons occur in showers with almost equal numbers of electrons. This finding, Blackett stated, confirmed the theory of pair production formulated by Paul Adrien Maurice Dirac (1902-1984). Blackett also discussed the discovery that gamma rays from radioactive materials produce positrons, the measurement of the momentum spectrum of cosmic rays, and the "penetrating," high-energy component of cosmic rays. Others later found the penetrating component to be new particles, mesons.

Throughout his lecture, Blackett generously credited others and readily admitted his errors. He made clear the contribution of cosmic-ray studies and the cloud chamber to knowledge of the nucleus.

Critical reception

Many of the first published announcements of Blackett's award in November, 1948, were bland summaries of the Nobel Committee's citation: Blackett had been chosen for his improvements of the Wilson cloud chamber and for his discoveries in cosmic radiation. *Time* (November 15) went further. Though not entirely correct in the details, the magazine's reporter noted Blackett's photograph of a nuclear transformation and his invention of an "electronic tripping device" for cosmic-ray research, also citing his war work on antiaircraft techniques and on the atom bomb.

The New York Times of November 6 used its announcement to discuss the importance of inventions to science, citing Blackett's refinements to the cloud chamber as a chief example. It asserted that Nobel Prizes in physics and chemistry usually went to those who are inventive in the laboratory. Moreover, it said, theories are nothing but inventions "conceived to explain what is observed or experienced."

The timing of the award is significant. Public interest in cosmic rays, after a lull lasting a decade, had been reawakened by discoveries of new subatomic particles since the end of World War II. As an article in *Science* stressed, on November 26, most of these discoveries had been made in the context of cosmic-ray studies. *Scientific American* of December, 1948, announced the discovery of a new particle on the same page with a note on Blackett's Nobel Prize. Moreover, the public's attention had been focused on nuclear physics by the development of the atom bomb and of ever-larger particle accelerators. Blackett, as a pioneer in cosmic rays and a scientist involved in nuclear physics, was a good choice for the award.

Another fortuitous circumstance was hinted at in the *Time* announcement. Blackett had achieved notoriety in 1947 for his suggestion that any spinning mass is necessarily magnetic. *Science News Letter*, on November 20, even suggested that the Nobel citation should be changed to "For the discovery of a connection between magnetism and gravitation." Such a discovery would indeed have been as significant as Albert Einstein's statement of the connection between matter and energy. Although Blackett later withdrew this idea, in 1948 it added to his fame.

If this background made him famous, another made him infamous and strongly affected the reaction to his Nobel honors. Blackett had published a book in October, 1948, titled *Military and Political Consequences of Atomic Energy*. This book was critical of both American and British nuclear weapons policies. It was viewed by some as pro-Soviet. *The Times* of London underscored that Blackett's prize was not for his book, but for his "physics." On November 23, both *The New York Times* and *The Times* of London published an attack on Blackett's ideas by General Frederick Osborne, the American deputy on the United Nations Atomic Energy Commission. Osborne stressed the heavy use of Blackett's book by the Soviet delegation to the commission and questioned how a man reared in Great Britain could support the Soviet Union's "peculiar view on human affairs." He accused Blackett of cynicism, factual errors, ignorance of history, and "tendentious arguments."

Blackett's Nobel Prize was virtually overshadowed after this by the reaction to his book. The *Bulletin of the Atomic Scientists* devoted a special issue (February 3,

1949) to commentary on it, as an American edition, *Fear, War, and the Bomb*, had just appeared. One of these articles was titled "Blackett's Apologia for the Soviet Position," but another, "Blackett's Analysis of the Issues," by Philip Morrison, defended his argument as moderate and coolly reasoned. Morrison also chastised Blackett's critics for their self-righteous personal attacks on him. *Scientific American* published an excerpt from the book and a critical, but balanced, response to it in their March, 1949, issue. Ironically, this same issue published a review article on cosmic rays which did not mention Blackett.

While some press accounts attacked Blackett for being a scientist dabbling in politics, others were aware that he had a long history in military tactics. *The New Republic* on November 29 published a detailed analysis by James R. Newman which stressed this background. Newman also reproached Blackett's critics for Red-baiting. Blackett's left-wing politics were well-known, and the Cold War was beginning.

Biography

Patrick Maynard Stuart Blackett was born on November 18, 1897, in London. His father was a stockbroker, and the family had long been Anglican. Patrick studied at Osborne Naval College, then at Dartmouth College. These naval schools stressed mathematics and science, which suited Blackett well.

During World War I, Blackett served as a midshipman in the south Atlantic and was in the Battle of Jutland. He became a lieutenant in 1918 and was sent by the Navy to the University of Cambridge in 1919. Soon after arriving, Blackett decided to resign from the Navy to study science. In 1921, he became a research student under Ernest Rutherford and attended lectures by Charles T. R. Wilson. He spent a year at the University of Göttingen in 1924-1925, on a Moseley Research Fellowship of the Royal Society, but returned afterward to Cambridge. In 1933 he left for Birkbeck College, to escape a heavy teaching load and to run his own laboratory. Many members of the cosmic-ray research team assembled there followed him to the University of Manchester in 1937. While there, he helped to establish Jodrell Bank. He moved to Imperial College in 1953, partly to be nearer the center of government.

During World War II, Blackett advised the government on technical issues. Though he fell from favor in 1947 because of his criticism of nuclear policy, he returned in the 1960's with the Labour government of Harold Wilson. He was instrumental in establishing science policy. He drifted away from government after becoming president of the Royal Society in 1965. He died in London on July 13, 1974.

Scientific Career

Blackett's interest in nature was well developed while he was still a student at Dartmouth College, where he explored the countryside, sailed, and watched birds. His technical inclination also developed while he was in the Navy. On active duty during World War I, Blackett noticed deficiencies in British gunnery and worked on inventions to improve it, even taking out a patent. He might have stayed on after the war but for what he believed was a lack of serious interest in technological improvement in the Navy. He considered seeking employment with an instrumentation company after the war but began studies at Cambridge instead.

Blackett entered Cambridge in January, 1919, and was accepted as a physics student in October. His course of studies was accelerated because of his war service, and he was graduated in 1921. Most of his work was done at the Cavendish Laboratory, which Rutherford was then guiding through a period of great importance in the history of physics. Even as an undergraduate, Blackett was surrounded by scientists engaged in intensive study of the atom and its nucleus. Rutherford had already discovered the disintegration of the atom and was continuing to bombard various light elements with alpha particles, attempting to learn about the nucleus.

Blackett became a research student just when Rutherford wanted someone to explore the utility of Wilson's cloud chamber for these studies. This project demonstrated Blackett's inventive abilities, a hallmark of his work in physics which ultimately earned for him the Nobel Prize. He inherited a cloud chamber from a former student, but he modified it to improve the trails left by charged particles and to improve the photographs taken of these trails. He published his first scientific article in 1922 in the *Proceedings of the Royal Society*. It contained no dramatic news, but it did extend knowledge of alpha particles somewhat. More important, this project introduced Blackett to the device and the scientific problems that would shape much of his career.

Blackett pursued many different projects with his cloud chamber over the next few years, and he assisted other scientists at the Cavendish Laboratory in many more. His main assignment, however, was to produce clear evidence of the events that occur during the transformation of the nucleus. He succeeded in 1924. He allowed alpha particles from a radioactive source to enter a cloud chamber filled with nitrogen gas and saturated with water vapor. The alpha particles entered the chamber just after it had undergone a rapid expansion, which was achieved through a combination of a piston, levers, cams, and springs. The expansion produced a supersaturated cloud, from which water droplets readily condensed. When an alpha particle collided with a nitrogen nucleus, the photograph indicated that a proton and an oxygen isotope remained. Rutherford's 1919 discovery had shown that a nuclear transformation takes place, but Blackett's now showed it in detail.

Blackett was also keenly aware of theoretical issues. He published a theoretical paper in 1923 which questioned what happens when an electron collides with an atom. How would the energy of the collision be allotted? What would the effective "target area" be? Blackett pursued related problems during his year in Germany (1924-1925) and returned to Cambridge awakened to developments in quantum mechanics.

Blackett frequently participated in team research projects, which were typical of most nuclear and cosmic-ray research. In 1925 he began a collaboration with Edmund P. Hudson on more problems related to alpha particle collisions with nuclei.

A little later, he worked with several physical chemists on a new technique for measuring the thermal properties of gases. Frequently, Blackett collaborated as a master of experimental technique, which he certainly was. In the late 1920's and early 1930's, he was constantly improving the cloud chamber, or its camera, or helping someone with an unrelated experimental problem.

In 1932 this activity took a new direction: Blackett abandoned alpha particle studies and switched to cosmic rays. The impetus for this switch was Occhialini's arrival from Italy. Occhialini brought with him the new techniques of Bruno Rossi (born 1905), which were based on the Geiger counter. From this collaboration emerged the "countercontrolled cloud chamber," the instrument that enabled Blackett and Occhialini to make their important discoveries about cosmic rays.

For three years, the two scientists photographed events triggered by cosmic rays. They photographed tracks of high-energy particles, the interaction of these particles with metal plates, and the behavior of the particles in a magnetic field. The curved tracks of the particles in the magnetic field indicated that some of them—the electrons—had negative charges and that others were positive and of about the same mass as the electrons.

This last observation, announced in 1933, verified Carl Anderson's 1932 discovery of a positive particle. Blackett and Occhialini, however, also observed "showers" of positive particles and electrons radiating from a single point. The discovery that nearly equal numbers of positrons and electrons are produced in cosmic-ray showers contradicted Robert Millikan's conclusion that the new positive particle was a proton ejected by the nucleus. Blackett and Occhialini left no doubt that it was a lighter particle, the positron, and that what had been witnessed was not ejection from the nucleus but the actual creation of matter from energy. Later, in 1933, Blackett connected this discovery to Paul Dirac's theory of pair production.

While at Birkbeck College in London, from 1933 to 1937, Blackett focused exclusively on cosmic-ray research. He mastered the breadth of current knowledge of cosmic rays and was acutely aware of the major questions yet unanswered. He planned cosmic-ray experiments to be conducted not only in his laboratory but also in airplanes at high altitudes and in the underground tunnels of London. Recently elected a Fellow of the Royal Society, he applied to the society to finance a huge electromagnet and a larger cloud chamber. With these, he studied the energy spectrum of cosmic rays and investigated whether their origin was near Earth or in space, terrestrial or cosmic.

Blackett, like most other cosmic-ray researchers, was greatly puzzled by a more penetrating form of cosmic rays discovered in the late 1930's. He thought, incorrectly, that these consisted of a high-energy electron which for some reason deviated from theoretical expectations. The work he began on this problem at Birkbeck was continued when he became Langworthy Professor of Physics at the University of Manchester in 1937. He soon accepted the view of Anderson and others that the penetrating radiation consisted of another new particle, which was called the "mesotron," because its mass was between that of a proton and an electron.

The main advantage to be found at Manchester was a better-equipped laboratory, which Blackett used effectively to attract a strong research team. Included on this team for six months was Rossi, who had fled Fascist Italy after it stripped him of his citizenship. The Manchester team undertook a wide variety of experimental studies, mostly aimed at a better understanding of the mesotron, which rapidly became known as the "meson."

As World War II developed, Blackett's attention was pulled progressively away from cosmic-ray research, though he never entirely abandoned it. Beginning in 1935, he served on several committees for the Air Ministry, to apply recent technological advances to improving Great Britain's defenses. Blackett drew on both his scientific qualifications and his long-standing interest in military affairs. These committees considered a wide variety of proposals for new defenses, but a most notable success was the improvement of radar. Blackett contributed personally to improving bomb sights, defense against U-boats, the coordinated use of radar and antiaircraft guns, and the statistical analysis of the expected results of alternative strategies. The latter activity, called operational analysis, was Blackett's wartime specialty. Indeed, he became director of Naval Operational Research.

Blackett's forthright statements about the wisdom or effectiveness of military actions sometimes attracted strong censure. In the 1930's, he resigned from the Tizard Committee of the Air Ministry in a disagreement over the priority to be given to the development of radar. During the war, Blackett criticized the bombing of German civilians, and he suggested that Great Britain could not practically develop an atom bomb alone, contrary to the majority position of the committee on which he served. After the war, while a member of the Advisory Committee on Atomic Energy, Blackett expressed nearly complete disagreement with British and American policy toward nuclear weapons. Some thought that he was a Soviet apologist. He was essentially ignored by government from 1947 until the election of a Labour parliament in 1964.

Blackett continued his scientific research after World War II, reinvigorating the cosmic-ray group at Manchester, with which he had never severed ties. Several important discoveries emerged, but none was more important than the detection of the first "strange particles" by George D. Rochester (born 1908) and Clifford C. Butler (born 1922) in 1947. Though Blackett did not adjoin his name to the announcement, he was active in the research.

Between 1947 and 1951, Blackett undertook a new research problem: the search for a possible fundamental relation between magnetism and the rotation of massive bodies. Scientists had long wondered what caused Earth's magnetism. One answer suggested was that magnetism was produced by any rotating body. Blackett noted that observations of the magnetism of Earth, the Sun, and some stars seemed to support the idea, and proposed experimental tests. One test involved the measurement of Earth's magnetic field in deep mines in South Africa and England. The other involved measuring the magnetic field of a stationary gold cylinder. Because this field was predicted to be extremely small, Blackett invented a magnetometer ten thousand times more sensitive than any then available. It was another instrumental tour de force. The results of these experiments, and of some conducted by other researchers, convinced Blackett that his theory was utterly unfounded.

Blackett's interest in magnetism continued into the 1950's. The sensitive magnetometer proved to be exactly what was needed for the new research field of rock magnetism. Because of developments in geophysics, it was becoming important to determine what Earth's magnetism had been like in earlier geologic eras. This knowledge was to be acquired by measuring the magnetism of small samples of rocks. Since this magnetism is generally quite weak, Blackett's magnetometer contributed to science in a way originally unintended. Ultimately, it provided data important for proving elements of the theory of continental drift.

With his move to Imperial College in 1953, Blackett faced his last academic post and the building of yet another research center. He presided over the growth of the physics department at the college, including the construction of a new building. He continued to stay abreast of developments in nuclear physics, cosmic rays, and magnetism. By 1960 he had become a most ingenious advocate of the continental drift theory, drawing on evidence concerning both ancient magnetism and ancient climate. After 1960, he became especially interested in the problem of the reversal of Earth's magnetic field and what this reversal implied about the cause of Earth's magnetism.

Blackett crowned his career as a scientist in the late 1960's and early 1970's. He was elected president of the Royal Society in 1965, a post which he felt honored to hold. He helped to direct international efforts to extend the benefits of science to developing areas of the world. He achieved this goal by a remarkable transformation of the Royal Society's program which involved it explicitly, for the first time, in international outreach. He died on July 13, 1974.

Bibliography

Primary

PHYSICS: "The Ejection of Protons from Nitrogen Nuclei, Photographed by the Wilson Method," *Proceedings of the Royal Society of London A*, vol. 107, 1925 (with Giuseppe Occhialini); "Photography of Penetrating Corpuscular Radiation," *Nature*, vol. 130, 1932; "The Craft of Experimental Physics," in Harold Wright, ed., *University Studies*, 1933; *Cosmic Rays: The Halley Lecture*, 1936; "Cosmic Rays: The 30th Kelvin Lecture," *Journal of the Institution of Electrical Engineers*, vol. 85, 1939; "The Magnetic Field of Massive Rotating Bodies," *Philosophical Magazine*, vol. 40, 1949; *Lectures on Rock Magnetism*, 1956; "Introduction to 'A Symposium on Continental Drift,'" *Philosophical Transactions of the Royal Society of London A*, vol. 258, 1965.

OTHER NONFICTION: *The Atom and the Charter*, 1946; *Science and the Welfare of Mankind*, 1946; *Military and Political Consequences of Atomic Energy*, 1948; *Atomic Weapons and East-West Relations*, 1956; "Atomic Heretic," *The Listener*, September 11, 1958; *Studies of War: Nuclear and Conventional*, 1962; *Science and*

Technology in an Unequal World, 1968; *Reflections on Science and Technology in Developing Countries*, 1970; *The Gap Widens*, 1970; *Science, Technology and Aid in Developing Countries*, 1971; *Aspects of India's Development*, 1973.

Secondary

Bromberg, Joan. "The Concept of Particle Creation Before and After Quantum Mechanics." *Historical Studies in the Physical Sciences* 7 (1976): 161-191. This article provides a clear treatment of the theoretical background to Blackett's experimental work in the early 1930's.

Browne, Laurie M., and Lillian Hoddeson, eds. *The Birth of Particle Physics*. Cambridge, England: Cambridge University Press, 1983. A sense of the level of debate and ambiguity in the 1930's and 1940's is provided by the reminiscences of scientists in this book. It must be noted that their discussions are often quite technical; their memories, however, also suggest the lively atmosphere of the research labs and the human side of discovery. Especially noteworthy are essays by cosmic-ray reseachers Dmitry Skobeltzyn and Carl Anderson.

Cassidy, David. "Cosmic Ray Showers, High Energy Physics, and Quantum Field Theories: Programmatic Interactions in the 1930's." *Historical Studies in the Physical Sciences* 12 (1981): 1-39. An essential study for understanding the relationship of nuclear physics and cosmic-ray studies during a critical period in Blackett's career.

Galison, Peter. *How Experiments End*. Chicago: University of Chicago Press, 1987. Blackett's work on cosmic rays is placed in the context of related work in quantum mechanics in chapter 3, "Particles and Theories." A major concern here is the interaction of observation and theory and the nature of proofs of the existence of new particles. An extensive bibliography of both primary and secondary sources is provided.

Lovell, Bernard. *P. M. S. Blackett: A Biographical Memoir*. London: Royal Society, 1976. A most detailed and informed discussion of Blackett's life and research. No other source is as comprehensive and informed. Included is a bibliography of works by Blackett, both scientific and nonscientific publications.

Sekido, Yataro, and Harry Elliot, eds. *Early History of Cosmic Ray Studies: Personal Reminiscences with Old Photographs*. Dordrecht, Netherlands: D. Reidel, 1985. This book consists entirely of the reflections of scientists who were involved in the development of the science of cosmic rays. It covers a period much wider than that of Blackett's active research in the field. The most useful sections for understanding Blackett's work are parts 3 and 4, "Positron and Mesotron: Early Discoveries of New Particles" and "Sea, Mountain, and Underground: Ultra-Penetrating and Extra-Terrestrial Aspects." References to Blackett, however, occur throughout the book.

Gregory A. Good

1949

Physics
Hideki Yukawa, Japan

Chemistry
William Glauque, United States

Physiology or Medicine
Walter Rudolf Hess, Switzerland
António Egas Moniz, Portugal

Literature
William Faulkner, United States

Peace
Lord Boyd-Orr, Great Britain

HIDEKI YUKAWA
1949

Born: Tokyo, Japan; January 23, 1907
Died: Kyoto, Japan; September 8, 1981
Nationality: Japanese
Area of concentration: Nuclear physics

Yukawa discovered how to modify the mechanism of the electromagnetic field in order to create a new field that would begin to explain the nature of nuclear forces. He predicted the existence of new particles called "mesons" that characterized this new field and that subsequently were found in cosmic radiation and by experimental means in the laboratory

The Award

Presentation

Professor Ivar Waller, a member of the Nobel Committee for Physics, presented the Nobel Prize in Physics to Hideki Yukawa at the Nobel ceremonies on December 10, 1949. Waller began his presentation speech by noting that scientists were trying to explain scientific observations in terms of elementary particles. For the past ten years, elementary particles called "mesons" had been observed and had received much attention from physicists. These particles were completely unknown until Hideki Yukawa, in 1934, predicted their existence while conducting a theoretical investigation of nuclear forces. The Nobel Prize was bestowed on him for this achievement.

Waller noted that the atomic nucleus was composed of protons and neutrons, which were collectively called "nucleons." Yukawa's overall plan had been to find the force that held one neutron and one proton together and then to generalize the theory to many nucleons. It was known that the electromagnetic field explained the long-range forces between charged particles. Using the idea that a proton and neutron were different states of a nucleon and modifying the electromagnetic field to obtain short-range forces, Yukawa discovered a relation which connected the mass of the field particles with the range of the force between the nucleons. Since the range of the force was approximately known, he was able to calculate the mass of these particles to be about two hundred times the mass of the electron. He called these field particles "mesons" and in 1934 suggested that they could be found outside the nucleus in cosmic radiation. Two types of meson were actually observed, one heavy and one light. It was the heavy meson that interacted strongly with nucleons, as Yukawa had predicted. It was this experimental verification that provided a brilliant confirmation of his theory.

Nobel lecture

In his lecture, "Meson Theory in Its Developments," Yukawa described the development of the meson theory up to 1949. He explained that the thrust of his work had been to expand the concept of the force field, which described gravitational and electromagnetic interactions, to include nuclear forces. After the discovery of the neutron, it was clear that an additional field of force was needed. Electromagnetic forces could be described by charges exchanging photons, the particles of the electromagnetic field. Therefore, it was suggested that the force holding the neutron and proton together could be described in terms of these nucleons exchanging an electron and neutrino pair. The nuclear forces calculated from this theory, however, proved to be much too small. Eugene Paul Wigner (born 1902) pointed out that the rapid increase in the binding energy from the deuteron to the alpha particle indicated that the nuclear forces were of very short range. To try to satisfy some of the requirements for a theory of nuclear forces, Yukawa postulated that the nucleons were exchanging an unknown particle, which he called the "meson."

He continued his lecture by describing the postulates of his initial meson theory and the results of the application of the theory. The mass of the meson could be related to the range of the nuclear force, estimated by Wigner, and the value was revealed to be about two hundred electron masses. Since these mesons produced the exchange forces, he knew that there must be positively and negatively charged mesons with a magnitude of charge equal to that of the electron. It was assumed that a positive (or negative) meson was emitted (or absorbed) when a nucleon went from the proton to the neutron state, and that a negative (or positive) meson was emitted (or absorbed) when a nucleon went from the neutron to the proton state. A neutron and proton, therefore, could "interact with each other by exchanging mesons just as two charged particles interact by exchanging photons."

This theory, however, had some contradictions with experimental results and, in addition, did not account for certain known properties of the deuteron (the nucleus of the deuterium atom, consisting of one proton and one neutron). Other scientists investigated in detail the application of various types of force field to this problem. It was subsequently found that only the "pseudoscalar" meson field theory predicted experimental results correctly. It was also necessary to postulate the existence of a neutral meson with a mass equal to that of a charged meson.

Yukawa suggested that experimental physicists look at the high-energy collisions of cosmic-ray particles with the upper layers of the atmosphere in order to search for the meson. The meson was an unstable particle and therefore would have a very short lifetime. In 1947, two differently charged mesons were found, one of which was heavier than the other. It was the heavier meson that was connected with nuclear forces. The lighter meson was the main constituent of cosmic rays at sea level. Later, using the cyclotron at the University of California at Berkeley, scientists discovered the neutral meson.

There is no doubt that the introduction of the meson to explain nuclear forces was a stroke of genius. It stimulated a tremendous amount of activity by other physicists in both the theoretical and experimental study of nuclear forces and elementary particles.

Critical reception

The response was overwhelmingly positive to Yukawa's winning the Nobel Prize in Physics. Before he won the prize, he was so highly respected that he became the first Japanese scientist to be invited to the United States after World War II. He spent the 1948-1949 academic year at the Institute for Advanced Study in Princeton, New Jersey, one of the most prestigious institutions of higher learning and theoretical research in the world. He was then invited to be a visiting professor of physics at Columbia University, starting at the end of his year at the institute. During his first year at Columbia, it was announced on November 3, 1949, that he had been chosen to receive the Nobel Prize. The next day, there was a picture on the front page of *The New York Times* showing Dwight D. Eisenhower, president of Columbia University, shaking hands with Yukawa. Physics journals all over the world printed research papers done by other physicists on meson theory and its applications.

J. Robert Oppenheimer was the director of the Institute for Advanced Study who had personally invited Yukawa to visit there. Oppenheimer was also past director of the atom bomb research team at Los Alamos during World War II, a giant in the world of physics. His statement lauding Yukawa represented the attitude of the entire physics community:

> Dr. Yukawa's anticipation of the meson is one of the few really fructifying ideas in the last decades. He played a great role in establishing the very, very high quality of physics in Japan. He was deeply loved by all his colleagues in his year here both as a scientist and a man.

Biography

Hideki Ogawa was born in Tokyo, Japan, on January 23, 1907. In 1908, his father, Takuji Ogawa, became a professor of geology at Kyoto University, and Hideki moved to Kyoto with his family. From 1913 to 1919, he attended the Kyogoku Primary School in Kyoto, and from 1919 to 1923 he attended Kyoto Prefectural First Middle School. He was a student at the Third High School from 1923 to 1926; thereafter, he began majoring in physics in the faculty of science at Kyoto University. He became an unpaid research associate at the university in 1929, and he wed Sumi Yukawa in 1932. Her family adopted him, a not uncommon tradition in Japan, and as a result he changed his last name to Yukawa.

Between 1932 and 1936, Yukawa was a lecturer at Kyoto University and Osaka University. In 1936, he was made an associate professor at Osaka, and in 1938 he received his doctoral degree from that institution. It is notable that he skipped the level of assistant professor, which is the next level above lecturer, and immediately became an associate professor. In 1939, he accepted a full professorship at Kyoto University. The next year, he was awarded the Imperial Prize of the Japan Academy, and in 1943 he received the Order of Decoration of Cultural Merit of Japan. He was a visiting professor at the Institute for Advanced Study in Princeton, New Jersey, in 1948 and 1949, and a visiting professor at Columbia University, in New York City, from 1949 to 1953. He received the Nobel Prize in December, 1949, while he was at Columbia University. He retired from Kyoto University in 1970 and was awarded the title of Professor Emeritus. He died in September, 1981, in Kyoto.

Scientific Career

In order to appreciate Yukawa's contribution to physics, one must have some historical perspective on the major steps in the development of theoretical physics. In the seventeenth century, Sir Isaac Newton discovered the law of universal gravitation, the first of the fundamental forces in nature. It stated simply that there was a force of attraction between any two objects, or masses, and that the mathematical expression of this law would be the same throughout the entire universe. Using this law, Newton was able to calculate the orbits of the planets around the Sun. Today, scientists use this law to determine the orbits of satellites around Earth and to solve many other problems.

The next basic force that was discovered was the law of force between electrically charged objects. It was found that there were two kinds of electrical charge: positive and negative. Charles-Augustin de Coulomb formulated the law of force between electrical charges, noting that like charges repel and unlike charges attract. For example, in the winter, when a person walks across a soft carpet, he becomes electrically charged, and when he reaches for a doorknob he will feel a spark jump between his hand and the knob as he discharges. The space around a stationary, electrically charged sphere is different from the space around a neutral sphere. Scientists say that the space around an electrically charged object contains an electric field. If one puts a compass in this space it would not be affected; if the charge is moved rapidly back and forth, however, a changing electric field would result, and the compass needle would continually change direction. A new kind of field has been created: a magnetic field.

This combination of the two kinds of field is called an electromagnetic field, and when it is made to travel in a certain direction, it constitutes an electromagnetic wave. Radio and television sets have antennae that receive electromagnetic waves from the station to which they are tuned, and the waves are then converted to sound or pictures on a screen. Light is also an electromagnetic wave; it constitutes a tiny portion of the spectrum of these waves, the portion that can be seen by human eyes. James Clerk Maxwell, in the nineteenth century, reformulated the electromagnetic laws of force in terms of the electric and magnetic fields.

In the early twentieth century, it became necessary to make another change in the laws of force. Instead of thinking of light as an electromagnetic wave, scientists began to perceive it as a collection of a huge number of tiny particles called "photons." These photons had properties of both waves and particles, and they were the basic units of the electromagnetic field. This new concept explained the attraction of unlike charges: These charges exchanged photons, and this constant exchange could be shown to create an attractive force.

Great strides were made toward discovering the structure of matter in the early twentieth century. Atoms were known to be the units of which all substances were composed; these units, however, also had structure. An atom had a central nucleus which contained all of its positive charge, and the space around the nucleus was filled with negatively charged particles called "electrons." The nucleus was composed of protons, which were positively charged, and neutrons, which had no charge. Physicists were trying to discover what held the neutrons and protons together in the nucleus. They knew that the protons repelled one another, because they had like charges, and that the protons and neutrons had no electrical attraction, because the neutrons were uncharged. What force, then, held these particles together so tightly in the nucleus? It is this question that Yukawa answered.

It was known in the 1920's that certain heavy, radioactive elements, such as radium, were unstable and that such an atom would spontaneously emit an electron and another, electrically uncharged, particle, called a "neutrino." Therefore, it was thought that electrons were inside the nucleus as well as outside it. Werner Heisenberg suggested that perhaps the force that holds a neutron and proton together is a consequence of these particles' exchanging an electron. This hypothesis followed the model of the electromagnetic field, in which unlike charges attract each other by exchanging photons. The force thus calculated, however, proved to be too small. Yukawa then had the brilliant idea that the neutron and protron were exchanging a hitherto unknown particle, called a "meson," that was providing the force binding the nucleus together. He devised equations that the mesons would have to satisfy; they were analogous to the Maxwell field equations that photons had to obey. In the process, Yukawa derived a new relationship between the meson's mass and the range of force between the neutron and proton. He used a scalar field variable to calculate the meson mass.

Yukawa suggested that mesons could be found outside the nucleus if strong enough collisions were made to occur between nuclei and particles that exist in the cosmic rays that come from outer space and bombard the upper atmosphere. He then developed a theory whereby he could calculate how long a meson would last before it changed into another particle (its lifetime). It was suggested on the basis of experimental evidence that there was a heavy and a light meson. Yukawa identified the heavy meson as the one responsible for the neutron-proton force, and his colleagues suggested that the heavy meson decayed into the lighter meson. Finally, he calculated the lifetime of the heavy meson; the result agreed with experimental measurements and was consistent with his calculations of the force between the neutron and proton.

Yukawa had the meson idea in 1934, and he delivered a talk entitled "On the Interaction of Elementary Particles I" at one of the monthly meetings of the Physico-Mathematical Society of Japan held at the University of Tokyo. He submitted an article on his theory that was published in the *Proceedings of the Physico-Mathematical Society of Japan* in 1935. There were many details left unanswered, and in 1937 he and a colleague, Shaichi Sakata, published "On the Theory of Elementary Particles II," wherein they presented a scalar meson theory of nuclear forces. Other scientists began trying different field variables to describe the mesons in order to get better and fuller results. Yukawa, Sakata, and M. Taketani published two more papers on the theory of elementary particles; in these studies, they tried pseudoscalar fields in their calculations, and they obtained better results. As a result of these publications, Yukawa was invited to the Solvay Conference on Elementary Particles and Their Interactions. Because of the outbreak of World War II, however, the conference was canceled. He then traveled to the United States, where he met many physicists and delivered lectures on the meson theory.

Now that many scientists were working on meson theory, Yukawa turned his attention to the mathematical structure of field theories in order to address some of the difficulties that these theories contained. He published in 1942 a series of articles on the foundation of the theory of fields in the Japanese journal *Kagoku* (science). These articles were his initial attempt to construct a field theory that did not contain quantities that became infinite in value in certain circumstances. These difficulties were called "divergences," and they plagued every field theory that had so far been mathematically formulated. Again, he was moving in the correct direction and would be joined by many others years later.

In 1946, Yukawa founded an academic journal in European languages called *Progress of Theoretical Physics*; it is now a leading international publication. J. Robert Oppenheimer, the director of the Institute for Advanced Study in Princeton, invited Yukawa to the institute to do his research in 1948. Columbia University invited him for the same reason in 1949. He received the Nobel Prize in December, 1949, and stayed at Columbia until 1953. Much of the work he did during his stay at these two institutions was a continuation of his effort to construct field theories that always give finite results. For example, in the theory of the neutron-proton system, variables are introduced to represent these two particles. There is also a field variable to represent the meson. The neutron-proton variables interact with the field variables via an interaction term, which contains all the variables. It is this term that causes the divergence difficulties. Yukawa introduced a way to "smear out" the interaction term over a small region of space. This technique was called "nonlocal field theory." His effort made things better but did not solve the whole problem.

In 1953, Yukawa returned to Japan. That same year, he was made director of the Research Institute for Fundamental Physics at Kyoto University. He assumed administrative duties and helped to direct fundamental research. He also became involved in outside activities. He was one of the eleven signatories to the Russell-Einstein Manifesto against the use of nuclear weapons and for the abolition of war. From 1956 to 1957, he was a member of the Atomic Energy Commission of Japan, and in the latter year he attended the first Pugwash Conference on Sciences and World Affairs, in Pugwash, Canada. He became president of the World Association of Federalists. In 1962, he helped organize the first Kyoto Conference of Scientists for nuclear disarmament. From 1965 to 1981, he was the honorary president of the World Association of Federalists.

In the 1970's, Yukawa published his last scientific papers, a collection of essays on creativity and intuition, and a volume of his collected works. In early 1981, he organized the fourth Kyoto Conference of Scientists. He died in September of that year.

Bibliography

Primary

PHYSICS: "On the Interaction of Elementary Particles, Part I," *Proceedings of the Physico-Mathematical Society of Japan*, vol. 17, 1935; *Butsurigaku ni kokorozashite*, 1944; *Ryōshī rikigaku josetu*, 1947; *Busshitsukan to Sekaikan*, 1948; "Hikyokushoba no riron," 1950 ("Quantum Theory of Non-Local Fields," 1950); *Yukawa Hideki jisenshū*, 1971.

OTHER NONFICTION: *Creativity and Intuition: A Physicist Looks at East and West*, 1973; *Tabibito, the Traveler*, 1982.

Secondary

Crease, Robert P., and Charles C. Mann. *The Second Creation: Makers of the Revolution in Twentieth Century Physics*. New York: Macmillan, 1985. A history of modern physics that focuses on the lives and personalities of the participants. About eight pages are devoted to Yukawa and his discoveries. The reactions of other physicists to his hypotheses are described, and his work is placed in the context of earlier and later developments in the field of nuclear and elementary particle physics. Suitable for high school and college students. Index and glossary.

Hawking, Stephen W. *A Brief History of Time*. New York: Bantam Books, 1988. This work contains a chapter titled "Elementary Particles and the Forces of Nature" that gives concise, clear explanations of the particles and forces that form the atomic nucleus. Quarks, mesons, electrons, and the strong and weak nuclear forces are discussed. Hawking spends some time explaining the notion that particles are "carriers" of the forces of nature.

Wilczek, Frank, and Betsy Devine. *Longing for the Harmonies: Themes and Variations from Modern Physics*. New York: W. W. Norton, 1988. This book attempts to explain the exotic theories of twentieth century physics in terms simple enough for the nonspecialist. Chapters 6, 7, and 8 describe the search for an understanding of elementary particles and the forces that govern them. Quarks, gluons, K-mesons, and virtual particles are discussed, as are the major experiments that shed light on their nature. The authors focus on the philosophy that underlies the physical discoveries.

Zukav, Gary. *The Dancing Wu Li Masters: An Overview of the New Physics*. New York: William Morrow, 1979. A treatment of advanced physics, from quantum mechanics to relativity theory, aimed at the college-level reader. Well illustrated. Bibliography, index, and particle table.

M. F. Soto

1950

Physics
Cecil Frank Powell, Great Britain

Chemistry
Otto Diels, West Germany
Kurt Alder, West Germany

Physiology or Medicine
Philip S. Hench, United States
Edward C. Kendall, United States
Tadeusz Reichstein, Switzerland

Literature
Bertrand Russell, Great Britain

Peace
Ralph Bunche, United States

CECIL FRANK POWELL
1950

Born: Tonbridge, Kent, Great Britain; December 5, 1903
Died: Near Milan, Italy; August 9, 1969
Nationality: British
Areas of concentration: Nuclear physics and cosmic radiation

Powell's development of the photographic emulsion method of recording the tracks of particles, along with the apparatus he devised for extracting precise quantitative information from the tracks, led to fundamental discoveries of new elementary particles occurring in cosmic radiation

The Award

Presentation

Professor A. E. Lindh, a member of the Nobel Committee for Physics, presented the Nobel Prize in Physics to Cecil Frank Powell on December 10, 1950, on behalf of the Royal Swedish Academy of Sciences and King Gustav VI, from whom Powell accepted the award. Lindh began his presentation with a brief description of the photographic method developed by Powell. He noted that although the method had been used in the early 1900's and developed in the 1930's, it had not been widely accepted in the field of nuclear physics; the "Wilson chamber" method had been used instead.

Powell was praised for having convinced nuclear physicists that the photographic method was an effective aid in investigating certain nuclear processes and cosmic radiation. Powell and his colleagues made significant improvements in the treatment of the material, the research technique, and the optical equipment used for particle trace analysis. The photographic method developed by Powell, Lindh said, had proved equal, if not sometimes superior, to the Wilson chamber method with respect to both time and material. The improved photographic method's greatest contribution, however, was to the study of cosmic radiation, especially at high altitudes. The discovery of new elementary particles, such as the neutral meson, resulted from Powell's studies in cosmic radiation.

The presenter concluded by commending Powell for making the photographic method one of the most efficient tools of modern nuclear physics.

Nobel lecture

Powell's Nobel lecture, titled "The Cosmic Radiation," began with a general definition and description of cosmic radiation. In terms comprehensible to the layman, he assessed the importance of the field of study. He then discussed the technical problems involved in cosmic-ray investigations and surveyed the major devices available for the detection of radiations. To aid his audience, he illustrated the lecture with slides and a film of the construction of the balloons that were part of his experiments.

Always giving credit to his colleagues, Powell went on to explain, in simple terms, his and his colleagues' work at Bristol University, emphasizing the technology involved in their experiments. He explained why the experiments were conducted at high altitudes and summarized the results of his investigations. Describing the nuclear collisions at high altitudes and the pi-mesons, or pions, which he studied, he mentioned that his discovery was similar to what Hideki Yukawa (1907-1981), the physics prizewinner for 1949, had predicted earlier. After discussing the transformation of pi-mesons into mu-mesons, Powell continued by giving credit to the work being conducted at other laboratories around the world regarding the existence of more massive mesons.

In the concluding two paragraphs of his address, Powell summarized his view of the significance of the study of cosmic radiation, which, he said, had been considered trivial only twenty-five years earlier. Stressing the richness of the field of discovery that had "contributed to the development of a picture of the material universe as a system in a state of physical change and flux . . . a picture which stands in great contrast with that of our predecessors," Powell placed his work in a larger context. He looked forward, he said, to future studies of cosmic radiation that could lead to the investigation of "some of the most fundamental problems in the evolution of the cosmos."

Critical reception

There was only a simple, brief announcement of Powell's award in *The Times* of London on November 11, 1950. In *The New York Times* (November 11), there was an article announcing the prize which mentioned that although Powell was accused of leftist tendencies, he had disavowed any connection with the Communist Party. *Time* magazine of November 20, nearly restating what had been said in *The New York Times*, referred to Powell as "the committeeman" and mentioned that Powell's political inclinations were leftist but that he said he was not a Communist. *Time* also alluded to Powell's belief that peace among nations was of the utmost importance.

Science News Letter of November 18, in the final paragraph of a very brief article on Powell's receipt of the Nobel Prize, stated that Powell had once been charged by Soviet scientists with ignoring their claims to have discovered new mesons. Shortly thereafter, two Soviet scientists, in a letter to *Nature*, a British science journal in which Powell often published articles, wrote that they had detected sixteen types of meson. Powell, in response to the controversy, recommended that the Soviets do further experiments to reduce statistical variations in their observations and give a decisive answer to the question of whether the many new particles they claimed to have discovered really existed.

On November 10, *Facts on File: A Weekly World News Digest*, after announcing Powell's prize, said,

Powell is a vice chairman of the British Peace Com., sponsor of the Communist-instigated World Peace Congress, but is not a Communist. His comment on Communist peace plans: "A good thing is not made worse by people who advocate it." He said that the U.S. and Russia should both stop making atomic bombs.

It appears that in the heyday of the McCarthy era, American publications tended to focus more on Powell's politics than on his physics.

Biography

Cecil Frank Powell was born on December 5, 1903, in Tonbridge, Kent, England. His father, Frank Powell, was one of a family of gunsmiths who had long practiced the trade in the town; his mother, of Huguenot descent, was the daughter of a schoolmaster.

Until the age of eleven, Powell attended a local elementary school. Then he won a scholarship to Judd School, a secondary school founded by the City of London Skinners Company. Next, he won a scholarship to Sidney Sussex College, the University of Cambridge, from which he was graduated second in his year in physics. Powell subsequently worked for two years as a research student under Charles Thomson Rees Wilson (1869-1959) and Ernest Rutherford (1871-1937) at the Cavendish Laboratory. In 1928 he was appointed research assistant to A. M. Tyndall, director of the newly opened H. H. Wills Physical Laboratory at the University of Bristol. There, except for a period in 1935 and 1936 when he traveled with an expedition to investigate seismic and volcanic activity in Montserrat, West Indies, he remained, filling in turn the posts of lecturer, reader, and Melville Wills Professor of Physics. In 1949, Powell was elected a Fellow of the Royal Society of London. The Physical Society of London awarded him its Vernon Boys Prize in 1947 and the Royal Society its Hughes Medal in 1949.

During the four years following his appointment as a research assistant at Bristol, Powell carried out, with Tyndall, an elaborate series of investigations into the mobilities of positive ions in gases. Their results, published in joint papers in 1929 and 1932, clarified a number of uncertainties which had previously existed and shed light on the formation of complex ions.

After World War II, Powell was active in movements for peace and scientific cooperation among all nations; he founded the Pugwash Movement for Science and World Affairs, which had those aims. He also served as president of the World Federation of Scientific Workers.

Scientific Career

After receiving his degree from Cambridge, Powell went on to do research under Wilson and Rutherford. His primary interest was Wilson's cloud chamber, and he spent years studying the mobility of ions in gases. (When water droplets condense around ions, they make visible tracks in the cloud chamber.) Powell and his colleagues, however, were interested in a method that entirely circumvented the cloud chamber technique, then much utilized as the chief tool of atomic nuclear research.

One of the major drawbacks of the cloud chamber was that it was sensitive only for brief periods; a photographic emulsion, however, could record the track of every particle that made contact with it. Hence, Powell, believing that the possibilities of emulsions merited the effort, embarked on extensive investigations into the technology of the problem.

By the early twentieth century, it was known that photographic emulsions could record the passage through them of certain charged particles. In traversing the emulsion, the particle ionized grains of silver iodide lying in its path; when the plate was developed, the grains that had been ionized were seen as relatively continuous dark lines. The faster the particle traveled, the more widely spaced were the developed grains, since the faster particles had less capacity to ionize. The distance between these grains was thus a measure of the particle's speed; consequently, the faster the particle, the more difficult it was to detect and measure it in the emulsion. In the late 1930's, photographic emulsions were still considered to be rather unreliable, and insufficiently sensitive, for effective use in nuclear physics.

Between 1939 and 1945, Powell and his colleagues at Bristol University experimented with the treatment and sensitization of emulsions, the development of the necessary photographic techniques, and the interpretation of the tracks left in the emulsion. This experimentation led to the use of the so-called Ilford half-tone emulsion, which, in experiments at high altitudes, proved capable of recording accurately and consistently the tracks of cosmic rays. When Powell and his associates used the plates to investigate cosmic-ray showers, a number of significant discoveries were made. The major advantages of the plates were the simplicity of the method of recording particle tracks, the completeness of the record left, and the connection between the length of a track and the speed of the particle that made it.

In 1947 the power of the above methods was increased by the development of the Ilford C2 emulsions, a further improvement on the original product. A group of these emulsions was exposed in the Pyrenees in a cosmic-ray experiment designed to detect new nuclear events. At this altitude, the fast, heavy atomic nuclei among the incoming primary cosmic-ray particles had already fragmented in collisions with nuclei in the air. Fast protons and alpha particles, however, penetrated to the lower altitude at which the plates were exposed, and it was among these that Powell and his colleagues hoped to detect certain new events, particularly those related to meson production.

An analysis of "disintegration stars" in the plates showed that mu-mesons, or muons, are created when cosmic primaries collide with atmospheric nuclei. Tracks recording the exact mechanism seemed to give evidence for a previously unknown stage in the meson formation process. Although the production of muons had been detected in cosmic radiation by Carl D. Anderson in 1937, the complete process was first described by Powell, who discovered that the muons decayed from slightly heavier mesons, which he called "pions." He noted that it was just such a particle that Hideki Yukawa, in 1935, had postulated as a theoretical necessity. Yukawa had concluded that there should exist a particle that functioned as the quantum of the "strong force" (the force that holds together the particles in the atomic nucleus) and described it as having a rest mass of about 250 electron masses. Yukawa's nuclear quantum was required to interact with nucleons (protons and neutrons), and the muon, which did not, was thus unsatisfactory for the role. The pion, however, suited Yukawa's requirements exactly, and Powell correctly concluded that it was the long-sought nuclear quantum. Powell found that muons were ejected when pions were brought to rest in the emulsions. In experiments involving other methods of detection, the short-lived pions had decayed in flight and thus had gone undetected.

Powell and his colleagues later discovered positive and negative pions and the modes of decay of the heavior K-mesons. In addition, he gave a detailed explanation of the production of cosmic-ray cascades in the atmosphere, classifying these cascades into "soft" components (electrons and photons) and "hard" components (muons and neutrinos).

Powell established a massive international network of laboratories to study elementary particles in the cosmic radiation by means of large stacks of emulsion in free balloons. He also continued to sponsor large-scale international collaboration in the use of accelerators in particle physics. In addition, he played a significant role in CERN, the laboratory of the European Organization for Nuclear Research, serving as chairman of its Scientific Policy Committee for three years. He had a passionate belief both in science as the great transforming force of society and in the social responsibility of scientists.

The study of the unstable elementary particles that have been found since Powell's discovery, many by means of the photographic emulsion method, continues to dominate high-energy physics and has led to the discovery of important properties of symmetry in nature: nonconservation of parity and charge conjugation in weak interactions, such as beta radioactivity and unitary symmetry in strong interactions, such as those related to nuclear forces. Powell's work was significant in marking the beginning of modern elementary particle physics.

Bibliography

Primary

PHYSICS: *The Study of Elementary Particles by the Photographic Method*, 1959; "Cosmic Radiation," *Proceedings of the Institution of Electrical Engineers*, vol. 107B, 1960; "The Role of Pure Science in European Civilization," *Physics Today*, vol. 18, 1965; "Promise and Problems of Modern Science," *Nature*, vol. 216, 1967; *Selected Papers of Cecil Frank Powell*, 1972.

Secondary

Barkas, Walter H. *Nuclear Research Emulsions*. Vol. 1, *Techniques and Theory*. New York: Academic Press, 1963. A two-part work that grew out of a need to answer questions asked by students. Part 1 gives practical information on the subject, which is first treated simply, then more deeply analyzed. The work includes charts, photographs, appendices on mounting and processing and mathematical and physical data, and an extensive bibliography. This volume, along with volume 2, provides a very thorough treatment of the field and Powell's contribution to it.

_____. *Nuclear Research Emulsions*. Vol. 2, *Particle Behavior and Emulsion Applications*. New York: Academic Press, 1973. Volume 2 continues the work of volume 1 and describes the behavior of elementary particles whose tracks are seen in emulsion. It uses mathematics and describes applications in cosmic-ray physics, nuclear physics, biology, and Earth sciences. Contains appendices and an extensive bibliography.

Glasstone, Samuel. *Sourcebook on Atomic Energy*. 3d ed. Princeton, N.J.: Van Nostrand Reinhold, 1967. This book describes, in simple language and with a minimum of mathematics, the most important developments in the areas of science covered by the term "atomic energy." The author uses a historical approach. He ends each chapter with a list of books and articles for further study. In the chapter titled "Elementary Particles," Glasstone talks about the discovery of mesons and Powell's contribution to that discovery. Includes numerous photographs and illustrations.

Leprince-Ringuet, Louis. *Cosmic Rays*. Translated by Fay Ajzenberg. New York: Prentice-Hall, 1950. This book seeks to acquaint the reader with the field of cosmic radiation and to show the nature of the problems involved. It emphasizes the great discoveries in the field, including Powell's, and covers the positron and meson in detail. Experimental processes of these discoveries are stressed. There are charts, graphs, and a brief bibliography on the major works in the field to date. In subsections of chapters titled "The Photographic Emulsion Method" and "Masses of Pi and Mu Mesons," Powell's work is comprehensively described.

Montgomery, Donald J. X. *Cosmic Ray Physics*. Princeton, N.J.: Princeton University Press, 1949. Published the year before Powell won the Nobel Prize, this book surveys the work done in the field (including a brief discussion of Powell's work) and indicates some promising lines of attack for the future. The book's purpose is to provide students who have an intermediate or advanced knowledge of physics with a specialized overview of the subject.

Wilson, John Graham. *Cosmic Rays*. New York: Springer-Verlag, 1976. There are several brief subsections on the development of nuclear emulsions and meson formation which discuss Powell's work, although not in great detail. The book provides a history of the understanding of cosmic particle radiation. A good general introduction to the subject.

Genevieve Slomski

1951

Physics
Sir John Douglas Cockcroft, Great Britain
Ernest Thomas Sinton Walton, Ireland

Chemistry
Edwin McMillan, United States
Glenn Seaborg, United States

Physiology or Medicine
Max Theiler, South Africa

Literature
Pär Lagerkvist, Sweden

Peace
Léon Jouhaux, France

SIR JOHN DOUGLAS COCKCROFT
1951

Born: Todmorden, Yorkshire, Great Britain; May 27, 1897
Died: Cambridge, Great Britain; September 18, 1967
Nationality: British
Area of concentration: Nuclear physics

The work of Cockcroft and his co-laureate Ernest Walton first demonstrated the feasibility of splitting the atomic nucleus by artificial means

The Award

Presentation

The 1951 Nobel Prize in Physics was awarded to Sir John Douglas Cockcroft and Ernest Thomas Sinton Walton on December 10, 1951. The presentation was made on behalf of the Royal Swedish Academy of Sciences by Professor Ivar Waller, a member of the Nobel Committee for Physics. Professor Waller first pointed out that the natural radioactivity of certain elements, which had been studied since the beginning of the century, had enabled scientists to investigate nuclear reactions. In particular, the pioneering work of Ernest Rutherford (1871-1937) in 1919 had shown that it was possible to transmute atomic nuclei—that is, to change one kind of chemical element into another through nuclear bombardment with alpha particles (the atomic nuclei of helium atoms). It was recognized, however, that the effectiveness of the technique was limited both by the relatively low energy of such projectiles and by the strong repulsion between them and the positive nucleus, which made nuclear penetration more difficult.

The Cockcroft-Walton accelerator employed beams of protons (the nuclei of hydrogen atoms), which, because of their smaller charge compared with that of the alpha particle, reduced the repulsion between the target nuclei and the projectile and thus increased the probability of penetration of the target by the projectile. The high-voltage accelerator operated up to about 600,000 volts. When the beam of protons struck a thin film of metallic lithium, the experimenters observed the simultaneous appearance of a pair of helium nuclei. This event was interpreted as resulting from the absorption of the proton by the lithium nucleus and the immediate fissioning of the unstable target-projectile system into two helium nuclei. The number of such fissions was seen to increase steadily with the accelerator voltage, as predicted by recently made theoretical calculations of George Gamow (1904-1968) and others.

Gamow's work, based on the revolutionary new ideas in the developing field of wave mechanics, had attributed wavelike properties to atomic particles such as protons. As a consequence, a proton of a given velocity would be able to penetrate the target nucleus even though it might seem to be forbidden by the electrical repulsion of the target nucleus. The experiments, suggested initially to Cockcroft and Walton by Gamow himself, produced good agreement with the new theory and therefore served as important corroboration for the theory. Waller also noted that the energy balances of these fission reactions were in good agreement with Albert Einstein's mass-energy relationship, $E = mc^2$.

Finally, Waller observed that the work of Cockcroft and Walton had been instrumental in opening up a new and fruitful field of physics research, one that was of profound importance for understanding the structure of the atomic nucleus.

Nobel lecture

Cockcroft's Nobel lecture began with a review of the work in nuclear physics that he had started in Rutherford's laboratory at the University of Cambridge in the 1920's and concluded with a survey of more recent work in nuclear physics that had been done under his supervision as director of the new Atomic Energy Research Establishment. It was titled "Experiments on the Interaction of High-Speed Nucleons with Atomic Nuclei."

Cockcroft began by citing the experimental work on the emission of alpha particles from radioactive nuclei; he mentioned the unexpected difficulty that had been encountered in interpreting the energies of such particles. The alpha particles from a substance such as uranium, for example, appeared to have a much lower energy, a lower velocity, than would have been expected on the basis of the results of Rutherford's scattering experiments that had shed light on the properties of the nuclear forces that bind together the nucleons (positive protons and neutral neutrons) within the nucleus. The expected energies of the alpha particles emitted spontaneously by elements such as uranium did not appear to be as high as the old classical physics would predict. The new quantum mechanical theory proposed by Gamow and others showed, however, that it was possible for alphas to leak out from the nucleus by tunneling through the "walls" that held its constituents together. In the new theory, which ascribed specifically wavelike qualities to atomic particles, the seemingly low energies of the emitted alphas came to be understood. Conversely, and this is what interested Cockcroft, the new theory implied that it would be somewhat easier for a bombarding positive projectile to overcome the electrical repulsion and be captured by a nucleus than was predicted by the old theory. Perhaps, Gamow suggested, it could tunnel its way in. This idea led Cockcroft to request from the head of the laboratory, Rutherford, permission to begin experiments in which protons would be allowed to strike the relatively light nuclei of the element lithium. Calculations showed that proton energies of less than 300,000 volts should suffice for penetration. Walton would design the proton accelerator.

Cockcroft continued his lecture by outlining the details of his experimental setup, which, by 1932, was able to accelerate protons to 500,000 volts—a unique achievement. The results quickly confirmed the new theory. The absorption of a proton by a lithium nucleus, for example, led to immediate fission of the nucleus into two identical fragments, which were soon identified as alpha particles. Having satisfied himself that the mass-energy balance of these nuclear reactions was in excellent agreement with Einstein's equation, the next step was to use the cloud chamber of

Charles Thomson Rees Wilson (1869-1959) to photograph these events. Wilson's technique would become increasingly important in the future, since it provided a graphic view of happenings at the atomic level and allowed physicists to determine both the natures and the energies of the particles involved in these otherwise invisible nuclear events. Cockcroft then went on to describe the experiments carried out subsequently in the laboratory by other groups of colleagues. Additional experiments were undertaken with targets of boron, heavy hydrogen (the hydrogen isotope deuterium), carbon, nitrogen, and oxygen. Deuterium nuclei (deuterons) were also used as projectiles.

Cockcroft went on to recount his post-World War II experiences as first head of the government's Atomic Energy Research Establishment at Harwell. In the nearly twenty years that had elapsed from the early accelerator experiments to the awarding of the Nobel Prize, Cockcroft's leadership at Harwell had resulted in the building of particle accelerators capable of producing beams of charged particles with many hundreds of times more energy than that of his early prototype. In addition, beams of neutrons (nuclear particles like protons, but without their electric charge), which do not suffer the disadvantage of being electrically repelled by target nuclei, were produced by reactions in which accelerated protons caused neutrons to be knocked forward from the target nuclei. Such neutron beams then became additional powerful tools for the further exploration of the nucleus.

The laboratory work outlined in detail by Cockcroft in his Nobel lecture was of crucial importance to the development of the relatively new field of experimental nuclear physics. That, however, was not all. The revolution in theoretical physics known as wave mechanics was beginning to throw light on events at the atomic level that the traditional, or "classical," physics had utterly failed to explain. Knowledge of the forces between the constituent particles, neutrons and protons, in the nucleus of an atom—what holds these particles together—was absolutely dependent on the experiments that Cockcroft and his colleagues had undertaken in those early years.

Critical reception

In general, the reaction of the press to the Cockcroft-Walton award was approving, though subdued. In view of the fact that the basic research for which the award was made had been completed some thirteen years earlier and that in the intervening time the science of nuclear physics had made tremendous strides—as evidenced by the new realities of nuclear weapons and nuclear power—the award may have been seen as somewhat overdue. *Physics Today* noted that the Swedish Academy's awards for that year in both physics and chemistry were for scientists working with the nuclei of atoms. "Nuclear science dominated the most recent awards in physics and chemistry," the journal announced. With respect to the physics award, it praised the Academy for drawing attention to the actual work of the two scientists rather than to the accelerator that had come to bear their names; it acknowledged also that the realization of the device itself had been crucial to those first machine-induced nuclear reactions.

The Times of London also emphasized the rapid growth in the nuclear physics field following the first nuclear transmutations by machine-accelerated projectiles and characterized the work as a "milestone" in nuclear research. The high degree of international tension at that time was highlighted in a note that the Communist Bloc diplomats had refused to attend the ceremonies in Stockholm because the Nobel Foundation had not given the prize to a Soviet scientist.

The New York Times, whose article announcing the winners was headlined "Nobel Scientists Created History," again acknowledged the retrospective character of the awards. It went on to provide its readers with a detailed summary of the achievements of the winning scientists, including their biographies. The article noted that Cockcroft and Walton had conducted their pioneering work in response to a call from the chief, Lord Rutherford, for a "million volts in a soap box" for smashing atoms—a reference, perhaps, both to the compactness of the accelerator and to the Cavendish Laboratory's somewhat parsimonious tradition of "string and sealing wax." The article emphasized the importance of the first experimental verification of the Einstein mass-energy balance equation.

An article in the magazine *Science* also drew attention to the pioneering nature of the work of the winners in 1951, noting the importance of the evidence for the transformation of nuclear mass into energy. *Scientific American* briefly noted the awards, remarking casually that Cockcroft and Walton had "in 1930 built one of the first high-energy accelerators" and highlighting the fact that by 1950, nuclear accelerators existed in many different forms and were capable of particle energies that were measured in millions, rather than thousands, of volts.

Biography

John Douglas Cockcroft was born into an old Yorkshire family of mill owners and weavers. At his birth, on May 27, 1897, in the village of Todmorden, his family still owned and operated a cotton mill. The eldest of five sons, John was educated in the local elementary and secondary schools. His interest in the physical sciences developed in secondary school, inspired, according to his own account, by both the quality of his science teachers and the contemporary discoveries that were dramatically changing the face of physics in the early twentieth century.

At age seventeen, Cockcroft was awarded a scholarship and admitted to study physics and mathematics at Manchester University. There, he attended physics lectures by Rutherford. Volunteering for military service in 1915 after he had completed barely one year of his university education, Cockcroft became a signaler with the field artillery and survived several severe engagements with the enemy. He was decorated for his service and appointed to the rank of second lieutenant at the end of the war. Cockcroft resumed his studies at Manchester at the relatively mature age of twenty-three, concentrating in the field of electrical engineering and earning the master of science degree in 1922. To further his education in mathematics, which was seen to be increasingly important for the sciences and engineering, Cockcroft enrolled at Cambridge, where, in 1924, he was awarded a bachelor of arts degree in mathematics. At that time, he was invited to join Ernest Rutherford's nuclear physics group at the Cavendish Laboratory, where he would accomplish the bulk of his scientific research. He received his doctorate in 1928, and five years later he was elected to an administrative position in the university which carried duties in addition to those of his teaching and research.

Cockcroft was married to his childhood friend, Eunice Elizabeth Crabtree, in 1925. They reared five children, all girls except the last, who, after obtaining his degree in engineering, returned to the family business in Yorkshire. It is said that their family life was exceptionally happy. Many honors were accorded Cockcroft in addition to the Nobel Prize, including numerous honorary degrees from universities around the world. He was knighted in 1948.

Scientific Career

John Cockcroft's scientific career was influenced to a significant degree by World War I, which had interrupted his university education. At age twenty-seven, he joined Rutherford as a research assistant in the university's renowned Cavendish Laboratory. Thus began Cockcroft's early professional interests in electrical machinery and electronics, interests which soon led him to particle accelerators. Among his first published works were some oriented toward problems in electrical engineering: the electrostatic fields surrounding conductors, the design of coils for the production of magnetic fields, and the confinement of very high-frequency electrical currents to the boundaries of conductors, the so-called skin effect. His early training in electrical engineering, as demonstrated in these early papers, would prove of great value when he and Walton undertook the design of their first accelerator.

During this early period, it is said, Cockcroft's congenial relationships with the university's professorial and technical staffs helped develop in him a lifelong appreciation for the knowledge that others from diverse fields bring to a research project. This collegial attitude apparently stood him in good stead during his professional career, particularly in later years, when he would be called on to play leadership roles in a variety of scientific and educational enterprises.

Two other primarily engineering-oriented projects were undertaken in the early years at the Cavendish. The first of these, launched at Rutherford's suggestion, involved a collaborative effort with the Soviet physicist Pyotr Kapitsa (1894-1984) for the design of coils to produce intense magnetic fields. The second led to the fabrication of an electromagnet for the analysis of alpha-particle energies in Rutherford's laboratory. Again, in this work Cockcroft's engineering and mathematical skills were of primary importance.

The next phase of Cockcroft's work at the Cavendish Laboratory provided him with an introduction to atomic beams and charged-particle accelerators. It was becoming increasingly clear that further work in nuclear physics would be hampered if the only tools of analysis were projectiles, such as alpha particles, from radioactive nuclei. Their velocities are fixed by nature and are beyond experimenters' control. What was needed for the exploration of the atomic nucleus was a controllable source of fast-moving charged particles. Following a suggestion made by George Gamow on the quantum mechanical tunneling phenomenon, Cockcroft calculated the probability of nuclear penetration by protons into boron and aluminum and found that a relatively low accelerating voltage—a few hundred thousand volts—should be sufficient to induce a nuclear reaction. Given a sufficient number of protons in the incident beam, Cockcroft showed, a reasonable number of direct hits would be expected to result in the capture of the proton and subsequent fission of the target nucleus. With these sketchy calculations in hand, he was able to persuade Rutherford to find the resources that would allow the laboratory to build an accelerator.

At this point, Ernest Walton, who had been working on an electron accelerator, joined forces with Cockcroft. Using a modification of a so-called voltage doubling circuit, which employed standard electronic devices known as transformers, capacitors, and vacuum tube rectifiers, they were able to transform a low alternating voltage of 220 volts into a steady, direct-current voltage of 600,000 volts. The idea was to apply this high voltage across the ends of a long tube from which the air had been removed, so that protons introduced at one end of the tube would be rapidly accelerated to the other end, where they would strike the target material. Using what by today's standards would be considered extremely primitive equipment, they were able to achieve a sufficiently high vacuum in their apparatus. (Without a reasonable vacuum, their proton beam would soon have been lost in collisions with air molecules.) Using a thin lithium film as a target, they soon saw the characteristic sparkles, or scintillations, produced on a zinc sulfide screen by alpha particles.

The experimenters were excited by their discovery. Evidently, some of the lithium nuclei had absorbed an incident proton, and the resulting unstable compound nucleus had promptly fissioned into a pair of alpha particles, each carrying slightly less than 50 percent of the proton-lithium mass. The slight mass decrease in the reaction was accounted for exactly by the energy possessed by the two alpha particles, a result that was in excellent agreement with the mass-energy equation. In this way, Einstein's equation received one of its first experimental tests. The two alpha particles, moreover, were observed to be ejected in exactly opposite directions, as required by the law of momentum conservation. On being called in to witness the alpha-particle scintillations, Rutherford is said to have remarked that they were "the most beautiful sight in the world."

As a result of these demonstrations of the possibility of fissioning light nuclei with artificially produced particle beams of fairly modest energy, an entirely new field of physics was opened. Furthermore, great impetus was given to the drive to build particle accelerators of many different designs; in the decades to come, accelerators would be capable of producing ever-greater energies. For this achievement, specifically, Cockcroft and Walton received the Hughes Medal of the Royal Society in 1938 and the Nobel Prize in Physics in 1951.

In 1933, the Cavendish Laboratory was able to acquire from the University of

California at Berkeley a small supply of the rare hydrogen isotope that is known as "heavy hydrogen," or "deuterium." (This form of hydrogen differs from the abundant common form in that it possesses a neutron and a proton in its nucleus, instead of the single proton or ordinary hydrogen. The nucleus of the deuterium atom is about twice as heavy as that of normal hydrogen, though it has the same single positive charge.) Beams of these more energetic deuterium nuclei were soon being accelerated in the Cockcroft-Walton machine, and early results with them led to the identification in the reaction of products of artificially radioactive forms of nitrogen and carbon.

The final phase of Cockcroft's experimental work resulted in the construction of another kind of particle accelerator at Cambridge: the cyclotron, a device for accelerating charged particles in circular rather than straight paths. The cyclotron was inherently capable of achieving far greater energies than the Cockcroft-Walton machine, because the increase in speed of the particles could be achieved by many small kicks as they executed circular orbits rather than by one large one as they moved in a straight line. Its principle had been successfully demonstrated in the United States by Ernest Orlando Lawrence (1901-1958). By the year 1936, Cockcroft had finally overcome Rutherford's reluctance to construct such a device at Cambridge, and on his return from a visit to the United States with a full set of drawings for the 36-inch-diameter Berkeley machine, construction was soon under way. Thus, a new era in nuclear physics began at the Cavendish Laboratory, which would continue to be an important center for nuclear physics research.

Cockcroft's contributions to Great Britain's effort in World War II were primarily administrative. He did critically important work in the development of radar—work that proved to be of enormous importance for his country's ability to destroy enemy aircraft and rockets—and was an effective proponent of American-British scientific collaboration. He was a member of the Tizard Committee, which was formed to discuss the exchange of technical and military information between Great Britain and the United States. In 1944, he headed the atomic energy research laboratory in Montreal, Canada, where, for security reasons, the British nuclear research center had been located. Throughout the war, he was an influential science policymaker and spokesman, and he subsequently did much to promote the peaceful uses of atomic energy. In 1946, he was appointed the first director of Great Britain's Atomic Energy Research Establishment at Harwell, where he was influential in developing a program for the design of high-energy particle accelerators which culminated in the 7 GEV proton synchrotron. In 1959 he was made head of Cambridge's new Churchill College.

Bibliography

Primary

PHYSICS: "An Electric Harmonic Analyser," *Journal of the Institution of Electrical Engineers*, vol. 63, 1925 (with R. T. Coe, J. A. Lyacke, and Miles Walker); "The Effect of Curved Boundaries on the Distribution of Electrical Stress Round Conductors," *Journal of the Institution of Electrical Engineers*, vol. 66, 1928; "On Phenomena Occurring in the Condensation of Molecular Streams on Surfaces," *Proceedings of the Royal Society A*, vol. 119, 1928; "The Design of Coils for the Production of Strong Magnetic Fields," *Philosophical Transactions of the Royal Society A*, vol. 227, 1928; "Skin Effect in Rectangular Conductors at High Frequencies," *Proceedings of the Royal Society A*, vol. 122, 1929; "Experiments with High Velocity Positive Ions," *Proceedings of the Royal Society A*, vol. 129, 1930 (with E. T. S. Walton); "A Permanent Magnet for β-Ray Spectroscopy," *Proceedings of the Royal Society A*, vol. 135, 1932 (with C. D. Ellis and H. Kershaw); "Experiments with High Velocity Positive Ions: Further Developments in the Method of Obtaining High Velocity Positive Ions," *Proceedings of the Royal Society A*, vol. 136, 1932 (with Walton): "Experiments with High Velocity Positive Ions: The Disintegration of Elements by High Velocity Positive Ions," *Proceedings of the Royal Society A*, vol. 137, 1932 (with Walton); "A Magnet for α-Ray Spectroscopy," *Journal of Scientific Instruments*, vol. 10, 1933; "Disintegration of Light Elements by Fast Neutrons," *Nature*, vol. 131, 1933 (with Walton); "Experiments with High Velocity Positive Ions: The Disintegration of Lithium, Boron, and Carbon by Heavy Hydrogen Ions," *Proceedings of the Royal Society A*, vol. 144, 1934 (with Walton); "Experiments with High Velocity Positive Ions: The Production of Induced Radioactivity by High Velocity Protons and Diplons," *Proceedings of the Royal Society A*, vol. 148, 1935 (with C. W. Gilbert and Walton); "Experiments with High Velocity Positive Ions: Further Experiments on the Disintegration of Boron," *Proceedings of the Royal Society A*, vol. 154, 1936 (with W. B. Lewis); "High Velocity Positive Ions: Their Application to the Transmutation of Atomic Nuclei and the Production of Artificial Radioactivity," *British Journal of Radiology*, vol. 10, 1937; "The Cyclotron and Betatron," *Journal of Scientific Instruments*, vol. 21, 1944; "Rutherford: Life and Work After the Year 1919, with Personal Reminiscences of the Second Cambridge Period," *Proceedings of the Physical Society*, vol. 58, 1946; "The Development of Linear Accelerators and Synchrotrons for Radiotherapy, and for Research in Physics," *Journal of the Institution of Electrical Engineers*, vol. 96, 1949; "Modern Concepts of the Structure of Matter," *Journal of the Institution of Electrical Engineers*, vol. 98, 1951; "Experiments on the Interaction of High Speed Nucleons with Atomic Nuclei," *Les Prix Nobel*, 1951; "The Scientific Work of the Atomic Energy Research Establishment," *Proceedings of the Royal Society A*, vol. 211, 1952; "High Energy Particle Accelerators," *Endeavour*, vol. 24, 1955 (with T. G. Pickavance); "Royal Society Discussion on Controlled Thermonuclear Reactions," *Nature*, vol. 181, 1958.

Secondary

Hartcup, Guy, and T. E. Allibone. *Cockcroft and the Atom*. Bristol, England: Adam Hilger, 1984. This work is the definitive biography of Cockcroft. In it, the authors trace Cockcroft's life in detail. Hartcup is a historian with special interests and insights into science and technology, and Allibone was associated with the scientist from their student days together at the Cavendish. Their collaborative work is rich in anecdotal and documentary evidence coupled with personal reminiscence, and it leaves the reader with great admiration for this eminent and humane scientist. Detailed source references and bibliography.

Oliphant, M. L. E., and W. G. Penny. "John Douglas Cockcroft." *Biographical Memoirs of Fellows of the Royal Society*, 14 (1968): 139-188. London: The Royal Society, 1968. Part of a lengthy series on prominent British scientists who have been elected fellows of the Royal Society, this entry was written by two individuals who were close to Cockcroft throughout his professional life. The article is divided into six major sections, covering periods from the scientist's early life, education, and scientific work through his later work on radar and atomic energy. The work includes a bibliography.

Snow, C. P. *The Physicists*. Boston: Little, Brown, 1981. This fascinating work by a prominent scientist-humanist was completed within months of his death in 1980. Snow is perhaps best known for his concern for the world's poor, coupled with the hope that science, with its enormous potential for both good and evil, will ultimately improve their condition. His last book, beautifully produced and illustrated, traces the growth of modern physics through the lives of its chief architects, starting with Michael Faraday and James Clerk Maxwell in the nineteenth century and concluding with the "younger masters," particle physicists and theoreticians, such as Richard Feynman. This book is accessible to the lay reader and provides an account of the development of knowledge of the atom on both the American and European continents.

Weart, Spencer R. *Scientists in Power*. Cambridge, Mass.: Harvard University Press, 1979. This book, written by the director of the Center for the History of Physics, American Institute of Physics, discusses the growth of physics in the twentieth century. Although the author is primarily interested in the story of the search for nuclear fission, he does so against the background of the political and social events of the period. Thus, wartime research in nuclear physics, in which Cockcroft played a major role, is described within a broader context that sheds light on the interaction of scientists with government, industry, and the military. Extended bibliography and end notes.

Wright, Stephen J., ed. *Classical Scientific Papers: Physics*. New York: Elsevier, 1965. This work is an important review which contains facsimile reproductions of twenty or so seminal works on twentieth century atomic physics. The papers begin with the early studies of radioactivity, proceed through the crucial experiments that led Rutherford to his nuclear atom model, and end with some special "tools of the trade" works, including Wilson's on the cloud chamber. The second Cockcroft-Walton paper listed above is included. This book is of great value to those who enjoy seeing the originals of works that have shaped science and society in this century.

David G. Fenton

1951

Physics
Sir John Douglas Cockcroft, Great Britain
Ernest Thomas Sinton Walton, Ireland

Chemistry
Edwin McMillan, United States
Glenn Seaborg, United States

Physiology or Medicine
Max Theiler, South Africa

Literature
Pär Lagerkvist, Sweden

Peace
Léon Jouhaux, France

ERNEST THOMAS SINTON WALTON
1951

Born: Dungarvan, County Waterford, Ireland; October 6, 1903

Nationality: Irish
Area of concentration: Nuclear physics

Walton, together with his colleague John Cockcroft, initiated a new era in nuclear physics with his invention of a high-voltage accelerator to produce a beam of protons, which were found to be very effective in producing a great variety of new nuclear reactions

The Award

Presentation

The Nobel Prize in Physics was presented jointly to Sir John Cockcroft and Ernest Thomas Sinton Walton by Professor Ivar Waller, a member of the Nobel Committee for Physics, at the Nobel ceremonies in December, 1951. The medal was presented by the King of Sweden on behalf of the Royal Swedish Academy of Sciences. Waller recognized Cockcroft and Walton for their construction in 1932 of a high-voltage accelerator which produced particles with a high enough energy to produce nuclear reactions. The first man-made nuclear reaction had been created in 1919 by Ernest Rutherford (1871-1937), who used natural radioactivity to accomplish a transmutation of nitrogen nuclei into oxygen. Only a few elements other than nitrogen could be made to undergo a transmutation with natural radioactivity, mainly because the beam intensity was too low. As Waller explained, "A more powerful stream of projectiles was needed."

By using a high-voltage transformer and rectifier system, Cockcroft and Walton had succeeded in building the first man-made accelerator for protons (hydrogen nuclei). In one experiment, they bombarded a target of the element lithium and showed that its nucleus was split into two helium particles. It was the first transmutation of an atomic nucleus by artificially accelerated particles. They also measured the energy of the two helium particles and demonstrated that there had been a mass-to-energy conversion, which verified Albert Einstein's theoretical equation $E = mc^2$. Subsequent work with other particle beams and targets opened up the possibility of creating many new radioactive isotopes, which would have practical applications in industry and medicine.

Nobel lecture

Walton's Nobel lecture, entitled "The Artificial Production of Fast Particles," was delivered on December 11, 1951. He gave an overview of the various nuclear particle accelerators that had been developed by physicists over a span of twenty-five years, including his own contribution to accelerator technology. Walton's colleague and cowinner, John Douglas Cockcroft, gave a companion lecture devoted to the experiments that they had conducted once their accelerator was running successfully.

Walton described six types of accelerator. The betatron uses a magnetic field that causes electrons to move in a circular orbit. The acceleration is produced by increasing the magnetic field strength with time while maintaining an electron orbit of constant radius. Walton made an important contribution in 1929 by showing how the magnetic field must vary. The modern betatron was developed in the 1940's and can produce electrons with several hundred million electron volts of energy.

The linear accelerator uses a series of hollow cylinders in a row with a voltage applied in the gaps between successive cylinders. No magnetic field is used. Very high final energies can be attained by making the accelerator tube very long.

The cyclotron uses a constant magnetic field to bend the path of charged particles into a circular orbit in which they cross the same accelerating gap over and over again. They spiral outward to a larger radius as they gain energy. Ernest Orlando Lawrence received the Nobel Prize in 1939 for his invention. The frequency-modulated, or FM, cyclotron was developed in the 1940's; it extended the operating range up to 350 million volts.

The Van de Graaff accelerator is an electrostatic machine having a single stage with several million volts. An electrical charge is sprayed onto a moving belt which carries the charge to a large, insulated, spherical electrode.

The synchrotron was developed in the late 1940's and is the basis for today's highest-energy accelerators. The particles follow a circular path with a radius of a kilometer or more. Walton predicted in his 1951 lecture that energies as high as 10,000 million electron volts were possible with the synchrotron. That estimate has been exceeded by a factor of one hundred.

The Cockcroft-Walton accelerator had a modest voltage output as compared with later developments, but it was a pioneer in its field. Starting in 1928, the Nobel laureates designed and built a first model that attained a maximum of 280 kilovolts, using a transformer and vacuum tube rectifier system. The technology of obtaining high voltages in this way had been developed earlier for X-ray apparatus. To increase the voltage further, an ingenious voltage doubler circuit was developed. In 1931, with the advantage of a better vacuum system, the authors were able to attain a maximum potential of 700 kilovolts. They demonstrated the disintegration of lithium nuclei with this device. A new era of using particle accelerators for nuclear physics had been launched.

Critical reception

Cockcroft and Walton were awarded the Nobel Prize in 1951 for the experimental work that they had done between 1927 and 1932, first building an accelerator and then using it to produce a new type of nuclear reaction. Several Nobel awards in physics have been given for work of the same general type: A new kind of accelerator was built and then used to initiate a fresh area of research. For example, Ernest Lawrence received the 1939 prize for his invention of the cyclotron and his application of it to the production of new radioactive isotopes. In 1959, Owen Chamberlain and Emilio Gino Segrè won the award for building the 6-billion-volt proton accelerator in Berkeley, California, which had just enough energy to produce a new type of particle, the antiproton. In 1961, Robert Hofstadter from Stanford University won the award for his experiments on nuclear structure using the electron beam from a new, more powerful linear accelerator that had been constructed especially for this purpose.

Cockcroft and Walton were held in high regard by scientists familiar with their experiments. Ernest Rutherford, who in the 1920's and 1930's had been head of the Cavendish Laboratory at the University of Cambridge, was quoted in the *Manchester Guardian* (November 16, 1951) as having said that two of his laboratory workers "had successfully disintegrated the nuclei of lithium and other light elements by protons entirely artificially generated by high electric potentials." The physicist Sir William Henry Bragg (1862-1942), one of the Nobel laureates for 1915, had said that "the experiments . . . opened up a new line of work of outstanding importance." A report titled *Atomic Energy for Military Purposes* noted the contribution made by this research: "The experimental results prove that the equivalence of mass and energy was correctly stated by Einstein." *The New York Times* announced the winners of the Nobel awards on November 16, 1951, stating that these men "stand out in the annals of science among the top architects of the atomic age."

Walton received the news of his award, "with the greatest surprise." He went on to say, "The atom bomb certainly could have been developed without the work we did, but our experiments did open up a new field." The atom bomb got its energy from the fission of uranium nuclei by means of neutrons; no high-voltage accelerators were involved. The only connection with Walton's 1932 experiments was that nuclear energy was released in both cases; the nuclear reactions and apparatus were entirely different. The work by Cockcroft and Walton stood on its own merits as a pioneering experiment which, according to Emilio Segrè, had had "an enormously stimulating effect on research in nuclear reactions."

Biography

Ernest Thomas Sinton Walton was born in Dungarvan, County Waterford, Ireland, on October 6, 1903. His father, the Reverend John A. Walton, was a Protestant pastor who later became president of the Methodist Church of Ireland. Ernest Walton showed an early interest in mathematics and physics at the Methodist College in Belford, Northern Ireland. After his graduation in 1922, he attended Trinity College in Dublin, where he received a master of arts degree in 1926 and a master of science degree later. For recreation, he enjoyed cross-country running and tennis. His first scientific paper was published in 1928 in the *Proceedings of the Royal Dublin Society*.

Walton received a scholarship to the Cavendish Laboratory of Cambridge to work as a research assistant in nuclear physics under Ernest Rutherford, the 1908 Nobel Prize winner in chemistry. He worked together with John D. Cockcroft to build a proton accelerator, which was successfully used for a series of nuclear reaction experiments between 1929 and 1934. Walton returned to Ireland in 1934, where he was married to Winifred Wilson, a kindergarten teacher and the daughter of a Methodist minister. Walton was a member of the physics department at the University of Dublin for forty years and served as the department chairman from 1947 until his retirement in 1974. He received a number of honors, including the Hughes Medal of the Royal Society, together with Cockcroft, in 1938 and honorary doctor of science degrees from Queen's University in Belfast in 1959 and Gustavus Adolphus College in Minnesota in 1975.

Scientific Career

Ernest Walton showed an early interest in a scientific career as a student at Trinity College in Dublin, which he attended from 1922 to 1927. He was an officer in the student societies for mathematics and experimental science. He won several student prizes at Trinity and held a scholarship that included the right to sit on the governing board of the college. After he received his master of arts degree, he was awarded the FitzGerald Memorial Scholarship, which enabled him to stay at Trinity one more year to earn an M.Sc. degree. His first scientific publication appeared in the January, 1928, issue of the *Proceedings of the Royal Dublin Society*; it was titled "Formation of Vortices Behind a Cylinder Moving Through a Liquid."

Because of his good record in physics at Trinity College, Walton received an Overseas Scholarship to work under Ernest Rutherford at the Cavendish Laboratory of Cambridge. Rutherford was the most famous British nuclear physicist of the time, having won the Nobel Prize in Chemistry in 1908 for his early work on radioactive transformations. He had earned an international reputation for the alpha-particle scattering experiment that established the nuclear atom model in 1911 and for the first man-made nuclear transmutation that converted nitrogen nuclei into oxygen using natural radioactivity. Walton was fortunate to be able to join a team of nuclear physicists at Cambridge who were working at the forefront of experimental research in this field.

The immediate goal of Rutherford's research group was to build an accelerator that could replace natural radioactivity as a source of bombarding particles for nuclear reactions. Rutherford called for "a million volts in a shoe box" to provide high energy and a greater intensity of "bullets" than radioactivity could supply. Walton's first project was to investigate how a magnetic field could be used to accelerate electrons in a circular orbit. Walton worked out the theoretical conditions for the way in which the magnetic field must vary in order to create a stable orbit for the electrons. The experimental apparatus was described in a 1929 publication in the *Cambridge Philosophical Society Proceedings*, titled "Production of High Speed Electrons by Indirect Means." Although the apparatus did not yield electrons with enough energy to produce X rays for nuclear reactions, it was recognized as the forerunner of the betatron accelerator that was successfully developed by Donald William Kerst in the 1940's. Walton also built an early experimental model of a linear accelerator, using cylindrical drift tubes arranged in a straight line.

In 1929 Walton began working with John Cockcroft to develop a proton accelerator that would use a transformer and rectifier system to reach a high voltage, similar to an X-ray tube. They developed an ingenious voltage doubler circuit which worked as follows: First, two capacitors were charged in parallel to the highest voltage of the transformer; then, the capacitors were disconnected and reconnected in series by a switching mechanism. The final voltage was the sum of the charges of the two capacitors. In 1930 the experimenters reached 280 kilovolts, and two years later they reached 800 kilovolts using a voltage quadrupler.

To produce a nuclear transmutation, a bombarding particle must have enough energy to enter the atomic nucleus. Both the nucleus and the bombarding particle, however, have a positive electrical charge, which causes them to repel each other. The repulsion becomes very strong at small distances, creating an electrical barrier which prevents the bombarding particle from penetrating the nucleus. A new theory was developed in the late 1920's by George Gamow and others; it suggested that atomic particles have some wavelike characteristics which might allow them to "tunnel through" the barrier instead of having to go "over the top." Gamow came to the Cavendish Laboratory in 1929 at Rutherford's invitation. He worked out the consequences of the tunneling concept and showed that nuclear reactions should be possible with bombarding particles with energies of less than a million volts, even though the barrier height was several million volts. This theoretical result provided strong encouragement for the experimenters, who now had reason to believe that an accelerator operating below a million volts could still be very effective.

The first element in the periodic table is hydrogen, the second is helium, and the third is lithium. The hydrogen nucleus cannot be subdivided, because it is a single proton. The helium nucleus is not a good candidate for being split either, because it has a very large binding energy. The third element, lithium, contains seven particles in its nucleus, three protons and four neutrons. Cockcroft and Walton chose lithium as their first target element for nuclear bombardment. Using 400-kilovolt protons, they were able to show that the lithium nucleus could be split into two helium nuclei. At higher voltages, up to 700 kilovolts, the reaction yield was increased greatly. It was the first time that an atomic nucleus had been split by artificial means.

Cockcroft and Walton were able to determine the energy of the two helium nuclei by measuring their penetrating power through very thin metal sheets. They showed that the helium nuclei had a combined energy of about 15 million electron volts, whereas the proton energy to initiate the reaction was less than 1 million electron volts. This large release of nuclear energy could perhaps be explained by Einstein's mass-energy equation, $E = mc^2$. The masses of the proton, lithium nucleus, and helium nuclei were already known from earlier measurements with a mass spectrometer; therefore, the experimenters were able to calculate a theoretical value for the conversion of mass to energy in this reaction. The measured experimental value was very close to the theoretically calculated value. This experiment, then, provided a convincing first demonstration that the Einstein equation was a quantitatively correct description of nature at the nuclear level.

Cockcroft and Walton developed an additional experimental test to verify that lithium was really being split into two helium nuclei. They set up two small zinc sulfide screens, which produce tiny light flashes, called "scintillations," when they are struck by helium nuclei. The nuclei would always be produced in pairs, so it was expected that the scintillations on the two screens would occur in coincidence, or simultaneously. The coincidence recording system made use of two separate observers, each one watching one of the scintillation screens through a microscope. Whenever they saw a light flash, they pushed a recording key. A high percentage of the recorded events showed simultaneous light flashes, giving Cockcroft and Walton strong experimental evidence to support the hypothesis that helium nuclei are emitted in pairs. This experiment was the crude beginning of a coincidence system for observing whether two particles are emitted simultaneously, a technique which was exploited much more fully later, with the development of modern electronics.

Cockcroft and Walton studied the disintegration of elements other than lithium using the same general method of proton bombardment. They were able to observe successful nuclear reactions with several other light elements: beryllium, boron, carbon, fluorine, and aluminum. For higher atomic numbers, the reaction yield became very small; in some cases, this effect may have been caused by impurities in the target material.

The year 1932 has been called the *annus mirabilis* for nuclear physics because of the remarkable coincidence of five new discoveries which occurred in close succession. Carl David Anderson discovered the positron (the positive electron), James Chadwick discovered the neutron, Cockcroft and Walton split the nucleus by artificial means, Ernest Lawrence built a successful cyclotron, and Robert Van de Graaff developed his high-voltage device.

A new development in chemistry at this time was the discovery of heavy water and the heavy isotope of hydrogen, deuterium. (Deuterium contains a proton and an extra neutron in its nucleus.) Cockcroft and Walton were able to obtain a sample of deuterium and to accelerate these particles in their apparatus, just as they could protons. By bombarding various targets with deuterium nuclei, they created a whole new class of nuclear reactions. They showed that deuterium bombardment is an effective method for producing neutrons, a discovery important to Enrico Fermi and to others who were studying what happens when uranium is bombarded by neutrons. A neutron generator that used the Cockcroft-Walton accelerator was an important experimental tool for the investigation of the uranium fission reaction, the basis of the atom bomb.

The Cockcroft-Walton method of accelerating protons would continue to be widely used. It forms the first stage in a sequence of devices that attains final energies of nearly one trillion electron volts. For example, the Fermi National Accelerator Laboratory, near Chicago, has a huge synchrotron accelerator, one of the largest in the world. The protons start as hydrogen ions in a Cockcroft-Walton device, which is followed by a linear accelerator, a small synchrotron ring, and finally a large magnet ring with a circumference of more than 6 kilometers.

Walton published a great many scientific papers during the seven years that he spent at Cambridge. In 1934 he returned to Dublin, Ireland, to join the physics department at Trinity College, where he had been a student. In 1938, he and Cockcroft were honored with the Hughes Medal of the Royal Society. In 1946 he was appointed the Erasmus Smith Professor of Natural and Experimental Philosophy, an endowed chair at Trinity College. He received the Nobel Prize in 1951 and became Fellow Emeritus of Trinity College on his retirement, in 1974. He later became an honorary life member of the Royal Dublin Society and an Honorary Fellow of the Institute of Engineers of Ireland.

Bibliography

Primary

PHYSICS: Most of Walton's publications had John Douglas Cockcroft and other scientists at the Cavendish Laboratory as coauthors. His major papers are "Production of High Speed Electrons by Indirect Means," *Cambridge Philosophical Society Proceedings*, October, 1929; "Experiments with High Velocity Positive Ions," *Proceedings of the Royal Society A*, vol. 129, 1930 (with John Cockcroft); "Experiments with High Velocity Positive Ions: The Disintegration of Elements by High Velocity Protons," *Proceedings of the Royal Society A*, vol. 137, 1932 (with Cockcroft); "Transmutation of Lithium and Boron," *Proceedings of the Royal Society A*, vol. 141, 1933 (with P. I. Dee); "Disintegration of Light Elements by Fast Neutrons," *Nature*, vol. 131, 1933 (with Cockcroft); "Experiments with High Velocity Positive Ions: The Disintegration of Lithium, Boron, and Carbon by Heavy Hydrogen Ions," *Proceedings of the Royal Society A*, vol. 144, 1934 (with Cockcroft); "Production of Induced Radioactivity by High Velocity Protons," *Nature*, vol. 133, 1934; "Experiments with High Velocity Positive Ions: The Production of Induced Radioactivity by High Velocity Protons and Diplons," *Proceedings of the Royal Society A*, vol. 148, 1935 (with Cockcroft and C. W. Gilbert); "Micro-electromagnetic Waves," *Wireless Engineer*, February, 1946; "High-Order Focusing by a Uniform Magnetic Field with Straight Line Boundaries," *Proceedings of the Royal Irish Academy*, vol. 57A, 1954; "Recollections of Physics at Trinity College, University of Dublin, in the 1920's," in Raikumar Williamson, ed., *The Making of Physicists*, 1987.

Secondary

Beyer, Robert T., ed. *Foundations of Nuclear Physics*. New York: Dover, 1949. A facsimile reprinting of thirteen original articles is presented, including some of the most important publications by physicists such as Rutherford, Fermi, and Chadwick. The reprint article by Cockcroft and Walton is the one titled "Disintegration of Elements by High Velocity Protons," originally published in the

Proceedings of the Royal Society of London, vol. 137, 1932.

Nobelstiftelsen. *Physics*. 3 vols. New York: Elsevier, 1964-1967. The Elsevier series of Nobel lectures is a reprinting of the complete address given by each laureate. It also provides brief biographies of the winners. Photographs and diagrams are included.

Pollard, Ernest C., and William L. Davidson. *Applied Nuclear Physics*. 2d ed. New York: John Wiley & Sons, 1951. Pollard was a contemporary of Cockcroft and Walton in England in the 1930's and later came to Yale University. This source is an elementary nuclear physics textbook; it describes apparatus and experiments using high-velocity protons. Written by a physicist who was a participant in the study of nuclear reactions.

Richtmyer, Floyd K., E. H. Kennard, and T. Lauritsen. *Introduction to Modern Physics*. 5th ed. New York: McGraw-Hill, 1955. This book was widely used as a text, going through five editions between 1928 and 1955. The work of Cockcroft and Walton is recognized in the sections that deal with particle accelerators and nuclear transformations.

Robinson, Timothy C. L., ed. *The Future of Science*. New York: John Wiley & Sons, 1977. Gustavus Adolphus College in St. Peter, Minnesota, has held an annual Nobel Conference since 1965, and this source covers the conference of 1975. The meeting brings together scientists and theologians to discuss leading topics in science. Although Walton was not one of the four main speakers at this conference, he received an honorary degree and participated in the discussion following the presentations. Twenty-seven Nobel laureates and six theologians spoke to an audience of about four thousand persons. The four main talks are reprinted here, along with selections from the subsequent discussions.

Segrè, Emilio, ed. *Experimental Nuclear Physics*. 2 vols. New York: John Wiley & Sons, 1953. These reference books contain a series of articles written by various authors who have personally contributed to nuclear physics. The presentation is aimed at physics students and experimenters. The contributions by Cockcroft and Walton are described and recognized for their importance.

Hans G. Graetzer

1952

Physics
Felix Bloch, United States
Edward Mills Purcell, United States

Chemistry
Archer Martin, Great Britain
Richard Synge, Great Britain

Physiology or Medicine
Selman A. Waksman, United States

Literature
François Mauriac, France

Peace
Albert Schweitzer, France

FELIX BLOCH
1952

Born: Zurich, Switzerland; October 23, 1905
Died: Zurich, Switzerland; September 10, 1983
Nationality: Swiss; after 1939, American
Area of concentration: Nuclear physics

Bloch's development of the induction method of nuclear magnetic resonance led to a more accurate description of nuclear magnetic moments and the ability to analyze the magnetic properties of a greater variety of substances

The Award

Presentation

Professor E. Hulthén, member of the Nobel Committee for Physics, presented the Nobel Prize in Physics to Edward Mills Purcell and Felix Bloch on December 10, 1952, on behalf of the Royal Swedish Academy of Sciences and King Gustav VI, from whom Purcell and Bloch accepted the prizes. Hulthén's presentation began with a discussion of the best-known magnetic instrument, the compass. The first uses of the compass are not clearly documented; however, the Chinese were apparently using such instruments as long ago as 2600 B.C. Hulthén went on to discuss how William Gilbert (1544-1603) had published the first scientific study of magnetism, *De Magnete* (1600). Thereafter, magnets were classified into three categories: ferromagnets, paramagnets, and diamagnets. In the 1930's a fourth category was found: the intrinsic magnetism of the atomic nucleus.

Hulthén proceeded to discuss a history of the measurement of magnetic moments of objects. Carl Friedrich Gauss (1777-1855) had measured magnetic moments of compass needles by measuring the oscillations of the needle when it was placed in a known magnetic field. On the atomic level, however, the magnetic moments are more like gyroscopes than compass needles in the way that they spin and precess. The method for determining nuclear magnetic moments through resonance with electromagnetic waves was found by Isidor Isaac Rabi (1898-1988), who won the 1944 Nobel Prize for it. Rabi's method required the substance to be in the form of a ray of molecules. Bloch's and Purcell's method could be used on materials in solid, liquid, or gaseous form. Since every type of atom has a particular nuclear frequency, any object could be placed between the poles of an electromagnet and analyzed to find all the various types of atom in the object. This procedure had no detectable effect on the object.

Nobel lecture

Bloch's Nobel lecture, delivered on December 11, 1952, and entitled "The Principle of Nuclear Induction," began with a historical sketch of the developments that had led to his work. He discussed the Zeeman effect, which demonstrated that magnetic fields were a part of spectroscopy, and the discovery of Wolfgang Pauli (1900-1958) that the hyperfine structure of spectral lines is a result of the nuclear magnetic moments of atoms. He then discussed the disadvantages of optical spectroscopy techniques for measuring magnetic moments and how Otto Stern (1888-1969) had determined magnetic moments by observing the deflections of particles in an inhomogeneous magnetic field. The next significant advancement was the magnetic resonance method, in which a beam of particles is passed through a homogeneous, constant magnetic field that is superimposed on a weak, oscillating field. At certain resonant frequencies in the radio range, absorption of the oscillating signal by the nuclei occurs. This method was much more accurate than previous methods and allowed for determination of the magnetic moments of the proton and deuteron.

Bloch went on to discuss his fascination with the possibility of an intrinsic magnetic moment of the neutron. Up to that point, the only explanations for magnetic moments were based on the intrinsic electrical charge of the particles, but if a neutron, which is electrically neutral, were to have a magnetic moment, its origin would have to be something other than charge. Bloch and Luis W. Alvarez first made such a measurement in 1939 at the University of California at Berkeley, but the accuracy was limited. Bloch, knowing that the magnetic resonance was based on the reorientation of nuclear moments, then realized that he could detect these reorientations using standard radio reception, in which the signal would be caused by electromagnetic induction and detected as a change in voltage (hence the name "induction method"). In his lecture, Bloch discussed induction and relaxation time, which is the time needed for the nuclear moments to reorient themselves.

Bloch ended his speech with a description of the approaches and equipment that had been applied to nuclear magnetic resonance. His particular arrangement was unique in that it allowed for the measurement of the sign of the nuclear moment, which until then had been unknown for many atomic nuclei.

The layperson of the time probably had little, if any, appreciation for the significance of Bloch's work. It was pure science, based on the results of previous scientific investigations. It would lead, however, to applications of the new technology in such fields as organic chemistry and diagnostic medicine.

Critical reception

The American press was quite receptive to the 1952 Nobel laureates, most likely because they were both American citizens. *The New York Times* ran several articles about the award. The first one (November 7, 1952) announced the prizewinners and discussed how Bloch and Purcell had independently invented the same general methods. It also gave a short biography of Bloch. The next article (December 11) provided a description of the awards ceremony itself. It noted that three of the prizewinners were American and that all six of the prizewinners had traveled to Stockholm to receive the award in person—a rare occurrence. The next article

(December 22) gave an account of Bloch's return to the United States. In this piece, Bloch discussed the world situation as it related to atomic physics. He believed that the United States had supremacy in atomic research but that the European nations were friendly despite that. He also favored as few restrictions as possible on publication results, to allow the exchange of information, and hoped that atomic energy would be used for peaceful purposes.

Magazines, especially those that were science-oriented, also made note of the award. In the science section of *Newsweek* (November 17), a short article described Bloch being awakened early on the morning of November 6 by a telephone call informing him that he was the winner. The article then gave a very short description of Bloch's work. *Science News Letter* (November 15) also printed a brief article announcing the award. *Nature* (November 29) printed a more thorough article that announced the award and then gave short biographies of Purcell and Bloch. The media seemed to focus its attention more on Bloch than on Purcell, even though they shared the prize equally. It is difficult to determine why; perhaps Bloch was more receptive to the media, or perhaps the media simply found him more interesting, given that he had been one of the scientists to emigrate from Europe. It is certain, however, that Bloch was the more renowned; only two years after his receipt of the Nobel Prize, he was unanimously appointed by representatives of twelve nations as the director of the Centre Européen de Recherche Nucléaire (CERN).

The British reaction to the physics winners was less enthusiastic than that of the American media. *The Times* of London ran a short article on the winners (November 7) that concentrated on the two British winners of the chemistry prize. Little was said in the American press about these chemistry winners. *The Times* also printed a short article on the presentation (December 11).

Biography

Felix Bloch was born in Zurich, Switzerland, on October 23, 1905, the son of Gustav Bloch and Agnes Mayer Bloch. His father was a wholesale grain dealer. When he was a boy, Felix showed an interest in math and astronomy. Seeing this, his father enrolled him in an engineering course at the Federal Institute of Technology. The first physics course that Bloch took convinced him to become a physicist. His first studies in physics were under Erwin Schrödinger (1887-1961), who introduced him to the then-new field of quantum mechanics. He received his training in theoretical physics there from 1924 to 1927.

In 1928, Bloch received his doctorate in physics from the University of Leipzig, Germany, under Werner Heisenberg (1901-1976), who was doing research there at the time. Bloch's dissertation introduced a theory of solids that provided a basic understanding of electrical conduction in solids. After receiving his degree, he returned home. He worked as a research assistant from 1928 to 1929. Then, in 1930, he went to the Netherlands on a Lorentz Fund Fellowship. In 1931 an Ørsted Fund Fellowship enabled Bloch to work with Niels Bohr (1885-1962) at the University of Copenhagen. In 1932 he returned to the University of Leipzig as a lecturer in theoretical physics.

In 1933, Bloch was awarded the Rockefeller Fellowship, which allowed him to travel to Rome and work with Enrico Fermi (1901-1954). This opportunity was welcome, for Adolf Hitler was coming into power in Germany and Bloch found Hitler's regime distasteful. In 1934, Bloch was admitted to the United States as a displaced scholar and offered a position at Stanford University as an associate professor. In 1936 he was promoted to the rank of full professor.

In March of 1940, Bloch wed a German-born physicist named Lore C. Misch. They had met while she was working as a research associate at the Massachusetts Institute of Technology. They would have three sons, George, Daniel, and Frank, and a daughter, Ruth.

From 1942 to 1944, Bloch worked with the team of physicists that was trying to develop an atom bomb, in Los Alamos, New Mexico. He then spent a year at Harvard University, working on radar. In 1945, he returned to Stanford. He became a member of the National Academy of Sciences in 1948, and in the mid-1950's, he served as the first director general of CERN. In 1971, he became a professor emeritus at Stanford. He died in Zurich on September 10, 1983.

Scientific Career

Felix Bloch—like many other physicists, such as Albert Einstein and Enrico Fermi—was very productive early in his career. He published papers and formulated several theories (that now bear his name) after he earned his doctorate and before he left Europe. In 1928 he discovered what is now known as the Bloch-Floquet theorem, which specifies what form the wave functions should take for electrons in a crystal. A wave function is a mathematical function that is used to predict the probability of a system's being in a particular state. This theorem is also named after Floquet because the physics problem that Bloch solved turned out to be identical to an abstract math problem solved years earlier by Floquet. Also in 1928, the Bloch-Grunseisen relationship was discovered. This relationship described the temperature dependence of the electrical conductivity of metals. Eduard Grunseisen did the experimental work that Bloch subsequently explained theoretically. Another theory that is named after Bloch is the Bloch T $^{3/2}$ law, which describes the dependence on temperature of magnetism in a ferromagnetic material. To explain the decrease in magnetism in a ferromagnet as temperature rises, Bloch postulated what is known as a "spin wave." A spin wave is a variation of the angular momentum caused by the spin of the electrons in a crystal lattice.

In 1932, Sir James Chadwick (1891-1974) discovered the neutron, a subnuclear particle that has no electrical charge. Bloch had a special interest in this particle. He became intrigued by the notion that even though it had no charge, it had a magnetic moment. Paul Dirac's explanation of the electron's magnetic moment was based on the electron's charge, and it was obvious that this theory would not suitably explain the magnetism of the neutron. Bloch set out to find a better explanation.

When Hitler came to power in 1933, Bloch, who was Jewish, found the new order uncomfortable and left Leipzig for Paris, where he was a lecturer at the Institut Henri Poincaré. Soon afterward, a Rockefeller Fellowship from the International Education Board allowed him to go to Rome to work with Fermi. From Rome, Bloch was admitted to the United States as a displaced scholar, much like many other European scientists of the time. It is generally believed that the European influx did not take place until the late 1930's, when scientists such as Bohr and Fermi came to America; however, there were many notables who preceded them and who helped to set the stage for successful interaction between European and American physicists. Bloch—along with others, such as Hans Bethe, Edward Teller, Victor Weisskopf, George Gamow, and Eugene Wigner—was one of these early arrivals who emigrated between 1930 and 1937. He was quite happy to come to the United States, as its academic system had advantages over the European system. One could become a professor more quickly and could more easily get graduate students and money for research. These advantages were what directed many of the European refugee physicists to the United States rather than other countries.

It was this influx of the most talented scholars from Europe that helped to bring the United States to the forefront of physics research. Up until the 1930's, America had had a shortage of theorists. In fact, some universities did not have any, and many American graduate students who wanted to train to be theorists went to Europe. Theorists such as Bloch were especially helpful to the American experimentalists, who were collecting more data than they could interpret. Bloch was a welcome arrival for the experimentalists at the Stanford Cyclotron, who until then had been forced to rely on J. Robert Oppenheimer (1904-1967), who was at Berkeley, for theoretical analysis of their data.

In 1936, Bloch predicted that the magnetic moments of the free electron and neutron could be verified experimentally by observation of the scattering of slow neutrons in iron. He also predicted that the magnetic scattering would lead to the polarization of neutron beams. The following year, a group of experimentalists at Columbia University confirmed these predictions.

In 1939, Bloch became a naturalized citizen of the United States. He also made a switch from theoretical physics to experimental physics when he and Luis Alvarez began conducting experiments to determine the magnetic moments of the neutron. They accomplished this task by passing a beam of polarized neutrons through a region where a weak, oscillating magnetic field was superimposed on a strong, constant magnetic field. Bloch was one of the relatively few physicists who showed a talent for working with experimentation as well as with theory.

During World War II, Bloch went on leave from Stanford. The first assignment he took was with Oppenheimer at Berkeley in the summer of 1942. The group of theorists gathered there were trying to study the physics of an atom bomb—specifically, how much fissionable material would be needed for such a bomb. When the Manhattan District was formed by the government to be one of three agencies that was working on the development of an atom bomb, Oppenheimer was chosen as the project director. Bloch went with him to work on this project in Los Alamos, New Mexico, and stayed there from 1942 to 1944. Bloch did not care for life on the Los Alamos mesa, where he had to cope with strict army rule, and decided to move on to something else. In 1944, he became an associate group leader in counter-radar research at Harvard University Radio Research Laboratory.

The large community of European refugee physicists had a definite impact on the United States' ability to progress in the field of atomic research, but this research was not the most crucial factor contributing to the Allied victory in the European war; developments in radar technology had a more decisive part. In the area of radar and radar countermeasures, the European refugees had a much smaller role than they had in atomic research. Bloch, along with such notables as Hans Bethe and Samuel Goudsmit, was one of the few Europeans who did work in this field.

After the war, Bloch returned to Stanford in the fall of 1945 and continued his investigation of nuclear magnetic moments. His work with radar had given him the familiarity with electronic equipment that he needed to be able to realize that the signals of the atoms could be detected through electromagnetic induction. In these new investigations, he worked with W. W. Hansen and Martin Packard. He published papers on neutron polarization by ferromagnetic media and started his studies of the behavior of atoms in time-varying magnetic fields. Not long after he and his colleagues had successfully made measurements, Bloch heard that Purcell had made the same discovery simultaneously and independently at Harvard. One of the indications of Bloch's success during this time was his admittance to the National Academy of Sciences in 1948.

The early 1950's marked the pinnacle of Bloch's career. It was during this time that he became a Nobel laureate and the first director general of CERN. In 1952 he shared the Nobel Prize with Purcell. They each received $16,500, as the total prize was worth $33,000. It is interesting that although most of Bloch's work was theoretical in nature, the Nobel Prize was awarded to him for work that had involved experimentation as well as theory. From 1954 to 1955, Bloch took another leave from Stanford to serve as the first director general of CERN, for which he had been unanimously selected.

After 1955 he continued his investigations into nuclear and molecular structure. In the latter years of his career, he led the life of a distinguished and respected member of the faculty of Stanford University. In 1961 he received an endowed chair through his appointment as Max Stein Professor of Physics. In 1971, he was named professor emeritus.

Much of Bloch's work is in the form of professional articles in technical journals. His early contributions beginning in 1927, include articles in publications such as *Zeitschrift für Physik* and *Physikalische Zeitschrift*. Starting in 1932, his papers appeared in journals such as *Nature*, *Physica*, and the *Physical Review*. It was in *Physical Review* that Bloch in 1946 published the papers describing the work that eventually won for him the Nobel Prize. The first paper, "Nuclear Induction," was written solely by Bloch and described the theory behind the induction method of magnetic resonance. The next article, "The Nuclear Induction Experiment," immediately followed Bloch's article and was written by Bloch, Martin Packard, and W. W. Hansen; it described the experimental setup and procedure.

The book *Spectroscopic and Group Theoretical Methods in Physics: Racah Memorial Volume* (1968), was edited by Bloch. This book is dedicated to Giulio Racah, an Israeli theoretical physicist who died in 1965. It consists of technical articles on subjects in the fields in which Bloch and Racah were involved.

Bibliography

Primary

PHYSICS: *Die Electronentheorie der Metalle*, 1933; *Les Électrons dans les métaux; Problèmes statistiques; Magnétisme*, 1934; "Nuclear Induction," *Physical Review*, vol. 70, 1946; "The Nuclear Induction Experiment," *Physical Review*, vol. 70, 1946 (with W. W. Hansen and Martin Packard).

EDITED TEXT: *Spectroscopic and Group Theoretical Models in Physics: Racah Memorial Volume*, 1968.

Secondary

Beyerchen, Alan D. *Scientists Under Hitler: Politics and the Physics Community in the Third Reich*. New Haven, Conn.: Yale University Press, 1977. This book discusses the relationship between the German physicists and the leadership of Germany during Hitler's rule. It addresses Nazi policies and their effect on the scientific community and also describes how the German scientists who worked under Hitler dealt with his Fascist regime.

Blakemore, John. *Solid State Physics*. Cambridge, England: Cambridge University Press, 1985. An undergraduate-level introductory text in solid-state physics. An excellent source for an introduction to the theories and formulas that Bloch conceived and that were named after him. The reader will find discussions of the Bloch-Floquet theorem, the Bloch T $^{3/2}$ law, and the work that Bloch did in magnetic resonance that eventually led to the Nobel Prize.

Chodorow, Marvin, ed. *Felix Bloch and Twentieth-Century Physics*. Houston: William Marsh Rice University Press, 1980. This book is a collection of mostly technical articles on subjects related to Bloch's field of study. It was dedicated to him on his seventy-fifth birthday. While most of the articles are geared toward people in the field, there are some that deal more personally with Bloch and his work at CERN.

Fermi, Laura. *Industrious Immigrants: The Intellectual Migration from Europe, 1930-1941*. Chicago: University of Chicago Press, 1968. This book, which was written by the wife of Enrico Fermi, is a study of the many gifted scholars who fled the Fascist governments of Europe. She concentrates on the physicists who emigrated, but she also discusses scholars in other fields—social scientists, artists, and writers.

Levitan, Tina. *The Laureates: Jewish Winners of the Nobel Prize*. New York:

Twayne, 1960. This book examines the people of Jewish faith that won the Nobel Prize for peace, science, or literature between the years 1905 and 1959. (There were forty such winners.) The science category is divided into sections on the laureates in chemistry, medicine, and physics.

Mark S. Gulley

1952

Physics
Felix Bloch, United States
Edward Mills Purcell, United States

Chemistry
Archer Martin, Great Britain
Richard Synge, Great Britain

Physiology or Medicine
Selman A. Waksman, United States

Literature
François Mauriac, France

Peace
Albert Schweitzer, France

EDWARD MILLS PURCELL
1952

Born: Taylorville, Illinois; August 30, 1912

Nationality: American
Area of concentration: Nuclear magnetic resonance

Purcell succeeded in designing and building microwave equipment that was capable of determining by resonance the magnetic moment of nuclei to a remarkably high degree of accuracy without disturbing the normal liquid or solid state of the material being studied. In addition, the fact that each kind of nucleus exhibited a characteristic magnetic moment made Purcell's method an extremely valuable tool for chemists analyzing unknown substances

The Award

Presentation

Professor E. Hulthén, a member of the Nobel Committee for Physics of the Royal Swedish Academy of Sciences, opened his presentation address with a summary of the history and importance of magnetism dating back to the third century before Christ. He noted that the old magnetic categories of ferro-magnetism, para-magnetism, and dia-magnetism had been joined in recent times by nuclear magnetism, and it was the accurate measurement of this new phenomenon by Felix Bloch and Edward Mills Purcell, working independently and using different techniques, that merited their being awarded the Nobel Prize in Physics for 1952.

Hulthén explained that as a charged particle, such as a nucleus, spins, it has a "magnetic moment" and its axis of spin precesses, as does a gyroscope, with a definite frequency. (The term "moment" as used here does not relate to time but is the term traditionally used for centuries to characterize the strength of a magnetic entity.) When the frequency of externally applied radio waves exactly matches the frequency of the rate of precession of the axis of the nucleus, a detectable resonance occurs if the nucleus is in a strong external magnetic field. This resonance occurs in a way analogous to a home radio responding—that is, resonating—with the incoming radio waves to which it is tuned.

Hulthén added that I. I. Rabi had been awarded the Nobel Prize in Physics in 1944 for his earlier discovery of this method of nuclear magnetic resonance (NMR) using a rarefied molecular beam of material. The innovations introduced by Bloch and Purcell consisted of a method of determining and precisely measuring the characteristic resonance frequency of each kind of nucleus present in a crystal sample without any disturbance of its crystal structure, thus making the NMR method valuable in many scientific and technical fields.

Hulthén then addressed Purcell individually, noting that Purcell's NMR work was an outgrowth of his wartime activity at the Radiation Laboratory and, in a sense, amounted to achieving the ancient goal of beating swords into plowshares. He particularly called attention to three aspects of Purcell's discoveries: his absolute (that is, not relative) determination of the magnitude of magnetic moments, his paramagnetic resonance work with Robert V. Pound that corresponded to negative absolute temperatures, and his contribution to radio astronomy from his discovery, with Harold Ewen in 1951, of the 21-centimeter hydrogen line coming from outer space. Hulthén then concluded his address with corresponding remarks directed to Bloch, and the two laureates' Nobel Prizes were presented to them by the King of Sweden.

Nobel lecture

Purcell began his address, "Research in Nuclear Magnetism," with a lyrical description of the wonder he had experienced when contemplating the surrounding world with new insight after his nuclear magnetic resonance experiments, saying, in part, "I remember, the winter of our first experiments . . . looking on snow with new eyes. There the snow lay around my doorstep—great heaps of protons quietly precessing in the earth's magnetic field. To see the world for a moment as something rich and strange is the private reward of many a discovery."

He then proceeded to a more technical discussion of his experience with nuclear magnetism, explaining that it was relatively easy to determine the ratio of the magnetic moments of two different nuclear species to a high degree of precision. Many magnetic moments had thus been determined, relative to the magnetic moment of the proton, with a degree of accuracy of one part in ten million. As one proceeds up the periodic table to increasingly heavy nuclei surrounded by more and more electrons, it is necessary to take into account the magnetic shielding effect of those electrons. Results for two isotopes (nuclei which have the same number of protons but different numbers of neutrons) are especially interesting, because of the light shed on the internal structure of the nuclei from the determination of their magnetic moments. In fact, all the results of nuclear magnetic moment experiments, Purcell noted, promise to be of great theoretical value.

With the aid of data determined by other investigators, Purcell was able to convert his relative values of magnetic moments into absolute values. In addition, the spin precession frequency of the electron can be determined and proves to be about seven hundred times greater than that of the proton.

Purcell also reported that the techniques of nuclear magnetism were able to throw considerable light on the problems of molecular motion and molecular structure in ways that he had never anticipated at the outset of his investigations. In a molecule there are local magnetic fields associated with each of the component nuclei which cause effects on the resonance responses that are particularly noticeable in crystal structure and are of great interest to physical chemists.

Another facet of Purcell's nuclear magnetic studies involved "nuclear relaxation," which he defined as the attainment of thermal equilibrium between the nuclear spins and their environment. He and his collaborators, Pound and Henry C. Torrey, devoted attention to this topic and found that the time required by different substances to attain this state varied from several hours to fractions of milliseconds. It involves the transfer of energy from the spinning nuclei to the crystal lattice of which they are part. This is a topic of theoretical and practical importance especially at low temperatures and has been studied at a number of laboratories in Europe and the United States.

In keeping with his characteristic modesty and generosity, Purcell made repeated reference in his address to the contributions to nuclear magnetism made by other workers in the field, which, he said, is not simply a new tool but also a new subject, one that has already proved itself to be rich in difficult and provocative problems and full of surprises.

Critical reception

The news of the awarding of the Nobel Prize in physics jointly to Felix Bloch and Edward Mills Purcell was widely reported in the popular and scientific press, usually without comment beyond some attempt to explain their achievements in layman's language.

Scientific American (December, 1952) likened their techniques to making the nuclei "literally dance in rhythm with a radio wave." It was noted that Purcell's method of "nuclear resonance" involved matching a high-frequency (short wavelength) radio wave to that of the nuclear precession rate, resulting in the nuclear spin reversing its direction. On the other hand, Bloch's method of "nuclear induction" involved using radio energy to stimulate the nuclei to send out radio waves of their own.

Physics Today (December, 1952) also compared and contrasted the methods of Bloch and Purcell, noting that both experimenters, working independently and unaware of each other's work initially, had achieved their results in 1945 after both had been involved in wartime radar projects—Bloch at the Radio Research Laboratory at Harvard (which was concerned with developing antiradar devices) and Purcell at the Radiation Laboratory of the Massachusetts Institute of Technology. The monetary value of their prizes was reported to be about $16,500 apiece.

The New York Times, for several days after the prize recipients were announced, had articles on all the Nobel Prizes awarded that year. Pictures of Bloch and Purcell were published (November 7) with an account of the simultaneity and independence of their precision methods, which constituted "an immense advance for atomic science." The following day, apparently after a telephone conversation with Purcell, *The New York Times* reported in almost incredulous tones, in a few paragraphs headlined "Physicist Worked Nights: Used Borrowed Supplies for Prize Winning Research," that most of Purcell's NMR study was done with borrowed equipment in his spare time. (This was essentially true. In December 1945 Purcell was about to leave the MIT Radiation Laboratory and return to Harvard. It was then that he, Pound, and Torrey did the initial NMR experiments. The large magnet they needed was borrowed from the Harvard Physics Department, where it was not then in use, and the smaller elements of their apparatus came from the Radiation Labo-

ratory, which was about to close down but still had skilled technicians and equipment not being fully utilized. Purcell and his coworkers developed and conducted
their experiment on their own time outside their official duties.)

The New York Times (December 11), in its coverage of the Nobel Prize ceremony,
mentioned Bloch and Purcell (along with an account of the sumptuous banquet that
followed the ceremony and the beautiful flowers that bedecked the platform), saying
that Professor Hulthén "eulogized the U.S. pair for their epoch making work."
Unfortunately, however, the reporter that day mistakenly identified their discoveries
as occurring in "the magnetic and nuclear fission fields."

George H. Waltz, Jr., in his chapter on Purcell in *What Makes a Scientist?* (1959),
quoted Pound as saying, "It [NMR] wasn't a spectacular thing like atomic energy. It
was nothing that was going to change our lives. However, this new technique does
give us a new and extremely accurate tool that can be used to investigate the very
inner nature of matter. It will help to fill in a lot of blanks on our knowledge." Waltz
also described the reaction of Purcell's colleagues at Harvard to the announcement
of his being awarded the Nobel Prize as "It couldn't have happened to a nicer guy."
Later, one of them commented, "He is the most *gracious* scientist I have ever
known," an evaluation shared by all who have come in contact with Purcell over the
years.

Biography

Edward Mills Purcell was born on August 30, 1912, in Taylorville, Illinois, the
older of two sons born to Edward A. Purcell and Mary Elizabeth (Mills) Purcell.
His father was manager of the local telephone company, first in Taylorville and later
in Mattoon. His mother, a graduate of Vassar College with a master's degree in
classics, had been a Latin teacher in high school before her marriage.

Yound Edward was educated in the local public schools before entering Purdue
University in 1929. At Purdue he took the course leading to a bachelor of science
degree in electrical engineering, which he obtained in 1933. During his junior and
senior years, however, he began serious work in the physics department and came
to realize that it was in physics that his interests really lay. He spent the year
following his graduation as an exchange student at the Technische Hochschule in
Karlsruhe, Germany. Upon returning to the United States in 1934 he enrolled as a
graduate student in the physics department of Harvard University. His Ph.D. in
physics was awarded in 1938, and he remained there as a faculty instructor until
1940. In 1937 he married Beth Busser, a Bryn Mawr graduate who had also been an
exchange student in Germany in 1933-1934. They would have two sons.

Between 1940 and 1946, Purcell was a member of the Radiation Laboratory at the
Massachusetts Institute of Technology, where the aircraft detection system radar
was being developed and perfected. He served as Head of the Fundamental Development Group of that laboratory. In 1946 he returned to Harvard as associate
professor of physics, dividing his time between teaching and research, and was
promoted to full professor in 1949. In 1958 he was named Donner Professor of

Science and later, in 1960, became Gerhard Gade University Professor at Harvard. For many years (1950-1971) he was also a senior member of the University-wide Society of Fellows, a prestigious group of scholars from many disciplines. He became professor emeritus in 1980. During his long career at Harvard, he also served the nation as scientific adviser to several groups for many years and was a member of the President's Scientific Advisory Committee under President Eisenhower (1957-1960) and under Presidents Kennedy and Johnson (1962-1966).

Scientific Career

As a young boy, Purcell had access to discarded telephone equipment by virtue of his father's position with the local telephone company. He made a number of simple electrical devices from the wires and coils he had available and, in the process, began his self-education in electricity and magnetism. When it came time to select a course of study in college, he chose electrical engineering, as it seemed to lead to a reasonable adult occupation. He had taken physics in high school, but at that time, although professional chemists were ordinarily visible to young persons, professional physicists were not.

While completing his electrical engineering program at Purdue, Purcell began taking courses in the physics department, although initially its offerings were limited. About midway through his undergraduate years, however, Purdue hired a Viennese physicist, Karl Lark-Horowitz, to establish a strong program in physics. Lark-Horowitz himself was doing research in the modern physics of the time and had graduate students working toward doctorates under his direction. During Purcell's junior and senior years he came to know these young graduate students, and they welcomed him into their laboratories. Purcell was an eager neophyte, glad to be helpful and increasingly fascinated by the physics they were doing. He learned new laboratory techniques and even came to coauthor, with Lark-Horowitz and one of the graduate students, a published paper on thin films while he was still an undergraduate. By the time he was graduated from Purdue, Purcell had resolved to become a physicist. The year that he spent in Germany, 1933-1934, allowed him to become better grounded in the basic physics he would need before embarking on formal graduate study the next year in the physics department of Harvard University.

After completing his required course work, Purcell conducted his thesis research under the guidance of Kenneth Bainbridge, an experimental physicist well-known for his work with mass spectrographs and who had recently joined the physics faculty at Harvard. Purcell's doctoral thesis, "The Focusing of Charged Particles by a Spherical Condenser," was completed and he received his Ph.D. in 1938. By that time Harvard was involved in building its first cyclotron, and Purcell was engaged for the next two years in building the power supply and the controls for the cyclotron's magnet; at the same time, he was teaching elementary physics courses. During his years of graduate study Purcell took a course on the theory of electric and magnetic susceptibilities with John H. Van Vleck, whose lifelong contributions to the study of magnetism were to be recognized with the Nobel Prize in Physics in 1977. One of the very few theoretical papers that Purcell ever published was the result of a project he undertook with a fellow graduate student in that course.

When Purcell left Harvard in 1940, he joined the Radiation Laboratory at the Massachusetts Institute of Technology, where radar (the acronym for *radio detection and ranging*), using very short-wavelength radio waves (microwaves), was being developed to aid the war effort by detecting enemy aircraft in order to prepare counteroffensive action. Over the next several years, such great progress was made in perfecting radar devices that it has been said that "radar won World War II—the atom bomb ended it." As leader of the Fundamental Development Group, Purcell made notable contributions to the progress that was made, but he also experienced considerable scientific development himself, since working with radio waves of that range was new to him and he was immersed in a totally new scientific environment—not only for him but for all the members of the "Rad Lab" as well.

A large number of established physicists from many institutions around the country were gathered together there to work toward a very important wartime goal. There were lively discussions and exchanges among them in and out of the laboratory. Notable among those contacts for Purcell was that with I. I. Rabi, who had developed a nuclear magnetic method and was awarded the Nobel Prize for it in 1944.

The war ended in August, 1945, and Purcell stayed until the end of the year, winding up the operations of the Radiation Laboratory and interacting with other members, such as Robert V. Pound and Henry C. Torrey. It was in this context that Purcell's work on nuclear magnetic resonance developed and led to his being awarded his Nobel Prize in 1952. In 1946, he returned to Harvard as an associate professor of physics, continuing his research, directing graduate students, and teaching courses. Among the graduate students with whom Purcell worked during the late 1940's was Nicolaas Bloembergen, a student visiting from the Netherlands. Bloembergen's thesis topic was related to Purcell's NMR work dealing with relaxation times, and resulted in the publication of an important joint paper coauthored by Bloembergen, Pound, and Purcell. After receiving his Ph.D. from the University of Leiden, Bloembergen would return to Harvard as a faculty member in the Division of Applied Science; he also won the Nobel Prize in Physics, in 1981.

Another of Purcell's graduate students who achieved notable results as part of his doctoral work was Harold Ewen. Working with Purcell, Ewen built a radio telescope which detected radiation coming from outer space which was identified as the 21-centimeter line of hydrogen. This achievement had been sought by radio astronomers around the world and made possible the mapping of the Milky Way. It also introduced Purcell to radio astronomy, a discipline to which he would return in later years and to which he would make significant contributions. In the 1970's, Purcell also became interested in the physics of biological systems. In general, Purcell's research interests have ranged wherever he has found interesting physical problems.

During his years at the Radiation Laboratory, Purcell developed an easy style of cooperating with members of the military, who were very appreciative of the value of the radar that scientists were then developing. When the war ended and Purcell returned to Harvard's physics department, cooperation with and funding from the military began to play an important role in the pursuit of physics at academic institutions. Purcell became a trusted scientific adviser to military and political leaders. He undertook some special projects for the military during summer months and served on several committees established to continue the cooperation that had worked so well in wartime. When, under President Dwight D. Eisenhower, the President's Scientific Advisory Committee (PSAC) was established, Purcell was one of the committee's first members. Ultimately, he served two periods of duty on PSAC under Presidents Eisenhower, Kennedy, and Johnson; he was able to do so without seriously disrupting his Harvard schedule, making frequent two- or three-day trips to Washington, D.C.

The years during which PSAC was most active were those during which the American space program was being launched. Purcell headed a subcommittee of PSAC charged with providing scientific and technical advice on space. He found that some basic physical concepts needed to be provided to the government's decision makers. His committee's report, presented in 1958, was formally titled "Introduction to Outer Space" and was informally known as "The Space Primer." It was a masterful exposition, in layman's terms, of the practical physics and technology that would be involved in the exploration of space. President Eisenhower was so pleased with this report that he urged its wide dissemination among all people of the United States and the world. Purcell also made many comparable oral presentations with charts and questioning before various Washington groups of congressmen and cabinet members. His committee's recommendations played a significant role in the establishment and organization of the National Aeronautics and Space Administration (NASA).

Throughout Purcell's professional career, he was a dedicated and highly successful teacher of physics. He authored or coauthored three college-level textbooks that were widely used. His *Electricity and Magnetism*, originally published in 1965 as part of a series being developed at the University of California at Berkeley and long regarded as a masterpiece of pedagogy, was reissued in a new edition in 1985. He supervised the doctoral research of eighteen graduate students at Harvard. In addition, he concerned himself with the teaching of precollege physics and was part of the team, based principally at the Massachusetts Institute of Technology, that developed the Physical Science Study Committee (PSSC) physics course in the late 1950's and 1960's to update and revitalize the physics being taught to high school students. In that context, he made two films about physics for classroom use.

Long a member of the American Association of Physics Teachers, Purcell was awarded their Ørsted Medal "for notable contributions to the teaching of physics" in 1966. Years earlier, soon after receiving his Nobel Prize, he had been honored by the same group with an invitation to deliver their annual Richtmyer Memorial Lecture at a joint meeting with the American Physical Society. His lecture on that occasion, titled "Nuclear Magnetism," has been called "a simple and elegant talk on NMR" and was published in the *American Journal of Physics* in 1954. Other honors bestowed upon Purcell were election to membership in the National Academy of Sciences and to the Presidency of the American Physical Society in 1970. In 1979 he was awarded the National Medal of Science.

Bibliography

Primary

PHYSICS: *Principles of Microwave Circuits*, 1948 (with C. G. Montgomery and R. H. Dicke); *Physics*, 1952 (with W. H. Furry and J. C. Street); "Introduction to Outer Space," 1958 (with others); *Electricity and Magnetism*, 1965, 1985.

Secondary

Bloch, Felix. "The Principle of Nuclear Induction." *Science* 118 (October 16, 1953): 425-430. Bloch's Nobel Prize acceptance address describing his approach to nuclear magnetism. This may be compared with Purcell's description of his related work in his Nobel Prize address, which was reprinted in the same issue of *Science*.

Killian, James R., Jr. *Sputnik, Scientists, and Eisenhower*. Cambridge, Mass.: MIT Press, 1977. This book carries the subtitle "A Memoir of the First Special Assistant to the President for Science and Technology," a post that Killian occupied during the period when Purcell was a member of the President's Scientific Advisory Council. Killian describes, in particular, the high level of respect in which Purcell was held especially when serving as chairman of the PSAC committee on space that led to the formation of the National Aeronautics and Space Administration (NASA). The report on space prepared by Purcell's committee and dubbed "The Space Primer" is reprinted as an appendix to this book. The entire book is a fine first-person account of the influence of scientists in government in the late 1950's and 1960's.

Pake, George E. "Magnetic Resonance." *Scientific American* 199 (August, 1958): 58-66. Pake, who received his Ph.D. under Purcell's guidance, has written an article summarizing the impact of magnetic resonance studies on such diverse fields as spectroscopy, molecular structure and identification, geomagnetism, and biophysics as these areas were being developed in the late 1950's.

Waltz, George H., Jr. *What Makes a Scientist?* Garden City, N.Y.: Doubleday, 1959. This is a collection of biographical sketches of twelve twentieth century American scientists who the author, a science writer, believes typify the kind of human beings scientists are. Edward M. Purcell is the subject of chapter 11, "Nuclear Explorer." This sketch provided is accurate for the most part and can be easily understood by the lay reader. Waltz was motivated to write this book by his observations of popular misconceptions concerning science and scientists.

Katherine R. Sopka

1953

Physics
Frits Zernike, Netherlands

Chemistry
Hermann Staudinger, West Germany

Physiology or Medicine
Fritz A. Lipmann, United States
Sir H. A. Krebs, Great Britain

Literature
Sir Winston Churchill, Great Britain

Peace
George C. Marshall, United States

FRITS ZERNIKE
1953

Born: Amsterdam, Netherlands; July 16, 1888
Died: Groningen, Netherlands; March 10, 1966
Nationality: Dutch
Area of concentration: Optics

Zernike opened new vistas in scientific research with his method of phase contrast and the phase contrast microscope. As a result, objects as small as a fraction of the wavelength of light could be seen better

The Award

Presentation

Professor E. Hulthén, a member of the Nobel Committee for Physics, gave the presentation speech for the 1953 Nobel Prize in Physics on behalf of the Royal Swedish Academy of Sciences and King Gustav VI. The prize was awarded to Frits Zernike, of the University of Groningen, for developing the phase contrast method and for inventing the phase contrast microscope. Hulthén noted that this particular award was remarkable because Zernike's contribution had been in the field of classical physics rather than in the more modern field of atomic and nuclear physics. The Nobel Prize in Physics had always been awarded for work done in modern physics, except for a few of the earliest prizes.

Hulthén went on to say that the microscope was one of the most important instruments of scientific research; consequently, improvements in the microscope could pave the way to great advances in such fields as the natural sciences and medicine. He gave a lucid description of the operation of this special instrument. Among the special capabilities of the phase contrast microscope, he said, were its abilities to render transparent microorganisms visible and to detect slight flaws in the mirrors and lenses of telescopes. Microscopic objects could now be located and measured so precisely that their atomic structures would begin to be observable.

Nobel lecture

Zernike's Nobel lecture, entitled "How I Discovered Phase Contrast," is a detailed account of the development and nature of the phase contrast method and the phase contrast microscope. Although he started work on the phase contrast method in 1920, in connection with diffraction gratings, an account of the method was only published in 1934, and his paper was concerned only with the detection of irregularities in the surfaces of telescope mirrors. One year later, however, Zernike published a description of the method's application to microscopes.

During the development of the phase contrast method, Zernike sought help from the prestigious Zeiss optical works facility in Jena, Germany. There the microscope had been developed, through the genius of Ernst Abbe, to a point where many believed that everything worth knowing in microscopy had been uncovered and everything worth trying had been attempted. Zernike's appeal for help was therefore greeted with little enthusiasm, and he was told by one of the senior scientific associates at Zeiss, "If [the idea] had any practical value, we would ourselves have invented it long ago." Zernike persisted with his research efforts on the microscope, however, and accomplished the "impossible" in two years.

Zernike's lecture included a description of the construction of a phase contrast microscope. This instrument is a standard microscope modified by the addition of a light-controlling diaphragm and a diffraction plate. The plate causes the object under the microscope to be seen in contrast to the surrounding background, even if the object is transparent. The object viewed need only have an index of refraction which is different from the background. Previous methods used for viewing transparent or colorless microorganisms had either introduced spurious structural features, if the "dark field illumination technique" was used, or killed living cells, if chemical staining techniques were used.

Critical reception

Many of the more widely read newspapers and technical periodicals, including *The Times* of London, *Nature*, *The New York Times*, and *Physics Today*, mentioned some of the practical uses of the phase contrast microscope at the time Zernike received the Nobel Prize. Most frequently mentioned were its applications in biological and medical research and its special promise in the field of cancer research. According to *Nature*, Zernike had a unique talent for combining mathematical insight and technical ability, a talent which allowed him to reduce problems to their simplest mathematical form. In fact, when he explained the principle of the phase contrast microscope, it was hard to understand why it had not been discovered earlier.

The technical periodical that had kept abreast of Zernike's achievements was the British journal *Nature*. Zernike was well-known in Great Britain even before he received the Nobel Prize, since he had delivered the Thomas Young Oration of the Physical Society and had been awarded the Rumford Medal of the British Royal Society. During the award ceremony for the Rumford Medal, Lord Edgar Douglas Adrian, a former Nobel Prize winner in physiology or medicine, noted that Zernike's work had been a great stimulus to the study of diffraction phenomena, which had led indirectly to important advances in the field of interferometry.

Although accounts of the award differed widely, they nearly always quoted or paraphrased the senior scientist at Zeiss who had been discouraging about the phase contrast microscope. It was *Physics Today* that recognized the irony of the German influence on the development of the phase contrast microscope. Because of the influence of Abbe and the unnamed scientist at the Zeiss optical facility, the development of the phase contrast microscope had been impeded and laboratories had been slow to adopt the device. Yet, during World War II, it was the German military that finally placed the microscope into production. As a result of a survey taken in

1941, it was decided that Zernike's microscope might have military applications.

In an article in *Nature*, two of Zernike's countrymen, J. A. Prins and N. G. van Kampen, provided insight into Zernike's personality. Even after conducting considerable research, he was not easily persuaded to publish his ideas; when he did, however, they were carefully and lucidly presented. He had a masterful way of using a simple analogy to throw light on an old problem. Zernike's contacts with other scientists were limited, partly because he was absorbed in his research and partly because he felt ill at ease with people. He was a gentle and humble man. When told that he had been selected for the Nobel Prize in Physics, he was overwhelmed. Unfortunately, Zernike's gentleness was unsuited to the turmoil of university politics. His friends would remember him for his great knowledge, broad scientific interests, and penetrating and unprejudiced views.

Biography

Frits Zernike was the second of six children of Carl Frederick August and Antje Dieperink Zernike. His father was the headmaster of a primary school in Amsterdam; he authored articles on pedagogy and compiled numerous elementary books on various subjects. While still in secondary school, Frits would spend time solving arduous mathematical problems with his parents, who were both mathematics teachers. He also conducted scientific experiments that often utilized homemade equipment and chemicals. Zernike entered the University of Amsterdam in 1905 and majored in chemistry, with a minor in physics and mathematics. His interest in mathematics soon won for him two gold medals: one from the University of Groningen, for an essay on probabilities, and another from the Dutch Society of Sciences, for a paper on critical opalescence. (Opalescence is the reflection of a rainbow display of color.) The latter work formed the basis for the doctorate he would receive from Amsterdam in 1915, and his dissertation made him a leading authority in his field at the age of twenty-seven. In 1913, Zernike became an assistant in the astronomical laboratory of J. C. Kapteyn at Groningen. After earning his doctor of science degree, he was appointed as a lecturer in theoretical physics. He was made a full professor only five years later, in the fields of theoretical and technical physics and theoretical mechanics.

Zernike was married to Dora van Bommel van Vloten; they had one son. In 1954, ten years after her death, he wed Mrs. L. Koperberg-Baanders.

Scientific Career

On receiving his doctorate, Zernike succeeded L. S. Ornstein at Groningen as a lecturer in mathematical physics. This appointment was the beginning of a fruitful collaboration with Ornstein on papers dealing with statistical mechanics. Zernike's doctoral dissertation, titled *L'Opalescence critique, théorie et expériments* (critical opalescence, theoretical and experimental), is still quoted in textbooks on thermodynamics and statistical mechanics.

In addition to working with Ornstein, Zernike conducted theoretical studies of galvanometers. In 1926 he published a paper on the natural observation limits of current strength which established the limits of measurements possible with galvanometers. For sensitive moving coil galvanometers, he found, the moment of inertia of the mirror must be approximately three times that of the moving coil for maximum sensitivity. These instruments are used in laboratories throughout the world for measuring extremely small currents. These findings are an example of the type of results that Zernike would deduce from first principles rather than from empirical experimentation with the instrument.

By employing Abbe's microscope theory, that images are interference effects of diffraction phenomena, Zernike first applied the phase contrast method in 1930 to explain certain errors in Rowland gratings. When finally developed in 1935, the phase contrast method was so sensitive that it enabled imperfections in reflectors as small as one-sixtieth of a wavelength of visible light to be detected, or about 0.0000001 centimeter. These developments also led Zernike to study the degree of coherence in light and to pioneer some ideas on the subject of holography, the three-dimensional formation of images.

The physical principle behind the phase contrast microscope is that light that passes through a transparent particle is shifted a quarter of a wavelength relative to light that does not. With the introduction of his phase plate, Zernike was able to increase the relative phase displacement to a half or a whole wavelength, causing the rays to cancel or reinforce each other and making the previously invisible particle appear dark or light in contrast to its surroundings. That a ray model is used to explain the interaction of light, rather than the quantized photon model used in spectroscopy, was the basis for Hulthén's describing Zernike's work as classical rather than modern.

When American troops arrived in Jena in 1945, they found micrographs taken at the Zeiss facility with the phase contrast microscope that had been dismissed years earlier. Zeiss, in fact, had done some developmental work with the instrument and succeeded in obtaining the first motion pictures of living cells dividing. These and other findings made by Arthur T. Bryce of the U.S. Army immediately aroused attention, and the Zernike microscope quickly became widely used throughout the scientific world. It was now possible to study such things as the fine structure of bacteria and living cells. Some recognition for his invention came to Zernike in 1946, when he became a member of the Royal Netherlands Academy of Sciences at Amsterdam.

Only a few years after Zernike had introduced the phase plate, he began to make further improvements. One was designed to increase the contrast of the details of the objects viewed, since they usually were not enhanced by the phase plate. Increased contrast was accomplished with the addition of a phase strip with the appropriate absorbing characteristics. Another improvement was the elimination of the asymmetric halo found around images with great contrast. That was achieved with an annular strip, which has the effect of spreading the halo in all directions, making it much fainter. For a number of years after the phase contrast microscope had been introduced, Zernike and B. R. A. Nijboer worked on another important developmental problem. They formulated a mathematical theory which determined the influence of small aberrations on the diffraction pattern in the image plane. By 1942 they had successfully completed their work and had invented a new mathematical tool, circle polynomials.

The impact of Zernike's microscope has been so great, it tends to obscure his other contributions which displayed his unusual versatility. From 1938 to 1948, he collaborated with his students on problems of the influence of lens aberrations on the diffraction pattern at a focus. In 1940 he published an extensive article on statistics. He also authored articles in the fields of chemistry and astronomy. Zernike never lost interest in chemistry, his undergraduate major. In 1939 he wrote an article on phase rules and allotropy, and a few years later, he was writing articles on the thermodynamics of alloys. In the field of astronomy, he introduced improvements in spectroscopy at infrared and ultraviolet wavelengths with thermopiles and photographic plates.

In an effort to develop the already very successful phase contrast microscope, Zernike became a visiting professor in 1948 at The Johns Hopkins University, in Baltimore. He and his colleagues developed a diffraction plate with a combination of plastics which allowed images to be produced in colors. They presented their findings at a meeting of the Optical Society of America in Buffalo in 1949. This effort was followed by Zernike's election to honorary membership in the Royal Microscopical Society of London in 1950.

Because Zernike's microscopes had such useful applications in the biological and medical research fields, his alma mater awarded him an honorary doctor of medicine degree in 1950. The impact of Zernike's work was now widely felt, and he soon received some of his most prestigious awards. In 1952, he was awarded the Rumford Medal; in 1953, the Nobel Prize. Five years later, at the age of seventy, he retired from the faculty at Groningen and with his second wife moved to Naarden, a town in the countryside near Amsterdam. He died in March, 1966.

The world has benefited greatly from Zernike's dramatic improvements in microscopic imaging. His unusual diversity and scientific genius were evident throughout his forty-eight-year affiliation with the University of Groningen.

Bibliography

Primary

PHYSICS: *L'Opalescence critique, théorie et expériments*, 1915; "Diffraction Theory of the Knife-Edge Test and Its Improved Form: The Phase-Contrast Method," *Monthly Notices of the Royal Astronomical Society*, vol. 94, 1934; "The Propagation of Order in Cooperative Phenomena," *Physica*, vol. 7, 1940; "A Precision Method for Measuring Small Phase Differences," *Journal of the Optical Society of America*, vol. 40, 1950; "How I Discovered Phase Contrast," in *Les Prix Nobel en 1953*, 1953; *Limitations of Interferometry*, 1960.

Secondary

Chu, Benjamin. *Laser Light Scattering*. New York: Academic Press, 1974. This source contains numerous references to Zernike's work with Ornstein on critical opalescence which appeared in *Proceedings of the Academy of Science (Amsterdam)* from 1914 to 1916. Suitable for college-level readers.

Cummins, H. Z., and A. P. Levanyuk. *Light Scattering Near Phase Transitions*. Amsterdam: North-Holland, 1973. This book touches on Zernike and Ornstein's fundamental work on light anomalies which appeared in *Physik Zeitschrift* in 1918. For college-level readers.

Kocinski, Jerzy, and Leszek Wojtczak. *Critical Scattering Theory: An Introduction*. Amsterdam: Elsevier, 1978. This publication is part of Elsevier's Phase Transition Phenomena, volume 1. Numerous references are made to Zernike and Ornstein's work on critical opalescence. Zernike and Prins's experiments on X-ray scattering in liquids are also discussed.

Nobelstiftelsen. *Physics*. 3 vols. New York: Elsevier, 1964-1967. The Elsevier series of Nobel lectures is a reprinting of the address given by each laureate. Brief biographies of the winners are provided. Illustrated with photographs and diagrams.

Schlessinger, Bernard S., and June H. Schlessinger, eds. *Who's Who of Nobel Prize Winners*. Phoenix, Ariz.: Oryx Press, 1986. This source contains a brief description of Zernike's life and work. The entry lists works by and relating to Zernike.

Louis Winkler

1954

Physics
Max Born, Great Britain
Walther Bothe, West Germany

Chemistry
Linus Pauling, United States

Physiology or Medicine
John F. Enders, United States
Thomas H. Weller, United States
Frederick Robbins, United States

Literature
Ernest Hemingway, United States

Peace
Office of the U. N. High Commissioner for Refugees

MAX BORN
1954

Born: Breslau, Germany; December 11, 1882
Died: Göttingen, West Germany; January 5, 1970
Nationality: British
Area of concentration: Quantum mechanics

Born's pioneering work in the development and formulation of the mathematical structure of quantum mechanics, together with his statistical interpretation of the quantum mechanical wave function, led to the first comprehensive treatment of atomic phenomena

The Award

Presentation

On behalf of the Royal Swedish Academy of Sciences, the Nobel Prize in Physics was presented to Max Born by Professor I. Waller, member of the Nobel Committee for Physics, on December 10, 1954 in Stockholm, Sweden. Waller's presentation carefully notes the distinction between the two primary formulations of quantum mechanics: the algebraic formulation of Born's assistant, Werner Heisenberg (1901-1976), and the wave mechanical formulations of the physicist Erwin Schrödinger (1887-1961). In this context, Waller observed that Born brought logical mathematical structure to Heisenberg's original theory. Furthermore, on the basis of that structure, Born, in collaboration with one of his students, Pascual Jordan (born 1902), and later also in collaboration with Heisenberg, developed Heisenberg's original formulation into the first comprehensive theory of atomic structure, called quantum mechanics. Schrödinger's separate formulation of the same theory treated matter as waves. Schrödinger, however, and all others except Born, failed to account for the nature of the connections between the waves and the material particles with which they were associated.

Born correctly understood that Schrödinger's waves could be used to predict the relative probability for each of the different possible results of any particular atomic experiment; thus, according to Born, quantum mechanics gives a statistical description of nature. From this it has been learned that nature is not, at its atomic root, deterministic. Waller states that such a fundamental change in the way physics is used to describe nature provoked much criticism and opposition. Nevertheless, it has come to be accepted. For these accomplishments and for his pioneering work in the study of crystals, Born was selected for the Nobel Prize.

Nobel lecture

Born's presentation was titled "The Statistical Interpretation of Quantum Mechanics." It consisted of a brief presentation of the historical setting and an explanation of both the Heisenberg and Schrödinger formulations of quantum mechanics. Following this, Born gives an account of the thinking which led to his "statistical interpretation." The tone of the piece is modest throughout, and every effort is made to credit all others whenever possible.

Born began his lecture by noting that even though his "statistical interpretation," the main work for which he was being cited, had won broad acceptance in the physics community, it still had many important critics. In this context, he listed four previous Nobel Prize winners as prominent critics of quantum mechanics: the 1921 laureate, Albert Einstein (1879-1955), the 1918 laureate, Max Planck (1858-1947), the 1929 laureate, Louis de Broglie (1892-1987), and the 1933 laureate, Schrödinger. All four had been major contributors to the development of the quantum theory yet they all had come to distrust it. Born then stated that "such weighty views cannot be ignored." Niels Bohr (1885-1962) went to great lengths to answer these important °critics; Born said that he too had some thoughts which he hoped might clarify the situation, thus establishing the theme of his lecture.

In preparation for his main point, Born briefly sketched the early work of Planck and Einstein on the absorption and emission of radiation. Their efforts, in this regard, led to light being considered as both corpuscle (particle) and wave. Born also discussed the early work of Bohr, which led to the idea of atomic energy levels; these researches had occurred before 1913. Born then credited a 1917 paper by Einstein, in which he introduced the idea of atomic transition probability, as a decisive step in the development of quantum theory. He also mentioned the work of many others in this connection and, in a rare break with modesty, correctly noted that he, Born, probably had been the first to use the term "quantum mechanics" in print.

Born next discussed Heisenberg's initial formulation of the quantum theory. Heisenberg did away with the traditional mechanical picture of the atom based on electron orbits and replaced it with a model based upon transition amplitudes. Transition amplitudes are in principle measurable and hence observable, whereas atomic orbits are not observable. Born compared this step to the one taken by Einstein in eliminating the concept for absolute (but unobservable) motion in relativity theory. Heisenberg's preliminary development was framed in terms of row and column arrays which needed to be manipulated in certain well-prescribed ways. Heisenberg, who was ill and had to leave Göttingen for a better climate, gave the work to Born, who recognized its value and submitted it for publication. Born allowed that, upon seeing Heisenberg's work, he came to realize that the arrays formulated by Heisenberg were the same as matrices which were well-known at the time to mathematicians but not to physicists. In Heisenberg's absence, Born first worked alone and later involved his pupil Jordan in a successful effort to develop and publish the main parts of the theory. Later Born and Jordan collaborated with Heisenberg to publish a definitive paper which, in the words of Born, "brought the formal side of the investigation to a definite conclusion." This section of the lecture ends with Born reporting that at the time he received a surprise, the news that Paul Dirac (1902-1984) had published, at about the same time, a similar but independent approach to quantum mechanics.

Born next shifted the discussion to Schrödinger's formulations of quantum mechanics, in which waves and differential equations replaced the matrices of Heisenberg. He noted that Schrödinger quickly proved the equivalence of the two different formulations. The wave function in Schrödinger's approach is usually given the symbol Ψ. The interpretation of this wave function was perplexing to all. Schrödinger advocated an approach which would have done away with the particle nature of electrons and other objects treated by quantum mechanics. This approach would have replaced the usual concept of an atomic particle as something isolated in space and localized in time by a continuous density distribution given by (for technical mathematical reasons) Ψ^2 rather than Ψ.

By contrast, Born's interpretation of Ψ (actually Ψ^2) preserved the traditional characteristics of particles. In his view, the particle interacted with matter in a conventional manner; it made a single spot upon striking a video screen. The role of the wave function was to predict where and when the particle would be most likely to interact. Specifically, at any given time, if one looks for a particle at those points or in those regions of space where Ψ^2 is large, there is a high probability of finding the particle; where Ψ^2 is smaller, however, the probability is also smaller, and it is zero where Ψ^2 is zero. Hence, Ψ^2 according to Born represented a "probability density," and that gave rise to a statistical interpretation of nature which was the very idea to which Planck, Einstein, and the others so strongly objected. Born stated that his critics had been (and in some cases were) concerned about both the explicit challenge to determinism and the implicit challenge to realism which were inherent in his interpretation.

In attempting to answer his critics, Born argued that classical physics, usually viewed as deterministic, was actually inherently statistical in practice, and hence that quantum mechanics was not a dramatic break with the usual practice. In his own words, "It [determinism] is an idol, not an ideal in scientific research and cannot, therefore, be used as an objection to the . . . statistical interpretation of quantum mechanics." Finally, he agreed with his critics on the second point: the "statistical interpretation" did challenge physicists' conventional notion of reality. Born ended his main argument by noting that each object we perceive, such as an electron, "appears in innumerable aspects. The concept of the [particle or] object is the invariant of all these aspects." From this point of view, the wave-particle duality of the electron could hardly be considered strange.

Critical reception

The reaction in both the popular press and the scientific press to Born's award could best be described as muted. This response probably can be attributed to two causes. The first was the question of time: As *Newsweek* (November 15, 1988) observed, "Rarely had the Swedish judges of the Nobel prizes in physics dipped so far into the past." Born and the corecipient, Walther Bothe (1891-1957) were both honored for work accomplished more than a quarter century earlier. The second reason for the comparatively mild reaction to the Born announcement was that it was overshadowed by the already legendary status of two of the other prizewinners for that year, Ernest Hemingway (1899-1961) for literature and Linus Pauling (born 1901) for chemistry. Hemingway's nomination was controversial because in literature the Nobel award is supposed to be for "work of an ideal tendency." The question of the appropriateness of Hemingway's work together with the status and controversial nature of the man himself guaranteed that much press coverage would be devoted to him. Similarly, Pauling, who received the prize for work done on chemical bonding, was very controversial as an individual. Politically active, associated with unpopular causes and people, Pauling always demanded attention. *Time* magazine devoted ten and a half column inches to him and only one inch to Born. Coverage in *The New York Times* was equally unbalanced. Even *Physics Today* gave as much attention to Pauling as to Born or his cowinner, Bothe.

The limited coverage given to the awarding of the Nobel Prize to Born amounted to little more than observations, such as "Born's main work . . . began in 1925 and resulted in the replacement of the original quantum theory . . . by modern wave electrons . . . an essentially mathematical description." (*The Times*, London, November 4, 1954). In this regard there was little difference between the popular press and the scientific press. One reason for this temperance may have been that the awards for the development of quantum theory (for which Born received recognition in 1954) had actually been distributed long before, in 1933. The 1932 award, which had been reserved, was given in 1933 to Heisenberg for his role in the development of quantum mechanics. This was presented in conjunction with the 1933 award given to corecipients Schrödinger and Dirac for their related work in the same field. At the time of Born's award, quantum theory was not a sensational new theory, as it had been in 1933; indeed, the coverage given the award in 1933 was much more extensive. Since Born was instrumental in Heisenberg's initial development and was the first to explain the Schrödinger theory correctly, it should have seemed surprising that the Nobel committee waited twenty-one years to include Born with his peers. This apparently was not discussed at the time of the 1933 award, at least not publicly. Einstein, in a letter to Born on the occasion of Born's award, observed that he was "very pleased to hear that you have been awarded the Nobel Prize, although strangely belatedly, for your fundamental contributions to the quantum theory." Born responded, "The fact that I did not receive the Nobel Prize in 1932 together with Heisenberg hurt me very much at the time, in spite of a kind letter from Heisenberg." Born believed that his formulation of the statistical interpretation of the Schrödinger theory provoked so much opposition from preeminent physicists that the Swedish Academy had chosen not to include him in the 1933 award along with Heisenberg. Instead, they waited two decades until Born's formulation was accepted by almost all physicists. By that time Born's achievement was hardly newsworthy.

Biography

Max Born was born in Breslau, Germany, to a professor of medicine, Gustav

Born, and his wife, Margarete. He received his university education primarily at Göttingen and completed the work on his doctorate there in 1907. He also attended the University of Breslau for three semesters, as well as the Universities of Heidelberg and Zurich (one summer term each). After completing his doctorate, he returned to Breslau and pursued, among other things, the study of relativity. This led to his return to Göttingen in 1909 to work with Hermann Minkowski (1864-1909). In 1912 he visited the United States to lecture on relativity. In 1915 he moved to Berlin University as a professor and, in addition, had to join the Germany army. He left Berlin in 1919 and assumed a similar post at Frankfurt. In 1921 he settled in Göttingen, where he completed work begun earlier on crystal theory and made most of his major contributions to quantum mechanics. During this period, he was director of the Institute for Theoretical Physics at Göttingen. Forced out of Germany in 1933 by the Nazis, he went first to Cambridge (during which time he became a British citizen) and then in 1936 to Edinburgh, where he stayed until his retirement in the early 1950's.

After retiring, Born returned to Germany, moving to Bad Pyrmout. He spent the rest of his life fighting for nuclear disarmament and urging his fellow scientists to assume responsibility for scientific and technological creations. Married in 1913 to Hedwig (Hedi) Ehrenberg, he and she had three children. One of them, Irene Newton-John, would become the mother of the popular singer of the 1970's and 1980's, Olivia Newton-John.

Scientific Career

Max Born's initial scientific interest was in what would come to be described as relativity. His earliest efforts were involved in the study of the self-energy of the electron. This type of inquiry was a cornerstone of the relativity theory of Hendrik Lorentz (1853-1928) and Henri Poincaré (1854-1912). In fact, it was not until 1909, four years after Einstein's sensational paper on the subject, that Born even became aware of the latter's work. He was immediately greatly impressed. Shortly afterward, Born met Einstein at a meeting in Salzburg where, ironically, Einstein was presenting a paper on light quanta and Born one on special relativity. The irony of the situation was not lost on Born. "This seems to me rather amusing," he would later write; "Einstein had already proceeded beyond special relativity which he left to minor prophets. . . ." Whatever the merits of the papers presented by these great men, the meeting led to a lifelong, challenging, and at the same time touching dialogue which ended only with the death of Einstein.

Born was to be frustrated by his work in relativity. First, the idea that the mass of the electron derives from it electrical self-energy leads to the concept of a velocity-dependent mass, a concept which had played a major role in the earlier forms of relativity. In the relativity theory developed by Einstein, however, relativistic mass assumed a rather insignificant role. Born himself observed that "all these efforts appear rather wasted." More important, circumstances intervened to frustrate his efforts. While a student at Göttingen in 1905, studying relativity under Minkowski, he took a seminar on the theory of elasticity from Felix Klein (1949-1925). He did so well in this that Klein, who had great influence, virtually dictated that he pursue this subject for his dissertation. Born actually wanted to study relativity but instead yielded to the pressure. Later, after completing his work at Göttingen, he returned to the study of relativity at Cambridge and at Breslau. He sent a paper on this subject to Minkowski and was invited to return to work at Göttingen in 1909 with this great mathematician. Unfortunately, soon afterward Minkowski died of complications from an appendicitis operation.

During this period, while he was at Göttingen, Born also pursued work on the theory of specific heat. This work was inspired by an earlier theory developed by Einstein and led to the publication of a superior theory of specific heat by Born and a collaborator, Theodor von Kármán (1881-1963). Unfortunately, a competing theory, one more easily understood, was published at the same time by Peter Debye (1884-1966), and it is this latter theory which became the standard. The Born-von Kármán theory, however, was more rigorously developed and is more accurate in its application. The work on specific heats naturally led Born into further, more general studies of crystal dynamics, which in turn led to comprehensive major publications in this field in 1915 and again in 1923. Born's work in the field of crystal properties was important to the development of the entire field of solid-state physics and was cited by the Nobel Prize Committee as contributing to his being selected for the award. As was the case with his earlier work in relativity, however, Born came to regret the time that he spent on these studies.

In 1922 Bohr visited Göttingen and presented a series of lectures on the problem of the atom. These lectures evidently greatly influenced Born and the others present (Heisenberg among them) to focus their attention upon this problem. Born investigated methods of converting the classical analysis of periodic systems to a quantum approach. In this work, he was assisted by Heisenberg. The work was published in 1924 under the title "On Quantum Mechanics." It was here that the term "quantum mechanics" first appeared in publication, and the paper also was the first step of many rapid steps in the formulation of modern quantum mechanics—the culmination of which would be its full development by the end of 1925. The next step was made by Heisenberg alone. Working secretly, he developed a method of analyzing atomic systems in terms of only their transition amplitudes. This was early in 1925. He then handed his results to Born for Born's advice and left for the seashore to seek relief from his hay fever. Born recognized the significance of Heisenberg's work and submitted it for publication. Heisenberg's paper, although the most important step in the development of quantum mechanics, was incomplete and involved an unrecognized form of mathematics.

Born was able to identify the exotic mathematics created by Heisenberg as matrix algebra, which at the time was a branch of mathematics unused by and unfamiliar to physicists. With the help of a student, Pascual Jordan, Born substantially generalized Heisenberg's work and rigorously formulated its mathematical foundation. Most notably, he and Jordan extended the matrix formulation to a treatment of momentum and were able to establish the commutation relationship between the momentum and the spatial matrices. This means that the order in which the matrices are applied is significant. This result is of the greatest importance in the development of quantum mechanics. In fact, its symbolic formulation, $pq - qp = h/2\pi i$ is so significant that it is included on Born's tombstone as his ultimate testament. This "commutation relationship," as it is called, is usually incorrectly attributed to Heisenberg. Similarly, the Born-Jordan paper also contained the correct quantization of the electromagnetic field, an accomplishment which is usually incorrectly attributed to Dirac. These are only two of the many difficulties Born had in getting proper credit for his contribution to quantum mechanics.

During this same period, Born consulted the great mathematician David Hilbert (1862-1943) about the matrix approach. Hilbert observed that he had seen such matrices arise from boundary value differential equations and advised Born to look for the differential equation associated with his matrices. Had he done so, he might have discovered the Schrödinger theory a year ahead of its actual discovery. Following the completion of the work of Born and Jordan, Heisenberg joined them and a third paper was published. This paper, to which Born referred as the "Three-Man Paper," essentially completed the matrix formulation of quantum mechanics.

Subsequently, Born visited the United States, lecturing at the Massachusetts Institute of Technology in 1925-1926. His lectures were published in a book titled *Probleme der Atomdynamik* (1926; *Problems of Atomic Dynamics*, 1926), the first published book on quantum mechanics. During his visit, he established a collaboration with Norbert Wiener (1894-1964), and together they generalized the matrix formulation of quantum mechanics into a more general operator formulation. In the process of doing so, Born and Wiener came very close to creating the yet-undiscovered Schrödinger formulation. A few months later, Schrödinger did indeed create his wave mechanics. This formulation became the standard presentation, probably because its mathematical structure, utilizing differential equations rather than matrix operations, was more familiar to physicists. At the time of its presentation, the problem with Schrödinger's approach was not related to the success of its predictions. Indeed, it was very successful. The difficulty lay in the underlying mechanism of the wave function itself. The existence of the wave function seemed to suggest that electrons and other atomic "particles" were in fact not particles in the classical sense, but instead some sort of diffuse wave.

Born's codirector at Göttingen was James Franck (1882-1964). Franck was performing definitive studies on atomic and molecular collisions. These studies served to convince Born that even at the atomic level well-defined particles exist. To analyze collision experiments, Born developed in 1926 the "Born approximation" theory of scattering, a general approach to collisions which would become the standard method for analyzing experiments at the atomic and subatomic levels. The theory, which was based on the Schrödinger wave equation, explained the results of a wide variety of existing atomic collision experiments, all of which, according to Born, could be understood in terms of a particle picture. Born used this fusion of wave and particle—the predictive power of the wave equation of Schrödinger and the particle nature of the experimental results—to arrive at his "statistical interpretation" of the wave function. He was led to it by a hint from some earlier work by Einstein and some implications he perceived in the mathematical formulation of quantum mechanics itself.

In Born's approach, the wave function became an expression for the "potential" of finding the particle—that is, where it probably is and where it probably isn't. Although this interpretation was to become the standard one, it has always provoked opposition. A wide variety of critics, then as now, have offered arguments against it. The most notable critics at the time were Planck, Einstein, de Broglie, and Schrödinger. When the 1932 and 1933 Nobel Prizes were awarded, the 1932 award to Heisenberg and the 1933 award jointly to Schrödinger and Dirac, Born was very hurt. He always believed that he should have shared in Heisenberg's prize, which had been awarded for the development of the matrix formulation. He believed that he was not included because of the quantity and quality of the opposition directed at his "statistical interpretation" of the Schrödinger formulation. Thus, if his assessment is true, there is considerable irony that twenty years later he was awarded the Nobel Prize for the very contribution to the Schrödinger formulation which excluded him in the first place from receiving the recognition he deserved for his considerable contribution to the competing matrix formulation.

Describing himself in 1928 as an "elderly man" (he was forty-six at the time) who was having a hard time keeping up with "the young ones" at his institute, Born reports that he had a nervous breakdown. This kept him from working for a year. Taking up a reduced load a year later, he began to commit his lecture notes on optics into a textbook. The ultimate success of this textbook, published in 1933, led Born to observe that one did not need to be a specialist to be a success. In fact, Born was proud of the fact that he was "always a dilettante." His life's work, which encompasses solid-state physics, atomic physics, optics, relativity, kinetic theory of liquids, nuclear physics, and the philosophy of science, speaks to the truth of this self-assessment. In this regard Max Born is perhaps unique among the company of the great physicists of this century.

Having been forced out of Germany in 1933 by the rise of Nazism, Born settled first in Cambridge and then in Scotland. He stayed in Scotland until his retirement. During this period he wrote many books, some popular science, some from a philosophic point of view, and some in physics. In this latter category, most note should be taken of his textbooks, *Atomic Physics* (1935), *A General Kinetic Theory of Liquids* (1949), and *Dynamical Theory of Crystal Lattices* (1954). He also kept busy in various research fields noting that "as usual, I changed from one field to another." More than most prominent physicists, Born was interested in a wide variety of nontechnical subjects. Consequently, he has extensive writings in the areas of philosophy of science, history of science, and general social concerns. Two notable books containing his writings in these areas are *Physics in My Generation* (1956, 1968) and *My Life and My Views* (1968). The first two chapters of the latter work contain a biographical sketch which is reproduced from the September and October, 1965, issues of the *Bulletin of Atomic Scientists*. Also noteworthy is his autobiography, *Mein Leben: Die Errinerungen des Nobelpreisträgers* (1975; *My Life: Recollections of a Nobel Laureate*, 1978), which provides great insight into the people and events which produced what is now called modern physics. Finally, the extensive correspondence between Born and Einstein, which covered the period 1920 to 1950, can be found in *The Born-Einstein Letters* (1971).

Upon retirement, Born returned to Germany, a move he notes that many of his friends, notably Einstein, resented. Owing to the time available to him in retirement as well as the general recognition brought to him by the Nobel Prize, Born turned his interests to a concern for the dangers of the nuclear age. He notes that, unlike almost all the other great emigrant physicists of the time, he never became involved with the development of the atom bomb. He implausibly attributes this lack of participation not to personal virtue but rather to the fact that his teacher in nuclear physics, Johannes Stark (1874-1957), was so bad "that I never learned nuclear physics properly and could not take part in its development," although he admits that the one paper he wrote in this area was "not bad." He was one of the first signers of the petition eventually signed by fifty-one Nobel Prize winners condemning the development of atomic weapons. Though he wrote and spoke brilliantly on the need of scientists to be responsible for the implications of their work, in the end he was apparently quite pessimistic with regard to the ability of society to deal with the creations of science: "Should the race not be extinguished by a nuclear war," he would be quoted as saying, "it will degenerate into a flock of stupid, dumb creatures under the tyranny of dictators who rule them with the help of machines and electronic computers."

Born considered himself to be a second-tier physicist, behind such notables as Einstein, Bohr, and Heisenberg. His writings also show that he felt intimidated by lesser notables, such as Wolfgang Pauli (1900-1958), J. Robert Oppenheimer (1904-1967), and Hans Bethe (born 1906). Perhaps because of this attitude, Born was always self-effacing in his speech and writings. As a result, he has not received proper credit for his personal contributions to the development of modern physics and, even more important, his contributions as a teacher, director, collaborator and organizer of all those who were led and inspired by him, men who would go on to restructure twentieth century physics.

Bibliography

Primary

PHYSICS: *Untersuchungen über die stabilität der elastischen Linie in Ebene und Raum, unter verschiedenen Grenzbedingungen*, 1906; *Zur Variationsrechnung*, 1906; *Dynamik der Kirstallgitter*, 1915 (*Dynamical Theory of Crystal Lattices*, 1954); *Die Relativitätstheorie Einsteins und ihre physikalischen grundlagen gemeinverstänlich dargestellt*, 1920 (*Einstein's Theory of Relativity*, 1922); *Die Aufbau der Materie: Dreis aufsätze über moderne atomistik und elektronentheorie*,

1920 (*The Constitution of Matter: Modern Atomic and Electron Theories*, 1923); *Atomtheorie des festen Zustandes (Dynamik der Kristallgitter)*, 1923; *Vorlesungen über Atommechanik*, 1925; *Zur Quantenmechanik*, 1925 (*Sources of Quantum Mechanics*, 1967); *Physical Aspects of Quantum Mechanics*, 1926; *Probleme der Atomdynamik*, 1926 (*Problems of Atomic Dynamics*, 1926); *The Mechanics of the Atom*, 1927; *Elementare Quantenmechanik*, 1930; *Chemische Bindung und Quantenmechanick*, 1931; *Moderne Physik: Sieben Vorträge über Materie und Strahlung*, 1933; *Optik: Ein Lehrbuch der elektromagnetischen Lichttheorie*, 1933; *Atomic Physics*, 1935; *The Restless Universe*, 1936; *Experiment and Theory in Physics*, 1943; *Atomic Energy and Its Use in War and Peace*, 1947; *Natural Philosophy of Cause and Chance*, 1948; *A General Kinetic Theory of Liquids*, 1949; *Continuity, Determinism, and Reality*, 1955; *Physics in My Generation: A Selection of Papers*, 1956; *Physik im Wandel meiner Zeit*, 1957; *Der Realitätsbegriff in der Physik*, 1958; *Principles of Optics: Electromagnetic Theory of Propagation, Interference, and Diffraction of Light*, 1959; *The Mechanics of the Atom*, 1960; *Zur Statistischen Deutung der Quantentheorie*, 1962; *Zur Begründung der Matrizenmechanik*, 1962; *Ausgewählte Abhandlungen, mit einem Verzeichnis der wissenschaftlichen Schriften*, 1963; *Von der Verantwortung des Naturwissenschaftlers*, 1965; *Naturwissenschaft heute*, 1965; *Atomtheorie des festen Zustandes (Dynamik der Krystallgitter)*, 1972.

OTHER NONFICTION: *Wo stehen wir heute?*, 1960; *Physik und Politik*, 1960 (*Physics and Politics*, 1962); *My Life and My Views*, 1968; *Ausblick auf die Zukunft*, 1968; *Errinerungen an Einstein*, 1969; *Der Luxus des Gewissens: Erlebnisse und Einsichten im Atomzeitalter*, 1969; *The Born-Einstein Letters*, 1971; *Mein Leben: Die Erinnergungen des Nobelpreisträgers*, 1975 (*My Life: Recollections of a Nobel Laureate*, 1978).

Secondary

Cline, Barbara Loveti. *The Questioners: Physicists and the Quantum Theory*. New York: Thomas Y. Crowell, 1965. A popular introduction to the history of the development of quantum mechanics, nonmathematical and interesting to read. Cline concentrates most of the discussion on the "major players": Einstein, Bohr, and Heisenberg. As a result, the book does not do full justice to Born's contribution (the fact that he formulated the statistical interpretation is relegated to a footnote).

Cropper, William H. *The Quantum Physicists and an Introduction to Their Physics*. New York: Oxford University Press, 1970. This extremely well-written book is meant to serve as a textbook. As such, parts of its are heavily mathematical, but the author's style is so illuminating that the text can be read and appreciated without an understanding of the mathematics. The volume also includes sections devoted to the primary individuals who helped the theory, including Born.

Dugas, Rene. *A History of Mechanics*. New York: Dover, 1988. Intended for the scholar who is a nonspecialist, the presentation is mathematical but not prohibitively so. Dugas carefully distinguishes between the different formulations of quantum mechanics and traces with great detail the ways in which various individuals contributed to the development of quantum mechanics. The treatment of Born is both accurate and fair.

Jammer, Max. *The Conceptual Development of Quantum Mechanics*. New York: McGraw-Hill, 1966. Jammer's is the most respected treatment of the topic. While the book deals with all the individuals who took part in this effort, it spends almost fifty pages on Max Born. Although mathematics is used in the discussions, it does not play a major role. The book, however, is scholarly in tone and does not lend itself to light reading.

March, Robert H. *Physics for Poets*. New York: McGraw-Hill, 1970. A general textbook, written for the nonscientist, containing extensive historical material and emphasizing twentieth century developments in physics. The author's approach is to display the creation of a physical theory as if it were the production of a work of art. The book's biggest drawback is that it deals almost exclusively with the Schrödinger formulation of quantum mechanics. Given this limitation, it does give an excellent introduction to this formulation and, in particular, discusses at length the statistical interpretation of Born.

Carl G. Adler

1954

Physics
Max Born, Great Britain
Walther Bothe, West Germany

Chemistry
Linus Pauling, United States

Physiology or Medicine
John F. Enders, United States
Thomas H. Weller, United States
Frederick Robbins, United States

Literature
Ernest Hemingway, United States

Peace
Office of the U. N. High Commissioner for Refugees

WALTHER BOTHE
1954

Born: Oranienburg, Germany; January 8, 1891
Died: Heidelberg, West Germany; February 8, 1957
Nationality: West German
Areas of concentration: Particle physics and nuclear energy

Bothe developed coincidence counting techniques and used them to study the collisions of photons and electrons. He then showed that energy and momentum are conserved in each collision, contrary to what some had supposed

The Award

Presentation

The presentation ceremony was held in Stockholm on December 10, 1954. Although Bothe was among those honored, he was unable to attend because of recent surgery. The presentation speech was made by Professor I. Waller, a member of the Nobel Committee for Physics.

Waller described Bothe's coincidence counting technique, which employed two counter tubes. The counter tubes were thin-walled cylinders fitted with electrodes and other devices. They were so constructed that if an electron or an X ray passed through a tube, the tube produced an electrical signal. Bothe fitted the tubes with a recording mechanism and then looked for events in which both tubes gave signals simultaneously. Using his coincidence counting technique, Bothe was able to show that each time a photon (a small particle of light) collided with an electron, both energy and momentum were conserved; that is, both the total energy and the total momentum had the same value before the collision as they did after the collision. This result was unexpected by some scientists and is of fundamental importance.

Later, Bothe applied his technique to the study of cosmic rays. By placing an absorber between two counting tubes, and by requiring signals from the tubes to be in coincidence, he was able to study the penetration power of cosmic rays. Among other things, he learned that at sea level, cosmic rays consist of at least some particles with enormous penetration power. Bothe's coincidence method would become very widely used in the study of nuclear reactions and cosmic rays.

Nobel lecture

Because of his convalescence, Bothe was unable to present his lecture orally, although he did submit it to the Nobel Foundation. Bothe began by acknowledging the efforts of his teachers, Max Planck (1858-1947) and Hans Geiger (1882-1945).

In 1924, Niels Bohr (1885-1962) and some coworkers had published a paper about the dual wave-particle nature of light. They sought to reconcile the wave nature and the particle nature of light by suggesting that photons (light "particles") do not behave like normal particles. Instead, Bohr and Planck proposed that features such as conservation of momentum and energy belonged not to individual photons, but only in some average fashion to large groups of them traveling in waves.

Prior to this time, Arthur Holly Compton (1892-1962) had successfully explained the Compton effect by assuming that energy and momentum were conserved in each individual collision. (In the Compton effect, a high-energy photon collides with an electron, losing momentum and energy to it. The "recoil" electron then flies off with more energy, while the "scattered" photon leaves with less energy.) Compton's work did not, however, preclude Bohr's new theory.

In order to decide the issue, Bothe and Geiger conducted an experiment which showed that the recoil electron and the scattered photon left the target within less than one ten-thousandth of a second of each other. They concluded that Compton was correct and that Bohr's latest theory was not.

Bothe next described how he and Werner Kolhörster (1887-1946) used the coincidence method to study high-energy cosmic rays. Because of their great penetrating power, it had previously been assumed that they were gamma rays (similar to X rays but with higher energy). In 1929, Bothe and Kolhörster placed two counter tubes so that one was above the other. By placing various amounts of absorbing material above the tubes and also between them, they were able to show that cosmic rays had the properties expected of particles, but not of gamma rays. Bothe's coincidence technique was used to determine when a particle penetrated the absorbers and both counter tubes. Bothe concluded with a brief discussion of the use of his method in other areas of nuclear physics.

Critical reception

Notice of Bothe's award was printed in *The New York Times* (December 11, 1954). It announced that he shared the prize with Max Born (1882-1970) but that Bothe had been unable to attend the ceremony because of the amputation of his leg. It stated that the award was for his coincidence method, which it called a method of measuring time with extreme accuracy. A more correct statement would be that it allows one to determine if two events occur within a very short time of each other; it usually does not measure the actual time between the events.

A similar brief notice in *Scientific American* noted that Bothe's coincidence method had become a universal technique in physics. *Science News Letter* (November 13, 1954) gave a few more details about Bothe's work. It republished a short article from *Science News Letter* (March 12, 1932) which described Bothe's work showing that cosmic rays were particles and not gamma rays.

Time magazine (November 15, 1954) carried the usual announcement and then added that Bothe was active in Germany's World War II attempt to build the atom bomb. It is only in this area where any controversy over Bothe's prize might have arisen. *Newsweek* (November 15, 1954) headlined the Nobel Prize article "timeless honor," a reference to the advanced ages of Born (seventy-two) and Bothe (sixty-three) and that they were being honored for work done a quarter of a century before. Bothe was described as relatively unknown to the public but well-known among physicists, who recognize his nuclear research experiments as "very beauti-ful," a reference to how Bothe conducted his scientific research: When confronted with various experiments which might be done, or various theories which might be correct, the most successful scientists are guided in their selection by an intuitive sense of beauty, elegance, and simplicity.

Newsweek mentioned Bothe's coincidence method, as well as the fact that he had barely missed discovering the neutron. Explaining that Bothe had completed Germany's first cyclotron (a machine for accelerating particles such as protons) in 1944, the writer noted that "Dr. Bothe was a key adviser, but no promoter, of confused Nazi wartime attempts to make an atomic bomb." In fact, however, Bothe was not a Nazi supporter, and it is thought that he may have actively undermined the German atom bomb project.

Biography

Walther Wilhelm Georg Bothe was born at Oranienburg, Germany, January 8, 1891. He was the son of Fritz (a merchant) and Charlotte Bothe. Bothe studied physics, chemistry, and mathematics at the University of Berlin. As a graduate student, he became one of the few ever to study under the famous Max Planck. After obtaining his doctorate in 1914, he began to work for Geiger in the radioactivity laboratory of the Physikalische-Technische Reichsanstalt (physical-technical institute).

World War I soon intervened, and Bothe became a machine-gunner in the German army. Captured by the Russians in 1915, he spent the next five years as a prisoner of war in Siberia. While there, he was able to continue his studies in mathematics and physics as well as learn Russian. He married a Russian, Barbara Below, in 1920 and returned to the Reichsanstalt in Berlin. The couple would have two daughters. His wife died in 1951.

Bothe accepted a professorship in physics at the University of Giessen in 1930. From there, he went to Heidelberg, directing the Physics Institute at the university from 1932 to 1934. Then, in 1934, he was named director of the Physics Institute of the Kaiser Wilhelm (later named Max Planck) Institute for Medical Research at Heidelberg. In 1945, he resumed his professorship at the University of Heidelberg and remained there until his death in 1957.

Bothe devoted the same intensity to his hobbies that he gave to his scientific studies. He was an excellent pianist and took special pleasure in playing the works of Johann Sebastian Bach and Ludwig van Beethoven. On holidays he liked to go to the mountains and paint, and he produced professional-looking oils and watercolors.

In addition to the Nobel Prize (1954), Bothe was decorated a Knight of the Order of Merit for Science and Arts (1952), received the Max Planck Medal (1953), and was awarded the Grand Cross of the Order for Federal Services of Germany (1954).

Scientific Career

Bothe's early work tended toward the theoretical side of physics. His doctoral thesis had been an attempt to explain reflection, refraction (bending), dispersion (separation into colors), and absorption in terms of interactions between light and molecules. In 1921, he published an important paper on a theory of refraction. Then his interest shifted to the scattering of alpha particles (helium nuclei) and beta particles (electrons). Bothe examined the case of an electron beam passing through a thin metal foil. Using statistics, he predicted what would most likely happen to the electrons as their paths changed during many close encounters with the atoms of the foil.

In 1924 Bothe and Geiger collaborated in an experiment of fundamental importance. Compton had treated the case (known as the Compton effect) wherein light impinges on an electron with the result that the electron recoils in one direction while the light scatters in a different direction with lowered energy. Compton treated the light as if it were composed of discrete bundles of energy called photons. The Compton effect thus joined the photoelectric effect (where photons can eject electrons from certain metals) as evidence that light can manifest a particle nature. It was unclear which features of the atom exhibited wavelike behavior and which acted like particles. Maybe the particles traveled in waves. If so, did they all work together and average out to the expected results? Bohr and others had formulated a new quantum theory, which predicted that energy and momentum were conserved only on the average as matter and light interacted.

Bothe and Geiger decided on a test. If energy and momentum are conserved each time an incident photon strikes an electron, then a recoil electron must always accompany a scattered photon. If Bohr's new theory were correct, light waves could be shined on target atoms, which would then absorb energy from the waves. From time to time, this energy would flow from various parts of the target to be concentrated in an individual recoil electron. Since the recoil electron had not gained its energy from a particular photon, it would not be specifically related to any particular scattered photon.

Instead of light, Bothe and Geiger used the higher-energy photons of an X-ray beam. The X rays struck the gas inside a counter tube. The tube was connected to a pointer that moved when a recoil electron was detected. A second counter tube was placed beside the first, with the hope that it would detect the scattered photon. If it did, its pointer also moved. Both pointers were continuously photographed on film moving through a camera at about ten meters per minute. Many hundreds of meters of film had to be developed, hung from the ceiling to dry, and then painstakingly inspected.

Bothe and Geiger were able to show that the tubes did indeed record coincident events, two events occurring at essentially the same time. The conclusion was that the recoil electron and the scattered photon were produced simultaneously, and hence, Bohr's new theory was wrong. In fact, energy and momentum were conserved in individual collisions. The coincidence method pioneered by Bothe went on to become a standard technique in nuclear physics.

In 1926, Bothe joined many other physicists of the day in studying radioactivity.

Heavy elements such as radium and uranium were known to emit alpha particles. These particles were allowed to strike targets of carbon, boron, or some other light element. Bothe was keenly interested in any radiation which the target might now emit, hoping that it would give him some insight into the structure of the atomic nucleus. Some of these reactions emitted protons, and Bothe was among the first to use electronic counters to detect them. In 1930, Bothe and H. Becker studied the radiation from a beryllium target. They found it to be surprisingly penetrating and assumed that it consisted of high-energy gamma rays. Not long after this, in 1932, Sir James Chadwick (1891-1974) showed that this radiation must consist of neutral particles, which he named neutrons.

At about the same time that he was working with beryllium, Bothe worked with Kolhörster in analyzing cosmic rays. Using Bothe's coincidence method, they placed one counter tube above a second counter tube and placed absorbing material between the tubes. If both tubes signaled a count at the same time, it was assumed that a single cosmic ray had gone through both tubes and had not been trapped in the absorber. Somewhat to their surprise, their results were not those expected from high-energy gamma rays. Instead, their experiments implied that cosmic rays are charged particles. Bothe pointed out that in order to penetrate Earth's atmosphere, the particles would need to have an energy equivalent to that when accelerated through a thousand million volts. Since this was a thousand times more energy than any process known then could produce, Bothe's was a very radical suggestion. History, however, has shown it to be correct.

During the 1930's, Bothe continued his studies of multiple scattering of electrons and began similar studies with neutrons. An article by him on both the experimental and the theoretical aspects of scattering appears in the 1933 edition of the *Handbuch der Physik*. In 1935, Bothe devised a simplified system of notation for nuclear reactions which would become widely used. He also studied the effects of high-energy gamma rays impinging on various nuclei. It was also during the 1930's, however, that the Nazis came to power. Part of the Nazi doctrine was that Einstein's theory of relativity, as well as the new theories of atomic structure (quantum mechanics), could not possibly be correct, since they had been fabricated by Jews. Scientists, such as Bothe, who continued to accept these theories were suspect. One of the few first-rate scientists to become an ardent Nazi was Philipp Lenard (1862-1947), at the University of Heidelberg. He gathered like-minded people around him, making the university a Nazi stronghold by the time he retired in 1931.

In 1932, Bothe was selected as Lenard's replacement, but increased Nazi influence resulted in his losing his professorship in 1934. It was then that he moved to the more politically comfortable Kaiser Wilhelm Institute. As the Nazi stranglehold tightened, many of the scientists left the country. Werner Heisenberg (1901-1976), one of the leading young physicists, went to Bothe's old teacher, Max Planck, asking if he and others should resign their positions. Planck advised against it. He said that an avalanche could not be influenced and that the most useful thing they could do would be to form islands of stability wherever they could. Perhaps he gave the same advice to Bothe, for that seems to be the course Bothe followed.

Bothe and Heisenberg were both patriotic Germans, although neither was sympathetic to the Nazis. By 1939, however, they had become two of the chief scientists in the German atom bomb project.

The Germans recognized two possible pathways to the atom bomb. The first way involved the separation of isotopes. Different kinds of the same element, which differ only in their weight, are called isotopes. The common isotope of uranium is number 238, but it does not explode well in a bomb. The isotope which does explode well is uranium 235, but natural uranium is only about 0.7 percent uranium 235. It is difficult to separate the two isotopes. After several attempts, the German scientists decided to concentrate their resources on a different method. If slow neutrons are collided with a uranium target, the uranium 238 will absorb a neutron and eventually become plutonium 239. Plutonium 239 works just as well as uranium 235 in a bomb, and since uranium and plutonium are different elements, they can be separated chemically. This is the route the Germans decided to take to the bomb. (The Americans developed both methods, not knowing in advance which one would work.)

In order to produce plutonium, one needs a reactor. The reactor must have appropriate shielding, cooling, controls, uranium fuel, and a moderator. When struck by a fast neutron, a uranium nucleus flies apart into fast neutrons, energy, and assorted radioactive substances. The purpose of the moderator is to slow down the fast neutrons. The Germans decided to use heavy water as a moderator. Heavy water is made from oxygen and heavy hydrogen, hydrogen atoms with a neutron as well as a proton in the nucleus. Heavy water is a great moderator, but it is hard to get.

The Americans used a graphite moderator. A good moderator must slow the neutrons but not absorb too many of them. In June of 1940, Bothe measured the absorption of neutrons in graphite. It seemed almost good enough to use, and he thought that a purer sample would show that it would make a good moderator. In January of 1941, Bothe made new measurements on supposedly very pure graphite. The results were worse than before, and graphite seemed clearly unsuitable. Because of Bothe's excellent reputation, no one rechecked his measurements.

Since the Allies continually sabotaged German efforts to obtain sufficient heavy water, Bothe's mistake proved to be enough to keep Germany from developing the bomb during World War II. The English made a similar mistake, but found that the error resulted from impurities. Because Bothe was such a meticulous experimenter, it is curious that he did not catch his mistake. Some have supposed that he allowed the mistake to stand because it would slow the effort to make the bomb. Bothe himself never explained it.

Another reason that the Germans did not develop the bomb was their belief that it would take too long. They expected to have won the war before an atom bomb could be produced. As it became clearer that Germany would lose the war, the scientists pushed research on nuclear reactors, hoping that the reactors would be a great aid in rebuilding Germany. Finally, the German scientists favored pure research rather than weapons research.

Bothe began work on a cyclotron in the late 1930's but was unable to complete it until 1944. (A cyclotron can produce beams of neutrons or other particles. Scientists can then study the effect of neutrons on uranium or some other target material.) After the fall of Paris to the Germans, and before his own cyclotron was working, Bothe visited Paris to use the cyclotron of Frédéric Joliot (1900-1958). The Allies were not aware of the German scientists' lack of enthusiasm for the bomb. There was a gentlemen's agreement that no research of military value would be done. Bothe did not consider himself bound by that agreement and insisted on making measurements on uranium. For some mysterious reason, the cyclotron overheated and shut down each time Bothe made the attempt, so that he obtained little useful data. (It later emerged that Joliot's chief mechanic was shutting off the cooling water.)

After the war, Bothe used the cyclotron he had constructed at Heidelberg for medical studies. He continued his work with cosmic rays and was senior author of *Nuclear Physics and Cosmic Rays* (1948), as well as many scientific articles. In 1940, Bothe coauthored along with Wolfgang Gentner and Heinz Maier-Leibnitz, *Atlas typischer Nebelkammerbilder*. In 1954 it was published as *An Atlas of Typical Expansion Chamber Photographs* with text in English, French, and German.

Bibliography

Primary

PHYSICS: "Ein Weg zur experimentellen Nachprüfung der Theorie von Bohr, Kramers, und Slater," *Zeitschrift für Physik*, vol. 26, 1924 (with Hans W. Geiger); "Über das Wesen des Comptoneffekts: Ein experimenteller Beitrag zur Theorie der Strahlung," *Zeitschrift für Physik*, vol. 32, 1925 (with Geiger); "Das Wesen der Höhenstrahlung," *Zeitschrift für Physik*, vol. 56, 1929 (with Werner Kolhörster); "Künstliche Erregung von Kern-γ-Strahlen," *Zeitschrift für Physik*, vol. 66, 1930 (with Heinrich Becker); *Atlas typischer Nebelkammerbilder*, 1940 (with Wolfgang Gentner and Heinz Maier-Leibnitz; *An Atlas of Typical Expansion Chamber Photographs*, 1954); *Nuclear Physics and Cosmic Rays*, 1948 (with others).

Secondary

Beyerchen, Alan D. *Scientists Under Hitler: Politics and the Physics Community in the Third Reich*. New Haven, Conn.: Yale University Press, 1977. This excellent work describes the political involvement (or noninvolvement) of many of Germany's top scientists. Nobel Prize winners become public figures and are often pressured into some kind of political action. Among the Nobel laureates discussed are Born, Bothe, Einstein, Franck, Heisenberg, Hertz, Lenard, Planck, Schrödinger, and Stark.

Born, Max. *Atomic Physics*. 7th ed. New York: Hafner Press, 1963. This classic work is written by one of the individuals who played a key role in founding the field of atomic physics. It discusses Bothe's work within this context. Although much of the work is quite technical, the author uses a historical approach.

Goudsmit, Samuel A. *Alsos*. New York: Henry Schuman, 1947. Reprint, Los Angeles: Tomash, 1983. Alsos was the code name for the intelligence mission to discover the status of the German atom bomb project. The book includes Goudsmit's interview and appraisal of Bothe at the war's end. The reader should be cautioned that Heisenberg believed that Goudsmit undervalued the German achievements. Keeping this in mind, the book is quite useful.

Irving, David. *The German Atomic Bomb*. New York: Simon & Schuster, 1967. A fascinating account which details Bothe's work on the project from its start to its finish. Irving shows how the allies sabotaged German efforts to procure heavy water and explores other reasons for the lack of success of the German project. Highly recommended.

Jammer, Max. *The Conceptual Development of Quantum Mechanics*. New York: McGraw-Hill, 1966. This work is similar to the one cited above by Born. While it is more historical and less technical than Born's work, it still requires a strong scientific background.

Rhodes, Richard. *The Making of the Atomic Bomb*. New York: Simon & Schuster, 1986. The most comprehensive book on the subject which is readily accessible to the lay reader. It includes references to Bothe from his production of neutrons in 1930 to his completion of Germany's first cyclotron in 1944.

Weart, Spencer R. *Scientists in Power*. Cambridge, Mass.: Harvard University Press, 1979. Weart describes the French World War II atom bomb project and follows its postwar development to the first plutonium production in 1949. He discusses Bothe's use of the French cyclotron as well as Bothe's error in measuring the absorption of neutrons by carbon. For the layman.

Charles W. Rogers

1955

Physics
Willis Eugene Lamb, Jr., United States
Polykarp Kusch, United States

Chemistry
Vincent Du Vigneaud, United States

Physiology or Medicine
Axel Hugo Theorell, Sweden

Literature
Halldór Laxness, Iceland

Peace
no award

WILLIS EUGENE LAMB, JR.
1955

Born: Los Angeles, California; July 12, 1913

Nationality: American
Area of concentration: Quantum electrodynamics

Lamb's discovery of the Lambshift provided a greater understanding of the structure of the hydrogen spectrum. Applying radio-frequency spectroscopy, Lamb was able to isolate an important trait of the hydrogen atom, thereby contributing to the reevalation and improvement of the theory of electrons and electromagnetic radiation

The Award

Presentation

Professor Ivar Waller, a member of the Nobel Committee for Physics, presented the Nobel Prize in Physics to Willis Eugene Lamb, Jr., and Polykarp Kusch on December 10, 1955, on behalf of the Royal Swedish Academy of Sciences and King Gustav VI. Lamb and Kusch, joint winners, each accepted a gold medal and roughly $18,000 in prize money.

Waller began his speech by noting that when Lamb had worked at the Radiation Laboratory of Columbia University, he had studied the spectra of the atom with radio waves. He had helped to outline (as did Kusch) how physicists could better understand the details of the structure and behavior of the atom. The fundamental research for this type of project had been done by Isidor Isaac Rabi (born 1902), who had won the Nobel Prize in Physics in 1944.

Lamb had studied the hydrogen atom, wherein a single electron moves around the nucleus in a series of orbits, each having a definite level of energy. These energy levels exhibit a fine structure; that is, they are arranged in groups of neighboring levels which are widely separated. It was for a reinterpretation of the explanation of this fine structure that Lamb was being honored.

In 1928, the English physicist Paul Adrien Maurice Dirac (1902-1984), a pioneer in the theory of quantum mechanics and the study of the atom, proposed a theory of the electron based on the requirements of the theory of relativity and quantum mechanics, then-new components of physics. From 1928 on, many physicists around the world attempted to check the Dirac theory of fine structure, without much success. Early evidence suggested that (as Lamb would later prove) the fine structure was not constant; there were deviations.

To study hydrogen's fine structure, Lamb used optical methods that had been developed at Columbia as part of radar research during World War II. These methods were based on Rabi's resonance technique, which Lamb modified. Lamb, said Waller, was an ideal scientist, because he could convert his theoretical knowledge into experimental success. In 1947, he found two fine structure levels in the next lowest group which should coincide, according to the Dirac theory, but in reality were shifted by a certain amount, appropriately labeled the "Lambshift." Lamb measured the shift with great accuracy and later made similar measurements of heavy hydrogen.

Although this finding seemed of little account, it had far-reaching effects. Lamb's discovery resulted in the reshaping of the theory of quantum electrodynamics.

Nobel lecture

Lamb's Nobel lecture, entitled "Fine Structure of the Hydrogen Atom," was a brilliant summary of the research that had led to his most important breakthrough. Experiments on the hydrogen atom, which is the union of the first known elementary particles, the electron and the proton, and the understanding of its spectrum taught the world much about the structure of all atoms. Lamb reviewed the history of the study of the spectrum of the hydrogen atom. In 1928, Dirac had postulated an equation that described an electron with wave properties and with a charge and mass as required by relativity theory. The energy levels of hydrogen were predicted by Dirac's formula with a high degree of precision.

Lamb then cited the influence of his teacher at the University of California at Berkeley, J. Robert Oppenheimer (1904-1967), an expert in quantum mechanics and the father of the atom bomb, and his mentor, Rabi, for teaching him the principles which had led to his developing the prizewinning experiment. He said that his work at the wartime laboratory at Columbia University Radiation Laboratory had been crucial. Although he was inspired to do the experiment by a class he taught, it took a year for the problem to come clear in his mind. He was then able, with the help of his graduate student Robert C. Retherford, to construct an apparatus (including a tungsten oven) with which to conduct the experiment. In his speech, he described the specifics of the experimental techniques and their theoretical foundation.

The final part of Lamb's lecture was concerned with the explanations that, up to 1955, had been developed to explain the Lambshift. In 1947, Hans Albrecht Bethe (born 1906), a German-born scientist who had emigrated to the United States, found that Dirac's theory of quantum electrodynamics had, hidden behind its divergences, a physical content which was in very close agreement with the results of Lamb's experiments. Bethe's new construction required a reinterpretation of the theory of mass and time as well.

As of 1955, Lamb remarked, much remained to be done. He ended his lecture by stating that it was "very important that this problem should receive further experimental and theoretical attention."

Critical reception

The immediate reaction to the awarding of the prize to Lamb was favorable. *The New York Times* (November 3, 1955) declared that he had won for "work in connection with atomic measurements." The newspaper, echoing accounts from across the United States, noted that Paul Dirac had won his Nobel Prize in Physics in 1933 for his creation of a basic theory and that Lamb had "corrected an error" made by Dirac. The press declared that Lamb had made an important contribution by properly calculating what actually occurs inside an atom.

It was noted that Kusch and Lamb shared the prize because they had independently attacked the same problem from different angles, both proving that Dirac's theories were invalid when confronted with certain experimental evidence. The theory known as "Dirac wave mechanics" had furnished directly a numerical value for the magnetic property of an electron. Lamb had uncovered errors of about one one-thousandth of the effect measured in Dirac's formula.

As early as 1947, accounts noted, Lamb's fellow physicists had recognized the importance of the Lambshift. In 1953, Norman F. Ramsey of Harvard had declared Lamb's experiments as among the most significant of the postwar era. I. I. Rabi had gone further and told *Newsweek* in 1947 that they represented "the most significant advance in fifteen years in the knowledge of the atom."

Lamb himself, it was reported in *The New York Times*, was nonplussed and went back to sleep for two hours after learning the news on the West Coast early in the morning. The first Nobel Prize ever won by a Stanford faculty member in residence had gone in 1952 to Felix Bloch, for physics. Lamb's award, even though given for work done at Columbia, was seen as an indication of the rise of a new, important physics department.

The New York Herald Tribune (November 4) summarized the nation's pride when it hailed Lamb's Nobel award as "fresh evidence of this nation's leadership in scientific development," and editorialized that "to the men who received it [including Lamb], it represents a culmination of years of research and study; to the rest of us, it signifies science's ever forward search for data and understanding that can be put to humanity's benefit." Looking back in 1977, on Lamb's sixty-fifth birthday, Freeman Dyson of the Institute for Advanced Study, Princeton, New Jersey, wrote, "You and Fermi [Enrico Fermi, the physics laureate for 1938] were the only physicists I have known who stood in the top rank both as theorists and experimenters."

Biography

Willis Eugene Lamb, Jr., was born in Los Angeles, California, on July 12, 1913, the son of Willis Eugene Lamb, born in Minnesota, and Marie Helen Metcalf Lamb, from Nebraska. His father worked as an electrical engineer with the Southern California Telephone Company, and his mother, a graduate of Stanford University, was a schoolteacher. Reared in Los Angeles (save for three years in Oakland, California), the young Lamb attended the local elementary schools and Los Angeles High School, where he was an enthusiastic student of chemistry. In 1930 he journeyed north to the University of California at Berkeley. There, he chose chemistry as his major and was graduated with a bachelor of science degree in 1934. He was a member of Phi Beta Kappa and Sigma Xi.

The physics courses he took as an undergraduate whetted his interest, and like many who were graduated in the middle of the Great Depression, Lamb decided to stay in school. He moved to the physics department at Berkeley and became a protégé of J. Robert Oppenheimer. Lamb stayed only the required four years, and on receiving his doctorate in 1938, he accepted a position at Columbia University, in New York City, as an instructor. At Columbia he quickly moved up through the ranks, becoming a research associate in 1943, an assistant professor in 1945, an associate professor in 1947, and a full professor in 1948. On June 5, 1939, he wed Ursula Schaefer, a history professor who taught at Barnard College (then the women's college of Columbia University) until 1951.

The work Lamb did at Columbia and its Radiation Laboratory was financed by the United States Army Signal Corps and the Office of Naval Research. From 1943 to 1946, he was engaged in research on radar and microwaves for the United States Office of Scientific Research and Development. At the end of World War II, Lamb returned to his peacetime researches at Columbia, and it was there he and his graduate student Robert C. Retherford built the device that would lead to the discovery of the Lambshift.

In 1951, Lamb moved west to his mother's alma mater, Stanford University, to become a professor of physics. During 1953 and 1954, he was Loeb Lecturer in Physics at Harvard University. In the years immediately prior to receiving the Nobel Prize, he won the Rumford Award of the American Academy of Arts and Sciences, was granted an honorary degree from the University of Pennsylvania, was elected to the National Academy of Sciences, and became a fellow of the American Physical Society. In 1960 he would receive a Guggenheim Fellowship.

In 1956, Lamb became Wykeham Professor of Physics and a Fellow of New College at the University of Oxford. In 1962 he moved to New Haven and became the Henry Ford II Professor of Physics at Yale. In 1974 he made another move to become a professor of physics and optical sciences at the University of Arizona, Tucson.

Scientific Career

Lamb's graduate work at the University of California at Berkeley was concerned with Charles-Augustin de Coulomb's law of electric fields and the relationships of charges. That was the type of research he conducted at Columbia. Several papers which he delivered during these early days of his career were at the time considered relatively unimportant; they would later, however, provide the means for calculating the correction for the induced magnetic field that was later hailed for changing the field of quantum electrodynamics.

Quantum electrodynamics is the fundamental theory of electromagnetic interactions. Its equations provide an explanation in precise mathematical terms of the interactions of electrons, muons, and protons—the quanta of the electromagnetic field. By extension, then, quantum electrodynamics (QED, to its theorists) offers the underlying theory of all electromagnetic phenomena, including atomic and chemical forces. Indeed, it seems, in part because of the famous Lamb experiments, that QED must be regarded as part of a more comprehensive theory unifying all the forces in the universe.

Despite the apparent correctness of Paul Dirac's hypotheses as to the basic structure of the interaction between the photon and the electron, and the elegance of the equations, there was a central problem in QED. This problem reflected the theory's "self-energy" corrections. For example, calculating the energy shift of a free electron caused by its emission and subsequent reabsorption of a single photon yielded an infinite number. Progress on this problem came only because of the extraordinary work performed by Lamb and his graduate students at Columbia.

The World War II years provided Lamb's introduction to experimental work. After 1945, he combined theory and practice in a set of famous experiments. Specifically, he began to test some of the hypotheses about the atomic hydrogen spectrum which he had first formulated before the war. After four attempts to construct an apparatus which would test the theories, Lamb and Retherford built a machine of glass tubes, copper wave guides, magnets, and an oven. It was known that the outside forces, when in contact with the hydrogen atom, could cause it to change the position of a single electron. By focusing the microwaves (excellent for emitting small quantities of energy) on a beam of hydrogen atoms, Lamb showed that the two levels of energy for the electron were not equal, as Dirac had theorized, but differed by a very small amount. The Lambshift required a revision of the theory of the interaction of the electron with electromagnetic radiation.

This experiment had its origins in much of Lamb's training. Lamb had studied theoretical physics with J. Robert Oppenheimer at the University of California at Berkeley from 1934 to 1938. His thesis under Oppenheimer dealt with field theories of the electromagnetic properties of nuclear systems. At Columbia after 1938, Lamb came into close association with I. I. Rabi and members of the Radiation Laboratory. His attention was drawn briefly to testing beams, and during the war he received some firsthand experience with microwave radar and the construction of vacuum tubes. One of the wartime projects was the determination of the absorption of waves in water vapor, and that spurred Lamb's postwar interest in microwave spectroscopy.

The precise inspiration for the famous experiment came while Lamb was teaching a summer-school class in atomic physics in 1945. He happened to read about some attempts made in the early 1930's to detect the absorption of shortwave radio waves in a gas discharge of atomic hydrogen, and he thought of repeating them with some greatly improved measurement apparatus developed at Columbia during World War II. His initial trials failed; it took a year of concentrated mental activity before he would find a solution.

Ultimately, with Retherford, Lamb devised an experimental apparatus in which molecular hydrogen was dissociated in a tungsten oven and a stream of hydrogen atoms emerged from a slit to be bombarded by electrons. This process brought one atom in a hundred million into a metastable state. After a small deflection, the excited atoms moved on to a metal surface from which they could eject electrons and so be detected and exposed to radio waves. By careful experimental study and analysis, it was possible to determine crucial energy separations which indicated departures from the expected fine structure pattern of hydrogen. The fine structure deviations were definitely established experimentally by May, 1947. (Lamb measured the shift with great accuracy and later made similar measurements on heavy hydrogen and helium.)

Lamb reported his results early in the summer of 1947. Soon thereafter, theoretical physicists began to realize the importance of the Lambshift to basic physics. A rough estimate which agreed with Lamb's measurements was made, and later Lamb and others carried out further, more precise calculations. Indeed, over the years, measurements of the Lambshift have been conducted with extraordinary precision.

Hans Bethe of Cornell laid much of the groundwork for the modern field of electrodynamics by partially explaining the Lambshift in the hydrogen spectrum. Bethe said that observed discrepancies between energy levels of different states of the element were caused by the interaction of the electron with its own electromagnetic field. Bethe found that quantum electrodynamic theory had hidden behind its divergences a physical content which was actually in close agreement with Lamb's microwave observations. (Bethe would go on to win his own Nobel Prize in 1967 for his work on atomic physics, especially with regard to energy production in stars.)

Most of the laureates in physics were concentrated at a select group of universities, two of which were the University of California at Berkeley and Columbia University. The former was where Lamb did his training as a graduate student, and the latter was where he made his crucial discovery. Three of Columbia's laureates in physics—Lamb, Polykarp Kusch (with whom Lamb shared the Nobel award), and Charles Townes (a winner of the Nobel Prize in physics in 1964)—were attracted to the university by the Radiation Laboratory and by Rabi, whose own research on magnetic properties of atomic nuclei had made him a Nobel Prize winner for physics in 1944.

Indeed, through the 1950's and 1960's, Rabi was a scientific "talent scout" for the Nobel Committee, and he was quite successful. Rabi surely drew attention to Lamb's pioneering work at Columbia. High-precision radio-frequency spectroscopy had begun in 1937 when Rabi, at Columbia, developed an apparatus which permitted very accurate measurements of the differences among energy fields of an atomic system. Lamb was one in a series of physicists at Columbia who used similar methods to study the atom and its properties.

Later, he and his associates at Stanford continued and extended the original experiments to obtain new data on higher energy levels of the hydrogen atom. This information led to further understanding of more complex atoms. Over the years, Lamb conducted research on the interactions of neutrons and matter, field theories of nuclear structure, fission, cosmic-ray showers, microwave spectroscopy, and the structures of molecules, helium, and electromagnetic energy. In the 1960's, he turned to the theory of lasers and made a contribution to that theory which is known as the "Lamb dip." His only book is a textbook on the theory of lasers coauthored with two of his colleagues at the University of Arizona.

Lamb's work is very difficult for the lay reader to understand. Possibly the best way to learn about his character, his theories, and his influence is to read the introductory pages of the festschrift published on the occasion of his sixty-fifth birthday.

Bibliography

Primary

PHYSICS: "On the Electromagnetic Properties of Nuclear Systems," *Physical Review*, vol. 53, 1938 (with Lenard I. Schiff); "On the Extraction of Electrons from a Metal Surface by Ions and Metastable Atoms," *Physical Review*, vol. 65, 1944 (with Amador Cobas); "Space, Charge, Frequency Dependence of Magnetron Cavity," *Journal of Applied Physics*, vol. 18, 1947 (with Mat Phillips); "Fine Structure of the Hydrogen Atom by a Microwave Method," *Physical Review*, vol. 72, 1947 (with Robert C. Retherford); "Resonant Modes of Rising Sun and Other Unstrapped Magnetron Anode Blocks," *Journal of Applied Physics*, vol. 19, 1948 (with Normal M. Kroll); "Formation of Metastable Hydrogen Atoms by Electronic Bombardment of H-2," *Physical Review*, vol. 75, 1949 (with Retherford); "The Fine Structure of Singly Ionized Helium," *Physical Review*, vol. 78, 1950 (with Miriam Skinner); "Fine Structure of the Hydrogen Atom," *Physical Review*, vol. 79, 1950 (with Retherford); "Fine Structure of the Hydrogen Atom III," *Physical Review*, vol. 85, 1952; "Fine Structure of the H Atom," *Physical Review*, vol. 86, 1952 (with Retherford); "Fine Structure of the H Atom," *Physical Review*, vol. 89, 1953 (with Sol Treibwasser and Edward S. Dayhoff); "Tryslet Fine Structure of Helium," *Physical Review*, vol. 98, 1955 (with Theodore H. Maiman); "Fine Structure of $n=3$ Hydrogen by a Radio-Frequency Method," *Physical Review*, vol. 103, 1956 (with Theodore M. Sanders, Jr.); "Measurement of Fine Structure Separation $3^3P_1 = 3^3P_2$ for Helium Atom," *Physical Review*, vol. 105, 1957 (with Maiman); "Microwave Technique for Determining the Fine Structure of the Helium Atom," *Physical Review*, vol. 105, 1957; *Laser Physics*, 1974 (with Murray Sargent III and Marlan O. Scully).

Secondary

Eastham, D. A. *Atomic Physics of Lasers*. London: Taylor and Francis, 1986. This book opens with a discussion of the Lambshift, one of the basic concepts in laser physics. Another of Lamb's discoveries, the Lamb dip, provides another essential point in laser theory. The book is advanced, but it does offer a thorough explanation of the important contributions of Lamb to modern physics.

Fain, Veniamin M., and Yakov I. Khanin. *Quantum Electronics*. Elmsford, N.Y.: Pergamon Press, 1969. A book of advanced theoretical physics, this text situates Lamb's work in the theory and practice of modern physics. Hans Bethe's theoretical explanation for the Lambshift is examined in some detail.

Grandy, Walter T. *Introduction to Electrodynamics and Radiation*. New York: Academic Press, 1970. In this very advanced book, aimed at physics graduate students, Lamb's work is allocated a complete chapter. The text is well illustrated and easy to follow in its basic argument, but some knowledge of graduate-level mathematics is necessary.

Haar, Dik T., and Marlan O. Scully, eds. *Willis E. Lamb, Jr.: A Festschrift on the Occasion of His 65th Birthday*. New York: North-Holland, 1978. A series of complex articles looking at the ideas that Lamb pioneered. Much interesting material on his teaching and intellectual influence is supplied by former colleagues at the beginning of the book. Includes some handwritten letters.

Svelto, Orazio. *Principle of Lasers*. 2d ed. New York: Plenum Press, 1982. A textbook covering the theory of lasers for undergraduate and graduate students of physics. The diagrams and discussions are extremely helpful, although the mathematics required is advanced. The book does, however, use Lamb's considerable contributions to illustrate how physical theory can lead to the betterment of the world—in this case, through the development of lasers.

Thirring, Walter E. *Principles of Quantum Electrodynamics*. Translated by J. Bernstein. New York: Academic Press, 1958. This basic textbook covers in some detail Lamb's famous experiments from the late 1940's and the 1950's. The Lambshift is explained in clear, concise terms with a number of valuable illustrations and diagrams.

Douglas Gomery

1955

Physics
Willis Eugene Lamb, Jr., United States
Polykarp Kusch, United States

Chemistry
Vincent Du Vigneaud, United States

Physiology or Medicine
Axel Hugo Theorell, Sweden

Literature
Halldór Laxness, Iceland

Peace
no award

POLYKARP KUSCH
1955

Born: Blankenburg, Germany; January 26, 1911

Nationality: American

Areas of concentration: Atomic and molecular physics

Kusch measured the magnetic strength of the electron with extremely high precision and showed that it did not agree with Paul Dirac's 1928 theory. This result led to a reshaping of one of the most fundamental theories in physics: that of the interaction of light and matter

The Award

Presentation

Polykarp Kusch received the Nobel Prize in Physics, jointly with Willis Lamb, on December 10, 1955, from King Gustav VI of Sweden. Professor Ivar Waller of the Nobel Committee for Physics made the presentation speech, in which he noted that Kusch's and Lamb's work had been performed independently, even though their separate research groups had had much in common: Both were in the physics department of Columbia University, both were using (different) postwar refinements of a magnetic resonance method developed before the war by Isidor Isaac Rabi, and both made their critical discoveries in the same year, 1947. Furthermore, both discoveries were later explained by the same new theory, quantum electrodynamics.

Kusch's achievement was a measurement of the magnetic strength of the electron with unparalleled precision. It had been known since the 1920's that the electron, one of the most basic constituents of matter, acted like a small magnet and also that its magnetic strength was, indeed, close to the value predicted for it by Paul Dirac's brilliant electron theory of 1928. Kusch, however, was able to measure that strength with such high precision that, in 1947, he became the first person to prove that the actual strength deviated slightly from the Dirac prediction, being larger by about one part in a thousand. Waller pointed out that this effect, though exceedingly small and measurable only with a very sophisticated technique, is of far-reaching consequence. Because it did disagree with Dirac's theory, it marked the boundary of that theory's validity and led to the development of an even more sophisticated theory of how light and matter interact, the theory that today is called quantum electrodynamics.

Waller ended his speech by praising Kusch's accomplishment:

Your work is marked not only by the beauty of your experiments but equally by the profound significance of your results. It does not often happen that experimental discoveries exert an influence on physics as strong and invigorating as did your work. Your discoveries led to a . . . development of utmost importance to many of the basic concepts of physics, a development the end of which is not yet in sight.

Nobel lecture

Kusch began his Nobel lecture, entitled "The Magnetic Moment of the Electron," by commenting (doubtless with tongue in cheek), "I must tell you, and with considerable regret, that I am not a theoretical physicist." He then gave a rather philosophical description of the role of experimental physicists in "interrogating nature."

Two sections on the historical background to his Nobel Prize-winning work followed. The first, entitled "Atomic and Molecular Beams," was on the experimental technique (radio-frequency spectroscopy) that he had used in his experiments: Beams of atoms or molecules were sent through magnetic fields that were changing direction a billion times a second and that sometimes caused the atoms to undergo slight changes in energy, which could then be measured with a high degree of accuracy.

The second section, "Electron Properties," explained that between 1925 and 1928, physicists had learned that the electron behaves in some ways like a small magnet and that the strength of its magnetic field, or magnetic moment, was at least approximately equal to a standard unit called the "Bohr magneton." The electron was also known to have a "spin" angular momentum; it behaved somewhat as if it were a small sphere spinning around its own axis. In 1928, Dirac's relativistic theory of the electron had tied these two properties together, and, to quote Kusch, "indeed, one of the great triumphs of the Dirac electron theory was the prediction of these postulated electron properties."

In the next section of his lecture, Kusch discussed "Early Measurements," performed by the group in Rabi's laboratory from 1939 to 1947, measurements which had initially been directed at studying magnetic properties of atomic nuclei, not of the electron. He explained, however that small discrepancies had appeared, and in 1947, Gregory Breit had suggested that the electron's magnetic moment might differ from Dirac's prediction (one Bohr magneton) by roughly 0.1 percent, presenting an anomaly.

This possibility led to Kusch's Nobel Prize-winning experiment, which he did in collaboration with his student H. M. Foley; it was described in the next two sections of the lecture, "Anomalous Magnetic Moment" and "Experimental Detail." One of the limiting factors which had threatened to restrict the high level of precision required for this experiment was that the laboratory magnetic fields could not be measured with great accuracy. Kusch described the clever design and intricate analysis used to extract results so that the answer did not depend on that poorly known magnetic field value; it was a masterful and complex piece of experimental research. "Experimental Detail" closed with this statement:

We may therefore conclude on the basis of all evidence that the electron does indeed possess an "intrinsic" or "anomalous" magnetic moment over and above that deduced from the Dirac theory and whose magnitude is very close to 0.119 percent of the Bohr magneton.

In the next section, "Theoretical Interpretation," Kusch compared that experimental result to the calculation that had been made in the same year by Julian Schwinger. Schwinger had used the new, evolving theory of quantum electrodynamics, which predicted an anomalous magnetic moment 0.116 percent above the Dirac value; his result was "in excellent agreement with experimental measurements of the same quantity." Kusch went on to describe the significance of his work: "The importance of the observation of the anomalous magnetic moment of the electron is in part in the demonstration that the procedures of quantum electrodynamics are, in fact, satisfactory in formulating a description of nature." The remainder of his lecture was devoted to a description of experimental and theoretical developments that had occurred between 1948 and 1955.

Critical reception

The passage of time has amply confirmed the view of Kusch's work expressed in Waller's presentation speech: "It does not often happen that experimental discoveries exert an influence on physics as strong and invigorating as did your work." In retrospect, therefore, the press coverage of the November 2, 1955, announcement of the physics laureates seems surprisingly subdued. This apparent lack of appreciation perhaps stemmed from the abstract, technical nature of the work, combined with its lack of practical applications.

The most extensive newspaper coverage was offered by *The New York Times*, which ran two related articles in its edition of November 3. The first, entitled "3 U.S. Scientists Get Nobel Prize," devoted most of its attention to the chemistry prizewinner, Vincent du Vigneaud. His work in synthesizing a pituitary hormone was described in some detail, and the article noted the hormone's role in the production of mother's milk and in the contraction of the uterus at the time of birth. In contrast, the work by Kusch—and Lamb, with whom he shared the prize—had no such easily grasped significance which could be readily conveyed to the lay public. Their work was first described by *The New York Times* (and almost the same phrasing appeared in other newspapers) as "correcting an error made by a Briton who previously had won the Nobel prize." This remark was as unfair to "the Briton" (Dirac, whose only "error" lay in making a brilliant discovery in 1928 that did not already incorporate the discoveries of the next generation) as it was to Kusch and Lamb, whose work consisted of much more than a simple correction to Dirac's work. Yet, a lack of appreciation for their work's importance ran throughout the newspaper accounts.

The second article in *The New York Times*, "How the Winners Reacted to News," successfully addressed the human-interest side of the award, describing Kusch as "a tall, slender, youthful, tweedy professor with an emphatic, witty gift of speech. He works in his laboratory 80 hours a week." It also brought out the lack of technological applications of his work, quoting Kusch: "It is of no practical value in the sense that that you can make a gadget or build anything. You can have the patent rights for 13 cents." Perhaps in response to this comment, *The Wall Street Journal* covered the

1955 prizes in three brief sentences; Kusch received one-half of one sentence.

The Washington Post, alone among major publications, introduced the story on page 1, with photographs of the three winners, but their story, presented on page 8, was brief. Like *The New York Times*, the Washington newspaper gave primary coverage to the chemistry award and repeated the false statement that Kusch and Lamb had essentially corrected a minor error of Dirac. *The Times* of London gave a similar treatment on page 10 of its November 3 edition.

The November 16 issue of *Time* magazine, which had had a few days instead of a few hours to prepare the story, managed to convey a more accurate impression of the significance of Kusch's measurement. It noted,

> This small change . . . meant that the theoretical physicists would have to modify their basic ideas of atomic behavior. For a while there was something like confusion on the upper levels of physics. But physicists enjoy this sort of confusion: it gives them a stimulating workout. Soon they found ways to reconcile—and reinforce—their theories with the Lamb and Kusch experiments.

Physics Today and *Scientific American* both provided informed and perceptive coverage in their December, 1955, issues, the latter concluding, "The discrepancy touched off a ferment in theoretical physics out of which emerged the new quantum field theory."

Biography

Polykarp Kusch was born on January 26, 1911, in Blankenburg, Germany. His father, John Matthias Kusch, was a Lutheran minister who named his son for Saint Polycarp, a second century bishop and martyr whose feast day is January 26. The family emigrated to the United States in 1912 and settled in the Midwest; Polykarp became a naturalized American citizen at age twelve. He was educated in the Midwest also, receiving his bachelor's degree from Case Institute of Technology in 1931 and his Ph.D. in physics from the University of Illinois in 1936. In 1935 he wed Edith McRoberts, with whom he would have three daughters. Family life and responsibilities have been an important theme in his life, often mentioned in interviews. His wife died in 1959, and in 1960 he was married to Betty Jane Pezzoni. Two more daughters would result from that marriage.

After receiving his Ph.D., Kusch spent one postdoctoral year at the University of Minnesota before going to Columbia University in New York City, where he remained, apart from interruptions caused by World War II, for thirty-five years. He rose through the faculty ranks from instructor, in 1937, to professor, in 1949, and then took on increasingly weighty administrative positions. In 1949 he began his first term as chairman of the physics department, and in 1969 and 1971, he served as academic vice president and provost for the entire university. In 1972 he left Columbia and went to the University of Texas at Dallas, joining a number of other eminent scientists of that period in a "brain drain" from the East Coast to the Sun Belt, where later mandatory retirement ages were among the inducements. Since 1982, he has remained Regental Professor Emeritus of Physics at the University of Texas at Dallas.

Kusch's Nobel Prize set loose an avalanche of other honors too numerous to list in detail. They include election to the National Academy of Sciences in 1956 and honorary degrees from eight colleges and universities, notably his alma mater, Illinois, in 1961 and Columbia in 1983. He has had a long-standing interest in societal issues and science education; these concerns led to his involvement with groups such as the Federation of American Scientists, the American Association for the Advancement of Science, the American Academy of Arts and Sciences, the American Philosophical Society, and the Democratic Party.

Scientific Career

Polykarp Kusch went to college intending to major in chemistry. He became a physics major instead, but during his long career he would often work in the border area of chemical physics, using the precise methods of physics to study the molecules that make up chemistry. In graduate school at the University of Illinois, he worked on optical molecular spectroscopy with F. Wheeler Loomis, a master of the field. This classic form of spectroscopy, which studies the small energy changes of molecules as they absorb and emit visible light, has been synonymous with high precision since the nineteenth century. In his first postdoctoral appointment, at the University of Minnesota, Kusch widened his experience to include another, newer, and very different form of spectroscopy, "mass spectroscopy." This method shoots a stream of electrically charged atoms and molecules through a laboratory magnetic field, with which they interact (in contrast to optical spectroscopy, in which stationary atoms interact with light waves). The interaction, or force, depends on the particles' mass, so molecules of different mass can be very precisely discriminated.

Kusch went from Minnesota to Columbia University to work in the laboratory of Isidor Isaac Rabi, one of the towering figures of twentieth century physics. As serendipity would have it, Kusch arrived in September of 1937, a time when Rabi's group was just beginning to attempt a new class of experiment. Kusch's background in other forms of spectroscopy was useful, so Rabi set him to work on the project along with Stuart Millman and Jerrold Zacharias. By January of 1938, they had obtained success in the first-ever "magnetic resonance" absorption experiment. In Kusch's own words, "It was a brand new mold of spectroscopy and you can learn all kinds of things about molecules, atoms, and nuclei. We knew this. We didn't underestimate our papers. . . . It seemed to be inevitable" that the work would bring Rabi a Nobel Prize, which it did in 1944. Four months after beginning a new job, a mere year and a half after finishing his thesis, Kusch was already a co-author of a Nobel Prize-winning paper. One can only assume that his appetite was whetted.

Magnetic resonance spectroscopy, which was fundamental to Kusch's own, later research, is based on the fact that, somewhat like a spinning top precessing in Earth's gravitational field, particles that have spin angular momentum will precess in laboratory magnetic fields. Moreover, they do so with a very definite frequency that depends both on the external magnetic field and on their own spin. The step that opened the door to the new method in 1937 was the addition of an extra, rapidly oscillating magnetic field to the apparatus. Dramatic shifts occurred when that field was tuned to oscillate at a frequency which exactly matched important frequencies of the particles in the beam; that matching is what constitutes resonance. It is analogous to pushing a child on a swing: If one wants to transmit energy efficiently and give a good, high ride, one must time the pushes carefully and match them exactly to the natural, back-and-forth frequency of the swing.

For these experiments to be successful, radio frequencies in the vicinity of one gigahertz (one billion oscillations per second) were required. Such frequencies, however, were at the time difficult to use, because there were no devices that generated much power at those high, "microwave" frequencies. Again, serendipity played a role in Kusch's career. World War II brought a halt to the molecular-beam research at Columbia, as virtually all the scientists there were enlisted in military work. For Kusch and many others, the wartime assignment was to develop the new technology of radar for use in high-altitude bombing. For this purpose, it turned out, the optimal radar wavelength was three centimeters, which implies a frequency of one gigahertz. The time and federal dollars invested in developing wartime radar therefore paved the way for Kusch to return to postwar physics research with the new weapon of microwave technology in his experimental arsenal. As described above, in "Nobel lecture," Kusch put that entire arsenal to use expeditiously and brilliantly in 1947 and 1948 to determine the anomalous magnetic moment of the electron. Thus, he secured his own Nobel Prize.

In those initial experiments, done with H. M. Foley, Kusch deduced the free electron's magnetic moment from measurements made on electrons situated in three different and rather complex atoms: sodium, which has eleven electrons; gallium, which has thirty-one; and indium, which has forty-nine. After completing that work, Kusch searched for another, independent method which would measure the electron's magnetic moment in a simpler, "cleaner," less complex environment. The ideal experiment would have been on a completely free electron, removed from all other particles, but that was unworkable for practical reasons. Kusch therefore began to work on the next-best system: the simplest of all atoms, ground-state hydrogen, which has only one electron (and that without any "orbital" angular momentum to interfere with the "spin" angular momentum). In 1952, Kusch published the result of that second, independent, and more accurate measurement. It indicated a magnetic moment of 1.001146 Bohr magnetons with an uncertainty of 0.000012, which was consistent with the 1948 Kusch and Foley result—1.00119 with an uncertainty of 0.00005.

The quantum electrodynamical calculations had also progressed beyond the 1948 results, and by 1952, the best theoretical value was 1.0011454. As Kusch commented in 1955, "The result of the experiment is in remarkable agreement with the calculation." Remarkable, certainly, but today one can see that it was also somewhat fortuitous, since the correct value is now known to be 1.001159652, with no uncertainty in the listed places. The theoretical calculation of 1952, it turns out, though more sophisticated, was also less accurate than the 1948 theoretical version. Kusch's experimental explorations, on the other hand, had indeed improved between 1948 and 1952; the latter result was more correct and had a smaller uncertainty than the former.

In the years after receiving the Nobel Prize, Kusch remained active in research in spite of often heavy administrative responsibilities. He continued to explore new areas of research, such as laser-induced fluorescence from molecules, and continued to publish widely cited papers in chemical physics throughout the 1970's and 1980's.

Bibliography

Primary
PHYSICS: "The Magnetic Moment of the Electron," *Physical Review*, vol. 74, 1948; "Hyperfine Structure by the Method of Atomic Beams: Properties of Nuclei and of the Electron," *Physics*, vol. 17, 1951; "Magnetic Moment of the Electron," *Science*, vol. 123, 1956; "Atomic and Molecular Beam Spectroscopy," in Siegfried Flügge, ed., *Encyclopedia of Physics*, vol. 37, *Atoms, Molecules*, 1959; "Analysis of the Band System of the Sodium Molecule," *Journal of Chemical Physics*, vol. 68, 1978.

Secondary
Cooley, Donald G. "Scientist's Show Goes on the Road." *The New York Times Magazine*, February 16, 1958: 38. A few months after the Soviet launching of the first artificial satellite, Sputnik, had aroused great concern in the United States about science education, Polykarp Kusch spent three days at Dartmouth College as part of a visiting scientist program sponsored by the National Science Foundation. This article chronicles his visit, during which he lectured, taught, and met formally and informally with students, faculty, and administrators. A very interesting and personal picture emerges of Kusch's views on teaching and research, on the rewards of life as a scientist, and on the role of science in contemporary society.
Feynman, Richard P. *QED: The Strange Theory of Light and Matter*. Princeton, N.J.: Princeton University Press, 1985. In this book, Feynman gives an informal, almost conversational description of quantum electrodynamics, the "strange theory of light and matter" that grew out of Kusch's experiments on the magnetic moment of the electron. Feynman himself shared the Nobel Prize in 1965 for his work in developing that theory and became well known to nontechnical readers in 1986, when his whimsical autobiography became a national best-seller. *QED* is written in the same enthusiastic, humor-filled style that made his autobiography popular and presents quantum electrodynamics in an elegantly simple form ideal

for nonphysicists. Fittingly, Feynman organizes his account of the subject around the measurements and theory of the magnetic moment of the electron, beginning with Kusch's 1948 value of 1.00119 and closing with the most precise value that had been identified by 1984, 1.00115965221.

Pfeiffer, John. "The Basic Need for Pure Research." *The New York Times Magazine*, November 24, 1957: 23. This article quotes extensively from an interview with Kusch about his views on pure research. Characteristically, he accepts as obvious pure science's technological applications to electronic communications, military systems, and the like and places his emphasis instead on the tremendous role of science in establishing "new modes of thought." He even speculates that "the spirit of pure inquiry may act primarily through an evolution of religious attitudes and religious points of view—a religion which will accept the rationality that science has injected into the thinking of men." This article complements the piece by Cooley cited above in fleshing out Kusch's personal and philosophical viewpoints.

Ramsey, Norman F. *Molecular Beams*. Oxford, England: Clarendon Press, 1956. A definitive reference work on molecular beams, the principal tool of Kusch's Nobel research. Ramsey was a colleague of Kusch during the early years at Columbia, and the author index of his book contains forty-four references to Kusch's work, many of them extensive. The discussion in chapter 9, section 5, "Atomic Moments and the Anomalous Electron Moment," is especially helpful to an appreciation of Kusch's research in this field. There is also a list of references which itemizes seventeen scientific papers written between 1939 and 1954 that had Kusch as the first or sole author; these works trace an outline of Kusch's research from his arrival at Columbia to the year before he won the Nobel Prize.

Rigden, John S. *Rabi: Scientist and Citizen*. New York: Basic Books, 1987. This very readable and thorough biography of Kusch's mentor provides a wealth of detail about the social milieu, laboratory, and university in which Kusch did the work that brought him the Nobel Prize. Includes descriptions of Kusch's research and comments by him. A valuable resource.

Ralph B. Snyder

1956

Physics
William Shockley, United States
John Bardeen, United States
Walter H. Brattain, United States

Chemistry
Nikolay Semyonov, Soviet Union
Sir Cyril Hinshelwood, Great Britain

Physiology or Medicine
Werner Forssmann, West Germany
Dickinson Richards, United States
André F. Cournand, United States

Literature
Juan Ramón Jiménez, Spain

Peace
no award

WILLIAM SHOCKLEY
1956

Born: London, England; February 13, 1910

Nationality: American
Area of concentration: Solid-state physics

Shockley's experiments on the control of current on the surface of a semiconductor was a major factor in the discovery of the point-contact transistor by Bardeen and Brattain. Soon afterward he developed the junction transistor, which is by far the most widely used type of transistor

The Award

Presentation

On December 10, 1956, Professor E. G. Rudberg, member of the Nobel Committee for Physics, presented the Nobel Prize in Physics to William Bradford Shockley and his corecipients, John Bardeen and Walter Houser Brattain, on behalf of the Royal Swedish Academy of Sciences and King Gustav Adolph. Rudberg began his presentation by using a seafaring analogy and an analogy to the life and work of Ben Franklin to explain the process of conduction of electricity, the reasons for adding slight impurities to semiconductors, and the operation of the transistor.

In the 1930's, attempts were made to use semiconductors to "rectify" electrical current—to allow it to pass easily in one direction but hinder it from passing in the other. It was also hoped that a solid-state device could be built which would amplify the current. Success was achieved with the invention of the transistor by William Shockley, John Bardeen, and Walter Houser Brattain. In a series of ingeniously conceived experiments, the trio disclosed many properties of "holes," which are what is left when impurity atoms in a semiconductor steal electrons. With these new tools, semiconductor research greatly expanded. Rudberg concluded with yet another analogy, this one involving comparing the work on the semiconductor problem and its eventual solution to the work of ardent mountain climbers who began at a high-altitude camp and were rewarded with breathtaking vistas from the summit.

Nobel lecture

Shockley began his lecture, entitled "Transistor Technology Evokes New Physics," with a brief discussion of the terms "pure" and "applied" research. He emphasized that many important developments had occurred as a result of quite practical considerations. The most outstanding case of the belief that fundamental research is worthwhile from a practical point of view was the Bell Telephone Laboratories, where Shockley, Bardeen, and Brattain performed the work which led to the development of the transistor. Although allowed to engage in "pure" research, Shockley in particular was always alert for possible practical applications. For Shockley it was not important whether his research might be classifed as pure or applied. The motivation for research may be purely aesthetic or distinctly practical, but what is important, he noted, is whether the research might yield new and perhaps enduring knowledge about nature.

Before he discussed a selected group of experiments in transistor physics, Shockley described five basic "imperfections" of semiconductors: electrons, holes, donors, acceptors, and deathnium. Semiconductors do not conduct electricity as well as metallic conductors but much better than insulators. The semiconducting materials, such as germanium and silicon, may have their electrical conductivity significantly altered by the addition of very small amounts of impurities. These impurities may contribute electrons to the material and be called "donors," or they may remove conduction electrons and be called "acceptors." An excess of donors makes the material have a majority of negative carriers of charge and be called an n-type semiconductor ("n" for negative). An excess of acceptors makes the material a "p-type" semiconductor ("p" for positive) since the impurities rob the material of electrons, leaving behind "holes" which are positively charged. "Deathnium," the last of the imperfections, speeds up the equilibrium of holes and electrons, restoring the normal level of electrical conduction.

The rest of the lecture was a discussion of several key experiments in transistor physics. The "field effect" experiment was a crucial early step in the development of the transistor: Shockley believed that rectification and amplification could be achieved by imposing an external field. Bardeen was able to explain why that did not work. Haynes' experiment attempted to answer unresolved questions of the operation of the point-contact transistor, discovered by Bardeen and Brattain. Shockley described in some detail the motivations behind and the experiments concerning the junction between two regions of differing conductive properties in the same semiconductor.

Brattain concluded his lecture with a description of the production and operation of junction transistors, which performed many of the same functions as the old vacuum tubes did but at a much higher efficiency, greater range of operating conditions, and occupying a much smaller amount of space. He touched on some of the many new areas in solid-state physics research that had been opened as a result of the development of the transistor.

Critical reception

Newsweek (November 12, 1956) greeted the announcement of the award with joy. Most of the previous Nobel Prizes, according to the article, had gone to those physicists whose work was far too complicated for the layman to understand. In a breezy and folksy style, the article states that, for once, the prize went to an eminently practical and understandable little American invention, the transistor. The transistor was probably the most important invention in electronics in forty years, according to the article. The fact that such a statement could be made only a few years after the transistor's invention is a mark of the speed at which it demonstrated its utility and practicality. *Time* magazine (November 12) ran a brief announcement of the award. The announcement endorsed *Newsweek*'s position that the transistor had already ushered in a revolution in electronics.

The scientific journals were more restrained in their rhetoric, but the sentiment was similar. *Scientific American* (December, 1956) ran a typically evenhanded account of the significance of the award. The article agreed that the transistor had initiated a revolution in electronics by replacing bulky vacuum tubes, which consume large amounts of power, with tiny, reliable transistors, which consume little power; a brief overview of the theory behind the operation of the transistor was included. The reaction of *Physics Today* (January, 1957) was even more subdued. A straightforward account of the development and an indication of the importance of the transistor were included. Bell Telephone Laboratories placed a full-page ad in that issue congratulating Shockley, Bardeen, and Brattain for their achievement and announcing that the company was "proud to have been able to provide the environment for their great achievement." (This was not the only time that Bell Telephone Laboratories had placed a full-page ad in *Physics Today*.)

The New York Times (November 2) joined in the chorus, proclaiming a revolution in electronics. Even though the transistor was "still in its youth, if not actual infancy," it had already demonstrated its ability to perform the work of vacuum tubes. In only a few years it had proven itself a "mighty mite." In 1967, the newspaper marked the twentieth anniversary of the discovery of the transistor with an article which hailed the transistor's positive benefit for humankind. The transistor had fostered a multibillion-dollar industry which employed hundreds of thousands of workers.

Biography

William Bradford Shockley was born in London, England, on February 13, 1910. His father, William Hillman Shockley, was a mining engineer, and his mother, May Bradford Shockley, had been a federal deputy surveyor of mineral lands. His parents moved back to the United States when he was three years old. He attended the University of California at Los Angeles in 1928 and transferred to the California Institute of Technology a year later. He was graduated with a B.S. in physics in 1932. His Ph.D. in physics was awarded in 1936 by the Massachusetts Institute of Technology. He was married to Jean Alberta Bailey in 1933; they were divorced in 1955. He wed Emmy Lanning the same year. Two sons and a daughter were produced by his first marriage.

Shockley joined the staff of Bell Telephone Laboratories immediately after obtaining his Ph.D. This decision was strongly influenced by the fact that his adviser was to be Clinton J. Davisson (1881-1958). Shockley began working on vacuum tube technology but soon was allowed to begin research on semiconductors. During World War II he worked on a variety of military projects, serving as director of the Antisubmarine Warfare Operations Research Group from 1942 to 1944.

He returned to Bell Telephone Laboratories as director of solid-state research in 1945 and continued his work on semiconductors. He left Bell Telephone Laboratories in 1955 to become director of Shockley Semiconductor Laboratories, later a subsidiary of Beckman Instruments. From 1963 until his retirement in 1975, he was Alexander M. Poniatoff Professor of Engineering and Applied Science at Stanford University. In 1965, Shockley put forth his controversial view of genetics called "dysgenics," which is, in his words, a "retrogressive evolution through the excessive reproduction of the genetically disadvantaged." His comments on human intelligence and genetics increasingly focused on race and caused public outcry.

Scientific Career

Before the introduction of vacuum tubes, semiconductors were used in early crystal radios to rectify current. A curl of wire (called a "cat's whisker") in contact with a semiconducting material (a galena crystal) accomplished this rectification. The introduction of vacuum tubes revolutionized electronics. Although the invention of the transistor made them obsolete, they enabled a wide variety of electronic devices to be developed. Vacuum tubes can rectify and amplify a current, but the tubes are bulky, prone to failure, require energy to be heated to operating temperatures, and operate over a limited range of current-carrying capability. Work in the 1930's held the promise of using semiconductors to perform the same functions much more efficiently, but much work needed to be done to understand the basic properties of semiconductors before a functional solid-state device could be created that would replace vacuum tubes.

Shockley's education prepared him for his later work. His Ph.D. thesis was titled "Calculation of Wave Functions in Sodium Chloride Crystals." His later research involved the solid-state physics that he had learned and the work on crystals that he had done as a student. He was well aware of the need for an electronic device that would rectify and amplify a current. As Shockley says in his Nobel lecture, he was continually alert for practical applications of his research. He began his work at Bell Telephone Laboratories in an indoctrination program in vacuum tube technology. The application that M. J. Kelley, his supervisor in his indoctrination, instilled in his mind was the replacement of mechanical with electronic telephone switches. After his indoctrination, he designed a vacuum tube that could rectify and amplify a current. In 1939 he proposed developing solid-state devices which would also perform these functions.

World War II interrupted his research program. He worked on the electronic design of radar equipment until 1942, when he became involved in antisubmarine warfare operations for the U.S. Navy. He worked in the new field of operations research, which applied scientific techniques to the solution of military problems such as the optimal deployment of depth charges. This work and work done later involving the productivity of laboratory workers introduced Shockley to sociological issues. He later claimed that his work during the war gave him the background necessary to make his controversial statements concerning race and intelligence.

Shockley returned to Bell Telephone Laboratories in 1945, Bardeen joined the organization the same year, and Brattain had been there since 1929. They were part of the group that began to study semiconductors in earnest. Since none of them had worked in that field during the war, they formed a study group to review work conducted in their absence. In addition to the restrictions inherent in the physical aspects of vacuum tubes mentioned above, tubes do not operate at the high frequencies required by radar. Advances had been made in the use of silicon and germanium as radar detectors during the war. The use of cat's whiskers and a semiconductor such as galenium to rectify current was revived, but the search was on for a more reliable device, one that would also be able to amplify the current.

As a direct result of trying to invent an amplifying semiconductor device, Shockley conducted some of the most important experiments in stimulating further research. He believed that an electric field applied to a semiconductor would control the flow of electrons. He believed that he could substantially affect the carriers of electric charge on the surface of the semiconductor. He also expected that this "field effect" would produce amplification of the current. When experiments failed to demonstrate the effect, Bardeen was able to account for the negative result by developing a theory of the behavior of electrons and holes on the surface of the material. These experiments played the greatest role in stimulating the research into semiconductors at the Bell Telephone Laboratories and led directly to the invention of the point-contact transistor by Bardeen and Brattain in 1947.

As with other transistors, in the point-contact transistor a current flowing between two contacts can be controlled by a voltage applied to a third contact. Their version consisted of a block of n-type germanium with two cat's whisker contacts on one side and an electrode on the other. A small positive voltage applied to one contact and a large negative voltage applied to the other contact both relative to the electrode establishes the electrical connections. Holes introduced to the germanium at one contact flow to the other contact and add to the current. A signal applied between one of the contacts and the base was amplified fifty times in their early versions of the point-contact transistor. The term "transistor" is a shortened version of "transfer resistor," so called because the device transfers current from a low-resistance input of a high-resistance output.

Transistors fall into two basic categories but differ only in the way in which the control of the current is achieved. Field effect transistors control the flow of current using an applied electric field, while the flow of current in "bipolar" transistors involves both holes and electrons. Following up on his experiments involving field effect transistors and using Bardeen's theory of surface states, Shockley demonstrated in 1948 that a field effect transistor was possible. Field effect transistors play a significant role in the measurement of the surface properties of semiconductors. The field effect has also been used to produce transistors with properties quite different from the far more numerous bipolar transistors.

The momentum in the research program shifted away from field effect and toward bipolar transistors. Within a month of the discovery of the point-contact transistor (a bipolar transistor), Shockley made a suggestion that led quickly to the development of the junction transistor (also a bipolar transistor). He suggested replacing the contacts with rectifying junctions between n-type and p-type regions in a single crystal. He decided to focus on this junction because it was a simpler structure than a point-contact transistor and its behavior was highly predictable on theoretical grounds. Shockley demonstrated in 1949 that fabrication of semiconductors whose compositional structure can be altered in a systematic and controlled way—necessary for the production of junction transistors—was feasible. The most common form of the junction transistor consists of a thin p-type region which is sandwiched between two n-type regions of the same semiconducting material. Electrical contacts are made to each of the three regions. This "n-p-n" transistor functioned as Shockley's calculations had predicted and proved to be as useful, as versatile, and as relatively easy to fabricate as had been hoped.

In his textbook of 1950 entitled *Electrons and Holes in Semiconductors*, Shockley predicted that many unforeseen inventions would be made based on the work conducted at Bell Telephone Laboratories, and that other new physical principles would be used to attain practical ends as the new science of transistors progressed. He left Bell Telephone Laboratories in 1955 to try to make that prediction come true. An early resident of Northern California's "Silicon Valley," the site of many companies working in the vanguard of electronics and computer technology, he became director of Shockley Semiconductor Laboratories, a subsidiary of Beckman Instruments. The company changed hands three times and finally closed in 1968. Shockley continued to work on semiconductors, as well as energy bands in solids, ferromagnetism, electromagnetic theory, and order and disorder in alloys. He also worked on new techniques of computer memory storage, called "bubble" storage.

In 1963, Shockley began teaching at Stanford. There he began to develop his controversial notion of dysgenics. He became concerned that overbreeding among the "genetically disadvantaged," including most blacks, would lead to an overall decline in intelligence. In the years after 1965, when he began to air his views publicly, and after his retirement in 1975, Shockley spent an increasing amount of time elaborating and defending dysgenics. When he would receive an award for his work in physics he would often talk about the threat of the breeding habits of the genetically inferior. One of his most controversial plans was to offer a cash bonus to encourage those with IQs below 100 to be voluntarily sterilized. His ideas on human intelligence and genetics were denounced in both the popular and the scientific press. Shockley spent his time after 1975 keeping his ideas before the public. Some of his public appearances were greeted with strong public protests, including being burned in effigy. In 1984 he sued the *Atlanta Constitution* for libel when a 1980 article compared his sterilization plan to Adolf Hitler's eugenics program. The jury found that Shockley had been libeled but awarded him only one dollar in damages.

William Shockley certainly earned a place in the history of physics for his significant contributions to the development of transistors. Not only do transistors outperform vacuum tubes on all measures of performance; they can also perform functions that tubes cannot. A tremendous change in all people's lives resulted from the applications of the tiny, seemingly innocuous transistor. In addition to a wide variety of consumer products, such as small, portable radios, they have made possible new devices in the fields of computer technology and communications which would have been impossible using vacuum tubes. Before the advent of the transistor, computers were restricted to large, expansive machines which processed data at very slow rates compared to today's computers. The transistor made computer technology available to business and can in large part be credited with initiating the "computer age."

Shockley's controversial views may also have earned for him a dubious place in contemporary history. To some he appears as a crackpot; to others, he is a speaker of truth. Still, whatever judgment may be passed on him for his controversial views, there is no doubt that Shockley serves as an example of how scientists interact with one another in the pursuit of particular goals in scientific research.

Bibliography

Primary

PHYSICS: "Investigation of Oxidation of Copper by Use of Radioactive Cu Tracer," *Journal of Chemical Physics*, vol. 14, 1946 (with John Bardeen and Walter Brattain); "Density of Surface States on Silicon Deduced from Contact Potential Measurements," *Physical Review*, vol. 72, 1947 (with Brattain); "Modulation of Conductance of Thin Films of Semiconductors by Surface Charges," *Physical Review*, vol. 74, 1948 (with G. L. Pearson); "Investigation of Hole Injection in Transistor Action," *Physical Review*, vol. 75, 1949 (with J. R. Haynes); *Electrons and Holes in Semiconductors*, 1950; "The Mobility and Life of Injected Holes and Electrons in Germanium," *Physical Review*, vol. 81, 1951 (with Haynes); "Statistics of the Recombinations of Holes and Electrons," *Physical Review*, vol. 87, 1957 (with W. T. Read); *Imperfections in Nearly Perfect Crystals*, 1952; *Mechanics*, 1966 (with Walter A. Gong).

Secondary

Bernstein, Jeremy. *Three Degrees Above Zero: Bell Labs in the Information Age*. New York: Charles Scribner's Sons, 1984. A popular account of the research work done at Bell Labs by a physicist who had added popular science writing to his list of accomplishments. Written in a highly readable style, the work provides a glimpse of the overall structure of an organization that employs thousands and conducts research in nearly every phase of modern physics. The chapter on solid-state physics goes into more detail on the work in the 1930's and 1940's than most other works.

Bode, Hendrik Wade. *Synergy: Technological Integration and Technical Innovation in the Bell System*. Murray Hill, N.J.: Bell Laboratories, 1971. Written by a former vice president of the labs, this work provides a reasonably detailed description of how technological innovation is accomplished in the Bell system. It analyzes the "technical integration" of the Bell system and how it has been shaped by technological and engineering problems.

Goodell, Rae S. *The Visible Scientists*. Boston: Little, Brown, 1977. The author discusses the interaction of scientists and the media. The fifth chapter deals with science "operators" (those who use the media for their own publicity) and the extent to which the "visible" scientists of the title are "operators." She illustrates her thesis with an account of how Shockley used the media to garner publicity for his dysgenics ideas.

Mabon, Prescott C. *Mission Communication: The Story of Bell Laboratories*. Murray Hill, N.J.: Bell Laboratories, 1975. This work is written from the perspective of a former vice president and assistant to the chairman of the board of AT&T. The fifth chapter relates the generally known facts of the discovery of the transistor and adds some "not so widely understood" information. Written by a former insider, this volume is a more popular account than those produced by Bell Labs itself.

Millman, S., ed. *A History of Engineering and Science in the Bell System: The Physical Sciences (1925-1980)*. Indianapolis, Ind.: AT&T Customer Information Center, 1983. The second chapter describes research on semiconductor physics and discusses how that research deepened the understanding of semiconductors. The material is moderately technical but only vaguely reads as though it were written by professional researchers. The chapter reprints an internal memorandum titled "The Genesis of the Transistor," an account of the thinking, work, and events that resulted in the development of the device. It also includes brief reminiscences of Walter Brattain and extensive references.

Smits, F. M., ed. *A History of Engineering and Science in the Bell System: Electronics Technology (1925-1975)*. Indianapolis, Ind.: AT&T Customer Information Center, 1985. The first chapter deals with the invention of the transistor, the public announcement and reception, and its further development. Includes reproductions of the pages from the notebooks of the scientists involved in the development of the transistor.

Roger Sensenbaugh

1956

Physics
William Shockley, United States
John Bardeen, United States
Walter H. Brattain, United States

Chemistry
Nikolay Semyonov, Soviet Union
Sir Cyril Hinshelwood, Great Britain

Physiology or Medicine
Werner Forssmann, West Germany
Dickinson Richards, United States
André F. Cournand, United States

Literature
Juan Ramón Jiménez, Spain

Peace
no award

JOHN BARDEEN
1956

Born: Madison, Wisconsin; May 23, 1908

Nationality: American
Area of concentration: Solid-state physics

Bardeen, the first person to be awarded two Nobel Prizes in Physics, shared the first with Walter H. Brattain and William Shockley for their development of the transistor, which made possible a broad range of electronic devices that have led to such scientific advances as supercomputers and space travel

The Award

Presentation

On December 10, 1956, Professor E. G. Rudberg of the Nobel Committee for Physics presented John Bardeen and his collaborators, William Shockley and Walter Houser Brattain, to King Gustav VI of Sweden to have bestowed upon them the Nobel Prize in Physics. They received the award for their work on semiconduction that led them ultimately to discover transistors, infinitesimally small control devices that replaced vacuum tubes.

Rudberg summarized the advance Benjamin Franklin had made in electricity 250 years earlier, when he flew his kite during a storm and pulled electrical energy from the thunderclouds. Franklin's wet kite string, serving as a conductor, was attached to a key tied to a dry silk ribbon that served as an insulator, the two requisites for a power line.

Rudberg noted that an atom of phosphorus, when forced upon an atom of silicon, will contribute a negative electron to the silicon. An atom of boron will have the opposite effect, contributing a positive charge and leaving in the atomic structure a hole that in semiconductors can migrate, thereby acting as a carrier of a positive charge. Holes and electrons can be simultaneous carriers in semiconductors, and the importance of semiconductors is derived from the interplay of these holes and electrons.

During the 1930's, rectifiers based on semiconductors came into being. Rudberg credited Bardeen, Brattain, and Shockley with building on this research, trying with other researchers to control rectifiers by adding an extra electrode. By finding how to make a probe positive close to a negative electrode, using the probe to inject holes, Bardeen and his immediate collaborators discovered transistor action as a means of controlling rectifiers, thereby discovering a fruitful way to deal with problems of semiconduction.

Nobel lecture

John Bardeen's Nobel address, "Semiconductor Research Leading to the Point

Contact Transistor," was the first of the three addresses delivered by the trio awarded the prize in 1956. Bardeen's speech was followed by William Shockley's, which concentrated on how injected minority carriers flow in bulk material. Walter Brattain's speech focused on research activities dealing with the surface properties of germanium and silicon, both of which were fundamental to semiconductor research.

Bardeen's speech is highly technical but fully amplified by appropriate formulae and diagrams. His basic aim was to describe the complex processes that had led to the discovery of the transistor effect. The work was conducted for three years that began in 1946 when Bardeen, Brattain, and Shockley were associated with Bell Telephone Laboratories in Murray Hill, New Jersey. Their charge from Bell was to gain an understanding of semiconductor phenomena based on atomic theory. Bell was obviously most interested in practical outcomes that would lead to enhanced amplification of sound.

Bardeen explained that he and his collaborators had begun their research from a fresh perspective, because none of them, although all were experienced scientists, had worked on semiconductors during the war years, 1941-1945. He acknowledged the experimental work that had been going on in conduction in terms of excess electrons and holes, flow by diffusion, and contact rectification—all well under way when the Bell researchers began their collaboration. Bardeen also noted the importance of germanium and silicon to semiconductor research, indicating that when chemical impurities are present in these elements, they begin to conduct either by means of excess electrons (negative charges) or holes (positive charges). The work leading to the transistor would not have been possible had not research conducted during World War II developed methods of purifying germanium and silicon and controlling their electrical properties. It was possible by 1946 to introduce into these two elements the necessary amounts of donor (negative) and acceptor (positive) impurities to implement the Bell experiments.

Bardeen elaborated on the need the trio had recognized to emphasize research on surface states, which at that time had been only tentatively and theoretically broached. The success of the work in semiconductors revolved around an ideal crystal that at a temperature of absolute zero serves as an insulator because its valence bonds are occupied. Because the crystal contains no excess (negative) electrons, the flow of current is impossible.

Bardeen went on to indicate how important the currents of both diffusion and conduction are to the transistor effect, after which he explained contact rectifiers and how they made possible the point-contact, bipolar transistor. He credited the surface state experiments with helping to explain properties of germanium and silicon that had not, to that time, been explained.

Bardeen closed his speech by commending the subsequent research of John Northrup Shive (born 1913), on the flow of energy through bulk materials, which had resulted in the development of junction transistors; this research, according to Bardeen, had surpassed point-contact transistors in most practical applications.

Critical reception

Most reports on the prize emphasized the work that the three Bell scientists had done, giving only brief sketches of the individual men and their work. A major portion of most articles in the popular press was devoted to explaining transistors and their practical applications in such devices as hearing aids, radios, and computers. John Bardeen, a retiring, self-effacing person, did not choose to use his position as a Nobel laureate to promote his personal social viewpoints; he was more reticent with the press than some winners of the prize have been.

The first announcements of the Nobel Committee's selections for the 1956 prize in physics were made in *The New York Times* (November 12) and *The Times* of London (November 12), which ran similar articles reporting that three Americans had been granted the award. The article in *The New York Times* identified the transistor as "a tiny and highly efficient substitute for the vacuum tube," pointing out that it is one-thousandth the size and one-hundredth the weight of a vacuum tube and that it can do the same work, as well as considerable work that the vacuum tubes could not. Moreover, the transistor operated using one-tenth the electricity required to power a vacuum tube.

After explaining the background of the award, both articles noted that the three laureates had been under consideration by the Swedish Academy for two years. The actual award came nine years after the invention of transistors in December, 1947. The article in *The New York Times* also described how the basic concept of the "cat's whisker," used in the crystal detectors that made the earliest radios possible, was modified by Bardeen and his colleagues and was used to introduce into germanium and silicon the small impurity that creates the electrons and holes necessary to semiconductivity and to the ensuing transistor effect.

There was essentially no negative response to the Academy's decision. The popular press applauded the Nobel Committee for making the award for something whose practical application could be understood by most laypersons. *Newsweek* (November 12) articulated this view while decrying the fact that so many past awards had been made for theoretical advances that defied explanation even by literate physicists. *Life* (November 12) ran a picture of the winners, noted how the transistor had revolutionized the electronics industry, and indicated that Bardeen, Brattain, and Shockley would share prize money of $38,633. *Science* (November, 1956), in its announcement, noted that Bardeen had left Bell Telephone Laboratories in 1951 to become professor of physics and electrical engineering at the University of Illinois at Urbana-Champaign.

On the day of the ceremony, *The New York Times* (December 11) ran an article outlining each award, indicating that the 1956 award celebration was subdued in part out of respect for the victims of the recent Hungarian rebellion and in part because the American-born wife of Juan Ramón Jiménez (1881-1958), that year's winner in literature, had died shortly before the ceremony, which prevented Jiménez from attending. The annual Nobel banquet was replaced by a private dinner for 150 people, including the Swedish royal family. *The Times* of London (December 11) ran full coverage of the award ceremony, including a picture of Bardeen and the other recipients on page 8.

Biography

Born in Madison, Wisconsin, on May 23, 1908, John Bardeen was the son of Charles R. and Althea (née Harmer) Bardeen. The father, a medical doctor, was a professor of anatomy and the first dean of the University of Wisconsin Medical School, serving from 1907 to 1935 in the latter capacity. Bardeen's mother died when her son was twelve.

Having skipped several grades of elementary school, Bardeen was graduated from Madison's Central High School in 1923 at the age of fifteen. He enrolled at the University of Wisconsin, from which he received bachelor and master of science degrees in electrical engineering in 1928 and 1929 respectively. Entering the work force just as the Great Depression was paralyzing the economy of the United States, Bardeen in 1930 became a geophysicist for Gulf Research and Development Corporation in Pittsburgh before returning to school at Princeton University, where he studied under Eugene P. Wigner; he received a doctorate in mathematical physics in 1936. He spent three years, from 1935 to 1938, as a Junior Fellow of the Society of Fellows at Harvard University, shortly before being appointed assistant professor of physics at the University of Minnesota, where he taught from 1938 to 1941. Also in 1938, he was married to Jane Maxwell; the union would produce two sons and a daughter.

Bardeen spent the war years as a physicist for the Naval Ordnance Laboratory in Washington, D.C., and then joined the Bell Telephone Laboratories in 1946 as a research physicist. There he and collaborators Shockley and Brattain did the work on semiconduction that would lead to the transistor in 1947 and their Nobel Prize in 1956. In 1951, Bardeen left Bell to become a professor of electrical engineering and physics at the University of Illinois. In 1957, with Leon N Cooper and John Robert Schrieffer, he discovered the cause of superconductivity, which would lead to his second Nobel Prize in Physics, awarded in 1972.

Along with the Nobel Prize, Bardeen is the recipient of many other awards, including the Franklin Institute's Stuart Ballantine Medal (1952), the American Physical Society's Buckley Prize (1955), the Soviet Academy of Sciences' Lomonosov Award (1987), and many honorary doctorates. He has been a member or officer of the President's Science Advisory Committee (1958-1962), the American Physical Society (serving as its president from 1968 to 1969), the Royal Society of Great Britain, the American Philosophical Society, and the Soviet Academy of Sciences.

Scientific Career

Bardeen's interest in science has been lifelong. His father's orientation was scientific and the young Bardeen was early exposed to a family environment that encouraged scientific inquiry. Upon completing his bachelor's degree in electrical engineering in 1928, Bardeen, who had already overcome the restrictive electrical engineering curriculum by undertaking extra courses in physics and mathematics, began his work with physics professor John H. Van Vleck (born 1899), who would win the 1977 Nobel Prize in Physics.

Quantum theory dominated physics in the mid-1920's, and quantum mechanics was coming into its own, although the University of Wisconsin did not emphasize it until 1928, when Van Vleck, whose main interest lay in atomic physics, joined the faculty. He introduced John Bardeen to quantum mechanics at a time when the youth was also studying kinetic theory and statistical mechanics with Peter Debye (1884-1966), who was a 1936 Nobel laureate in chemistry. Bardeen studied with such eminent visiting professors as 1932 Nobel physics laureate Werner Heisenberg (1901-1976) and the 1933 recipient, Paul Dirac (1902-1984).

During his two years in the master's program, Bardeen became interested in geophysical prospecting by electrical means, a relatively new field at that time. In 1930, his application for a fellowship at Cambridge University turned down, Bardeen, having completed the master's degree, followed his professor of geophysical prospecting to the Gulf Research and Development Corporation in Pittsburgh. Bardeen remained with Gulf until 1933, when he entered the doctoral program at Princeton University, whose mathematics and physics departments had gained an enviable reputation. Another attraction Princeton offered was the newly established Institute for Advanced Study, whose eminent faculty was easily accessible to graduate students. Princeton offered doctorates in mathematical physics in both the mathematics and physics departments, and Bardeen chose to take the Ph.D. in the mathematics department.

Albert Einstein (1879-1955) joined the Institute for Advanced Study in 1933, and among his colleagues were such giants as John von Neumann (1903-1957), Oswald Veblen (1880-1960), and Eugene Wigner (born 1902). Wigner directed Bardeen's doctoral research, which sought to determine the energy necessary to remove an electron from the interior of metals to positions outside one of the crystal faces, research intimately related to Bardeen's later work on semiconduction and on transistors. During his two years at Princeton, Bardeen became extremely interested in the solid-state physics that underlay much of his later work. He also came to understand how, in low densities, electrons form a lattice (Wigner's lattice), information vital to later work in semiconduction.

Harvard University offered Bardeen a three-year Junior Fellowship in 1935. Although he had not completed his doctoral dissertation, he accepted the fellowship and arranged to complete his dissertation from Cambridge. The excellence of Harvard's physics department and Harvard's proximity to the Massachusetts Institute of Technology (MIT) helped Bardeen reach his decision. In Cambridge, Bardeen met Shockley, then finishing his doctoral work at MIT.

In 1937, Bardeen produced a significant paper elucidating a first-principles calculation of electron-phonon interaction in monovalent metals. This research led him to the concept of random phase approximation. Bardeen also became interested in alkali metals because they change substantially in their ability to compress under certain conditions. More important than any of these interests, however, was Bardeen's interest, first stimulated during the Harvard years, in superconductivity, and this interest engaged him during his three years at the University of Minnesota (1938-1941). He was diverted for one decade from pursuing fully his interest in superconductivity, first being forced to work at the Naval Ordnance Laboratory during World War II and then by the demands his work on semiconduction at Bell Telephone Laboratories imposed on him for five years after the war.

Bell wanted Bardeen to continue his work with them, but by 1951 he was becoming intrigued with news of experiments that demonstrated the occurrence of superconductivity when conduction electrons couple with the lattice. Research was going on that emphasized the role of electron-phonon interaction in the superconducting ground state. Out of these experiments emerged the isotope effect. When Bardeen learned of it in May, 1950, he resurrected his superconductivity work of more than a decade earlier and in a matter of days devised a new theory of superconductivity modified by the new findings. He reported the revision of his earlier theory of superconductivity in an article he submitted to *Physical Review* on May 22, 1950, one week after he first learned of the isotope effect. Bardeen resigned from his position at Bell in 1951 to become professor of physics and electrical engineering at the University of Illinois, where he could pursue his theoretical research unfettered by the pressure of being expected to arrive at immediate, practical outcomes in his work. He was now at the turning point in his life that would result in his collaborating with colleagues who with him would develop the superconductivity theory that resulted in his being awarded a second Nobel Prize in Physics in 1972. Although his work on semiconduction and on the transistor effect had been a detour from the course his work might have taken had the war not interfered with his career, it was nevertheless a most fruitful detour with enormous and immediate practical and theoretical outcomes.

Bardeen worked for the next few years on superconduction with physicist David Pines and others at the university. In 1955, Leon Cooper joined the faculty, sharing an office with Bardeen. Along with graduate student John Robert Schrieffer, they began a series of investigations into the different aspects of the superconductivity phenomenon, in which certain metals, at very low temperatures, not only exhibit reduced electrical resistance (as predicted by understood physical laws) but inexplicably, at a certain low temperature several degrees above absolute zero, lose electrical resistance suddenly and entirely. The phenomenon had been observed for decades but had promised to remain a mystery until the 1950 discoveries surrounding electron coupling and the isotope effect. These discoveries paved the way for Bardeen, Cooper, and Schrieffer. Finally, in 1957, they were successful in confirming experimentally their theory that the electrons within the metals, when subjected to the appropriate low temperatures, were aligned and moving in such a way as to create a huge coherent state, as opposed to the normal random motion, resulting in the observed superconductive effect. Other experimental confirmations of the "BCS theory" came pouring in soon thereafter.

After the discovery of the BCS theory, Bardeen continued his investigations into the properties of superconductors, especially with a view to finding a way to produce the superconductive state in materials at higher temperatures, where the practical applications are broad. He has also served in many professional and government organizations to further research in this area, including the American Physical Society, the President's Science Advisory Committee, and the Commission on Very Low Temperatures of the International Union of Pure and Applied Physics.

Bibliography

Primary

PHYSICS: "Diffraction of a Circularly Symmetric Electromagnetic Wave by a Circular Disk of Infinite Conductivity," *Physical Review*, vol. 36, 1930; *The Solution of Some Theoretical Problems Which Arise in Electrical Methods of Geophysical Exploration*, 1930 (with Leo J. Peters); "Some Aspects of Electrical Prospecting Applied in Locating Oil Structures," *Physics*, vol. 2, 1932 (with Peters); "Theory of the Work Functions of Monovalent Metals," *Physical Review*, vol. 48, 1935 (with Eugene P. Wigner); "Theory of the Work Function: II. The Surface Double Layer," *Physical Review*, vol. 49, 1936; "On the Density of Energy Levels of Heavy Nuclei," *Physical Review*, vol. 51, 1937; "Conductivity of Monovalent Metals," *Physical Review*, vol. 52, 1937; "Compressibilities of the Alkali Metals," *Journal of Chemical Physics*, vol. 6, 1938; "An Improved Calculation of the Energies of Metallic Li and Na," *Journal of Chemical Physics*, vol. 6, 1938; "Symmetry Effects in the Spacing of Nuclear Energy Levels," *Physical Review*, vol. 54, 1938 (with Eugene Feenberg); "Expressions for the Current in the Bloch Approximation of 'Tight Binding' for Metallic Electrons," *Proceedings, National Academy of Sciences*, vol. 25, 1939 (with John H. Van Vleck); "Concentration of Isotopes by Thermal Diffusion: Rate Approach to Equilibrium," *Physical Review*, vol. 51, 1940; "Electrical Conductivity of Metals," *Journal of Applied Physics*, vol. 11, 1940; "The Image and van der Waals Forces at a Metallic Surface," *Physical Review*, vol. 58, 1940; "The Production of Concentrated Carbon (13) by Thermal Diffusion," *Journal of Chemical Physics*, vol. 9, 1941 (with Alfred O. Nier); "Investigation of Oxidation of Copper by Use of Radioactive Cu Tracer," *Journal of Chemical Physics*, vol. 14, 1946 (with Walter Brattain and William Shockley); "The Quadrupole Moments and Spins of BR, Cl, and N Nuclei," *Physical Review*, vol. 71, 1947 (with C. H. Townes, A. N. Holden, and F. R. Merritt); "Surface States and Rectification at a Metal Semi-Conductor Contact," *Physical Review*, vol. 71, 1947; "Calculation of Nuclear Quadrupole Effects in Molecules," *Physical Review*, vol. 73, 1947 (with Townes); "Second-Order Corrections to Quadrupole Effects in Molecules," *Physical Review*, vol. 73, 1948 (with Townes); "The Transistor, a Semi-Conductor Triode," *Physical Review*, vol. 74, 1948 (with Brattain); "Nature of the Forward Current in Germanium Point Contacts," *Physical Review*, vol. 74, 1948 (with Brattain); "Physical Principles Involved in Transistor Action," *Physical Review*, vol. 75, 1949 (with Brattain); "Zero-Point Vibrations and Superconductivity," *Physical Review*, vol. 79,

1950; "Wave Functions for Superconducting Electrons," *Physical Review*, vol. 80, 1950; "Choice of Gauge in London's Approach to the Theory of Superconductivity," *Physical Review*, vol. 81, 1951; "Relation Between Lattice Vibration and London Theories of Superconductivity," *Physical Review*, vol. 81, 1951; "Criterion for Superconductivity," *Physical Review*, vol. 82, 1951; "Change in Superconducting Penetration Depth with Field," *Physical Review*, vol. 87, 1952; "The Interaction of Excitons and Phonons," *Physical Review*, vol. 87, 1952 (with Paul Leurgans); "Superconductivity and Lattice Vibration," in *Low Temperature Physics: Four Lectures by F. E. Simon*, 1952; "Theory of the Meissner Effect in Superconductors," *Physical Review*, vol. 97, 1955; "Theory of Superconductivity," in S. Flugge, ed., *Encyclopedia of Physics*, vol. 15, 1956; *Superconductivity*, 1956; "Microscopic Theory of Superconductivity," *Physical Review*, vol. 106, 1957 (with Leon N Cooper and John Robert Schrieffer); "Theory of the Anomalous Skin Effect in Normal and Superconducting Metals," *Physical Review*, vol. 111, 1958 (with D. C. Mattis); "Theory of Superconductivity," *Physica*, vol. 24, 1958; "Ground-State Energy and Green's Function for Reduced Hamiltonian for Superconductivity," *Physical Review*, vol. 118, 1960 (with G. Rickayzen); "Recent Developments in Superconductivity," in Cornelius J. Gorter, ed., *Progress in Low Temperature Physics*, vol. 3, 1961 (with Schrieffer); "Tunneling and Superconductors," *Physical Review Letters*, vol. 9, 1962; "Developments of Concepts of Superconductivity," *Physics Today*, vol. 16, 1963; "Superconductivity," in Maurice Levy, ed., *Cargèse Lectures in Theoretical Physics*, 1963; "Theory of Motion of Vortices in Superconductors," *Physical Review*, vol. 140, 1965 (with M. Stephen); "Superconductors and Superfluids," in Per-Olov Lowdin, ed., *Quantum Theory of Atoms, Molecules, Solid State*, 1966; "Effective Interaction of He^3 Atoms in Dilute Solutions of He^3 and He^4 at Low Temperatures," *Physical Review*, vol. 154, 1967 (with Gordon Baym and David Pines); "Advances in Superconductivity," *Physics Today*, vol. 223, 1969; "Electron-Phonon Interaction and Superconductivity," *Science*, vol. 181, 1973; "History of Superconductivity Research," in Behrman Kursunoglu and Arnold Perlmutter, eds., *Impact of Basic Research on Technology*, 1973; "Superconductivity: Past and Future," *Industrial Research*, vol. 18, 1976; "Beginnings of Solid State Physics and Engineering," *The Bridge*, vol. 14, 1984.

Secondary

Hoddeson, Lillian. "The Discovery of the Point-Contact Transistor." *Historical Studies in the Physical Sciences* 12 (1981): 41-76. This lucid, well-researched article details Bardeen's work on transistors and gives details about his life. Particularly valuable is the material that Bell Telephone Laboratories made available to Hoddeson, especially the notebooks of those who worked on semiconduction and transistors.

Pines, David. *Solid State Physics*. New York: Academic Press, 1955. Pine, who became Bardeen's colleague at the University of Illinois, explains well Bardeen's contributions to solid-state physics and shows how he and others applied the theories of solid-state physics to their work in semiconduction and later in superconduction.

Shockley, William. *Electrons and Holes in Semiconductors*. New York: Van Nostrand, 1950. Although this book is intended for the specialist, it provides some insights into Bardeen's contributions to transistor technology that the layperson will find accessible. Shockley covers in detail much of the material that Bardeen summarizes in his acceptance speech and presents in his articles on semiconductors.

Slater, John Clarke. *Solid States and Molecular Theory: A Scientific Biography*. New York: Van Nostrand, 1975. Slater recalls how he taught large numbers of young physicists about the quantum theory of solids during his years at MIT. Among his students was William Shockley. Slater details in this book some of the early theory leading to research in semiconduction that resulted in a Nobel Prize for Bardeen, Brattain, and Shockley.

Stuckey, William K. "John Bardeen: A Profile." *Saturday Review of the Sciences* 1 (February 24, 1973): 30-34. A satisfactory overview of Bardeen and his work, this article is intended for the nonspecialist. Although it is simplified, it offers useful insights into Bardeen's method of working through problems in physics.

R. Baird Shuman

1956

Physics
William Shockley, United States
John Bardeen, United States
Walter H. Brattain, United States

Chemistry
Nikolay Semyonov, Soviet Union
Sir Cyril Hinshelwood, Great Britain

Physiology or Medicine
Werner Forssmann, West Germany
Dickinson Richards, United States
André F. Cournand, United States

Literature
Juan Ramón Jiménez, Spain

Peace
no award

WALTER H. BRATTAIN
1956

Born: Amoy, China; February 10, 1902
Died: Seattle, Washington; October 13, 1987
Nationality: American
Area of concentration: Solid-state physics

Brattain conducted experiments to test theories developed by William Shockley and John Bardeen concerning the surface properties of semiconductors. These experiments led unexpectedly to the discovery of the point-contact transistor

The Award

Presentation

Professor E. G. Rudberg, member of the Nobel Committee for Physics, presented the Nobel Prize in Physics to Walter Houser Brattain and his corecipients, William Shockley and John Bardeen, on December 10, 1956, on behalf of the Royal Swedish Academy of Sciences and King Gustav Adolph. Rudberg began his presentation by explaining the process of conduction of electricity, the reasons for adding slight impurities to semiconductors, and the operation of the transistor by using an amusing seafaring analogy and an analogy to the life and work of Ben Franklin.

In the 1930's, attempts were made to use semiconductors to "rectify" electrical current—to allow it to pass easily in one direction but hinder it from passing in the other. It was also hoped that a solid-state device could be built which would also amplify the current. Success was achieved with the invention of the transistor by Shockley, Bardeen, and Brattain. In a series of ingeniously conceived experiments, the trio disclosed many properties of "holes," which are what is left when impurity atoms in a semiconductor steal electrons. With these new tools, semiconductor research greatly expanded. Rudberg concluded with an analogy comparing the trio to ardent mountain climbers who began at a high-altitude camp and were rewarded with breathtaking vistas from the summit.

Nobel lecture

Walter Brattain's concentration in the field of surface phenomena was evident from his Nobel lecture, titled "Surface Properties of Semiconductors." He began by acknowledging his coworkers, teachers, and those researchers upon whose work he had built, saying that his success had been the result of being in the right place at the right time.

Most of the lecture is devoted to a description of the model of the surface of germanium, one of the simplest semiconductors. Surfaces are vitally important in nature, but little was understood of even some of the simplest surfaces before the development of quantum mechanics in the 1920's. Chemical reactions are catalyzed on a surface, most electrical circuit elements involve phenomena occurring at the surface, and much of biology is concerned with reactions going on at the surface of the cell. Brattain showed how calculations of such physical properties as the changes in electrical potential, changes in the concentration of electrons at the surface, and how fast equilibrium is reached could be made. He did not deal with abstract, ideal surfaces, but "complex and dirty" ones—the kinds of surfaces which really exist. At the surface there are both slow and fast changes.

When a light is shined on a surface, he noted, there is a measurable change in the electrical conductivity of the surface. The conductivity is also changed when an external electric field is applied. From these events and a knowledge of some of the physical characteristics of the semiconducting material, a host of physical quantities can be derived. The surface properties of the material depend on the surface treatment and not on the properties of the bulk of the material.

Brattain concluded his lecture by noting that the understanding of the relatively simple surface of germanium would ultimately contribute to the understanding of other surface phenomena and that it was the original attempts to understand surface phenomena of this nature that had led to the discovery of the transistor effect. He also mentioned the names of colleagues who had continued the work on the understanding of surface phenomena.

Critical reception

Time magazine (November 12, 1956) ran a brief announcement of the award, saying that the transistor had already ushered in a revolution in electronics. *Newsweek* (November 12) greeted the announcement of the award with joy: Most of the previous Nobel Prizes, according to the article, had gone to those physicists whose work was far too complicated for the layman to understand. The article applauded the awarding of the prize to an eminently practical and understandable American invention, the transistor—perhaps the most important invention in electronics in forty years.

The scientific journals were more restrained in their rhetoric, but the sentiment was similar. *Physics Today* (January, 1957) provided a straightforward account of the development of the transistor and an indication of its importance. Bell Telephone Laboratories placed a full-page advertisement in that issue, congratulating Shockley, Bardeen, and Brattain for their achievement, including a self-promoting statement that it was "proud to have been able to provide the environment for their great achievement." *Scientific American* (December, 1956) ran a typically evenhanded account of the significance of the award, noting that the transistor had initiated a revolution in electronics by replacing bulky, energy-eating vacuum tubes with tiny, economical transistors.

The New York Times (November 2) proclaimed a revolution in electronics. Even though the "mighty mite" transistor was "still in its youth, if not actual infancy," it had already demonstrated its ability to perform the work of vacuum tubes. In 1967, the same newspaper would mark the twentieth anniversary of the discovery of the transistor with an article which hailed the transistor's positive benefit for humankind. The transistor had fostered a multibillion-dollar industry that employed thousands and benefited all.

Biography

Walter H. Brattain was born in Amoy, China, on February 10, 1902. His father, Ross R. Brattain, taught at a private school for Chinese boys. A year later, the family moved back to their native state of Washington, where Ross Brattain became a stockbroker. When Walter was nine, the family moved to a homestead in Tonasket to become cattle ranchers and flour millers. Brattain enjoyed mathematics and science and was allowed to skip a year. English and foreign languages did not come easily to him. With the financial support of his aunt, he was able to attend a private school to complete his high school education, which had been interrupted by work on the homestead. He entered Whitman College and in 1924 received his bachelor's degree in mathematics and physics. At Whitman, he was the student of Benjamin Brown, a famous teacher of physics. He earned his master's degree in physics at the University of Oregon in 1926.

Brattain migrated via sheep train to the University of Minnesota where he studied under John H. Van Vleck (1899-1980), who would win the Nobel in 1977. Brattain took Van Vleck's course on quantum mechanics in 1927-1928, the first year the course incorporated the wave mechanics of Erwin Schrödinger (1887-1961) and the matrix mechanics approaches to quantum theory of Werner Heisenberg (1901-1976) and Max Born (1882-1970), which had appeared only a few years before. Brattain completed his Ph.D. in 1929 and spent a year at the National Bureau of Standards as he finished his thesis. In 1929, he was invited to join the staff at Bell Telephone Laboratories. He remained there until he had reached the mandatory retirement age in 1967. During his last five years there, until 1972, he taught a laboratory course and a course for the nonscience major at Whitman College. He began research on the surface properties of cells in 1965 at Whitman and continued that work for several years. He died after a long illness on October 13, 1987.

Scientific Career

While pursuing his doctorate at the University of Minnesota, Brattain took one of the first courses offered in the United States on quantum mechanics, based on the recently developed wave mechanics of Schrödinger and the matrix mechanics of Heisenberg and Born. Quantum theory held the promise of accounting for the properties of solids which had eluded classical physics. Brattain then worked briefly at the National Bureau of Standards. While there, he helped design a temperature-controlled oscillator. During a tour he was giving to an official from Bell Telephone Laboratories, the official offered him a job. Brattain accepted and began working under Joseph A. Becker in 1929, when Bell Labs was only four years old. It was Becker who, as Brattain put it, "dried my ears off as a green young Ph.D."

Brattain's work before 1935 included research on electron collisions in mercury vapor, magnetometers, frequency standards, and infrared phenomena. On the theoretical side, he heard Arnold Sommerfeld's lectures on the new electron theory of metals (which used quantum mechanics as a starting point) in 1931 and learned about the quantum mechanical explanation of the conduction of electrons from A. H. Wilson's papers. On the experimental side, the importance of the development of solid-state circuit elements was clear to those working in the field by the mid-1920's. Vacuum tubes were still a fairly new invention, but their high operating temperatures, fragile construction, bulkiness, and the relatively limited range of current and voltages at which they could operate meant that there would be quite a market for an efficient and reliable replacement.

Vacuum tubes can rectify and amplify a current. Sealed inside an evacuated glass container, a hot filament boils off electrons, which are attracted to a positively charged plate placed near the filament. A battery connects the two together outside the tube. Because the current can flow in only one direction (from the filament to the positive plate), the current is "rectified." In this operation, an alternating current is converted to a direct current. A wire mesh can be inserted between the filament and the positive plate. By adjusting the voltage across the mesh, the electrons can either be encouraged or discouraged from moving to the plate. In fact, a small change in the voltage can make a large change in the amount of the current, thus making an amplifier. The search for materials that could perform the vital functions of rectification and amplification was complicated by the fact that the theory was insufficiently developed and that the materials then considered, such as copper oxide and selenium, had a complex structure. Throughout the 1930's, quantum theory was beginning to make progress on the theoretical side, but progress on the materials engineering side was slow, and the experimentalists were not making much progress either.

Brattain and Becker recognized, as did others, the potential of developing a solid-state circuit element which could replace vacuum tubes, but the problems seemed insurmountable in the 1930's. In a direct analogy with the vacuum tube, physicists considered inserting a wire mesh inside a piece of copper oxide. Calculations indicated, however, that the thickness of the mesh and other operating characteristics made actual construction quite impractical. The Great Depression also threatened to take its toll: Brattain, a bachelor in 1932, would have been the next to go if the Depression had worsened.

Semiconductors held the promise of replacing vacuum tubes. Semiconductors do not conduct electricity as well as metals, but much better than insulators. In general, the structure of semiconductors is simpler than that of metals. Silicon and germanium in particular have simple structures. Semiconductors had been used years earlier in crystal radio sets to rectify a current. A "cat's whisker," a curl of wire, in contact with the mineral galena (a semiconductor) would rectify a current. Brattain and William Shockley, who joined Bell Telephone Laboratories in 1936, looked for semiconducting materials that would amplify as well as rectify. Among the many problems in fabricating semiconducting samples was that a small change in the impurities in the material could drastically alter the conductivity.

Semiconductors come in two types: "p-type" and "n-type." In crystals of silicon and germanium, four electrons are needed to make the bonds that hold the crystal together. If an impurity atom is added which has five electrons available, then there is one left over after the impurity atom has displaced one of the original atoms. This electron is then free to move around and conduct electricity. This type of semiconductor is called "n-type" because there are more negative charges than in the pure material. If the impurity atom has only three electrons, then there is a "hole" left in the crystal. This hole (an absence of an electron) acts like a positive charge but is not as mobile as electrons. This type of semiconductor is called "p-type" because there are more positive charges than normal.

World War II interrupted the search for a rectifying and amplifying semiconductor but perhaps paved the way for the discovery of the transistor. First, the impressive gains in the field of radar brought with them advances in the understanding and fabrication of semiconductors which could operate at the high frequencies radar required. Second, scientists were uprooted and exposed to new professional pressures and relationships. Brattain worked on, among other things, the magnetic detection of submarines. Third, neither he nor Shockley worked on semiconductors during the war. Perhaps their separation from the field during the war allowed them some new perspective on the problem.

After the war, a research team was formed at Bell Telephone Laboratories to perform basic research on semiconductors with the intention of constructing a solid-state device that would rectify and amplify a current. The goal was not new but the approach was different. Because the team, including Brattain and Bardeen and headed by Shockley, had been out of touch with developments during the war, they decided to review that progress. It was decided that the first goal was to understand the simplest semiconductors, since copper oxide and selenium had proven intractable. Then they could search for a practical replacement for vacuum tubes.

A theory of rectification based on quantum mechanics led Shockley to believe that an electric field applied to a semiconductor could increase the conductivity of the surface and thus amplify a current. Calculations indicated that a suitable arrangement of the circuit could produce amplification. Rectification was achieved by the very nature of the semiconductor. Brattain conducted experiments in 1945 to test Shockley's belief. All the attempts failed to show amplification. Bardeen developed a theory involving the electrons on the surface of the material. He reasoned that charges induced by the field could screen the interior of the material from the electric field. Brattain and his team members conducted the experiments which demonstrated the effect Bardeen had predicted. At this point, it was decided that Brattain would concentrate on the surface of the material and that Gerald Pearson would concentrate on the bulk properties. The key at this point was to bypass the surface states predicted by Bardeen's theory and control the conductivity some other way.

Brattain and other members of the team tried heat, cold, light, and submersion in liquids in order to bypass the surface effect. Some progress was made in achieving the field effect. Brattain and Bardeen attempted to demonstrate the validity of the field effect by immersing the semiconducting material in an electrolyte (a liquid that can conduct electricity) in an attempt to bypass the surface state. They used a cat's whisker to make contact to one face of a block of germanium and a broad plate on the bottom to make the second contact. A drop of water, later glycol borate, surrounded the cat's whisker, which was coated with wax to insulate it from the electrolyte. Another cat's whisker was placed in the drop and made the third contact. They believed that the current in the contact could be controlled by controlling the voltage applied to the drop of fluid. The experiment worked, but only at frequencies too low for practical use. For the electrolyte they substituted a layer of germanium oxide and a small amount of gold to serve as the contact, but the oxide washed off, so they tried another cat's whisker placed near the gold spot.

The experiment showed a small effect, but exactly opposite to the one expected from the field effect. With a certain voltage, they expected the current to decrease, but in fact the current increased. They reasoned that holes were flowing into the germanium from the gold spot. Some holes went to the cat's whisker contact to increase the current. The effect was not very strong, but they could increase the effect if they could get the contact closer so that more of the holes would flow to the other contact. They used gold foil and cut two lines about two one-thousandths of an inch apart. The experiment was repeated and an amplification of about 50 was obtained. The current was now controlled not by an external field but by the action of the holes.

The term "transistor" was coined by an electrical engineer at Bell, John Pierce. It is a combination of "transfer" and "resistor" which symbolizes the physical operation of transferring current from a low-resistance input to a high-resistance output. The device that Brattain and Bardeen discovered is called a "point-contact" transistor, because the cat's whisker makes contact with the semiconductor at a point. The term "bipolar" was attached to the phenomenon because both electrons and holes are involved in the effect.

The significance of the unexpected result must be emphasized. Before this experiment, the role of the holes in conduction was not considered significant. Now it was clear that their role was crucial. In a sense, the discovery of the transistor effect was an accident. In an experiment designed to demonstrate the validity of the field effect, Bardeen and Brattain had stumbled upon the point-contact transistor. Their primary goal, however, was to develop a device that would amplify and rectify a current more easily and reliably than vacuum tubes, and that they had accomplished. It was not completely accidental that Bardeen and Brattain discovered the transistor effect—they were part of a team that had been working on the problem for years. What was accidental and unexpected was the route which the discovery took.

The experiments of Bardeen and Brattain were conducted in late 1947. Soon after that, Shockley proposed the idea of the junction transistor, in which the contacts are replaced with rectifying junctions between different regions in the same crystal. An "NPN" transistor has a p-type region sandwiched between two n-type regions all in the same crystal. The junction transistor rapidly took its place as the most widely used form of transistor. Bipolar and field effect transistors are used in more specialized applications. Public announcement of the discovery was not made until July of 1948 because of concerns that other researchers might be near to developing the transistor. Bell Telephone Laboratories wanted to verify the discovery and establish the patent before announcing it to the public. Thereafter, transistors rapidly became a mainstay of the electronics industry and fundamentally altered daily life for people all over the world.

Brattain continued to work at Bell Labs until mandatory retirement in 1967. He worked on the surface properties of semiconductors, piezoelectric frequency standards, magnetometers, infrared detectors, and blood clotting. After his return to his alma mater as a teacher, he began research with David Frasco on modeling the surface of living cells. He once said that the most gratifying outcome of transistors to him was the small battery-operated radio, which allows even the most underprivileged peoples the opportunity to gather together and listen to what they want to hear, independent of what their leaders may wish them to hear. The most deplorable outcome, he found, was rock and roll musicians' use of solid-state electronics to amplify sound to the point where it is both painful and injurious.

Bibliography

Primary

PHYSICS: "Investigation of Oxidation of Copper by Use of Radioactive Cu Tracer," *Journal of Chemical Physics*, vol. 14, 1946 (with John Bardeen and William Shockley); "Density of Surface States on Silicon Deduced from Contact Potential Measurements," *Physical Review*, vol. 72, 1947 (with Shockley); "Nature of the Forward Current in Germanium Point Contacts," *Physical Review*, vol. 74, 1948 (with Bardeen); "The Transistor, a Semi-Conductor Triode," *Physical Review*, vol. 74, 1948 (with Bardeen); "Physical Principles Involved in Transistor Action," *Physical Review*, vol. 75, 1949 (with Bardeen); "Development of Concepts in Semiconductor Research," *American Journal of Physics Teachers*, vol. 6, 1956; "Surface Properties of Semiconductors," *Science*, vol. 126, 1957; "The Distribution of Potential Across the Los-Index Crystal Planes of Germanium Contacting on Aqueous Solution," *Proceedings of the National Academy of Sciences*, vol. 48, 1962 (with P. J. Boddy); "One Researcher's Personal Account," *Adventures in Experimental Physics*, vol. 5, 1976.

Secondary

Bernstein, Jeremy. *Three Degrees Above Zero: Bell Labs in the Information Age*. New York: Charles Scribner's Sons, 1984. This popular account of the research work done at Bell Labs is written in a highly readable style and provides a glimpse of the overall structure of the organization. The chapter on solid-state physics is particularly appropriate here.

Bode, Hendrik Wade. *Synergy: Technological Integration and Technical Innovation in the Bell System*. Murray Hill, N.J.: Bell Laboratories, 1971. A detailed description of how technological innovation is accomplished in the Bell system, by a former vice president of Bell Labs. He analyzes the "technical integration" of the Bell system and how it has been shaped by technological and engineering problems.

Braun, Ernest, and Stuart MacDonald. *Revolution in Miniature: The History and Impact of Semiconductor Electronics*. Cambridge, England: Cambridge University Press, 1978. This book is aimed at the lay reader and presents a fairly complete account of how the main inventions in semiconductor electronics came about, how a major new industry grew up, and how our lives have been affected. Technical language was avoided.

Mabon, Prescott C. *Mission Communication: The Story of Bell Laboratories*. Murray Hill, N.J.: Bell Laboratories, 1975. Written from the perspective of a former vice president and assistant to the chairman of the board of AT&T. The fifth chapter narrates the development of the transistor and adds some little-known facts as well.

Millman, S., ed. *A History of Engineering and Science in the Bell System: The Physical Sciences (1925-1980)*. Indianapolis, Ind.: AT&T Customer Information Center, 1983. Chapter 2 describes research on semiconductor physics and how that research deepened the understanding of semiconductors. Reprints an internal memo entitled "The Genesis of the Transistor," which recounts the events that led up to the development of the transistor, including Brattain's participation.

Smits, F. M., ed. *A History of Engineering and Science in the Bell System: Electronics Technology (1925-1975)*. Indianapolis, Ind.: AT&T Customer Information Center, 1985. The first chapter covers the invention of the transistor, the public announcement and reception, and its further development, including reproductions of pages from the notebooks of the scientists involved in the development of the transistor.

Weaire, Denis L., and Colin G. Windsor, eds. *Solid State Science: Past, Present and Predicted*. London: Taylor and Francis, 1987. The preface, introduction, and first chapter of this book present an overview and discuss the state of historical research of the field of solid-state physics in nontechnical terms.

Weart, Spencer R. "The Birth of the Solid-State Physics Community." *Physics Today* 41 (July, 1988): 38-45. Written by the director of the Center for the History of Physics of The American Institute of Physics, this nontechnical article includes a sidebar which describes the International Project in the History of Solid State Physics.

Roger Sensenbaugh

1957

Physics
Chen Ning Yang, China and United States
Tsung-Dao Lee, China and United States

Chemistry
Sir Alexander Todd, Great Britain

Physiology or Medicine
Daniel Bovet, Italy

Literature
Albert Camus, France

Peace
Lester B. Pearson, Canada

CHEN NING YANG
1957

Born: Hofei, Anhwei, China; September 22, 1922

Nationality: Chinese; after 1964, American
Areas of concentration: Particle physics and statistical mechanics

Yang and Tsung-Dao Lee made a fundamental theoretical breakthrough by demonstrating the nonconservation of parity. Because of their work, all scientific theories based on parity had to be reexamined

The Award

Presentation

The Nobel Prize in Physics was presented to Chen Ning Yang by Professor O. B. Klein, a member of the Nobel Committee for Physics. Klein's presentation speech emphasized the revolution in theoretical physics that had been created when Yang and his corecipient, Tsung-Dao Lee, disproved a principle that had been accepted for three decades: the conservation of parity.

Klein began his presentation with the assertion that quantum theory assumes that the laws of earlier physics are correct but greatly oversimplified. By way of paying tribute to the winners' Chinese origins, Klein introduced Yang and Lee's discovery by paraphrasing the Chinese philosopher Lao-tse: "The elementary particles, which could be defined, are not the eternal elementary particles." He then observed how Yang and Lee's experimental discoveries had overturned Paul Adrien Maurice Dirac's deceptively natural assumption that the best-known elementary particles possessed no feature which would permit a distinction between right and left.

Yang and Lee's revision of the question of right-left symmetry in elementary-particle reactions began with the discovery of a new kind of particle, called a "K-meson," which seemed to contradict Dirac's assumption. Most physicists were merely puzzled by these particles; only Yang and Lee took them seriously enough to subject them to intense scientific scrutiny. The result of their investigation was the conclusion that the symmetry assumption had no experimental support, because all experiments had been designed to give the same result whether the assumption was valid or not.

Not content to confine themselves to this negative statement, Yang and Lee proposed a series of experiments which could test the right-left symmetry assumption in different elementary particle transformations. The Chinese physicist Chien-Shiung Wu and her colleagues carried out the first of these experiments. When atomic nuclei of a radioactive isotope of cobalt were exposed at a very low temperature to a magnetic field, they became just like compass needles, thereby allowing the direction of the electrons to be analyzed. The experiment's results indicated that certain atomic processes lack right-left symmetry.

Klein ended by praising Yang and Lee for breaking a "most puzzling deadlock in the field of elementary particle physics."

Nobel lecture

Yang delivered his lecture, "The Law of Parity Conservation and Other Symmetry Laws of Physics," on December 11, 1957. He began by explaining that symmetry laws, which seem to be verified by daily experience, generate the law of conservation. He pointed out that one of the symmetry principles—the symmetry between left and right—was as old as human civilization. Even though right and left are distinct from each other in everyday life, the laws of physics have always shown a complete symmetry between right and left. After the introduction of quantum mechanics, the law of right-left symmetry contributed to the formulation of the law of conservation of parity in 1924 by O. Laporte. Eventually, this law of conservation was extended to other aspects of physics until its validity was taken for granted by most physicists.

In 1956, however, experiments conducted in many laboratories indicated that one of the newly discovered mesons seemed to decay into configurations of differing parity. To resolve this paradox, Yang was forced to consider the faultiness of the law of parity conservation for the weak interactions, the forces that cause elementary particles to disintegrate. Yang then attributed the dearth of information on the conservation of parity to the fact that the parity conservation of the entire nuclear decay process had never been observed. The violation of the parity laws was proved by Wu and her team, who conducted experiments suggested by Yang. Yang praised them in his lecture for their courage and skill and said that their work had called into question other symmetry laws.

Critical reception

The importance of Yang and Lee's discovery is reflected in the large number of periodicals that reported it. *Time* magazine (January 28, 1957) predicted that the abolition of parity would relieve some of the confusion into which physics had fallen since the end of World War II as a result of the large number of puzzling subatomic particles that had been discovered. *Life* of January 28 also noted that the excited scientists who were rushing to the laboratory to verify Yang and Lee's discovery would have to reexamine other theories based on the erroneous concept of parity. *Life* even foresaw the attainment of a goal which had eluded Albert Einstein: a unified field theory encompassing all the laws of matter and energy. *Science News Letter* of January 26 likened Yang and Lee's discovery to Einstein's theory of relativity in the impact that it would have on the laws of atomic matter. One could say that Yang and Lee had become media heroes as a result of their monumental find.

Some periodicals also commented on the confusion that the discovery would create in the world of physics. *Life* said that many physical theories would be restructured if Yang and Lee could stand up to the attacks that would be made against them. *Newsweek*, while agreeing that Yang and Lee's discovery would spur much-needed reform, observed that many scientists were baffled as to where the discovery would lead. In 1964, Isaac Asimov said that the discovery "broke like a bomb" on the world of nuclear physics and that men such as Wolfgang Pauli, who had proposed the neutrino, found it difficult to accept the new development.

Yang and Lee's award was unique in other ways, which were also reported in the media. They were the first scientists of Chinese birth to win a Nobel Prize. *Scientific American* of December, 1957, included them among the youngest men ever to receive a Nobel award. *Science News Letter* took note of the year that had elapsed between the discovery and the conferring of the award, which was at the time the shortest interval ever between a discovery and the award of the Nobel Prize. Neither *Scientific American* nor *Science News Letter* criticized Yang and Lee's award on the basis of their youth or the Nobel Committee's timing.

Biography

Chen Ning Yang was born on September 22, 1922, in Hofei, Anhwei, China. While still young, Yang adopted "Franklin" as his first name after reading the autobiography of Benjamin Franklin. In 1929, his family moved to Peiping, but in later years they had to move again to stay out of the way of the Japanese invaders. Yang enrolled in the National Southwest University in Kunming, where he met Tsung-Dao Lee. After obtaining his bachelor's degree in 1942, Yang entered Tsinghua University, because his father was a professor of mathematics there. He admitted that the "academically inclined atmosphere" of his childhood was denied to most of the Chinese of his generation.

Yang completed his master's degree in 1944 and then taught at a Chinese high school. Finding that Enrico Fermi had moved from Italy to the University of Chicago, Yang decided that he would go there too, so that he could study under him. He won a Boxer fellowship, which was derived from funds returned to China by the United States after the Boxer Rebellion, and he used it to finance his studies in the United States. In 1946, he enrolled at the University of Chicago. Less than two years later, Yang completed his doctorate, writing his thesis under the supervision of Edward Teller. He remained in Chicago for a year as an assistant to Fermi, who probably influenced Yang's scientific development more than any other scientist. Lee had also come to Chicago on a Boxer fellowship, and the two men began the collaboration that eventually led to their Nobel Prize work on parity.

In 1949, Yang went to the Institute for Advanced Study in Princeton, New Jersey, and he became one of the very small number of professors on the institute's permanent staff in 1955. In 1968, he was appointed Albert Einstein professor of physics and director of the Institute of Theoretical Physics at the State University of New York at Stony Brook. During the 1970's, he was a member of the board of Rockefeller University, the American Association for the Advancement of Science, and the Salk Institute for Biological Studies, San Diego. In addition, he was on the board of Ben Gurion University, Beersheba, Israel. Yang received the Einstein

Award in 1957 and the Rumford Prize in 1980.

In 1950, he wed Chih Li Tu, a former student of his in China who was studying in Princeton. They would have two sons and one daughter. As one of the forty-five hundred Chinese students stranded in the United States as a result of the Communist takeover of 1949-1950, Yang was the subject of much interest on the part of officials of the Communist Chinese Embassy in Sweden, who wanted to return him to China on the eve of his acceptance of the Nobel Prize. In his acceptance speech, however, Yang left no doubt that he would remain in the United States because of his devotion to modern science, which, he believed, is primarily of Western origin. He became an American citizen in 1964.

Scientific Career

Even from his earliest days as a physicist, Yang made significant contributions to the theory of weak interactions, the forces that had long been thought to cause elementary particles to disintegrate. Yang first became skeptical of the law of conservation of parity after 1953, when it became apparent that it contained a fundamental paradox. According to this law, it made no difference whether mesons spiraled with a left-handed or a right-handed twist. The spin was considered random, and so the particles were thought to be essentially the same. In the mid-1950's, however, R. H. Dalitz, an Australian physicist, pointed out a fundamental problem with this law. One of the newly discovered mesons, the K-meson, exhibited decay modes into configurations of differing parity. Sometimes, these K-mesons decayed into two or three smaller particles without warning. Yang realized that much of the bafflement regarding these strange properties of the K-mesons was caused by the fact that the law of conservation of parity, which had been built into physical theories since 1925, was so deeply rooted.

After considering every conceivable alternative, Yang, along with his fellow physicist at the Institute for Advanced Study at Princeton, Tsung-Dao Lee, decided to test the experimental foundations of the conservation of parity. After discovering in early 1956 that there was no experimental evidence against parity nonconservation in the weak interactions, Yang reported his findings to the Sixth Annual Rochester Conference on High Energy Nuclear Physics at the University of Rochester in April, 1956. For the next three weeks, Yang at Brookhaven and Lee at Columbia picked a given experiment and worked out the theory for it, allowing for the fact that parity might not be conserved. Late in June at Brookhaven, Yang and Lee wrote a brilliantly reasoned paper titled "Question of Parity Conservation in Weak Interactions." In this paper, they suggested a series of experiments that would test their hypothesis that there were certain decay paths in weak particle interactions that were preferred and that remained constant despite the reversal of other relevant parameters. They also reexamined the consequences of removing the parity law for radioactive disintegration of nuclei and particles.

Having challenged other researchers to look into the problem, Yang and Lee could do nothing but wait. While they were waiting, they began working at Brookhaven on an entirely different branch of physics: statistical mechanics. Statistical mechanics is the study of systems, such as gases, that are composed of a large number of particles. Yang and Lee did not try to analyze the particles; instead, they attempted to develop a statistical theory of large numbers of particles. It is important to note that while they were waiting for others to verify their reservations regarding parity, they made significant contributions in this field.

Among the research groups that accepted Yang and Lee's challenge was one representing a collaboration between Columbia University and the National Bureau of Standards. Another Chinese physicist at Columbia, Chien-Shiung Wu, went to Washington, D.C., to work with the first-rate physicists at the National Bureau of Standards. Wu and her team devised an apparatus that cooled radioactive cobalt 60 to a temperature of 0.01 degree Celsius above absolute zero. Even though the cobalt nuclei continued to spin under the extreme cold, their random thermal motions were reduced to almost nothing. By applying a magnetic field, Wu made the spinning cobalt nuclei align themselves, like small magnets, parallel to the applied magnetic field. Since temperature had no effect on radioactivity, the aligned cobalt atoms continued to disintegrate, giving off electrons. When the number of electrons emitted along the direction of the spin was compared to the number going in the opposite direction, the numbers were found to be different. According to the conservation of parity, half of them should have emitted their electrons toward the "north" end of the magnetic field and the other half toward the "south" end. Actually, however, more electrons came out of the south end of the nuclei. When the test was repeated under varying conditions, it was proved that cobalt nuclei emit electrons from one particular end. This phenomenon indicates the favoring of a direction associated with the spin. Thus, Wu and her associates proved not only that particles have "handedness" but also that that may be their most distinctive property. Yang and Lee were in constant communication with Wu, and as the evidence accumulated, they became convinced that parity conservation was a false concept.

After the cobalt experiment, Leon M. Lederman of Columbia and his research team tried a second test. A pi-meson decayed into two other particles, a neutrino and a rapidly spinning mu-meson. Passing through a carbon block, the mu-meson entered a second block wrapped in wire that produced a magnetic field. At this point, it disintegrated into an electron and two neutrinos. Instead of going in random directions, as parity dictated, the electrons always went in a particular direction. This experiment also supported Yang and Lee's objection to the law of parity.

In addition to working on weak interactions and statistical mechanics, Yang, in collaboration with Lee and others, later investigated the nature of elementary-particle reactions at extremely high energies. In collaboration with R. L. Mills, Yang proposed a non-Abelian gauge theory, which is also known as the Yang-Mills theory. This theory involves a mathematical principle describing fundamental interactions for elementary particles and fields.

Bibliography

Primary
PHYSICS: "Interaction of Mesons with Nucleons and Light Particles," *Physical Review*, vol. 75, 1949 (with T. D. Lee and M. Rosenbluth); "Reflection Properties of Spin ½ Fields and a Universal Fermi-Type Interaction," *Physical Review*, vol. 79, 1950 (with J. Tiomno); "Mass Degeneracy of the Heavy Mesons," *Physical Review*, vol. 102, 1956 (with Lee); "Question of Parity Conservation in Weak Interactions," *Physical Review*, vol. 104, 1956 (with Lee); "Parity Nonconservation and a Two-Component Theory of the Neutrino," *Physical Review*, vol. 105, 1957 (with Lee); "Remarks on Possible Noninvariance Under Time Reversal and Charge Conjugation," *Physical Review*, vol. 106, 1957 (with Lee); *Selected Papers, 1945-80, with Commentary*, 1983.

Secondary
Asimov, Isaac. *Asimov's Biographical Encyclopedia of Science and Technology.* Garden City, N.Y.: Doubleday, 1964. A very brief introduction to Yang's life, career, and research.

Bernstein, Jeremy. "Chen Ning Yang." In *Encyclopædia Britannica*, 15th ed., vol. 12. This entry provides an excellent history of Yang's career. Divided into two sections, life and work, the article contains most of the essential information relating to this physicist. It includes a short bibliography.

———. *A Comprehensible World*. New York: Random House, 1967. Written by a colleague of Yang and Lee, this books contains a chapter that is invaluable for its month-by-month explanation of the scientific work conducted by Yang and Lee in 1957. Bernstein's descriptions of the scientific conversations they had at a Chinese restaurant and of Yang's view as to how his work reflects Chinese philosophy are essential to an understanding of the human side of this brilliant scientist.

"Cherished Law of Physics Gets Repealed." *Life* 42 (January 28, 1957): 59-60. This indispensable article not only describes Wu's experiment by means of illustrations and pictures but also explains the impact that Yang's discovery would have on the world of physics.

"Death of a Law." *Time* 69 (January 28, 1957): 59-60. An excellent article that illustrates the theory of parity and its disproof by means of a diagram. It also describes Wu's experiment in detail and predicts the consequences that Yang's work would have for the scientific world.

"New Atomic Matter Laws." *Science News Letter* 71 (January 26, 1957): 50. This article explains the parity principle and Yang's experiment in technical terms. Analogies help to clarify the material for the layman.

"Nobel Prizes." *Scientific American* 197 (December, 1957): 59. This very brief essay comments on the youth of the winners and explains why their findings were accepted so quickly.

"Physicists Win Prize: Nobelist Studied Life Particles." *Science News Letter* 72

(November 9, 1957): 293. Describes the discovery which won for Yang the prize and comments on the award's timing.

Schlessinger, Bernard S., and June H. Schlessinger, eds. *Who's Who of Nobel Prize Winners*. Phoenix, Ariz.: Oryx Press, 1986. This reference book contains a very brief description of Yang's life and publications. The entry is valuable because it includes a list of works relating to Yang. The "commentary" section explains the nature of Yang's research and discusses why Yang won the Nobel Prize.

"Secrets of the Universe." *Newsweek* 49 (January 28, 1957): 56. Describes Yang's discovery in terms understandable to the layman. Contains a good illustration which helps the reader to grasp the implications of the experiment.

"These Chinese Choose." *Newsweek* 50 (December 23, 1957): 36. This article is very interesting, because it details an attempt by Communist leaders to return Yang and Lee to China. It also includes a statement by Yang concerning his decision to stay in the United States.

Alan Brown

1957

Physics
Chen Ning Yang, China and United States
Tsung-Dao Lee, China and United States

Chemistry
Sir Alexander Todd, Great Britain

Physiology or Medicine
Daniel Bovet, Italy

Literature
Albert Camus, France

Peace
Lester B. Pearson, Canada

TSUNG-DAO LEE
1957

Born: Shanghai, China; November 25, 1926

Nationality: Chinese; after 1962, American
Areas of concentration: Particle physics and statistical mechanics

Lee and Chen Ning Yang determined that prior experiments had not tested the law of conservation of parity. They suggested experiments that could, and did, show that parity was not conserved, which led to greater theoretical understanding and experimental discoveries in the physics of elementary particles

The Award

Presentation

Professor O. B. Klein, a member of the Nobel Committee for Physics, presented the Nobel Prize in Physics to Tsung-Dao Lee and Chen Ning Yang on December 10, 1957, on behalf of the Royal Swedish Academy of Sciences and King Gustav VI, from whom each received the prize. Klein, in Swedish, pointed out that the modern atom, hardly the indivisible, unchanging entity postulated by the ancient atomists, had constituents which were themselves complex. Theories describing these "elementary" particles assumed that their reactions were left-right symmetric, that, in fact, nature made no distinction between right and left.

In attempting to explain puzzling reactions of K-mesons, Lee and Yang searched for experimental support for left-right symmetry. They found none for this type of reaction; past experiments would have given identical results if the symmetry principle did not hold. They therefore suggested experiments which would test the symmetry assumption. Klein described one experiment performed by C. S. Wu and her collaborators, in which radioactive cobalt atoms were oriented, like compass needles, by a magnetic field. The electrons, they observed, were emitted from the cobalt not symmetrically with respect to the orientation direction, but in a preferred direction. One could, Klein said, relate this direction to directions significant to the experiment and thereby communicate to an alien being what humans mean by "left," although that would be possible only if the alien's atoms were identical to those on Earth. If his atoms consisted of antiparticles, rather than particles, there would be additional considerations.

In closing, Klein said that lack of time prevented him from mentioning "the many other beautiful contributions to theoretical physics" made by Lee and Yang.

Nobel lecture

Just as they shared the prize, Lee and Yang shared the explanation of the role their discoveries had played in physics. Both presented their lectures on December 11, 1957, Yang preceding Lee. Lee began "Weak Interactions and Nonconservation of Parity," a lecture directed at listeners with substantial knowledge of physics, by stating that Yang, in his lecture, had discussed symmetry principles in physics in the light of their work. Because the work had stimulated new experiments, Lee said, he would review the subject of elementary particles and their interactions to facilitate understanding of the new results.

He described the two main particle groups—"heavy particles," such as protons, and "light particles," such as electrons—and the three interactions (other than gravitational) to which they are subject: strong, electromagnetic, and weak. Lee said that he would focus on the recent experiment that indicated parity was not conserved in weak interactions and would discuss their direct theoretical implications and possible consequences.

The first weak interaction process he considered was the beta (electron) decay of a nucleus. The first experiment to establish nonconservation of parity was performed by C. S. Wu and her colleagues on the beta decay of cobalt 60 nuclei aligned in a magnetic field. The electrons were emitted by the nuclei not symmetrically in all directions, but in a "preferred" direction with respect to the plane of the current in the electromagnet producing the field. Next, Lee sketched mathematically the reasoning leading to the conclusion that the experiment also indicated that beta decay is not invariant under charge conjugation; that is, the mathematical expressions describing the process are not identical when antiparticles are substituted for the particles. He said that it would be interesting to learn whether the beta-decay interaction was invariant (whether the mathematical description remained the same) under simultaneous parity transformation and charge conjugation (mirror reflection and antiparticle substitution).

The remainder of the lecture dealt with other weak interaction processes: a pi-meson (pion) decaying into a mu-meson (muon) and a neutrino; a K-meson decaying into a muon and a neutrino; and a lambda particle decaying into a proton and a pion. Experiments on these interactions also exhibited asymmetries, indicating that neither parity nor charge conjugation is conserved in the weak interactions.

Lee noted that the new results might be used to probe the structure of the physical world but that the most significant consequence might relate to the reexamination of old concepts. He discussed two of these. One, the two-component theory of the neutrino, a 1929 theory postulating fixed directions for the spin of the neutrino and its antiparticle relative to their direction of travel, had been discarded because it violated parity conservation, an objection no longer valid. The second, conservation of leptons, states that in all physical processes the sum of light particles remains constant. Lee showed that if the two-component theory and conservation of leptons were taken together, they would lead to the conclusion that the mass of the neutrino must be zero. He outlined experiments that could test the validity of both assumptions.

Lee concluded by noting that scientific progress results from the interplay between concepts of the universe and observations of nature, the former evolving from the latter. Sometimes, however, concepts can influence observations; as in the case involving parity, certain properties may be observed only when basic concepts have been altered.

Critical reception

Reaction to the award was, in general, as swift and favorable as the award itself had been. On November 1, 1957, *The New York Times* stated that Lee and Yang's contribution was to destroy for all time what had been considered a basic law of nature. The newspaper began its editorial in the more widely read Sunday edition (November 3) by saying, "The world of physics is unanimously applauding the award"; it went on to state that the two Chinese-born, American-trained physicists were among the youngest ever to receive the Nobel Prize and that "the recognition of their revolutionary theoretical concepts . . . [was] the quickest for any work in the history of the prizes."

Physics Today, the general-interest magazine of the American Institute of Physics, pointed out that speedy recognition had taken the form of the earliest available Nobel Prize and, in a departure from its customary matter-of-fact language, said the award had been given "for work in demolishing the notion that parity conservation can never be violated." The magazine gave its own speedy recognition in the form of a cover (December, 1957) which reproduced a page from Lee's scratch pad of the summer of 1956.

In contrast to the approval expressed by *The New York Times*, *The Times* of London exhibited a response that could be characterized as a kind of nationalistic disgruntlement. It announced the awards for both chemistry and physics (the former to Sir Alexander Todd, professor of organic chemistry at the University of Cambridge, for his work on nucleotides and nucleotide enzymes) and then stated, "The two Nobel awards are in striking contrast . . . the one for more than a quarter of a century of sustained original research, the other for a single brilliant—and successful— suggestion." *The Times* went on to say that Lee and Yang's main contribution was to suggest experiments by which conservation of parity could be tested. "Apart from the suggested experiments," it said, "the main theoretical contribution by the two was paralleled by Professor A. Salam of the Imperial College, London, and Professor Landau in the Soviet Union, papers by all of these physicists giving similar results." Most physicists would agree that these comments minimized the importance of the experiments. The reaction of the Chinese press—from mainland China to Taiwan—was, as could be expected, overwhelmingly enthusiastic, as Lee and Yang were the first Chinese citizens to be awarded a Nobel Prize.

Just how shocking the concept of nonconservation of parity was can be assessed from reactions to Lee and Yang's suggestion that parity was not universal and, later, reactions to the experimental confirmation of that fact. Before the results of the experiments had been announced, Wolfgang Pauli, a giant among Nobel laureates who had postulated the existence of the neutrino to explain an earlier physics puzzle, wrote to his former postdoctoral student, Victor F. Weisskopf, in regard to the weak interactions: "I do not believe that the Lord is a weak left-hander,"

Pauli said, "and I am ready to bet a very high sum that the experiments will give symmetric results." After the experiment showed asymmetry, Pauli wrote, "I am shocked not so much by the fact that the Lord prefers the left hand as by the fact that he still appears to be left-right symmetric when he expresses himself strongly," the last comment referring to the fact that parity is conserved in processes involving the strong interactions. Pauli was said to have stated later that he was glad he had not bet money, which he could ill afford to lose, but only part of his reputation, which he could. Two other Nobel laureates were also willing to bet against parity nonconservation: Felix Bloch, who said he would eat his hat if it were experimentally confirmed and Richard Feynman, who bet fifty dollars to one.

Nobel laureate Isidor Isaac Rabi presided over a press conference at which the experimental confirmation was presented. He recollected, at a 1986 symposium, "When I first heard what the result was, I was completely flabbergasted. It was so unbelievable." The day after the press conference, *The New York Times* carried, on the front page, the headline "Basic Concept Upset in Tests." Professor O. R. Frisch of the University of Cambridge stated in a talk at that time, "The obscure phrase 'parity is not conserved' circled the globe like a new gospel."

Biography

Tsung-Dao Lee was born in Shanghai, China, on November 25, 1926, the third of six children of businessman Tsing Kong Lee and Ming Chang Chang. He attended the Kiangsi Middle School in Kanchow, Kiangsi, graduating in 1943. He entered the National Chekiang University in Kweichow province, but the Japanese invasion prompted his evacuation to Kunming, Yunnan, where he attended the National Southwest Associated University. With the aid of Professor Ta-You Wu, he received a Chinese government fellowship, enabling him to study in the United States, where he enrolled in the graduate school of the University of Chicago. There, he became fast friends with fellow student Chen Ning Yang, whom he had met in Kunming. He received his doctorate in 1950, his thesis adviser having been Enrico Fermi. The same year, he was married to (Jeannette) Hui Chung Chin. They would have two sons, James and Stephen.

A brief period at the Yerkes Observatory was followed by one year as a research associate and lecturer at the University of California at Berkeley and two years as a member of the Institute for Advanced Study, in Princeton, New Jersey. Lee became an assistant professor at Columbia University in 1953 and a full professor in 1956, the youngest on the Columbia faculty. In 1957, he shared the Nobel Prize in Physics with Yang. Except for the years 1960 to 1963, which he spent as a professor at the Institute for Advanced Study, he has been associated with Columbia University since 1953, having been named Enrico Fermi Professor of Physics in 1964 and a university professor in 1984. Lee has received numerous honors and awards in addition to the Nobel Prize.

In 1980, he established the China-United States Physics Examination and Application (CUSPEA) Program to enable qualified Chinese physics students to study for the doctoral degree at American universities. Much of Lee's energies after 1980 would be devoted to this program.

Scientific Career

Tsung-Dao Lee, known to fellow physicists as T. D., made his mark on physics early. He received the Nobel Prize within weeks of his thirty-first birthday, the only younger scientist having been Sir Lawrence Bragg, who shared the award with his father in 1915. Although his subsequent work has not had the dramatic impact that his Nobel work on the downfall of parity did, he has remained one of the world's leading theoretical physicists, doing fundamental work in a broad range of fields.

Lee's scientific career can be said to have begun at the National Southwest Associated University in Kunming. There, he studied with Ta-You Wu, who obtained a Chinese government fellowship for Lee and took him with him to the United States in 1946. Wu wrote letters on Lee's behalf but had difficulty getting him admitted to a graduate program, as he had completed only his sophomore year. The University of Chicago, at that time, accepted students without formal degrees if they were familiar with the great books designated by then-President Hutchins. Lee has said,

> Luckily for me, the system was so fluid that it was possible to be admitted even if one had not heard of the great books. I convinced the admissions officer that I was quite knowledgeable in the oriental equivalent of such classics (Confucius, Mencius, Laotse, etc.), which she accepted without verification.

The science departments at the University of Chicago were, perhaps, the best in the world then, with a distinguished faculty that included five members who were or would become Nobel laureates and equally impressive students, four of whom had won the Nobel Prize by the late 1980's. One of these students was Yang, with whom Lee developed a close friendship. In 1948, Lee began his thesis research under Enrico Fermi, whose reputation as a teacher matched his reputation as a researcher. Fermi was a great inspiration and a considerable influence in the scientific lives of his students. While still a graduate student, Lee, together with Yang and M. Rosenbluth, both students of Edward Teller, wrote a paper which was, in effect, an extension of Fermi's theory of beta (electron) decay to other interactions. Lee's doctoral thesis, on white dwarf stars, was completed in 1949.

On Fermi's recommendation, Lee worked with astrophysicist Subrahmanyan Chandrasekhar (a Nobel laureate for 1983) for eight months at the Yerkes Observatory, then worked at the University of California at Berkeley for a year. This period was followed by two years at the Institute for Advanced Study in Princeton, where Yang had a position. In collaboration with Yang, Lee wrote two important papers on statistical mechanics. In 1953, Lee took a position as an assistant professor of physics at Columbia University. Except for three years, beginning in 1960, spent as a professor at the Institute for Advanced Study, Lee has been on the Columbia faculty, becoming an associate professor in 1955, a professor in 1956, Enrico Fermi Professor of Physics in 1964, and a University Professor in 1984.

At Columbia, Lee first worked in field theory, on what is now known as the Lee model, a mathematically solvable model against which new computational techniques or theorems can be checked. He then turned to particle physics, in particular to the major problem of the mid-1950's, the theta-tau puzzle. The puzzle concerned a particle, called a "K-meson," which seemed to appear in two guises. One, the theta-meson, decayed into two pions; the other, the tau-meson, decayed into three pions. Yet, the theta and the tau were the same in other respects: They had the same mass, the same charge, and the same lifetime before decay. What prevented physicists from saying that the theta and the tau were the same particle was that to do so would mean parity was violated; a particle that could decay into two pions could not decay into three if parity were conserved.

Physically, parity is related to right-handedness and left-handedness—that is, to an object and its mirror image, for a person wearing a ring on her left hand will see her image in a mirror wearing the ring on the right. It had always been assumed that the laws of physics were the same whether described by a right-handed system of coordinates or by a left-handed system, the mirror image of a right-handed system. In other words, nature was thought to be symmetric with respect to left and right; object and image could not be distinguished, because they behaved in the same manner. An analogy devised by Lee consists of two cars made exactly alike except that one is the mirror image of the other. Car A has the driver's seat on the left with the gas pedal near the driver's right foot; car B has the driver's seat on the right and the gas pedal near his left foot. Car A's driver starts the car by turning the ignition key clockwise; car B is started by turning the key counterclockwise. If the gas and the pressure on the gas pedal are the same for both, one would expect the two cars to move forward at the same speed. Since both arrangements behave in the same way and are identical except for the original right-left difference, what is called "right" and what is called "left" are entirely relative. That is the right-left symmetry principle in physics, which was accepted until 1956.

In trying to solve the theta-tau puzzle, Lee and Yang were led to examine experiments already performed. They found that the symmetry, or parity, law held in two of the three types of interaction they examined—the strong and the electromagnetic interactions—but that experiments already performed did not test the law for the weak interactions: The results would have been the same whether parity was conserved or not, but this had not been recognized. Lee and Yang then suggested experiments that would really test the law. In the first one, by C. S. Wu and her collaborators shortly after the suggestion had been made, nuclei of cobalt 60 atoms were aligned by a magnetic field at very low temperatures. If the nuclei are thought of as small spheres, each spinning on its axis in the manner that Earth turns about its axis, then alignment means spinning, say, clockwise with respect to the direction of the magnetic field. The mirror image would spin counterclockwise with respect to the field. Atomic nuclei emit electrons in the weak interaction process called beta decay. If symmetry held, as many electrons would be emitted in the hemisphere moving in the direction of the field as in the opposite hemisphere, so that the mirror image could be said to behave in the same manner as the object. In fact, however, the emission of electrons was asymmetric; there was a preferred direction. In terms of Lee's car analogy, the two cars, one the mirror image of the other, moved at different speeds. One might even have gone backward.

Thus, a law of physics was overturned: Parity was not conserved in the weak interactions. Laws are not overturned with great frequency. Ordinarily, they are not overturned at all; hence, the designation "law." When they are overturned, there are important consequences. The effects of parity nonconservation and the reconsideration of other symmetry principles such as time reversal (in which particles have their motions reversed) and charge conjugation (in which antiparticles are substituted for particles) dominated particle physics for the next decade, with Lee and Yang playing a prominent role, either directly or in providing theoretical impetus for experiments such as were performed with high-energy neutrinos, a major source of information about weak interactions. Lee and Yang shared the first Nobel Prize in Physics awarded after the experimental confirmation of their findings.

At the same time that they were working on symmetry principles in particle physics, from 1957 to 1960, Lee and Yang wrote some papers in the field of statistical mechanics, one of which has been termed a classic. Through the next decades, Lee, with several different collaborators, worked in a variety of fields and produced some two hundred papers. Beginning in 1960, he returned to an idea suggested in his very first paper: that the weak interactions might result from the exchange of a particle called the intermediate vector boson. He wrote several papers on the properties of these particles, which were hypothetical at the time. Next, he analyzed mathematical problems associated with particles that have no mass, which play an important part in the field called "quantum chromodynamics." In the 1970's, Lee, together with G. Wick, studied symmetry properties in a heavy nucleus and found that under certain circumstances, a new type of matter, having greater density, would result. This suggestion has, thus far, not been testable experimentally. Some work in field theory led Lee to consider the possibility that space and time are not continuous but discrete. After investigating the consequences of this idea for classical and quantum physics, Lee turned, in the late 1980's, to its application to the field of general relativity.

Noted for being a superb lecturer, Lee has, throughout his career, been invited to lecture before physics audiences composed of nonspecialists. A fine example of this work is *Symmetries, Asymmetries and the World of Particles*, published in 1987 from lectures given at the University of Washington. Another part of Lee's scientific career began in 1974 and is captured dramatically in that book, which begins, "Tell me, why should symmetry be of importance?" The words were uttered by Chairman Mao Zedong of the People's Republic of China shortly after a 6 A.M. telephone call to Lee's hotel in Beijing, summoning him to Mao's residence. Symmetry was, to Mao, a static concept; he believed dynamic change was the basis of society, so he was puzzled by the importance physics attached to symmetry. Lee placed a pencil on a pad and tipped the pad toward Mao, then back toward himself, causing the pencil to roll first in one direction, then in the other. He pointed out that this was a dynamic process, yet one which had symmetry. Mao apparently appreciated the demonstration, for he accepted Lee's proposal—made at the time of the Cultural Revolution, when education had been virtually suspended—that the education of the most brilliant students be maintained and strengthened. With the support of Zhou Enlai, this program led to the "youth class," an intensive educational program for talented young people, and ultimately to the China-United States Physics Examination and Application (CUSPEA) Program, established in 1980 by Lee to enable highly qualified Chinese physics students to study in American universities. In discussing CUSPEA in the essay "Reminiscences," contained in a symposium volume celebrating his sixtieth birthday, Lee said that the fellowship for American study that his Chinese teacher had helped him to obtain had changed his life. He said:

> Among all the relevant factors for creativity, "luck" is perhaps the most important; yet by its very nature it is also the least understood. While it is not possible to order a chance happening, probability can be improved, at least in a statistical sense. Appreciation of the important chance that I had in 1946 led me to organize the CUSPEA program in recent years, so that similar good fortune might come to others.

Bibliography

Primary

PHYSICS: "Interaction of Mesons with Nucleons and Light Particles," *Physical Review*, vol. 75, 1949 (with C. N. Yang and M. Rosenbluth); "Mass Degeneracy of the Heavy Mesons," *Physical Review*, vol. 102, 1956 (with Yang); "Question of Parity Conservation in Weak Interactions," *Physical Review*, vol. 104, 1956 (with Yang); "Parity Nonconservation and a Two-Component Theory of the Neutrino," *Physical Review*, vol. 105, 1957 (with Yang); "Remarks on Possible Noninvariance Under Time Reversal and Charge Conjugation," *Physical Review*, vol. 106, 1957 (with Yang); *Particle Physics and Introduction to Field Theory*, 1981; *T. D. Lee: Selected Papers*, 1986; *Symmetries, Asymmetries and the World of Particles*, 1987; "Happiness Is When Old Friends Come from Far Away," in *Thirty Years Since Parity Nonconservation: A Symposium for T. D. Lee*, 1988.

OTHER NONFICTION: "Reminiscences," in *Thirty Years Since Parity Nonconservation: A Symposium for T. D. Lee*, 1988.

Secondary

Gardner, Martin. *The Ambidextrous Universe*. New York: Basic Books, 1964. This book gives an excellent, entertaining survey of the entire subject of parity, in clear, understandable prose with no recourse to mathematics. With the aid of illustrations by John Mackey, Gardner starts with an examination of mirror reversals and a discussion of left and right in magic and art; he then explores left-right symmetry and asymmetry in the natural world. The climax is the description of the fall of parity and its consequences for modern physics. The book is intended for the general reader, but readers at all levels of scientific sophistication can profit from it.

Lee, T. D. *T. D. Lee: Selected Papers*. Edited by Gerald Feinberg. 3 vols. Boston: Birkhäuser, 1986. This work is the same as that listed in the primary bibliography; it is repeated here for the editor's assessments of the different papers and the introductions to the different areas of physics covered. These commentaries are intended for physicists, but the reader need not be a specialist in the particular fields covered.

Novick, Robert, ed. *Thirty Years Since Parity Nonconservation: A Symposium for T. D. Lee*. Boston: Birkhäuser, 1988. A collection of lectures celebrating Lee's sixtieth birthday. Along with highly technical surveys of several fields in the forefront of physics at the time of the symposium, there are reminiscences by Lee's early mentors and by the participants in the experiments that proved parity nonconservation. In "The Discovery of Nonconservation of Parity in Beta Decay," C. S. Wu gives the insider's account of that first experiment on cobalt 60 and gives the reader a good idea of how experimental physics is performed at this level. In "Demonstration of Parity Nonconservation in the π-μ-ϵ Chain," Richard Garwin re-creates the excitement of young physicists performing what they know to be a crucial experiment. Remarks by Isidor Isaac Rabi show the impact of the parity experiments on the scientific community.

Grace Marmor Spruch

1958

Physics
Pavel Alekseyevich Cherenkov, Soviet Union
Ilya Mikhailovich Frank, Soviet Union
Igor Yevgenyevich Tamm, Soviet Union

Chemistry
Frederick Sanger, Great Britain

Physiology or Medicine
George W. Beadle, United States
Edward L. Tatum, United States
Joshua Lederberg, United States

Literature
Boris Pasternak, Soviet Union

Peace
Dominique Georges Pire, Belgium

PAVEL ALEKSEYEVICH CHERENKOV
1958

Born: Novaya Chigla, Russia; July 28, 1904

Nationality: Soviet
Areas of concentration: Nuclear physics and particle physics

Cherenkov's researches into the glowing of liquids bombarded by gamma rays, undertaken in the early 1930's, led to the conclusion that the phenomenon is caused by the activity of nuclear particles moving faster than light. This discovery proved to be of extreme importance to the physicists of the atomic age, aiding in the discovery of the antiproton

The Award

Presentation

On December 10, 1958, the year's Nobel Prize in Physics was presented by Professor Karl Manne Georg Siegbahn of the Royal Swedish Academy of Sciences to three Soviet scientists: Pavel Alekseyevich Cherenkov, Ilya Mikhailovich Frank, and Igor Yevgenyevich Tamm. They were given the prize for their research into and description of the so-called Cherenkov radiation. The three men accepted the prize from the hands of King Gustav VI.

In his presentation speech, Siegbahn noted that Cherenkov had been attracted to the problem of the fluorescence of liquids bombarded by gamma rays while a graduate student under the tutelage of the famous Soviet physicist Sergei Ivanovich Vavilov in the early 1930's. For years, the bluish glow that appears under such conditions was thought to be akin to the fluorescence used by radiologists in X-ray fluoroscopes. Cherenkov, however, eliminated the possibility of the glow's being dependent on the composition of the bombarded liquid by experimenting with doubly distilled water. Eventually, he came to the conclusion that the radiation responsible for the glow was caused by incoming secondary radium electrons.

Although Cherenkov had been given the most credit for the explanation of this physical phenomenon, Siegbahn was quick to point out that it was Frank and Tamm who had provided the scientific world with acceptable mathematical reasoning to support Cherenkov's theory.

The implications of Cherenkov's theory are indeed startling. At first, the assumption that under certain circumstances atomic particles exist which possess a velocity greater than that of light seems impossible, given Albert Einstein's dictum that the speed of light is the fastest possible velocity. Yet, as Siegbahn noted, Einstein's theory applies to the speed of light in a vacuum. When light is introduced into a liquid or transparent solid, its velocity decreases dramatically, and thus, the bluish glow noted by Cherenkov is actually "the bright blue magic shine from the hectic race of the electrons with the out-distanced light."

Siegbahn ended his speech by mentioning the great importance that Cherenkov's discovery had had for modern physics. He said that scientists were better able to study the world of the atom thanks to the development of the Cherenkov counter, and he congratulated the Nobel recipients for the great theoretical and practical advances in science that their research had helped to bring about.

Nobel lecture

In his Nobel lecture, delivered on December 11 and titled "Radiation of Particles Moving at a Velocity Exceeding That of Light, and Some of the Possibilities for Their Use in Experimental Physics," Cherenkov said that the phenomenon that bore his name had been noticed and researched by generations of physicists. Lucien Mallet and the French-Polish team of Pierre and Marie Curie were noted as being among the first to have observed and investigated the Cherenkov effect the luminescence emitted by water bombarded by gamma rays.

Cherenkov went on to explain, however, that this luminescence had traditionally been regarded as nothing more than another manifestation of the phenomenon of fluorescence, noted in X-ray research, whereby particles present in the liquid are greatly responsible for the ensuing glow. Yet, experiments carried out in an attempt to "quench" the luminescence of the liquids were unsuccessful in cases where Cherenkov radiation was found. (Parallel experiments with more familiar examples of luminescent fluids succeeded.) Therefore, the possibility of the Cherenkov effect's being but another occasion of a familiar happening was eliminated.

In 1936, Cherenkov explained, an experimental breakthrough occurred which greatly helped him to solidify his theory: The asymmetrical nature of gamma radiation was documented. In the familiar case of polarized fluorescence, the main direction of the vector of electrical vibrations runs perpendicular to the beam of bombardment; with Cherenkov radiation, the vector runs parallel to the beam. Thus was born the theory that the light observed is produced by electrons moving in the substance at a speed surpassing the velocity of the light in that same medium. Cherenkov here mentioned the extreme significance of the mathematical researches of his colleagues Frank and Tamm.

The superfast phenomenon of Cherenkov radiation, which the physicist compared to the sonic boom of a jet which exceeds the speed of sound and the "bow wave" of a ship which moves faster than the waves on which the vessel travels, seems to be in conflict with Einstein's theory of relativity. This difficulty, however, is reconciled by the fact that light's velocity is actually much slower in a liquid or a transparent solid than it is in a vacuum. Totally in agreement with Einstein's theory is the postulate that the velocity of a superfast particle in a liquid can surpass the speed of light while yet remaining less than light's speed in a vaccum. Cherenkov insisted that his theory was actually less surprising than it seemed. Earlier in the twentieth century, he explained, theoretical work was already being undertaken which delved into the possibility of electrons moving at higher velocities than light, even in a vacuum.

Cherenkov concluded his lecture with a brief mention of the significance that his discovery had had for the scientific community. It had established, for example, a new discipline in physics: the study of the optics of rays moving at velocities which exceed the speed of light. He closed on an optimistic note, expressing hope that, given the ever-quickening pace of scientific research and the ever more sophisticated tools at the disposition of physicists, new and practical applications for his important discovery would be found.

Critical reception

The recognition of Cherenkov's discovery by the Royal Swedish Academy, coming when it did, is of special importance. During this period, the world was polarized into two camps dominated by the United States and the Soviet Union. The Cold War was in full swing, and the race for space was just beginning. Cherenkov's researches into high-speed optics had great significance for the Soviet space program, and instruments developed to execute experiments based on his work in physics had been sent into orbit aboard the Sputnik 3 satellite. It is not surprising, then, that American newspapers did not wax rapturous over Cherenkov's selection. Nevertheless, the importance of his research was fairly and scrupulously noted, both in the popular press and in the American scientific journals, which had followed Cherenkov's career with interest since the early 1940's.

In the Soviet Union, which prided itself on the successes of its academicians and scientists, the selection of Cherenkov, Frank, and Tamm was regarded by the press as an unusually inviting opportunity for propaganda. For the second time in five years, Soviet scientists had been singled out for recognition by the world's most prestigious learned society. It was an especially sweet moment for the Soviets: In 1956, Nikolai Semenov had shared the Nobel Prize in Chemistry with Great Britain's Sir Cyril Hinshelwood; in 1958, however, Moscow alone was in the limelight.

Western European newspapers, generally more receptive toward the Soviet Union than their American counterparts, were also more generous with praise for the laureates, perhaps partly because a great number of important articles on Cherenkov's work had first appeared in British and continental scientific publications.

Biography

Pavel Alekseyevich Cherenkov was born in the village of Novaya Chigla, Russia, on July 28 (July 15, Old Style), 1904. His parents, Aleksei and Mariya Cherenkov, were peasants. Novaya Chigla is situated in that part of the Russian Soviet Socialist Republic known as the Voronezh Oblast.

Cherenkov was thirteen years old when the October Revolution brought the Communist regime to power in Russia. His peasant background was no hindrance to his social and educational advancement; in fact, it began to open doors for him. Above all, however, the future Nobel Prize winner's academic successes and quick rise to the top of the Soviet scientific world resulted from his sharp intellect, innate curiosity, and intuitive talent for solving the most complicated problems. At the age of twenty-four, he was graduated from the State University of Voronezh and in 1940 was awarded the degree of doctor of physicomathematical sciences.

Six years later he joined the Communist Party of the Soviet Union, and in that same year (1946) he was awarded his first State Prize, sharing the honor with Sergei Vavilov, Frank, and Tamm. He was to receive the same laurels in 1952 and 1977; he also has two Orders of Lenin to his credit. In 1930, Cherenkov wed Marya Putinseva, daughter of A. M. Putinsev, a literary critic and professor of Russian literature. He has one son, Aleksei, and one daughter, Elena.

Scientific Career

Cherenkov began his scientific career as a senior scientific officer at the P. N. Lebedev Institute of Physics in the year 1930. Four years later, while doing graduate work under the direction of Soviet physicist Sergei Vavilov, the young researcher became interested in discovering the nature of the faint bluish glow that makes its appearance in liquids bombarded with gamma rays. (This phenomenon may also be noticed today in the pools of water that shield some nuclear reactors.) For years, the genesis of this glow had been misunderstood by physicists, and Cherenkov was the first to prove that it was actually caused by the emission of light by a charged particle when that particle is moving in a medium, such as a liquid, at a speed greater than the velocity of light waves traveling in the same medium.

Cherenkov's coworkers, Ilya Frank and Igor Tamm, in 1936 provided a solid mathematical grounding for the theory of "Cherenkov radiation," as the phenomenon later became known. The famous Italian nuclear physicist Enrico Fermi generalized the theory of Cherenkov radiation, taking into account the ability of the medium to absorb light in several spectral regions. Fermi's experiments greatly improved the understanding of ionization losses by charged particles, which in turn affect the polarization of a medium.

Fermi's adjustment of Cherenkov's theory came in 1940, the same year in which Cherenkov obtained the degree of doctor in physicomathematical sciences. With the development of Cherenkov's scientific career came a parade of academic honors. In 1953, he attained the rank of professor of experimental physics, and he has since been one of the key figures in the Soviet world of science. His teaching posts have included a professorship at the Moscow Physical Engineering Institute and the directorship of an important photo-meson processes laboratory.

A corresponding member of the Soviet Academy of Sciences since 1964, Cherenkov was raised to full membership in 1970. The Soviet government, so enamored of scientific progress, was not lax in recognizing this chief nuclear physicist. Cherenkov was decorated by his government a number of times, and his honors, besides the Nobel Prize, include three State Prizes of the Soviet Union and two Orders of Lenin.

Cherenkov's contribution to contemporary physics is impressive indeed. He has carried out important research in nuclear physics, high-energy particle physics, the study of cosmic rays, and the development of electron accelerators. The work for which he was awarded the Nobel Prize has initiated developments in the fields of "faster than light" optics, electromagnetic studies, Doppler effects, and Mach waves in acoustics.

Of far-ranging significance to scientific progress was the invention of the Cherenkov counter, which detects the presence of charged, subatomic particles moving at high speeds. Earlier scintillation counters could not locate particles with the exactitude of Cherenkov counters, which, because of the asymmetry of Cherenkov radiation (the bow wave effect), make it possible to measure only the particles that are moving in one direction and eliminate the interference of other particles. This characteristic of Cherenkov's instrument proved especially useful in the determination of the albedo of cosmic rays present in the upper layers of Earth's atmosphere. ("Albedo" signifies the ratio of the amount of reflected visible radiation to the amount falling on a given body.) With earlier counters, only certain amounts of particles falling in a shower of cosmic rays could be measured. With Cherenkov's instrument, however, even particles which had developed in an early stage of the shower and already disappeared could be detected and taken into account.

The Cherenkov counter is useful in determining the mass of a particle via exact measurement of its speed and momentum. Particle energy can also be accurately measured with the Cherenkov counter, which is widely employed in experiments making use of particle accelerators. The discovery of the antiproton in 1955 owed much to the work of this Nobel laureate and the practical applications of the theories that have issued from his laboratory. Seldom has a scientist contributed so fully to both the progress of abstract scientific endeavor and the useful application of scientific theory.

Bibliography

Primary

PHYSICS: Most of Cherenkov's major articles were originally published in *Doklady Akademii Nauk SSSR*, which appears in translation as *Soviet Physics-Doklady*. Some of his publications are "Vidimoe svechenie chistykh zhidkostei pod deistviem γ-radiatsii," *Doklady Akademii Nauk SSSR*, vol. 2, 1934; "Visible Radiation Produced by Electrons Moving in a Medium with Velocities Exceeding That of Light," *Physical Review*, vol. 52, 1937; *Nobelevskie lektsii*, 1960 (with I. E. Tamm and I. M. Frank).

EDITED TEXT: *Tsiklotron*, 1948.

Secondary

Barclay, F. R., and J. V. Jelley. *The Oxford Conference on Extensive Air Showers*. Harwell: A.E.R.E., 1956. An interesting description of the experimental usage of the Cherenkov counter and its performance vis-à-vis earlier scintillation counters in the measurement of cosmic phenomena. As in the book by Jelley noted below, this work is of importance to those interested in the further research possibilities into Cherenkov radiation and the application of the Cherenkov counter, though some information given out in the work by Barclay and Jelley may be outdated.

Birks, J. B. *Scintillation Counters*. New York: McGraw-Hill, 1953. Birks's book provides the reader with a good overview of the nature and usage of scintillation counters and gives an adequate assessment of Cherenkov's importance to the development of this scientific tool. An indispensable text for those interested in the practical applications of Cherenkov's theories and research achievements. Includes specific descriptions of the photomultiplier, an optical instrument of great significance for the development of Cherenkov's device.

Curran, Samuel C. *Luminescence and the Scintillation Counter*. New York: Academic Press, 1953. Like the foregoing volume, Curran's text underscores the importance and practical applications of Cherenkov's researches into the luminescence of liquids. Curran is the coinventor of the first scintillation counter, which, like Cherenkov's machine, was greatly indebted to the photomultiplier.

Jelley, John V. *Cherenkov Radiation and Its Applications*. Elmsford, N.Y.: Pergamon Press, 1958. Perhaps the greatest reference source on Cherenkov and his famous discovery, Jelley's book was written in the same year that the Soviet physicist received his Nobel Prize. Composed in highly readable scientific prose, the work will be satisfying to expert and layman alike. It contains information concerning the historical development of research into fluorescence before Cherenkov's discovery, clear synopses of the scientist's research and the latter researches undertaken on the basis of his work, and a discussion of the scientific tools invented for further work in high-speed optics and related fields. The practical applications of Cherenkov's results are also covered. Generous quotes and suggestions for further reading.

Charles S. Kraszewski

1958

Physics
Pavel Alekseyevich Cherenkov, Soviet Union
Ilya Mikhailovich Frank, Soviet Union
Igor Yevgenyevich Tamm, Soviet Union

Chemistry
Frederick Sanger, Great Britain

Physiology or Medicine
George W. Beadle, United States
Edward L. Tatum, United States
Joshua Lederberg, United States

Literature
Boris Pasternak, Soviet Union

Peace
Dominique Georges Pire, Belgium

ILYA MIKHAILOVICH FRANK
1958

Born: St. Petersburg, Russia; October 23, 1908

Nationality: Soviet
Areas of concentration: Nuclear physics, particle physics, and optics

. *Together with Igor Tamm and Pavel Cherenkov, Frank was responsible for demonstrating the nature of, and formulating a theory to explain, the phenomenon of Cherenkov radiation. Instruments based on this principle are critical to the study of elementary particles and cosmic radiation*

The Award

Presentation

Professor Karl Manne Georg Siegbahn, a member of the Royal Swedish Academy of Sciences, presented the Nobel Prize in Physics to Pavel Alekseyevich Cherenkov, Ilya Mikhailovich Frank, and Igor Yevgenyevich Tamm on December 10, 1958, on behalf of the Academy and King Gustav VI. Siegbahn began his presentation by noting that the phenomenon of Cherenkov radiation had been observed by many scientists, and that the contribution of the three Soviets consisted in their recognizing the unique nature of the effect and following through with a detailed theoretical analysis of its origin.

Cherenkov radiation is a weak bluish glow which emanates from substances under radioactive bombardment. Previous observers had assumed that the effect was caused by fluorescence: the excitation of atoms and molecules in a medium by incident, invisible radiation and subsequent spontaneous reradiation at optical wavelengths. In the early 1930's, Cherenkov, then a graduate student at the Lebedev Physics Institute in Moscow, made a number of observations which indicated that the effect could not be attributed to fluorescence. He demonstrated that the source was, instead, fast electrons moving through the medium. These results, published in 1934, established the unique nature and properties of Cherenkov radiation; it remained for Ilya Frank and Igor Tamm, colleagues of Cherenkov, to provide an explanation and mathematical model of the effect. They showed that it was produced by electrons moving in a medium at a speed greater than that of light in the same medium. Under these conditions, light waves, analogous to the bow wave of a ship and the sonic boom of a supersonic aircraft, are produced.

The discovery that Cherenkov radiation is produced only by particles traveling faster than light and that the angle of propagation depends on the velocity of the particle allowed scientists to construct sensitive instruments capable of measuring the passage of single elementary particles. Cherenkov counters were to play an important role in the discovery of the antiproton and are an essential part of the instrumentation in atomic laboratories.

Nobel lecture

Ilya Frank delivered his Nobel lecture, titled "Optics of Light Sources Moving in Refractive Media," on December 11. His address consisted of a detailed and largely theoretical analysis of radiation from moving point sources of light, of which the Cherenkov effect is but one example.

After a brief introduction, Frank touched on the phenomenon of transition radiation, which occurs when a particle crosses the boundary between two substances with different refractive indices. In this case, the mechanism for producing radiation is the difference between the change in the phase velocity of light and the change in the velocity of the particle at the boundary. The predicted effect was slight and had not been demonstrated experimentally, but it was presumed to be part of the experimentally observed Cherenkov radiation, since the apparatus used invariably involved interfaces where such transitions would be expected to occur.

Next, Frank considered the general equation for a radiating source light:

$$\frac{n\omega}{c}\cos\Theta = \frac{\omega \pm \omega_0}{v}$$

where c/n is the velocity of light of frequency ω in the medium, Θ is the angle of propagation relative to the direction of motion of the source, v is the velocity of the source, and ω_0 is the frequency of internal oscillation of a radiating source. Cherenkov radiation occurs when ω_0 is equal to zero, in which case the equation reduces to the formula for determining the direction of propagation of Cherenkov radiation.

If $n/c(v)(\cos\Theta)$ is less than unity (which in turn implies that the speed of the particle is less than the velocity of light in the medium), it follows that the term ω_0 is negative. The general equation then describes the Doppler effect for a moving source of light in a medium. The Doppler effect is the decrease in wavelength of waves propagated in front of a moving source and the corresponding increase in wavelength behind the source; it is readily observed as a change in pitch as a sound source moves rapidly past an observer.

The term $n/c(v)\cos\Theta$ will be greater than unity if a system with an internal frequency ω_0 is moving at a speed greater than the phase velocity of light in the medium; in this case, the system will radiate at "superlight" Doppler frequencies. The model predicts that internal oscillations of the system will be damped by Doppler radiation at sublight velocities, but that at superlight velocities the internal oscillations of the system will be excited at the expense of the kinetic energy of the particle.

Frank then presented a graphic representation of the three equations to demonstrate the threshold for appearance of each effect and the condition under which it would be complex, or when light of more than one frequency would be emitted at a given angle Θ. Since the function describing the variation of the refractive index of a medium with respect to wavelength is nonlinear, while the quantity ω plus or minus $\omega_0/(v)\cos\Theta$ is linear, it is possible to have more than one wavelength which satisfies the general equation. At the threshold particle velocity, which is equal to the phase velocity of light at the emitted frequency, the slope of the line is tangential to the wave function, and a single frequency is emitted. At higher particle velocities, complex Cherenkov and super-Doppler effects are possible. At particle velocities below the group velocity of light, the tangent to the wave function governs the upper limit of the appearance of complex Doppler effects.

In the final section of the lecture, Frank considered Cherenkov radiation in an optically anisotropic medium, such as a crystal, in which the magnitude of the refraction index depends not only on the frequency of light but also on its angle and polarization. Qualitatively, this can be visualized as follows: In an optically isotropic medium, a narrow beam of electrons traveling at superlight frequencies produces a cone of Cherenkov radiation which would appear in projection as a ring centered on the axis of the beam. In an optically anisotropic medium, the ring becomes distorted, because the angle of propagation that satisfies the basic equation varies with direction. Cherenkov radiation had not at the time been studied in anisotropic media, but the general theory was of interest because it also applied to the propagation of radio waves in the ionosphere. The ionosphere behaves as an anisotropic medium under the influence of Earth's magnetic field, and the theory would therefore apply to the radio output of a moving object, such as a satellite, orbiting Earth.

Critical reception

The awarding of the Nobel Prize in Physics to three Soviet physicists in 1958 attracted considerable attention both in the Soviet Union and abroad. Several factors contributed to this unusual interest. Cherenkov, Frank, and Tamm were the first Soviet scientists to be awarded a Nobel Prize in the sciences which was not shared with any Western scientists. (There had been an award in chemistry, which had been shared by Cyril Hinshelwood and Nikolai Semenov in 1956, and two awards which predated the Russian revolution.) They were not, however, the first Soviet citizens to be awarded a Nobel Prize, for in the same year, 1958, Boris Pasternak was awarded the Nobel Prize in Literature for his poetry and for *Doktor Zhivago* (1957). The literature prize was announced a week before the physics prize, and a profoundly embarrassing situation resulted for the Soviet government. The honor bestowed on Pasternak was greeted in the Soviet press with a torrent of criticism of both Pasternak and the Nobel Committee, whose motives were denounced as bourgeois and politically motivated. Faced with a choice between refusing the prize and forced emigration, Pasternak declined the prize.

It was then announced that the physics prize had been awarded to three of the most highly respected scientists in the Soviet Union. The importance of the prize to the prestige of Soviet science was such that the Soviet government was unwilling to forgo accepting the prize, notwithstanding its earlier position on the motives of the Nobel Committee. *Pravda* (as reported by *The New York Times*, October 30, 1958) featured the physics award prominently, including photographs of the three scientists and testimonials by colleagues. Parenthetically, the article mentioned that the Nobel Prizes in science had always recognized true merit, while those for literature had sometimes been inspired by reactionary political motives.

Although the irony of the juxtaposition of the awards attracted the most attention in the Western press, reaction to the physics award was generally favorable. The claims of a French professor, Lucien Mallet, to have anticipated Cherenkov's discovery attracted brief attention, but, as the science correspondent of *The Times* of London pointed out (November 1), the award had been given not for observing the effect but for thoroughly investigating it and providing a theoretical analysis which would form the basis for future uses of the phenomenon in instrumentation.

The New York Times (October 24) summed up the Western attitude in an editorial titled "Science and Internationalism." In it, the editor discussed the relationship between the work of the Soviet laureates and that of contemporary American nuclear physicists and between the work of Frederick Sanger, winner of the 1958 chemistry prize, and that of the Soviet botanist Mikhail Tsvett. He concluded, "These latest Nobel Prizes not only honor distinguished men of science but also reassert the concept of scientific internationalism as one which transcends all barriers of nation, politics and ideology."

Biography

Ilya Mikhailovich Frank was born October 23 (October 10, Old Style), 1908, in St. Petersburg, Russia, the younger of two sons of Mikhail L. Frank, a professor of mathematics, and Yelizaveta M. Gratsianova, a physician. His older brother, Gleb Mikhailovich Frank, was a noted biophysicist and a member of the Soviet Academy of Sciences. Ilya Frank married Ella Abramovna Beilikhis, a historian, in 1937; they would have one son, Alexander.

Frank was graduated from Moscow State University in 1930, and he subsequently joined the laboratory of A. N. Terenin at the Vavilov State Optical Institute. The work that he did there served as the basis for awarding him the doctoral degree in 1934, when he was only twenty-six years old. At Sergei Vavilov's suggestion, he then transferred to the Lebedev Physics Institute, which had just separated from the Physics and Mathematics Institute. It was there, from 1934 to 1937, that he, together with Vavilov, Vavilov's graduate student Pavel Cherenkov, and their senior colleague Igor Tamm, commenced his renowned studies of Cherenkov radiation. At the same time, he was one of a group of young physicists studying atomic nuclei.

Frank became a professor of physics at Moscow State University in 1940. He became the organizer and head of the Laboratory of the Atomic Nucleus, Physics Institute of the Academy of Sciences, and the organizer and director of the Laboratory of Neutron Physics at the United Institute of Nuclear Research in Dubna. Between 1946 and 1956, he also headed the Laboratory of Radioactive Radiation and the Scientific Physics Institute of Moscow State University.

Frank's accomplishments as a physicist have been well recognized and rewarded in the Soviet Union. He was elected a corresponding member of the Soviet Academy of Sciences in 1946 and a full member in 1968. He received the State Prize of the Soviet Union in 1946, 1954, and 1971, and he was awarded three Orders of Lenin and several other orders and medals. He has continued to be active in his profession well past the usual retirement age of sixty, making a major contribution to the 1984 events commemorating the fiftieth anniversary of the discovery of Cherenkov radiation.

Scientific Career

Frank's scientific career began in the field of optics, in which he worked as a graduate student, but gradually shifted into nuclear physics. It was during the course of the shift that he became interested in the problem of Cherenkov radiation, which might be said to embody aspects of both fields. While still at Moscow State University, he carried out an experimental study of luminescence quenching in fluids under the direction of Sergei Vavilov. After that, he spent several years studying photochemical reactions by optical methods; this work earned for him the doctoral degree in 1934.

Because he had earlier worked on luminescence problems with Vavilov, it was natural that he should be included from the outset in Cherenkov and Vavilov's experiments on the emissions produced by various substances under gamma-ray bombardment. In his 1984 paper on the conceptual history of Vavilov-Cherenkov radiation, Frank recalls how the experimenters would sit in total darkness discussing theories while waiting for their eyes to become sufficiently adapted to the dark to serve as instruments to measure the threshold for Cherenkov radiation. Tamm's association with these experiments came somewhat later, when it became clear from the experimental data that some unusual physical principle was involved.

The four physicists eventually came to the conclusion that the radiation was produced by electrons traveling at a speed greater than that of the light in the medium. This theoretically derived explanation of Vavilov-Cherenkov radiation, presented to the Soviet Academy of Sciences in January of 1937, initially met with disbelief, despite good agreement with additional experimental results obtained by Cherenkov in 1936 and 1937. As Tamm recalled in his Nobel Prize lecture, it was not until after the paper had been delivered that he and Frank realized the full implications of the theory. Cherenkov's results and their theoretical interpretation were at first noted only by Soviet physicists, although the Soviet journal in which they were published was available to Western scientists. In 1937, a paper by Cherenkov comparing the experimental and theoretical results was sent to the prestigious British journal *Nature*, which turned it down, presumably because the results seemed to the editors doubtful at best. The paper, titled "Visible Radiation Produced by Electrons Moving in a Medium with Velocities Exceeding That of Light," was eventually published in *Physical Review*. Further experimental confirmation of the effect was provided in 1938 by B. Collins and V. G. Reiling in the United States, who coined the term "Cherenkov radiation."

The explanation of the Cherenkov effect became for Frank a starting point for a series of theoretical investigations on the optical properties of light sources moving in a medium; some of this work was summarized in his Nobel lecture. Of the range of problems he investigated, the most widely noted was the phenomenon of transition radiation, predicted and theoretically described in 1945 in a paper written with V. L. Ginsberg and subsequently experimentally verified in the 1960's. Transition radiation is the radiation that occurs because of the change in velocity of a relativistic particle at the boundary between two media with different refractive indices. It has potential uses in investigations of the optical properties of matter and in measurements of the energy of relativistic particles. Other papers published by Frank dealt with the Doppler effect in refractive media, Doppler effects at superlight velocities, Cherenkov radiation of multipoles, and the scattering of light by fast electrons moving in a refractive medium.

· During World War II, the Physics Institute of the Academy of Sciences was evacuated from Moscow to Kazan, and Frank, along with other members of the institute, worked predominantly on practical problems of immediate concern to the war effort, such as using gamma rays to measure tube thickness.

From the mid-1940's onward, although he continued to work and publish in the field of optics, Frank's attention was increasingly devoted to nuclear physics. His prewar research in this area had been directed toward electron-positron pairs produced by gamma rays in krypton and nitrogen. After the war, the focus of Soviet nuclear research shifted, and in the words of the testimonial biography in *Soviet Physics-Uspekhi* (1968), Frank "energetically participated in the study of the problems confronting the Soviet nuclear physics in connection with the urgent need to solve the atomic problem"—that is, the need to develop a Soviet atom bomb. He conducted a program of theoretical and experimental research into the propagation of neutrons in heterogeneous uranium-graphite systems and performed experimental studies of light-nucleus reactions during which neutrons are emitted. Initially he used a stationary neutron source for his neutron-propagation experiments, but in 1952 he showed that a pulsed neutron source gave better results. That led to the discovery of the diffusion cooling of neutrons. Frank was also instrumental in building a pulsed fast-neutron reactor at Dubno, in the Ukraine. This installation has been used to study polarized neutrons and neutron resonance; similar facilities have been built in other countries.

In the late 1970's and early 1980's, although he continued to produce technical papers, Frank increasingly devoted his attention to popular articles on nuclear physics and Cherenkov radiation. He produced a number of memoirs, testimonial biographies, and reviews on the history of science. His career has been characterized by great scientific productivity and superior organizational ability, as witnessed by his roles in the founding of laboratories and the organizing of conferences.

Bibliography

Primary

PHYSICS: Some of Frank's papers, originally published in Russian, have appeared in the *Bulletin of the Academy of Sciences of the USSR, Physical Series* and *Soviet Physics-Doklady*. Selected works in English are "Coherent Visible Radiation of Fast Electrons Passing Through Matter," *Comptes rendus (doklady) de l'Académie des sciences, U.S.S.R.*, vol. 14, 1937 (with Igor Tamm); "Einstein and Optics," *Soviet Physics-Uspekhi*, vol. 22, 1980; "Conceptual History of the Vavilov-Cherenkov Radiation," *Soviet Physics-Uspekhi*, vol. 27, 1984.

Secondary

Barit, I. Ya., B. M. Bolotovskii, L. E. Lazareva, L. I. Luschikov, Yu. P. Popov, and E. L. Feinberg. "Il'ya Mikhailovich Frank on his Seventieth Birthday." *Soviet Physics-Uspekhi* 21, no. 10 (1978): 887-892. This brief testimonial biography covers much of the same ground as the biography published in the same journal ten years earlier, but it contains more information on Frank's research with fast neutrons. It also covers the period from 1968-1978, when Frank turned his attention toward historical and popular writing.

Barit, I. Ya., L. E. Lazareva, E. L. Feinberg, and F. L. Shapiro. "Il'ya Mikhailovich Frank (In Honor of His Sixtieth Birthday)." *Soviet Physics-Uspekhi* 11 (1968): 782-784. A chronological account of Frank's scientific career and professional accomplishments, written by colleagues as an official tribute. It contains sketchy personal information, an abbreviated bibliography of technical papers written by Frank, and some discussion of the nature and importance of his discoveries.

Medvedev, Zhores. *Soviet Science*. New York: W. W. Norton, 1978. Although this is a standard reference on science in the Soviet Union, it is principally a critique of the Soviet scientific establishment; written by a biologist, it concentrates on biology, a weak point in Soviet science, particularly in the Stalin era. It is a useful reference for understanding the scientific hierarchy in the Soviet Union and the significance of awards and titles. The grim picture it paints of Soviet scientific life in the 1930's makes the accomplishments of Frank and his coworkers during the period seem particularly remarkable.

Weber, Robert L. *Pioneers of Science: Nobel Prize Winners in Physics*. Edited by J. M. A. Lenihan. Bristol, England: Adam Hilger, 1980. This book consists of brief sketches of all Nobel Prize-winning physicists to 1980. Its chief use is as a source of biographical data, and it includes personal data on Soviet scientists which Soviet sources do not include. Since it is complete to 1980, it is helpful for charting the careers of living physicists. The entry on Frank is brief and concentrates on the nature of Cherenkov radiation rather than on the physicist's career.

Martha Sherwood-Pike

1958

Physics
Pavel Alekseyevich Cherenkov, Soviet Union
Ilya Mikhailovich Frank, Soviet Union
Igor Yevgenyevich Tamm, Soviet Union

Chemistry
Frederick Sanger, Great Britain

Physiology or Medicine
George W. Beadle, United States
Edward L. Tatum, United States
Joshua Lederberg, United States

Literature
Boris Pasternak, Soviet Union

Peace
Dominique Georges Pire, Belgium

IGOR YEVGENYEVICH TAMM
1958

Born: Vladivostok, Siberia; July 8, 1895
Died: Moscow, Soviet Union; April 12, 1971
Nationality: Soviet
Areas of concentration: Particle physics and plasma physics

Tamm's analysis, achieved with Ilya Frank and Pavel Cherenkov, of the properties of energy radiated by particles traveling at a speed faster than that of light in a medium, demonstrated a new and unanticipated physical phenomenon and was decisive in the development of instrumentation to study the structure of matter

The Award

Presentation

Professor Karl Manne Georg Siegbahn, a member of the Royal Swedish Academy of Sciences, presented the Nobel Prize in Physics to Pavel Alekseyevich Cherenkov, Ilya Mikhailovich Frank, and Igor Yevgenyevich Tamm on December 10, 1958, on behalf of the Academy and King Gustav VI. Siegbahn began his presentation by noting that the phenomenon of Cherenkov radiation had been observed by many scientists but that the three Soviets had been the only ones to follow through with a detailed analysis of the properties of the effect, which in turn had led to recognition and a theoretical analysis of its unique nature.

Transparent substances, regardless of their chemical composition, emit a weak glow under radioactive bombardment. Early observers attributed this to fluorescence produced by excitation of atoms in the medium. Cherenkov, a graduate student at the Lebedev Physics Institute in Moscow, made a number of observations which indicated that the effect could not be attributed to fluorescence and that the source was, instead, fast electrons moving through the medium. These results, published in 1934, established the unique nature and general properties of Cherenkov radiation.

In 1937, Igor Tamm and Ilya Frank published a detailed theoretical analysis of Cherenkov radiation. They showed that it was produced by electrons moving in a medium at a speed greater than that of light in the medium. Under these conditions, waves of visible light, analogous to the bow wave of a ship and the roar of a supersonic aircraft, are produced.

The knowledge that Cherenkov radiation is produced only by particles traveling faster than light and that the angle of propagation depends on the velocity of the particle and the wavelength of the light makes it possible to construct sensitive instruments capable of measuring the passage of single elementary particles. Cherenkov counters played a decisive part in the discovery of the antiproton and became an essential part of the instrumentation in atomic laboratories.

Nobel lecture

Tamm began his Nobel lecture, titled "General Characteristics of Radiations Emitted by Systems Moving with Super-Light Velocities with Some Applications to Plasma Physics," with a brief historical background, a general description of Vavilov-Cherenkov radiation (as it is called in the Soviet literature, in recognition of the contribution of Cherenkov's graduate adviser, Sergei Vavilov, to the initial discovery), and two derivations of the formula for its propagation. He concluded with a theoretical discussion of the properties of Cherenkov radiation in a plasma, a topic then being investigated for its possible relevance to the production of controlled thermonuclear reactions.

The principle behind Cherenkov radiation is actually a simple one. The equation governing radiation by a system inherently capable of radiating, moving at a constant velocity v, is $\cos \Theta = c'(\omega)/v$, where $c'(\omega)$ is the speed, in the medium, of radiation of frequency ω and $\cos \Theta$ is the angle of propagation of the radiation. For high-energy electrons traversing a range of transparent media, the radiation is produced in a continuous, relatively narrow band centered in the blue region of the visible spectrum (hence the characteristic color of the emission) at a small angle relative to the direction of the electron's path. This relationship had already been demonstrated for sound waves (Mach waves) produced by objects moving at supersonic velocities and had been derived on purely theoretical grounds by the German physicist Arnold Sommerfeld in 1904 for an electron moving at superlight velocities in a vacuum. It was difficult for physicists to make the connection between theories derived from classical electrodynamics and aerodynamics and the observed phenomenon, because they had been taught that electromagnetic radiation in general is produced only by the nonuniform motion of charges, and because, according to the general theory of relativity, particles are incapable of moving at superlight velocities in a vacuum. Even Tamm and his coworkers were at first reluctant to trust the formulas they had derived, despite agreement with experimental results, and it was only after they had presented their paper that they perceived that it was possible for a particle to move *through a medium* at a speed faster than that of light *in the medium*. The fundamental equation governing Cherenkov radiation was also derived by Ilya Frank, in 1943, from the laws governing the kinetic energy and internal energy of a moving particle. At low velocities, internal energy is transformed into radiative energy; at velocities exceeding those of the wave being propagated, kinetic energy is transformed into radiative energy and self-excitation. This relationship applies to supersonic aircraft as well as to moving particles.

In a plasma, such as a highly ionized gas, longitudinal plasma waves, in which oppositely charged plasma particles oscillate along the direction of propagation of the wave, can be induced by a moving charged particle by a mechanism equivalent to the Vavilov-Cherenkov effect. This phenomenon has potential applications to the problem of heating plasmas to very high temperatures, an important process in thermonuclear research. Electrical heating of plasma becomes impracticable as the plasma becomes increasingly hot and rarefied. Since energy transfer caused by the propagation of Vavilov-Cherenkov waves is not dependent on close collisions, it ought to be a more effective method of energy transfer at high temperatures.

In plasmas, it is also possible for the reverse of the Cherenkov effect to occur: An electron traveling through the plasma at a speed equal to or greater than that of the plasma wave can "ride the crest of the wave," absorbing energy until its velocity increases so much that it drops out of phase with the wave. This damping effect was described by L. Landau in 1946. A. Morozov and L. Soloviev proposed designing vessels containing plasma in such a way that the recoil produced by the propagation of Cherenkov radiation into the wall would stabilize a current within the plasma.

In his concluding remarks, Tamm noted that his discussion of the applications of the general theory had been intended as a survey of possibilities and that he would not comment on their advantages or feasibility.

Critical reception

An unusual amount of attention, both in the West and in the Soviet Union, attended the awarding of the 1958 Nobel Prize in Physics. Several factors contributed to this situation. Cherenkov, Frank, and Tamm were the first Soviet scientists to be awarded a Nobel Prize in Physics and the first to win an award in any scientific discipline which was not shared with Western scientists. As such, they were justifiably lauded in the Soviet press. *Pravda* (as reported by *The New York Times*, October 30, 1958) featured the physics award prominently, including photographs of the three scientists and testimonials by prominent colleagues.

The reaction of the Western press to the physics prize per se was also favorable. In the words of *The New York Times* (October 30), the award gave "definitive recognition to the high quality of the experimental research in physics being done in the Soviet Union." This and other sources commented particularly on the high regard in which Tamm was held in international circles, not only for the excellence of his research in physics but also for his candor and independence as an individual.

Ironically, much of the controversy surrounding the physics prize was generated by a presumably unrelated action. In the same year, 1958, Boris Pasternak was awarded the Nobel Prize in Literature for *Doktor Zhivago* (1957), a politically unacceptable book which had been banned in the Soviet Union. The Soviet government was quick to denounce both Pasternak and the Nobel Committee, who were subjected to scathing attacks in the Soviet press.

A week later, it was announced that the physics prize had been awarded to three of the most highly respected scientists in the Soviet Union. The importance of this to the prestige of Soviet science was such that the Soviet government was unwilling to forgo acceptance of the prize, notwithstanding its earlier position on the motives of the Nobel Committee. When honoring the physicists, Soviet officials belatedly mentioned that the Nobel Prizes in science had always recognized true merit, while those for literature had sometimes been inspired by reactionary political motives. Tamm, himself a critic of political hypocrisy, must have been struck by the irony.

A minor controversy was generated by the claims of a French professor, Lucien

Mallet, that he had anticipated Cherenkov's discovery. It was quickly pointed out, however (for example, by the editors of *Science*), that Mallet, among others, had merely observed the phenomenon, while Cherenkov and his colleagues had analyzed it and placed it at the disposal of physicists.

In an editorial titled "Science and Internationalism," *The New York Times* (October 24) summed up the generally hopeful attitude of the time concerning East-West scientific cooperation, pointing out that the discoveries of Cherenkov and his colleagues were critical for contemporary American high-energy physics and that the discovery of the structure of insulin, which had won the chemistry prize for Frederick Sanger, had built on Soviet antecedents.

Biography

Igor Yevgenyevich Tamm was born in Vladivostok on July 8, 1895, the son of Evgenii Tamm, an engineer, and Olga Davydova Tamm. After completing his secondary education in Elizabethgrad (later Kirovgrad), in southern Russia, he studied for a year at the University of Edinburgh, where he learned to speak fluent English with a Scottish accent. He then returned to Russia to study physics at the University of Moscow, where, despite the interruptions of World War I (he served as a nurse on the eastern front), the Russian Revolution, and civil war, he received the *kandidat nauk* (doctoral) degree in physics in 1918.

While teaching physics at the Crimean University and the Odessa Polytechnical Institute from 1922 to 1924, Tamm formed a friendship with L. I. Mandelstam which greatly influenced his scientific career. In 1924 he moved to Moscow and joined the department of theoretical physics of Moscow University, becoming its head soon thereafter. In 1934 he organized the theoretical division of the Lebedev Physics Institute, which he directed until the last years of his life. He was elected a corresponding member of the Soviet Academy of Science in 1933 and a full member in 1953, and he was awarded the Order of State Prize for his services to science in 1946 and 1953. He was also elected to the Polish Academy of Sciences, the American Academy of Arts and Sciences, and the Swedish Physical Society.

The picture of Tamm that emerges from the recollections of those who knew him is one of an intellectually, physically, and socially energetic man: a man whose friendship and moral leadership were valued along with his intellectual qualities and an athlete whose hobbies included mountain climbing and waterskiing. It seemed to his colleagues a cruel twist of fate that he spent the final years of his life crippled by a painful and degenerative disease, through which, to the last, he retained his dignity and lucidity.

Scientific Career

The elucidation of the theory behind Cherenkov radiation was only one of several major discoveries made by Tamm during the course of his long scientific career; indeed, he himself believed that his contribution to the theory of beta forces was more significant. A widely used and celebrated textbook on the theory of electricity was the first of many contributions to widely divergent branches of physics. In the early 1930's, Tamm addressed his attention to solid-state physics, publishing internationally recognized work on the combination scattering of light in crystals. In papers on Paul Dirac's theory of the electron, he demonstrated the inevitability of states of negative energy. Investigations in 1932 into the quantum theory of metals led to the discovery of bound electron crystal-surface states (now known as "Tamm levels"), which are important in the theory of semiconductors.

Tamm's theory of beta forces, formulated in 1934, was the first systematic, quantitative analysis of interactions within the atomic nucleus. He deduced that the forces were weak and could not explain the stability of the nucleus, but the work served as a prototype for subsequent theories. In 1938, Tamm showed that although the neutron is neutral electrically, it has a magnetic moment whose sign is negative.

In his 1984 paper "Conceptual History of the Vavilov-Cherenkov Radiation," Ilya Frank gives an interesting picture of Tamm's role in that discovery. The investigations proceeded in the face of two major obstacles: the inadequacy of laboratory instrumentation at the time and the apparent contradiction between the observed effects and accepted physical theories. Because the most sensitive instrument for detecting light at the time was the human eye, the researchers were constrained to sit for an hour in total darkness before conducting their experiments, and the effects observed were near the limit of visibility even for a dark-adapted human eye. The setup, in Frank's words, had "something of the nature of a spiritualist seance" and left the experimental results open to question to a degree that would have been unlikely had photographic recording been possible.

From 1934, when the results of Cherenkov's experiments were published, until the end of 1936, Cherenkov, Vavilov, Frank, and Tamm groped for a theoretical explanation for the observed phenomena. Initially it was suggested that *Bremsstrahlung*—energy emitted as a result of the acceleration of a high-energy electron in the region of an atomic nucleus—was responsible for Cherenkov radiation, but this did not account for the observed lack of dependence of the glow's intensity on the atomic number and the refractive index of the medium. Frank recalls how Tamm telephoned him late one night in 1936, summoning him to his house, where he laid out before him the derivation of the final, correct formula. The equation was derived for a path of limited extent (eliminating the objection that a uniformly moving electron cannot radiate) but proved to be valid for a uniformly moving electron traveling faster than light.

In the early 1950's, Tamm, together with his younger colleague Andrei Sakharov, conducted important research on controlled thermonuclear reactions and thermonuclear fusion; they share the distinction of being the "fathers" of the Soviet hydrogen bomb. Like many other nuclear physicists (among them Albert Einstein and Enrico Fermi), Tamm and Sakharov were appalled by the prospect of thermonuclear war but believed, at least initially, that a balance of nuclear capability would act as a deterrent to war; they were also optimistic about the prospects for nonmilitary uses of nuclear energy.

Tamm was universally admired by his colleagues not only for the breadth and excellence of his command of physics but also for his qualities as a leader and teacher. His weekly seminars in theoretical physics were for many years a center of attraction for many of Moscow's physicists, and he served as teacher and mentor to many younger colleagues in widely varying branches of physics. The impact of Tamm's life cannot be communicated by a mere enumeration of his scientific accomplishments and awards, significant and numerous as they were. The impact of his character was also profound, and it extended beyond the realm of theoretical physics.

In the Soviet Union, scientists play a more prominent role in the impetus for reform than they do in Western countries. That can be attributed partly to the high status of distinguished scientists in the Soviet Union and to a consciousness that they are irreplaceable, which makes authorities reluctant to impose ordinary sanctions on them. Soviet scientists are therefore somewhat freer to express their opinions, although less so than their Western counterparts. Tamm himself directed his efforts for reform primarily toward the scientific community; he espoused Einstein's theory of relativity, sometimes regarded in the Soviet Union as anti-Marxist idealism, and he revised university course materials to reflect "bourgeois" advances in science. In 1956 he spearheaded a movement for reform within the Soviet Academy of Sciences, advocating abiding by majority rule and reallocating resources in a more prudent manner. He successfully fought against the diversion of promising science students from their courses of study into unskilled work programs, something which the authorities of the time thought promoted proletarian consciousness but was actually more effective in building resentment and dissipating the energies of young would-be scientists. He was also a thoughtful opponent of arms proliferation who participated in the 1957 Geneva conference on the detection of nuclear explosions; in a CBS interview in 1963, he advocated a "drastic change in our political thinking which starts from the point of view that no war at all is possible."

His example of personal integrity and advocacy of the truth had a profound effect on his students and colleagues. It is not accidental, then, that while Tamm trained many young physicists, the most internationally famous individual to come from his laboratory was the winner of the 1978 Nobel Peace Prize, Andrei Sakharov, who is noted for his outspoken advocacy of nuclear disarmament and human rights in the Soviet bloc. Sakharov himself acknowledges a debt to Tamm which goes beyond his role as a physicist.

Tamm's professional career proceeded against a backdrop of unprecedented political and social upheaval. A student during the Russian Revolution, he established himself as a distinguished physicist during the 1920's, when Soviet intellectual life was experiencing a brief, intense burst of creative expansion. The position and international reputation that he had established left him able to continue his work during the purges of the 1930's, which numbered many scientists among their victims and which had a profoundly adverse affect on the course of Soviet scientific inquiry. Tamm's groundbreaking research on Cherenkov radiation, bound electron states in crystals, and the magnetic moment of the neutron was accomplished during this bleak period. After World War II came recognition for his work in the form of state prizes, full membership in the Soviet Academy of Sciences, and generous support for research in atomic physics. Finally, under Nikita Khrushchev in the late 1950's, there came a thaw, and it was possible to speak more freely. That Tamm survived, produced, and maintained his integrity amid all of this is testimony to the strength of character that his admirers cite, even above his mastery of physics, as his essential quality.

Bibliography

Primary

PHYSICS: "Exchange Forces Between Neutrons and Protons, and Fermi's Theory," *Nature*, vol. 134, 1934; "Coherent Visible Radiation from Fast Electrons Passing Through Matter," *Comptes rendus (doklady) de l'Académie des sciences, U.S.S.R.*, vol. 14, 1937 (with Ilya Frank); "Izluchenie elektrona pri ravnomernom dvizhenii v prelomlyayushchey srede," *Trudy fizicheskogo instituta*, vol. 2, 1944; "K reliativistskoi teorii vzaimodeistvia nuklonov," *Zhurnal eksperimentalnogo i teoricheskogo fizika*, vol. 24, 1954; "Teorii magnitnykh termoyadernykh reaktsky," in *Fizika plazmy i problemy upravlyaemykh termoyadernykh reaktsky*, 1958; "General Characteristics of Vavilov-Cherenkov Radiation," *Science*, vol. 131, 1960; *Sobranie nauchnykh trudov*, 1975; *Vospominaniya*, 1981.

Secondary

Frank, I. M. "A Conceptual History of the Vavilov-Cherenkov Radiation." *Soviet Physics-Uspekhi* 27 (May, 1984): 385-395. This review, by one of the discoverers of the Cherenkov effect, is written for the historian of science rather than for a specialist in the field; although the language is at times technical, the article is basically a chronological account of research leading to the discovery, with some interesting personal insights about experimental conditions and the interactions among the individuals involved.

Frank, I. M., A. V. Shubnikov, B. A. Vredinskij, A. L. Mints, V. I. Veksler. "Sketches for a Portrait of S. I. Vavilov." *Soviet Physics-Uspekhi* 16, no. 5 (1974): 702.

Frank, I. M., S. N. Rzhevkin, N. N. Malov, G. P. Faerman, and A. A. Lebedev. "Sketches for a Portrait of S. I. Vavilov." *Soviet Physics-Uspekhi* 17, no. 6 (1975): 950-962. These two collections of short papers devoted to the memory of Sergei Vavilov, who directed Cherenkov's research, also include material on the early history of the Lebedev Physics Institute and provide a picture of working conditions and personal interactions in Soviet science in the 1920's and 1930's.

Ginzburg, V. L., M. A. Markov, A. D. Sakharov, and E. L. Feinberg. "In Memory of Igor Evgen'evich Tamm." *Soviet Physics-Uspekhi* 14 (1972): 669-670. In this official memorial biography, colleagues of Tamm trace his scientific career and give a sketch of his personality and his influence on Soviet physics. The high esteem in which Tamm was held by his colleagues, both as a scientist and as a person, is evident.

Sakharov, Andrei. *Sakharov Speaks*. Edited by Harrison Salisbury. New York: Alfred A. Knopf, 1974. A collection of Sakharov's major political statements from 1968 to 1974, including the pioneer *samizdat* essay "Progress, Coexistence, and Intellectual Freedom." The foreword by Salisbury contains an analysis of the role of the Soviet intelligentsia, especially the scientific intelligentsia, in the defense of intellectual freedom and human rights in the Soviet Union. Both this foreword and Sakharov's introduction discuss the professional association of Tamm and Sakharov and their role in the Soviet H-bomb effort.

Weber, Robert L. *Pioneers of Science: Nobel Prize Winners in Physics*. Edited by J. M. A. Lenihan. Bristol, England: Adam Hilger, 1980. This book consists of brief sketches of all Nobel Prize-winning physicists to 1980. Like other Western sources, it focuses on Tamm's independent spirit and his attempts at reform within the Soviet scientific community.

Martha Sherwood-Pike

1959

Physics
Emilio Gino Segrè, United States
Owen Chamberlain, United States

Chemistry
Jaroslav Heyrovsky, Czechoslovakia

Physiology or Medicine
Severo Ochoa, United States
Arthur Kornberg, United States

Literature
Salvatore Quasimodo, Italy

Peace
Philip Noel-Baker, Great Britain

EMILIO GINO SEGRÈ
1959

Born: Tivoli, Italy; February 1, 1905
Died: Lafayette, California; April 22, 1989
Nationality: American
Area of concentration: Nuclear physics

The discovery of the antiproton confirmed Paul Dirac's prediction that to every elementary subatomic particle there must correspond an antiparticle. At the Bevatron in Berkeley, California, Segrè, Owen Chamberlain, and others detected the first known antiprotons in 1955

The Award

Presentation

Professor E. Hulthén, Chairman of the Nobel Committee for Physics, presented the Nobel Prize in Physics to Emilio Segrè and Owen Chamberlain (born 1920) on December 10, 1959, on behalf of the Royal Swedish Academy of Sciences and King Gustav VI, from whom they accepted the prize.

Hulthén pointed out that the very successful relativistic theory of quantum mechanics developed in 1928 by Paul Adrien Maurice Dirac (1902-1984) predicts that for every subatomic particle there is a corresponding antiparticle. The antiparticle is expected to have the same mass as the original particle and the opposite electrical charge. When a particle encounters its antiparticle, the two are likely to annihilate each other, the energy of their masses being converted into kinetic energy, radiation, or the masses of lighter particles. In this part of the universe, where the prevalent particles of matter are electrons, protons, and neutrons, any antielectrons (known as "positrons"), antiprotons, or antineutrons are not likely to survive long before they undergo an annihilating collision.

With sufficient energy available, however, it is possible to create particles and antiparticles in pairs. The 1932 discovery by Carl David Anderson (born 1905) of the positron, which was created in the collisions of energetic cosmic-ray particles with air molecules, led to the general acceptance of Dirac's ideas. The Bevatron, a synchrotron which could accelerate protons to kinetic energies of 6 billion electron volts, was built at the Radiation Laboratory at the University of California at Berkeley, directed by Ernest Orlando Lawrence (1901-1958). Using Edwin M. McMillan's principle of phase synchronization, scientists designed the Bevatron to achieve energies sufficient to produce proton-antiproton pairs.

The actual detection of the first antiprotons was announced by Chamberlain, Segrè, Clyde Wiegand (born 1915), and Thomas Ypsilantis (born 1928) in 1955. Subsequently, antineutrons and the antiparticles of many subnuclear entities were created and detected, putting Dirac's conjecture on very firm ground and leading to a more complete understanding of the subatomic world.

Nobel lecture

Segrè began his Nobel lecture, entitled "Properties of Antinucleons," by acknowledging his debt to two previous Nobel Prize winners. Enrico Fermi (1901-1954) had been Segrè's teacher, mentor, and source of inspiration. Ernest Orlando Lawrence had organized a laboratory at which were designed and built the high-energy accelerators that were essential to Segrè's later work, most notably the discovery for which he was being honored by the Nobel Committee.

By 1959, the antiparticles of objects more massive than the proton had also been found in experiments using the Bevatron. Antineutrons were detected soon after antiprotons. Antiparticles to hyperons, which are unstable baryons more massive than protons and neutrons, had also been seen. The existence of hyperons themselves had been known for barely a decade. Antilambda hyperons were announced in 1958. Segrè reported the recent discovery of antisigma hyperons at Berkeley, a result that had not been published at the time of the lecture.

The possible reactions that can take place when an antiproton collides with a normal proton include elastic scattering, in which the proton and antiproton emerge unchanged but moving with different momentum; charge exchange, in which they are changed into a neutron and an antineutron; and annihilation, in which proton and antiproton disappear, and in their place two or more mesons are created out of the energy released. At higher energies of the incident antiprotons, each of these processes can be accompanied by additional mesons, a reaction known as inelastic scattering.

The rate at which a given reaction takes place is characterized by nuclear physicists by a reaction cross section. The cross section is defined as the number of reactions of a given type which take place per incident projectile particle divided by the number of target nuclei per square centimeter. One can visualize that each target nucleus has a certain size and that if the projectile hits that small area, the specified reaction will occur; otherwise, it will not. This visual model cannot be strictly correct, since it is known that nuclear cross sections depend on such factors as the energy of the incident beam, the angle of scattering, and the particular reaction being studied.

Segrè presented data for the various antiproton-proton reactions at all the energies that were available at the Bevatron. He asserted that these data could be adequately accounted for by existing models of particle physics. He illustrated the lecture with photographs of events in nuclear emulsions and bubble chambers, in which antiprotons were seen to annihilate with protons or neutrons bound in the nuclei of carbon or heavier atoms. In each case, a "star" of subatomic particles, including mesons and hyperons, was seen to radiate from the annihilation site as the particles left their tracks in the visual detector.

The number of mesons produced in an annihilation event is not fixed. Some events release only two or three mesons, each with relatively high kinetic energy; other events produce six or more rather slower mesons. The average number of pi-mesons produced per annihilation when the antiproton is nearly at rest is about five, equally divided between positively charged, negative, and neutral mesons. This multiplicity was not explained well by the theories available in 1959.

The mesons produced in annihilation reactions decay within a few nanoseconds into lighter particles, including mu-mesons (muons), electrons or positrons, and neutrinos. The muons themselves decay within microseconds into electrons or positrons and neutrinos. The positrons soon find electrons with which to annihilate. In a very brief time, there is nothing left of the annihilating pair except their energy and a few light particles. It is also possible for a proton and antiproton to annihilate directly into gamma rays rather than mesons. This process is thought to be rare, however, and has not been observed.

Segrè alluded to the discovery in 1957 of processes involving weak nuclear interactions which break the symmetry between right- and left-handed systems and between particles and antiparticles. He speculated that this asymmetry might enable one in principle to determine whether a distant star is composed of normal matter or of "antimatter," in which positrons orbit about antinuclei composed of anti-protons and antineutrons. The properties of antimatter should be very similar to ordinary matter as long as the two are kept out of contact. According to the 1957 discovery and the ideas that followed it, however, a star consisting of antimatter might emit more antineutrinos than neutrinos, which (if the antineutrinos were detectable) would enable an observer to distinguish the two cases.

In his conclusion, Segrè acknowledged the important contributions of others to his work. In addition to his coauthors, Wiegand and Ypsilantis, he singled out Oreste Piccioni (born 1915), Edward J. Lofgren (born 1914), and Herbert M. Steiner (born 1927).

Critical reception

It was clear even before the experiment was proposed that the detection of antiprotons was likely to lead to the Nobel Prize. Several groups competed for access to the Bevatron, while the machine was still under construction, for the purpose of discovering the antiparticles of the proton and the neutron. When the synchrotron began operation, there were at least four parallel efforts under way. The Segrè-Chamberlain-Wiegand-Ypsilantis group was not even the first of these to collect data.

The antiproton was hardly an unexpected discovery. As *Scientific American* put it in December, 1959, "For 25 years physicists had been confident that the antiproton existed." In the same month, *Physics Today* noted that "one of the original sup-positions in planning for the Berkeley Bevatron, in fact, was that its projected 6.2 billion electron volts would prove more than adequate for production of proton-antiproton pairs."

While the discovery of antiprotons was a great triumph in confirming the predictions of a generally accepted theory, it was a project of such near-certain outcome that an expensive accelerator could be designed with this goal in mind and several experimental groups could compete to achieve the same result. The group headed by Segrè was clever enough, and fortunate enough, to achieve the first success with the Bevatron. Although there was never any doubt that the discovery of antiprotons was worthy of a Nobel Prize, there must still have been some question on the part of the Nobel Committee about which members of the experimental group would be honored. Segrè went out of his way to give special mention to Clyde Wiegand for his "indispensable" role in the investigation. Ypsilantis was a graduate student at the time, and students who helped in some great discovery typically did not share the full honors with their thesis sponsors. In Segrè's case, it is possible that he was also being indirectly honored for his many achievements in nuclear physics before the antiproton discovery.

Others who were not members of the final discovery team also came forward to claim their shares of the credit. The physicists who sponsored, designed, and built the Bevatron certainly contributed as much to the discovery of antiprotons as the ones who made the actual detection. Lawrence, McMillan, and Lofgren had an extensive organization working with them to construct the accelerator.

Oreste Piccioni filed a suit in 1972 against Segrè and Chamberlain, claiming that they had used his ideas in the successful design of the experiment but had then excluded him from their work. In his Nobel lecture, Segrè acknowledged Piccioni's contribution. The latter's absence from Berkeley—in part because of immigration and security clearance problems—during crucial phases of the experiment account for his not being part of the discovery team. The lawsuit was dismissed on grounds that Piccioni had delayed too long before filing it.

Biography

Emilio Gino Segrè was born in Tivoli, Italy, near Rome, on February 1, 1905. He was the son of Giuseppe Segrè, an industrialist, and Amelia Treves Segrè. He went to school in Tivoli and Rome and entered the University of Rome as a student of engineering in 1922. He transferred to the study of physics in 1927 and took his doctor's degree in 1928 under Enrico Fermi. His was the first doctorate conferred under Fermi's sponsorship.

Segrè served in the Italian army in 1928 and 1929. Subsequently, he entered the University of Rome as a research assistant. In 1930 he received a Rockefeller Foundation Fellowship and worked with Otto Stern at Hamburg, Germany, and Pieter Zeeman at Amsterdam. In 1932 he returned to Italy and became an assistant professor at the University of Rome, working continuously with Fermi. Other members of the group were Eduardo Amaldi, Bruno Pontecorvo, O. D'Agostino, and Franco Rasetti. The young theoretical physicists Giulio Racah and Ettore Majorana were also in Rome during this period. It was a very productive time, during which they made important investigations into the reactions of neutrons with various atomic nuclei, including uranium.

In 1936, Segrè was appointed director of the physics laboratory at the University of Palermo; he remained there until 1938. In February, 1936, he wed Elfriede Spiro, a young German-Jewish woman who had fled Breslau to escape the Nazis. Segrè's family was also of Jewish descent, and this fact was to make it impossible for them to remain in Italy after Benito Mussolini issued racial decrees in 1938. Segrè and his wife made repeated visits to the United States during his tenure at Palermo. In the summer of 1935, he visited Ann Arbor, Michigan, with Fermi and then continued to Columbia University in New York, where he found Rasetti. In 1936, he and Elfriede, then pregnant with their son Claudio, went again to Columbia and then to the University of California at Berkeley. As he was leaving for Palermo, Segrè asked Lawrence if he could take with him some radioactive molybdenum reflectors from the cyclotron. In his laboratory at home, he discovered the missing element 43, technetium, which exists only in radioactive forms.

In 1938, Segrè returned to Berkeley without his family. Almost immediately on his arrival, he read in the newspaper that Mussolini had embraced anti-Semitism and was firing all state employees who did not satisfy his newly discovered criteria of racial purity. "It was clear to me," he wrote, "even without a letter from the Italian authorities, that I had lost my job and that there was no future for me in Italy." Lawrence offered Segrè a temporary position at Berkeley. His family was sent for, and thus began a lifelong association with the University of California. Until 1946, when he became a professor of physics, his appointments at Berkeley were always temporary. In 1941, when Italy declared war on the United States, he became an "enemy alien." Nevertheless, he became a group leader in the Manhattan Project. From 1943 to 1946, he was a leader in the effort at Los Alamos, New Mexico, to build the first atom bomb. Once more he was working with Fermi. The results of that project are well-known.

In 1944, Segrè was naturalized as an American citizen. In Berkeley, after the war, he became the leader of a group doing experimental research using the high-energy accelerators that were being built at Lawrence's laboratory. The 184-inch synchrocyclotron was the leading research instrument until the Bevatron was completed in 1954. The antiproton discovery was the result of the first experiment to be done at the Bevatron, but a long series of experiments followed, both at the Bevatron and at the synchrocyclotron.

Elfriede Segrè died in 1970. She had borne one son and two daughters. In 1972, Segrè married Rosa Mines, a native of Uruguay. That year, he became a professor emeritus at Berkeley. In 1974 he received an appointment as professor at the University of Rome. He would continue to give occasional lectures at both these universities.

Scientific Career

Segrè began his career as an atomic physicist—that is, he dealt with problems that involved the atom as a whole, and in particular the electrons that orbit the nucleus. The energy involved in a transition between atomic states is typically of the order of 1 electron volt, and the radiation emitted in such a transition is visible light. Later, Segrè would become more involved with the nucleus itself, and still later with subnuclear particles. The energy scale shifted to millions and then to billions of electron volts, and the radiation emitted was more likely to be gamma rays.

Segrè's doctoral thesis was about "anomalous dispersion of lithium vapor." His first original work concerned "forbidden" transitions in the optical spectra of alkali metals; later he investigated several types of forbidden lines, including X-ray spectra. Until 1934, he worked mainly in atomic spectra, spending two fruitful periods abroad in Zeeman's laboratory in Amsterdam. He joined with Fermi to produce a paper on hyperfine structure that included the well-known "Fermi-Segrè formula" and went to Hamburg to learn vacuum techniques and molecular beams from Otto Stern. He returned to Rome to work on atoms in very high quantum states.

In 1934 the Rome group learned of the beautiful results of Irène Joliot-Curie and Frédéric Joliot on artificial radioactivity. Fermi realized that it would be easier to use neutrons as projectiles than the charged particles that the French team had been using. Segrè and the other young physicists joined him, and they began going systematically through the table of elements, producing new artificial isotopes with regularity. They were able to show by chemical methods that the atomic numbers of the new substances they obtained were either the same as the target or one or two less. One or two protons were presumably knocked out of the target nucleus by the incident neutron.

One of Segrè's tasks was to procure samples of every element to use as targets for the neutrons. When he tried to obtain some "masurium," which was the name then given to element number 43, the supplier told him that it was not available. Before long, Segrè was to explain to the world why it was not. Element 43 does not exist in any nonradioactive form; it therefore cannot be found on Earth, except for when it has recently been created in a nuclear reaction.

The Rome group was having trouble reproducing some of their reactions. On October 24, 1934, around noon, they discovered that the filtration of neutrons through paraffin greatly increased their efficiency for activating certain substances. They stopped for lunch and a siesta. (Fermi always stopped for lunch, even when he was testing the first uranium pile reactor.) When they returned, Fermi had the answer: The paraffin slowed the neutrons down, and the slow neutrons were more easily absorbed by the target nuclei. "The scales fell from our eyes," Segrè later wrote of that day's experiences.

In 1936, Segrè took a position at Palermo. From then on his work would be independent of Fermi. In the summer of that year, he and his bride took a trip to Berkeley, California, to visit Ernest O. Lawrence's laboratory, where the first cyclotrons were operating. Inside the cyclotron were some deflector plates, used to bring out the beam. They were made of molybdenum, a metal with a high melting point, because the deflectors became quite hot during operations. They also became very radioactive and had to be replaced regularly. Segrè asked for some scraps from the latest molybdenum deflectors and took them home to Italy with him, packed in his steamer trunk.

The cyclotron scrap proved to be a fertile mine of radioactivity. Segrè isolated some radioactive phosphorus, which was used in biological investigations. Most important, he discovered element 43, which his old chemical supplier had not been able to give him. It was formed when the molybdenum (element 42) absorbed a neutron, which later decayed within the nucleus into a proton, thus raising the atomic number of the nucleus by one. The element was named technetium because it was the first artificial element. Later, in Berkeley again, Segrè and Glenn Seaborg found the element's isomer, technetium 99m, which became one of the mainstays of nuclear medicine. Segrè returned to Berkeley in 1938, expecting to spend the summer studying isotopes that were too short-lived to take back to Palermo. Political events forced him to remain permanently in California.

His work at Berkeley was equally outstanding. In 1940, D. R. Corson, K. R. Mackenzie, and Segrè found astatine, element 85, also an artificial element. After the announcement of nuclear fission in 1939, Segrè and his students worked on fission fragments. In 1941, in a result that was not published until 1946, J. W. Kennedy, Seaborg, A. C. Wahl, and Segrè discovered plutonium 239 and the fact that it, like uranium 235, is fissionable by slow neutrons.

During the war, Segrè became a group leader at Los Alamos. Among his group's important discoveries there was the spontaneous fission of plutonium (Pu) 240. This isotope profoundly affected the design of the plutonium bomb. Plutonium produced in a reactor, where there are many neutrons around, will inevitably contain Pu 240 along with Pu 239. The spontaneous fission of Pu 240 would tend to make the chain reaction start prematurely. A bomb made of a critical mass of plutonium, assembled normally, would fizzle rather than explode. To make a plutonium weapon explode, it is necessary to force the material together rapidly; consequently, the "implosion" technique was developed.

Segrè had a reputation for gruff unsentimentality. His nickname in Rome was the "basilisk," a mythical creature whose look can turn one to stone. J. Robert Oppenheimer, who was the wartime director of Los Alamos, told the story of the day he, Segrè, and some others went to inspect the site that was to become the Los Alamos laboratory. They traveled on horseback and at the end of the day came to a spot on the top of the mesa. An afternoon thunderstorm was just clearing, and a sunset was illuminating the desert in all its painted glory. As the others sat silently awestruck at the scene, Segrè spoke up: "You will come to hate it."

After the war, Segrè returned to Berkeley as a professor. Some members of his group at Los Alamos remained with him, including Wiegand and, after earning his doctorate at the University of Chicago with Fermi, Chamberlain. Segrè and Wiegand did an experiment using beryllium 7 to show that at least one nuclear process, electron capture by the beryllium nucleus, could have its rate affected by the state of chemical combination of the atom. The experimental work moved to a higher energy scale with the completion of the 184-inch cyclotron and then the Bevatron. The Bevatron was designed with an energy sufficient to produce proton-antiproton pairs. It began operation in 1954.

Several groups competed to be the first to detect antiprotons. Some of them based their technique on being able to measure the large energy release when the antiprotons annihilated against normal protons in the materials they encountered. These methods did not work at first, because the antiprotons were greatly outnumbered by negatively charged mesons, from which they could not be separated. The Segrè group chose to identify the antiprotons by simultaneously measuring their momentum and their speed. From these two quantities, the mass of the particles can be calculated. The momentum was determined by using a magnetic beamline, including magnetic focusing elements to keep the beam from spreading. The speed was measured both by time of flight and by using a newly designed velocity-selecting Cherenkov counter. By using this method, the group was able to isolate antiprotons when they were outnumbered ten million to one by less interesting particles in the beam.

In the excitement of preparing the data for publication, one graph was submitted with the data two channels out of place. The time of flight of the negative pi-mesons should have been shown peaking at the position of 40 millimicroseconds (nanoseconds.) The value of 40 is given in the written text, and a simple calculation based on the time of flight of the antiprotons shows that 40 is where the mesons should peak. The graph as published, however, seems to show the meson time of flight peaking at 38. This discrepancy has led some amateurs to claim that the mesons were traveling faster than the speed of light, which is nonsense. For Segrè, it was simply another incident in a career that throve on controversy.

Emilio Segrè has been a world leader in nuclear physics. He entered the field when it was newly born and participated in Fermi's discoveries of neutron-induced fission and the remarkable properties of slow neutrons. With the discoveries of technetium, astatine, and plutonium, he filled in and extended the periodic table of chemical elements. His wartime work on the Manhattan Project led to important insights. The discovery of the antiproton was a fitting climax to a career that was already distinguished.

Bibliography

Primary

PHYSICS: *Nuclei and Particles: An Introduction to Nuclear and Subnuclear Physics*, 1964; *Enrico Fermi, Physicist*, 1970; *From X-Rays to Quarks: Modern Physicists and Their Discoveries*, 1980; "Fifty Years up and down a Strenuous Trail," *Annual Review of Nuclear and Particle Science*, vol. 31, 1981; *From Falling Bodies to Radio Waves: Classical Physicists and Their Discoveries*, 1984.
EDITED TEXT: *Experimental Nuclear Physics*, 1953.

Secondary

Alfvén, Hannes. *Worlds-Antiworlds: Antimatter in Cosmology.* San Francisco: W. H. Freeman, 1966. An account intended for the layman, this book is written on the level of *Scientific American*. The author explains the theory of antiparticles and tells the story of their discovery. He then offers his own ideas about the possible existence of galaxies of antimatter; the reader should be warned, however, that his views are not generally accepted by cosmologists.

Fermi, Laura. *Atoms in the Family*. Chicago: University of Chicago Press, 1954. The story of life with Fermi, related by his wife with flair and drama. The same general material is covered, and naturally Segrè figures prominently, but events are described from the point of view of someone who is not a scientist.

—————————. *Industrious Immigrants: The Intellectual Migration from Europe, 1930-1941*. Chicago: University of Chicago Press, 1968. This volume is an imposing study of the huge number of gifted scholars forced to flee the advance of Fascism. It concentrates primarily on scientists known to the Fermis and is written with a feeling for the drama of the period. It also considers how world history might have been changed had these individuals been either allowed or forced to continue research in their native countries.

Forward, Robert L., and Joel Davis. *Mirror Matter: Pioneering Antimatter Physics*. New York: John Wiley & Sons, 1988. A physicist and a science writer have collaborated to describe the theories and events that led to the discoveries of antielectrons, antiprotons, and antineutrons. Details and colorful anecdotes about the scientists and the machines that made the discoveries are plentiful, as are discussions about the possible use of antimatter in the future—including its imaginary uses, such as powering the "warp drive" engines of the USS *Enterprise* on the television program *Star Trek*.

Libby, Leona M. *The Uranium People*. New York: Crane, Russak, 1979. An account, flavored with numerous personal anecdotes, of the people who worked at the Los Alamos laboratory. The author used Segrè as one of her major sources, and comments attributed to him are sprinkled throughout the book. In chapter 7, there is a revealing description of Segrè himself.

Gilbert Shapiro

1959

Physics
Emilio Gino Segrè, United States
Owen Chamberlain, United States

Chemistry
Jaroslav Heyrovsky, Czechoslovakia

Physiology or Medicine
Severo Ochoa, United States
Arthur Kornberg, United States

Literature
Salvatore Quasimodo, Italy

Peace
Philip Noel-Baker, Great Britain

OWEN CHAMBERLAIN
1959

Born: San Francisco, California; July 10, 1920

Nationality: American
Area of concentration: Nuclear physics

Chamberlain and Emilio Segrè developed the experimental method and analytical technique that made possible the discovery of the antiproton

The Award

Presentation

Professor E. Hulthén, Chairman of the Nobel Committee for Physics, presented the physics prize to Owen Chamberlain on December 10, 1959, on behalf of the Royal Swedish Academy of Sciences and the King of Sweden. Hulthén began his presentation speech with the observation that since ancient times, there had been the notion of an indivisible atom; more recently, it had been found that the atom is both divisible and made up of many "elementary particles."

With an alarming number of particles being discovered by a variety of means, Paul Adrien Maurice Dirac (1902-1984) had offered the theory that there were only two families of particles: particles and antiparticles, mirror images of each other. Evidence supporting this theory came from Carl David Anderson (born 1905), who in 1932 found the positive electron, or positron, in cosmic radiation. As a result of this success, there began a series of searches for other antiparticles, including the most logical one, the antiproton. Unfortunately, an energy level two thousand times greater than the one required for the positron was necessary for the antiproton. This discovery therefore had to wait for the construction of the particle accelerator at the University of California at Berkeley by Ernest Orlando Lawrence. Although technological achievements provided the means for the discovery, Chamberlain and Emilio Segrè (born 1905) developed the experimental method and system of analysis that made the discovery of the antiproton possible.

Hulthén concluded his remarks with a reference to Enrico Fermi (1901-1954), who had received his prize twenty-one years earlier, and reminded both recipients of Fermi's role as teacher, friend, and colleague.

Nobel lecture

Chamberlain's lecture was titled "The Early Antiproton Work" and described in some detail the contributions of other scientists that had made the detection of the antiproton possible. The search for the antiproton began with a mathematical theory proposed by Dirac in 1930. In looking at the relativistic equation relating the energy and momentum of particles, Dirac observed that the value of a particle's energy could be either positive or negative. Ordinarily, one never sees particles with negative energy; nevertheless, Dirac was able to deduce that an electron (which is negatively charged) in a negative energy state would have characteristics of a positively charged particle. That raised questions about the proton, which is normally positively charged, and suggested that there may be a negatively charged proton, or antiproton. Anderson took Dirac's theory seriously and in 1932 detected the first antielectron, which he called a "positron." The positron has the same mass as the electron but the opposite electrical charge.

Although Dirac's theory explained the electron-positron pair successfully, extending the theory to the proton created certain complexities. Nevertheless, physicists believed that there was an antiproton exactly like the proton except for electrical charge and magnetic moment. The initial search for the antiproton was centered on cosmic radiation, since there was enough energy in space to produce the particle, but the few observations that could be attributed to antiproton activity proved inconclusive. At this juncture, Ernest O. Lawrence (1901-1958) was working on the design of the Bevatron, a particle accelerator, at the University of California at Berkeley. In collaboration with Edwin McMillan (born 1907), he decided to build a machine that could produce 6 billion electron volts of energy, enough to produce the antiproton. As scientists increasingly doubted the existence of this particle, the decision was made to use the Bevatron to attempt to find it.

Chamberlain described a series of experiments in which high-energy protons were fired at a target and the resulting particles from this collision were aimed through a magnetic field, with positive particles deflected in a different direction from the negative ones. The investigating group collected the positive particles and measured those particles that possessed the momentum and velocity predicted by the mathematics of the antiproton. To identify those particles as antiprotons, a Cherenkov counter was employed, because it could distinguish between antiprotons and mesons (particles with a velocity profile similar to that of the antiproton). Given the arrangement of the magnets, it was possible to determine the momentum of the particles. In addition, a separate experiment was set up with photographic emulsions, which would provide a visual check on the counter. The life of an antiproton was short, and when one encountered a proton, there was a mutual annihilation that could be captured on film.

Chamberlain explained why this work was considered such an accomplishment. The production of an antiproton in the Bevatron was a comparatively rare event, on the order of one antiproton among one hundred thousand other particles. During Chamberlain and Segrè's experiment, more antiprotons were produced: one for every thirty thousand particles, or about one antiproton every fifteen minutes. By the end of the experiment, there was no doubt as to the existence of the antiproton. Chamberlain concluded his lecture with the observation that because antiprotons are born in pairs with protons or neutrons, like electrons and positrons, there is a strong probability that antiparticles exist for all particles. Chamberlain closed his remarks by thanking those associated with his work, including his immediate collaborators, Emilio Segrè, Clyde Wiegand, and Thomas Ypsilantis.

Critical reception

The existence of antiparticles opens the imagination to science-fiction concepts of separate universes and the production of unlimited power. There is an aesthetically pleasing concept in physics called "symmetry," according to which every particle in the universe is balanced by another particle that is its mirror image. For every positively charged particle, there is a similar one, except for the charge; for every particle that has a magnetic momentum in one direction, another has the same momentum, except in the opposite direction. If one combines this idea of symmetry with an awareness of the energy necessary to produce these antiparticles, energy achieved by the Bevatron, one can understand the exhilaration associated with the announcement of the 1959 Nobel Prize. Moreover, this award marked the beginning of an international cooperation which would become a common aspect of scientific investigation. The work being honored had begun with an abstract mathematical theory on electrons and antielectrons conceived by the Englishman Dirac in 1928; it had culminated with the discovery of the antiproton by an American and an Italian using high-energy technology developed in the United States.

In an extended article, *The New York Times* of October 25 greeted the announcement of the award to Chamberlain and Segrè with references to the power of the "atomic smasher" and to the fact that both recipients had worked on the atom bomb at Los Alamos as "pioneers of the atomic age." Chamberlain was quoted as saying in 1956, at the time of the discovery of the antiproton, that this particle could not be used to build a superbomb, because the energy needed to produce the particle was equal to the energy released through the annihilation of a proton and antiproton. The article described how the scientific community had welcomed this step in the "endless quest into the nature and the construction of the universe" and how the discovery had opened the possibility that entire galaxies were made from antimatter. Later in the article, there were biographies of both men and a mention of their association with the creator of atomic energy, Enrico Fermi. Both men had worked on the Manhattan Project, which developed the first atom bomb, and Chamberlain had been present at Alamogordo, New Mexico, when the bomb was exploded.

Time magazine of November 9 covered similar territory in a brief announcement of the award that described the discovery of the "long-sought antiproton, key particle of the stranger-than-fiction world of antimatter." On October 27, when a reporter for *The New York Times* asked the recipients for their reactions to the award, Chamberlain could only reply that he was "stunned." Segrè more matter-of-factly stated that the future of antiproton physics lay not in the search for "strange particles" but in looking more deeply into the nature of matter.

Biography

Owen Chamberlain was born on July 10, 1920, in San Francisco. His father had come to San Francisco shortly after the 1906 earthquake; he became one of the early practitioners in the medical field of radiology. During Chamberlain's youth, his father practiced in San Francisco and was on the staff of Stanford University

Hospital. When Chamberlain was ten years old, his family moved to Philadelphia and Owen attended the Germantown Friends School. Chamberlain's interest in science was encouraged and developed by his family, his schooling, and a friend of the family who brought him puzzles and games. He attended Dartmouth College and was graduated, with a major in physics, in 1941.

Chamberlain decided to continue his education in physics and began his graduate work at the University of California at Berkeley. With the outbreak of World War II, he interrupted his graduate work and joined the Manhattan Project, working on isotopes of uranium under the direction of Ernest O. Lawrence. In 1943, Chamberlain was transferred to Los Alamos, where a large team of scientists were assembled to build the first atom bomb. In 1945, he was present during the first test of the atomic weapon.

At the end of the war, Chamberlain worked for Argonne National Laboratory in Chicago and also continued his graduate work under the direction of Enrico Fermi. He received his doctoral degree in 1948 and returned to Berkeley as an instructor in physics. He became an assistant professor two years later and in 1950 was promoted to associate professor. Over the next several years, Chamberlain would concentrate on high-energy neutrons and protons. Working with Emilio Segrè and others, he demonstrated the existence of the antiproton in 1955, ending a twenty-five-year search for this elusive particle. For this work, Chamberlain and Segrè received the Nobel Prize in 1959. Chamberlain was awarded a Guggenheim Fellowship in 1957, was promoted to professor of physics at Berkeley a year later, and was chosen as the Loeb lecturer for physics at Harvard University for 1959. Chamberlain has continued to teach physics at Berkeley and has also contributed to research into high-energy particles.

Scientific Career

Owen Chamberlain's contribution to science lay in his intense dedication to furthering the understanding of nuclear particles. He came to Berkeley as a graduate student to do research in physics at a time when the existing theories predicted a number of possible particles and the experimenters possessed only limited technology with which to demonstrate the existence of such particles. It was also the time when the U.S. government began seriously to fund fundamental research in atomic physics via the Manhattan Project. Chamberlain arrived at Berkeley to begin his graduate work only to find his country at war; he joined the Manhattan Project to work under the direction of Ernest Lawrence, who was investigating uranium isotopes. Atomic theory had predicted that one of the isotopes of uranium, uranium 235, could be compressed to produce an atomic explosion, but more precise information concerning the amount and the purity of the isotope was necessary. Since work on the Manhattan Project was scattered at research centers throughout the country, it was decided to concentrate all the projects at Los Alamos, New Mexico, and Chamberlain would spend the period from 1942 to 1945 working with Emilio Segrè on neutrons.

The period Chamberlain spent at Los Alamos was to be important in his later life. Many of the most talented and promising American physicists were brought here, along with a large contingent of emigrant scientists from Western Europe. They were kept in isolation to prevent the outside world from identifying them and their work. Los Alamos was miles from any urban center, and the entire operation was organized by the U.S. Army.

Chamberlain assisted Segrè with measuring the number of neutrons produced in the spontaneous fission of one uranium isotope, uranium 238, and found the number to be small. In making nuclear weapons, one must take half of what is called the "critical mass" of the nuclear material and push it against a little more than half of another critical mass. A few neutrons are injected, and fission begins. If, however, there exists a background level of neutrons, then fission will begin early and there will be no explosion.

Chamberlain would gain practical experience working on experiments that had rigid time constraints. He would later recall that it was his patriotic duty to assist in the making of the atomic weapon, but after the explosion of the first atomic device at Alamogordo in 1945, Chamberlain and a number of his colleagues collected the fused sand from the explosion and sent samples of the destructive power of this new weapon to one hundred mayors throughout the country. Chamberlain thought it was also his patriotic duty to warn American leaders of the dangers of nuclear weapons, and he would work on nuclear disarmament throughout his career.

After the war, Chamberlain continued to work on atomic physics at the Argonne National Laboratory at Chicago and at the same time completed his doctoral dissertation under the direction of Fermi. Segrè was an old friend of Fermi, and Chamberlain was in close contact with both at Los Alamos. Thus, it seemed appropriate for Chamberlain to complete his graduate work at Chicago, under the sponsorship of the most eminent physics teacher of the time. Later, during his acceptance speech for the Nobel Prize, Chamberlain would remember Fermi with gratitude and call him the most intelligent man he had ever met. After completing his work on slow-neutron diffraction in liquids in 1948, Chamberlain was invited to return to Berkeley as an instructor in physics and was quickly promoted to assistant professor.

At Berkeley, Chamberlain began his work on the scattering of high-energy neutrons and protons in the Bevatron. Ernest Lawrence, who had begun in 1931 to build a cyclotron, a device to accelerate particles through a circular path, found that after the war federal money was available to build bigger and more powerful cyclotrons. It was natural that Chamberlain, who had worked so extensively on the nucleus of the atom, would attempt to discover the antiproton using a cyclotron. In 1928, Paul Dirac had developed a mathematical theory to describe the properties of the electron. Although the equation for the electron accounted for all the observable properties, it also predicted the existence of an electron with a positive charge, a positron. The positron was discovered by Carl Anderson in 1932; since that time scientists had searched for a negative proton, but none could be found. Indeed, in some scientific circles, it was suspected that predicting antiprotons on the basis of Dirac's equation was unwarranted. Although cosmic-ray observations gave some indications on this subject, a clear and final answer was required. Other experimental attempts had failed, because the antiproton was a heavy particle and required more energy than existing accelerators could produce. It was hoped that Berkeley's new Bevatron, capable of producing 6.2 billion electron volts, would produce the answer to the problem.

Thus, in the early 1950's, working in collaboration with Segrè and assisted by Clyde Wiegand and Thomas Ypsilantis, Chamberlain began to fire protons at a copper target. From the target came an assortment of subatomic particles, and this beam was directed through a series of lenses to select out the antiprotons. Over a number of months, the team reviewed the results of these experiments and found some events that seemed to result from proton-antiproton annihilation. On plates covered with emulsion, these events could be recorded; they left a "star" pattern that is unique to the annihilation of a pair of matter-antimatter particles.

The team's success rested on the ability to solve the intricate problem of detecting and identifying the antiproton. They created a system of magnetic focusing devices to select out each antiproton, specially constructed electron counters and timers to measure the velocity of the particles, and devices that could photograph the proton-antiproton's annihilation. In 1955, after they had made forty confirmed detections—which came to about one antiproton every fifteen minutes—they announced their results to the world. The discovery of the antiproton completed a chapter in the understanding of nuclear structure that had begun twenty-five years earlier. Not only did it confirm the Dirac equation and its implications that for every particle there would exist an antiparticle, but it eliminated the need to find all possible particles as well. Nuclear physics could now move from the subatomic level toward an investigation of even deeper structures.

Chamberlain would remain at Berkeley after the discovery and continue to teach and contribute to the field. In addition to being awarded a Guggenheim Fellowship in 1957 and the Loeb lectureship at Harvard in 1959, he was promoted to full professor at Berkeley in 1958. In 1960, he was elected to the National Academy of Sciences. He became a Fellow of the American Physical Society, as well. Chamberlain has shared his knowledge of the intricate world of atomic physics with a generation of students. In addition, he opened the door to a complex and subtle field in modern physics.

Bibliography

Primary

PHYSICS: "Observation of Antiprotons," *Physics Review*, vol. 100, 1955 (with Emilio Segrè, Clyde Wiegand, and Thomas Ypsilantis); "Antiproton Star Observed in Emulsion," *Physics Review*, vol. 101, 1956 (with W. W. Chupp, G. Goldhaber, Segrè, and Wiegand); "Antiprotons," *Nature*, vol. 177, 1956 (with Segrè, Wiegand, and Ypsilantis); "Example of an Antiproton Nucleon Annihilation," *Physics Review*, vol. 102, 1956 (with Chupp, A. G. Ekspong, G. Goldhaber, S. Goldhaber, E. Lofgren, Segrè, and Wiegand).

Secondary

Alvarez, Luis W. *Alvarez: Adventures of a Physicist*. New York: Basic Books, 1987. Although Chamberlain is mentioned only a few times, this book is relevant because it records the period and many events familiar to Chamberlain. Chapters 6, 7, and 9 deal with Fermi, Los Alamos, the bomb, and the period at Berkeley after the war.

Del Regato, Juan A. *Radiological Physicists*. New York: American Institute of Physics, 1985. Chapter 10 gives a brief description of the career of Enrico Fermi. The chapter covers the subject in greater detail than the standard reference work; it provides information on the building of the first chain reactor and the period when Chamberlain was studying at Chicago.

Kevles, Daniel J. *The Physicists: The History of a Scientific Community in Modern America*. New York: Alfred A. Knopf, 1977. Kevles tells the story of the rise and establishment of modern American physics. Chapters 20 through 23 cover the period of the Manhattan Project through the beginnings of federal funding of large physics projects. These chapters make clear the intimate relationship between the creation of the atom bomb and the new research policies that began after the war.

Ne'eman, Yuval, and Yoram Kirsh. *The Particle Hunters*. Cambridge, England: Cambridge University Press, 1983. The two authors have put together a relatively elementary text on the history of atomic particles. Although there are some equations, large segments of the narrative can be understood without reference to them. Chapters 3 and 4 are particularly relevant to antiprotons, since they cover the discoveries of the 1930's and 1940's and discuss particle accelerators.

Trefil, James S. *From Atoms to Quarks: An Introduction to the Strange World of Particle Physics*. New York: Charles Scribner's Sons, 1980. An excellent introductory text to the world of subatomic particles. Strongly recommended are chapter 4, on antimatter; chapter 6, on accelerators; and chapter 7, on the discovery of particles.

Victor W. Chen

1960

Physics
Donald A. Glaser, United States

Chemistry
Willard Libby, United States

Physiology or Medicine
Sir Macfarlane Burnet, Australia
Peter B. Medawar, Great Britain

Literature
Saint-John Perse, France

Peace
Albert Lutuli, South Africa

DONALD A. GLASER
1960

Born: Cleveland, Ohio; September 21, 1926

Nationality: American
Area of concentration: Particle physics

Glaser's invention and subsequent development of the bubble chamber revolutionized high-energy nuclear physics. An analog to the low-energy Wilson cloud chamber, the bubble chamber allows for detailed calculations and analyses of fundamental particles and their decay products, lifetimes, and reaction schemes, all of which are central to the understanding of nuclear structure

The Award

Presentation

Professor K. Siegbahn, of the Royal Swedish Academy of Sciences, presented the Nobel Prize in Physics to Donald A. Glaser at the award ceremonies on December 10, 1960, on behalf of the Academy and the King of Sweden. Siegbahn's presentation, delivered in Swedish, introduced the idea of a cloud of vapor particles used in viewing the pathway of an energetically moving object. Awarded the Nobel Prize in 1927, Charles Thomson Rees Wilson (1869-1959) had developed the cloud chamber, using a supersaturated water vapor to track radioactive decay products as they moved with fairly low energies.

In modern accelerators, however, particles are driven to energies much higher than can be handled by such cloud chambers. Glaser solved the problem by developing a bubble chamber. He used liquid heated to just below its boiling point. The passage of an atomic particle through such a superheated, unstable medium causes boiling to occur, marked by the formation of bubbles along the pathway. In 1952, Glaser was able to photograph the tracks of such high-energy particles, having analyzed the physics of bubble formation from both theoretical and experimental viewpoints. Since then, much larger bubble chambers have been built, using liquid hydrogen cooled nearly to absolute zero. Such chambers are surrounded by powerful electromagnets and equipped with complex computer instrumentation. They have led to huge advances in the investigation of the strange new particles of modern nuclear physics.

Nobel lecture

Glaser's Nobel lecture, titled "Elementary Particles and Bubble Chambers," was a careful summation of the invention, development, and subsequent uses of the bubble chamber for the investigation of the most fundamental particles in nature. Noting the finding of thirty such bodies over the previous several years, Glaser described his early interest, awakened by cosmic-ray studies, in elucidating the basic constituents of matter. He had attempted to develop a method for experimentally observing the strange particles and their interactions that would augment the older standbys, cloud chambers and nuclear emulsions.

Investigating amplifying track mechanisms, such as dielectric breakdown, Glaser decided on the thermodynamic instability of superheated liquid as a convenient mechanism for displaying extensive ionizing-particle track schemes. First solving the problem mathematically, by considering the bubble formation and energy losses of the traversing nuclear particles, Glaser located two detailed mechanisms for bubble formation: formation by mutual electrostatic repulsion and formation by superelastic collisions. Using as the test liquid diethyl ether superheated to 140 degrees Celsius under one atmosphere of pressure, Glaser began with bubble chambers a few cubic centimeters in size, taking pictures at a rate of three thousand per second. The experiment was highly successful.

Glaser decided to use liquid hydrogen in a larger, aluminum chamber, which also performed well. Using xenon in still-larger versions of the chamber, Glaser gathered precise information on various nuclear quantities, such as mass, spin, and lifetime, and on particle production rates, interactions, and decay rates. Literally millions of photographs, several examples of which were supplied in Glaser's lecture, have been taken of tracks in bubble chambers; indeed, it has been difficult to develop computer techniques fast enough to analyze all the information being made available.

Critical reception

The immediate reaction to the Nobel Committee's choice was extremely positive. Mentioning two earlier winners involved with elementary particle studies, *Science* (November 11, 1960) acknowledged that Glaser had bridged the gap between the earlier techniques by evolving a process in which nuclear particles left traces in superheated liquids, the trails appearing as strings of fine bubbles. *Science* also made a point of mentioning that, for the first time in the sixty-year history of the Nobel awards, two scientists (Willard Libby and Glaser) from the same university (the University of California at Berkeley) had won the chemistry and physics prizes simultaneously and exclusively.

Newsweek of November 14, 1960, interviewed Glaser, who had "always wanted to do something with particle physics." The magazine noted that California was the home of the greatest number of Nobel Prize winners in physics and chemistry—twelve. *The New Yorker* of November 19 attributed Glaser's success to his ability to build chambers of a size and shape that allowed him to take sophisticated pictures of his targets, the elementary particles of nature.

The popular press was enthusiastic about Glaser's award. *The New York Times* of November 4 and the *New York World-Telegram* of November 3 noted his success in developing elegant, complex techniques for understanding the fundamental nature of matter. *Time* and *The Christian Science Monitor* proudly pointed to the work Americans were doing in advancing the fields of chemistry and physics. *Life* of

January, 1961, mentioned that on November 28, about a week before leaving for Sweden to attend the official Nobel Prize ceremonies on December 10, Glaser had wed Ruth Louise Thompson, whom he had met when she was a Berkeley graduate student in the Lawrence Livermore Radiation Laboratory.

In the scientific journals, the response was also positive. *Nucleonics* of December reported that Glaser had been swamped with congratulatory telegrams on the night of the announcement. In his first experiments, the article said, Glaser had used beer. The subsequent failure had made him turn to diethyl ether, and his basic theory was proved when particles from a cobalt 60 source produced the requisite bubbles. The magazine quoted him as saying, "I am planning to propose more experiments with the Bevatron here. Frankly, I'm a little bored with the bubble chamber."

Physics Today (January, 1961) did a briefing of Glaser's works, noting that his original idea had been based on the observation that boiling commences in a superheated liquid if a foreign object is put in as a source, or concentration point, for the vapor. After demonstrating the feasibility of the idea, Glaser had developed the bubble chamber, which became an indispensable accessory of high-energy particle accelerators.

Biography

Donald Arthur Glaser was born in Cleveland, Ohio, on September 21, 1926, the son of William J. Glaser, a businessman, and his wife, Lena. Both were Russian immigrants. Glaser received his early education in the public school system of Cleveland Heights, Ohio. For college, he chose to attend Case Institute of Technology to study mathematics and physics. As a child, his interests and talent had been in music, which he studied for a time, playing the viola and violin, at the Cleveland Institute of Music. At Case, however, he did his first original scientific research, an electron diffraction study of the properties of thin metallic films evaporated onto crystalline metal substrates.

On receiving his bachelor of science degree in 1946, and after teaching mathematics at Case in the spring of that year, Glaser went to the California Institute of Technology (Caltech) for graduate studies. He finished his doctoral work in 1949, receiving his degree in physics and mathematics in 1950 while already working as an instructor in physics at the University of Michigan. His doctoral thesis research marked the beginning of his major work in physics; it concerned an experimental study of the momentum spectrum of high-energy cosmic rays and mesons at sea level. The University of Michigan awarded him an assistant professorship in 1953, an associate professorship in 1955, and a full professorship in 1957, when he was only thirty-one years old.

Glaser has received many honors for his work. Among them are the Henry Russell Award of the University of Michigan, the Charles V. Boys Prize in Physics of the Physical Society of London, the American Physical Society Prize, a National Science Fellowship, and a Guggenheim Fellowship. He has written widely for professional and scientific journals in the United States and Europe and is a member of the American Physical Society and Sigma Xi. In addition, he has served as a consultant to the Institute for Nuclear Studies at the University of Chicago.

Scientific Career

Glaser began his greatest scientific work while at the University of Michigan. In 1952, after having worked with Carl David Anderson (the 1936 physics prizewinner) at Caltech on cosmic-ray particles, he became extremely dissatisfied with the tools then available for the detection and measurement of nuclear particles. The Wilson cloud chamber, although improved by many physicists, had major flaws for doing high-energy work. It held a gas rarefied enough that all the particles passing through it could form only a relatively small number of ions. Rare or short-lived nuclear events were, therefore, bound to be missed. Glaser also found that photographic or spark emulsions worked extremely poorly when confronted by the energetic particles being accelerated out of the new billion-volt atom accelerators.

Glaser started along traditional lines, examining various experimental techniques and constructing numerous diffusion cloud chambers and parallel-plate spark counters before finally deciding that something new was necessary: a device that would accept large volumes of heavy-density materials and have a brief turnover time. In considering amplifying processes sensitive to very minute amounts of energy carried by fast, charged bodies, he arrived at the idea of instabilities involving liquids and solids. Examples of such instabilities include monomers' tendency to polymerize, instabilities caused by intense electric fields, and thermodynamic instabilities found in supercooled liquids or superheated solids and liquids.

Glaser's idea was based on a well-known observation: Boiling will start quickly in a superheated liquid if a foreign object, such as a seed, droplet, or gasket, is introduced to serve as a point of concentration of energy for the vapor. He reasoned correctly that the charged ions produced when a fast-moving charged body passed through the solution would have the same effect, producing bubbles. Glaser devised two models of bubble formation: The first involved like-signed clusters of ions forming bubbles by mutual electrostatic repulsion, and the second involved the transference of energy from the excited atoms and molecules into localized heating via superelastic collisions. Instead of allowing supercooled vapor to condense about ions, then, Glaser decided that it would be best to get superheated liquid to boil around ions, forming drops of gas in a sea of liquid. (It is said that he had this revelation while watching bubbles form in a glass of beer.) For this proposed effect to occur, the liquid had to be nonconductive, allowing the ions to retain their charges. Glaser also showed, both mathematically and experimentally, that the liquid had to have a low surface tension and high vapor pressure so that the bubbles would not collapse before there was time to photograph them.

In 1952, Glaser constructed his first bubble chamber; it was only several inches in diameter. His first experiments, in which he used beer exposed to gamma rays, failed, but later attempts with diethyl ether were quite successful. Filling a heavy-walled capillary tube with pure vapor and liquid, he cooled the vapor, causing the pressure to drop to one atmosphere and superheating the liquid to 140 degrees Celsius. When the liquid was exposed to gamma rays from a cobalt 60 source, the ether boiled violently and instantaneously. Glaser found that the bubbles grew to a millimeter in diameter in 300 microseconds and were easily seen when photographed at a rate of three thousand pictures per second. Such photography allowed for precise measurements of the particles to be made. After proving the feasibility of his idea at the University of Michigan, Glaser built an improved chamber, with liquid propane as the fluid, and tested it at the Brookhaven National Laboratories. There, in the first ten minutes, he obtained pictures of nuclear events seldom seen in their entirety by other detection methods.

Calculations showed that greater efficiency could be obtained with lower temperatures, so Glaser soon switched to liquid hydrogen, going to the University of Chicago to use its cryogenic facilities. He worked on liquid hydrogen bubbles, showing that superheated liquid hydrogen was radiation-sensitive. He also found that any liquid, tested seriously, would work as a chamber medium. Fabricated of aluminum, with flat glass windows and rubber gaskets, the bubble chambers were soon being built in much larger sizes.

The original bubble chambers were useful only for showing the paths of charged particles. In 1956, however, Glaser began using xenon for the internal fluid and vapor. Subatomic events never before revealed were photographed for the first time. The xenon gas could be used to take pictures of neutral as well as charged particles, the greater density of the liquid making it possible for more high-energy particles to react with nuclei and leave distinct visual trails behind. Copious quantities of data on particles and their interactions were produced, including precise measurements of mass, spin, lifetime, and polarization. A completely new reaction, nuclear fusion catalyzed by mu-mesons, was discovered in the hydrogen bubble chamber.

In 1959, Glasser became professor of physics at Berkeley, where he developed larger and more computer-oriented bubble equipment. The chamber had become a necessary accessory to cyclotrons. The largest of Glaser's time, built at Berkeley, was the 180-centimeter, 500-liter hydrogen chamber, constructed under the direction of Luis W. Alvarez (born 1911). Because of xenon's high density and the rapid cycling times of the large chambers, abundant information was generated on particle production, interaction, and decay, particularly for the neutral lambda hyperon, the neutral K-meson, and the neutral sigma hyperon. Other experiments provided valuable information on pion-proton scattering, parity violations in nonleptonic hyperon decay, and the branching ratios in positive K-meson decay.

Bubble chambers were shown to be far more sensitive and efficient than the old cloud chambers or spark devices. Particularly useful for very high-energy particles, the equipment made practical experiments that would otherwise have been extremely difficult or even impossible to conduct. In a bubble chamber, the energetic bodies strike more targets per unit of distance in the dense liquid and so are more quickly slowed, forming shorter and more highly curved paths that can be studied in their entirety. The Berkeley chamber could measure tracks every fourteen seconds, with three photographs taken for stereoscopic purposes. In 1959 and 1960 alone, half a million photographs were taken; for one experiment, Glaser's group analyzed 160,000 pictures.

After receiving the Nobel Prize in Physics, Glaser announced that he was going to the University of Copenhagen and changing his focus from nuclear physics to molecular biology. Later, he returned to the United States to accept a position in the molecular biology department of the University of California at Berkeley.

Bibliography

Primary

PHYSICS: "Some Effects of Ionizing Radiation on the Formation of Bubbles in Liquids," *Physical Review*, vol. 87, 1952; "Progress Report on the Development of Bubble Chambers," *Nuovo Cimento Supplement*, vol. 11, 1953; "Characteristics of Bubble Chambers," *Physical Review*, vol. 97, 1955 (with D. C. Rahm); "Bubble Counting for the Determination of the Velocities of Charged Particles in Bubble Chambers," *Physical Review*, vol. 102, 1956 (with Rahm and C. Dodd).

Secondary

Asimov, Isaac. *The History of Physics*. New York: Walker, 1984. This work offers an all-inclusive overview of the history of physics. Without mathematics, Asimov treats in a lucid fashion the structure of the nucleus and the numerous particles found in nature. Recommended to the layman who would like to ramble in the historical development of a science.

Goldsmith, Maurice, and Edwin Shaw. *Europe's Giant Accelerator: The Story of the CERN 400 GeV Proton Synchrotron*. London: Taylor and Francis, 1977. Details the history and evolution of the ideas leading to the CERN 400 giga-electron volt proton accelerator and its associated equipment, including the bubble chamber. Illustrates knowledge gained and sought, with emphasis on the types of research done and the particles and forces investigated. Thoroughly illustrated with great pictures and diagrams.

Mauldin, John H. *Particles in Nature: The Chronological Discovery of the New Physics*. Blue Ridge Summit, Pa.: TAB Books, 1986. This work traces the history of particle physics and the people and ideas involved. Major ideas considered include particles as fundamental blocks of matter, indeterminacy, duality, symmetry, and the nature of science itself. Includes a collection of superb questions to test the reader's comprehension. Excellent list of references. Illustrated.

Mulvey, John H., ed. *The Nature of Matter*. Oxford, England: Clarendon Press, 1981. A collection of eight lectures, this book takes the nonspecialist through the progress in understanding the basic structure of matter in the 1970's. The chapters on particles and forces and on research tools for high-energy physics are particularly good. Well illustrated and presented. Bibliography included.

Park, David A. *Contemporary Physics*. New York: Harcourt, Brace, and World,

1964. This book covers the physics developments of the twentieth century, paying special attention to particles and their behavior. High-energy accelerators and the equipment, such as the bubble chamber, needed to photograph trails are explained in some detail. An older book, but well written, it ends with a discussion of laser and maser principles.

Trefil, James S. *From Atoms to Quarks: An Introduction to the Strange World of Particle Physics*. New York: Charles Scribner's Sons, 1980. Dealing with the ultimate nature of matter, this work traces the development of nuclear physics. Accelerators and bubble chambers are discussed, and muons, quarks, and other strange particles are related to the everyday world. Glossary provided. Good explanatory pictures.

Weisskopf, Victor F. *Knowledge and Wonder: The Natural World as Man Knows It*. Cambridge, Mass.: MIT Press, 1979. An enchanting overview of the large and small phenomena that make up the universe. The work describes how knowledge is obtained and explains various natural observations. Clearly written, it presents the wonders of nature in a scientific light. Well illustrated.

Arthur L. Alt

1961

Physics
Robert Hofstadter, United States
Rudolf Ludwig Mössbauer, West Germany

Chemistry
Melvin Calvin, United States

Physiology or Medicine
Georg von Békésy, United States

Literature
Ivo Andrić, Yugoslavia

Peace
Dag Hammarskjöld, Sweden

ROBERT HOFSTADTER
1961

Born: New York, New York; February 5, 1915

Nationality: American
Area of concentration: Nuclear physics

Using very high-energy electrons as bombardment tools, Hofstadter obtained detailed information on the internal structure of atoms, including the distribution of charge for the enclosed particles in the nucleus. In the process, he invented complicated new technology necessary to make precision measurements

The Award

Presentation

Professor Ivar Waller, of the Royal Swedish Academy of Sciences, presented the Nobel Prize in Physics to Robert Hofstadter on December 10, 1961, on behalf of the Academy and the King of Sweden, from whom Hofstadter accepted the prize. In his presentation speech, Waller briefly mentioned early investigations of the structure of the atomic nucleus. It had been discovered, he said, that the nucleus consists of protons and neutrons, and Hideki Yukawa (1907-1981) had provided a theory of the forces that hold those particles together.

Waller drew attention to Hofstadter's development of a new experimental method for dealing with the totally unknown interior structure of both atomic nuclei and the individual protons and neutrons. By measuring the scattering of very high-energy electrons with a precision magnetic spectrometer, Hofstadter had been able to obtain detailed knowledge of the electric charge distribution within the atom and the magnetic moment distribution within the individual particles. To perform this research, begun in 1950, Hofstadter had built a complex experimental installation for measuring the electron scatterings with extreme accuracy.

Hofstadter's pioneering work, Waller said, had been confirmed in experiments at Cornell University and had led to new advancements in the science of operation and information retrieval with electron accelerators. The success of his various measurements also led to investigations of extremely small systems to a degree of precision previously unobtainable in high-energy physics research. Hofstadter's results stimulated discoveries of new particles, discoveries necessary for a more complete understanding of the forces acting within the atom's nucleus.

Nobel lecture

Hofstadter's Nobel lecture, entitled "The Electron-Scattering Method and Its Application to the Structure of Nuclei and Nucleons," was a concise summary of his major work in physics. He began by noting that in physics, new experimental techniques often uncover the structure of particles that were thought "elementary."

He acknowledged the work of Ernest Rutherford (1871-1937), particularly his study of deviations from Coulomb scattering, and then introduced his own experimental technique: the use of high-energy electron scattering to explore the nature of nuclear particles. Hofstadter defined several important quantities, including the differential cross section for scattering, a structure factor F, and the momentum-energy transfer g. The most important of these was F, which indicates the interference effects generated by the nucleus and relates to the electron charge density.

Beginning at the University of Illinois in 1951 with low-energy electrons and continuing at Stanford University and the University of Michigan, experiments were done to fix the nuclear charge density distribution using an electron accelerator and two magnetic spectrometers for separating electrons of different energies. Hofstadter gave examples of electron scattering curves for several elements, showing the types of graphs derived for elastic and inelastic scattering peaks. From these curves and additional theoretical calculations, the charge density distribution could be obtained. Hofstadter evolved a simple scheme for spherical nuclei construction; it was based on the measured distance from the nucleus to the 50 percent scatter point and the interval between the 90 percent and 10 percent ordinates. From those derivations, he was able to find the size of a nucleus and describe the behavior with increasing atomic weight of a nuclear radius. He found that there was some property of nuclear matter causing the outer nuclear region to develop an essentially constant surface thickness, independent of size.

Beginning in 1954, Hofstadter designed experiments to work with hydrogen, helium, and protons. Among his discoveries was the fact that the proton is an object of finite size, not merely a point source. Knowing that the proton had spin and a magnetic moment, Hofstadter was able to explain electron scattering behavior via mathematics developed in 1950 by M. Rosenbluth. Work done on the neutron, however, seemed to indicate a radius of zero. Working with M. R. Yearian on the deuteron and proton, Hofstadter showed that the neutron was not a point object and that its magnetic moment was distributed in a manner similar to the proton's. This finding eventually led Y. Nambu to predict the omega-meson and W. R. Frazer and J. R. Fulco to predict the rho-meson. A third form, the nu-meson, was found by A. Pevsner.

Hofstadter showed eventually that the proton and neutron are two different aspects of a single entity, a nucleon. They are distinguished by their isotopic spin. Identical, charged mesonic clouds appear in both the neutron and the proton, adding together in the proton and canceling each other in the neutron. The mesonic cloud theory of the structure of the nucleons can explain most of the particles' characteristics. Hofstadter closed his lecture, however, by expressing the belief that smaller and ever more fundamental particles would continue to be found as equipment became better and stronger.

Critical reception

Immediate reaction to the announcement of Hofstadter's award was subdued.

During the 1950's, many of the major discoveries in physics and chemistry—the development of new instruments, such as the bubble chamber and the radio telescope, or the organic synthesis of important molecules necessary for the advancement of American technology—were either ignored or simply mentioned in passing in the press. Nuclear physics was associated with hydrogen bombs, particle accelerators, or the use of nuclear energy for sustained space travel; indeed, the scientific awareness of the average person and of the press was so minimal that space achievements of the 1950's caught Americans completely by surprise. Few outside the realm of high-energy physics, either at universities or working for the federal government, seemed to have an understanding of the importance of Hofstadter's work. The *New York Herald-Tribune* and *Newsweek* said that his experiments had been confined to measuring the size and shape of the proton and neutron in order to prove certain theoretical calculations. Other reports, equally brief and lacking in substance, summarized his award-winning works as presenting the first "reasonably consistent picture of atomic nuclear structure" (*The New York Times*, November 3, 1961) and as providing a clarifying image of the basic constituents of matter (*Time*, November 10, 1961).

The scientific magazines and journals offered similarly brief reports. *Physics Today* of December, *Nature* of December 2, and *Science* of November 10 mentioned Hofstadter as one of the physicists sharing the award, citing the marvelous experiments at Stanford in which he had used high-energy electron scattering techniques to determine the electromagnetic structure of nucleons. *Physics Today* also gave a brief summation of Hofstadter's career, but it did not comment on his fitness for receiving the prestigious award. *Chemical & Engineering News* of November 13 stressed Hofstadter's proof that the nucleus does not have a sharp boundary but rather is characterized by a charge density that is constant for some distance from the center and then decreases so that the outer layers become more diffused. Altogether, it was a sparse collection of articles for work recognized as deserving a Nobel Prize.

Biography

Robert Hofstadter was born February 5, 1915, in New York City, New York. His father was Louis Hofstadter, a salesman, and his mother was Henrietta Koenigsberg Hofstadter. The third of four children, he was reared in New York City proper, attending first the local public schools and then the College of the City of New York. He was graduated in 1935, magna cum laude, with a bachelor of science degree in physics. He had won the Kenyon Prize for outstanding work in physics and mathematics, which resulted in his being elected to Phi Beta Kappa. He had started college with the intention of majoring in literature and philosophy, but he converted to physics when an instructor convinced him the laws of physics could be tested and those of philosophy could not.

In 1935, he began graduate work at Princeton University, his expenses covered by a Coffin Fellowship from the General Electric Company and a Procter Fellowship of the college. He earned both a master's degree and a doctorate in physics. His very creative doctorate project was concerned with the infrared spectra of simple organic molecules, and in particular with the elucidation of the structure of the hydrogen bond. In 1938, as a Procter Fellow for postdoctoral work, he began studying the photoconductivity of crystals, particularly willemite. He did additional work at the University of Pennsylvania as a Harrison Fellow in 1939, where he helped to construct a large Van de Graaff machine for nuclear research. He then became an instructor in physics at Pennsylvania and at the City College of New York.

Hofstadter worked as a physicist at the National Bureau of Standards in Washington, D.C., during the first part of World War II. There he helped to develop the proximity fuse, an important antiaircraft weapon that detonated a shell when it detected approaching objects by radar. From 1943 to 1946, he was the assistant chief physicist at the Nordan Laboratories Corporation in New York.

Scientific Career

After World War II, Hofstadter left industry to become assistant professor of physics at Princeton University. There, he did original research on crystal conduction counters, on the Compton effect of wave-particle scattering, and on scintillation counters. In 1948, he discovered that sodium iodide, activated by thallium, made an excellent scintillation detector of gamma rays and showed further that gamma-ray energies could be accurately measured. Carrying the research further, by 1950, working with J. A. McIntyre, he had found that well-formed crystals of thallium provided remarkable energy-measuring devices for higher-energy gamma rays, X rays, and other energetic particles, being a particle counter of high efficiency. The thallium crystal scintillation spectrometer has been of immense importance in the development of modern nuclear physics.

In 1950, Hofstadter accepted the position of associate professor of physics at Stanford University. There, he took advantage of the school's large linear accelerator, invented by W. W. Hanson. This instrument accelerated charged elementary particles by moving them with successive pushes in a straight line, rather than in a spiral, as in the cyclotron, or a circle, as in the betatron. In straight-line accelerators, high-energy electrons can be produced more easily than in the other machines. Using the "linac," Hofstadter instituted an experiment on the scattering of energetic electrons on atomic nuclei as they came out of the linear accelerator. While developing and building equipment for the electron scattering experiments, he continued working on scintillation counters and developed means of detecting neutrons and X rays.

From 1953 on, Hofstadter's principal interests centered on electron scattering experiments, including more and more precise measurements. Fascinated by the idea of discovering the material universe's ultimate constituents, he began soon after coming to Stanford to investigate the atomic nucleus. With students and other physicists, he investigated the charge distribution in the nucleus and then the charge and magnetic moment distribution in the proton and neutron. In 1953, he announced that the two particles composing the nucleus were less uniformly packed than had been supposed. Instead of being a solid, uniformly composed sphere, he found, the nucleus had a densely packed core of component particles which gradually thinned toward the edge of the nucleus, the core being some 130 trillion times denser than water. These discoveries were performed using a procedure pioneered by Ernest Rutherford (1871-1937): particle scattering. Hofstadter, however, had developed a more advanced accelerator and scattering machine. Unlike Rutherford, who had aimed alpha particles resulting from radioactive decay at gold foil, Hofstadter used the linear accelerator to shoot electrons at extremely high energies down a path controlled by magnets toward atomic nuclei targets of gold, lead, tantalum, and beryllium. The electron, on entering the nucleus, was deflected from its original path by the electrical fields of the particles constrained in the core itself. Hofstadter's creation, the scattering machine, consisting essentially of a microscope built with a gigantic magnet, counted the number of electrons coming through and measured their angles of deflection. Hofstadter then used these measurements and theoretical calculations to determine the position of particles in the nuclei to within one hundred-trillionth of an inch. This knowledge allowed him to formulate a much clearer idea of the innermost structure of the nucleus.

As envisioned and improved by Hofstadter, the electron scattering method was used to find the size and surface-thickness parameters within the nuclei. Many of his principal results concerning the proton and neutron were obtained between 1954 and 1957 as better equipment became available. Hofstadter decided to examine, if possible, individual protons and neutrons. He set up his machinery to delineate the charge distribution, or the internal structure, of the two fundamental bodies. In 1956, he was able to determine that the proton measured 0.00000000000003 inch in diameter and was constructed as a dense sphere, apparently soft on the outside and hard on the inside, like an apricot. It came as something of a shock to realize that the proton was not merely a point object but had a surprisingly large size. In December, 1957, Hofstadter announced that his group had also measured the size and shape of the neutron. Further developments, however, had to await the building of even more accurate equipment.

In April, 1961, Hofstadter announced to the American Physical Society that the proton and neutron were made up of a central core of positively charged matter, about which were two shells of "Yukawa clouds," containing mesons. In the proton, the meson shells were both positively charged. In the neutron, one of the shells was negatively charged, so the overall charge was zero. Further experiments showed that in the proton, 28 percent of the positive charge is in the outer cloud, 60 percent is in the denser inner cloud, and the remaining 12 percent is in the pointlike core. The neutron's two outer mesonic clouds are the same as the proton's, except that the charge of the inner cloud is negative. The two nucleons, then, are really the same particle, differentiated only by the component of isotopic spin. Hofstadter's findings were verified in later experiments.

The Nobel Prize is not Hofstadter's only award. He was elected to the National

Academy of Sciences in 1958 and was named California Scientist of the Year in 1959. He was a Guggenheim Fellow in 1958 and 1959 at the European Organization for Nuclear Research in Geneva. He was made Max H. Stein Professor of Physics at Stanford University in 1971 and a professor emeritus in 1985. The Townsend Harris Medal of the City College of New York was awarded to him in 1961, the Röntgen Medal of Germany in 1985, the U.S. National Science Medal in 1986, and the Prize of the Cultural Foundation of Fiuggi, Italy, in 1986.

Hofstadter is a Fellow of the American Association for the Advancement of Science and a member of the American Physical Society, the Physical Society of London, the Italian Physical Society, and Sigma Xi. He has written more than seventy-five papers on molecular structure, solid-state physics, nuclear physics, crystal structures, electron scattering, and subnuclear structures. He was the editor for *Investigations in Physics* from 1958 to 1965 and associate editor for the following journals: *Physics*, *Review of Modern Physics*, *Physical Review*, and *Reviews of Scientific Instruments*.

Bibliography

Primary
PHYSICS: "High-Energy Electron Scattering and the Charge Distributions of Selected Nuclei," *Physical Review*, vol. 101, 1956 (with B. Hahn and D. G. Ravenhall); *High-Energy Electron Scattering Tables*, 1960 (with Robert C. Herman); *Electron Scattering and Nuclear and Nucleon Structure*, 1963.
EDITED TEXT: *Nucleon Structures*, 1964 (with Leonard I. Schiff).

Secondary
Dodd, James E. *The Ideas of Particle Physics: An Introduction for Scientists.* New York: Cambridge University Press, 1984. This work, beginning with twentieth century discoveries, treats scientists' understanding of the basic four forces of nature governing the known universe and of the multitude of particles produced by scattering experiments. Reaching to the quark level, it ends with a discussion of the search for a grand unified theory of matter. Well written. Numerous diagrams.
Mulvey, John H., ed. *The Nature of Matter.* Oxford, England: Clarendon Press, 1981. A series of lectures depicting modern views on how the universe is structured. Particularly important are articles on the inside of the proton, elementary particles and the tools used to reach quark levels, and the tools of high-energy physics in general. Well written, with a good glossary.
Nambu, Y. *Quarks: Frontiers in Elementary Particle Physics.* London: Taylor and Francis, 1985. Explaining how elementary particle physics has evolved since the 1930's, this work traces the development of ideas that have shaped the understanding of matter and its ultimate constituents, the quarks. Accelerators and other tools are described, as are the people who were involved in great discoveries. Well written and easily assimilated.

Polkinghorne, John Charlton. *The Particle Play: An Account of the Ultimate Constituents of Matter.* San Francisco: W. H. Freeman, 1979. Written to illustrate the marvels of discovery, this book treats the world of the subatomic particles and the machines necessary to make them visible. The particles' interaction with the forces of nature to create the universe is stressed. Detailed, but written for the intelligent layman.

Segrè, Emilio. *From X-Rays to Quarks: Modern Physicists and Their Discoveries.* San Francisco: W. H. Freeman, 1980. A historical overview of the people and ideas involved in subatomic physics. The ultimate bodies of nature are investigated in a journey through the ideas that unfolded as advanced equipment and knowledge became available. Excellent illustrations.

Weinberg, Steven. *The Discovery of Subatomic Particles.* San Francisco: W. H. Freeman, 1983. Delightfully written, detailed history of particle-force discovery, with explanations of how the numerous subatomic bodies interact to create the universe. The author captures the trials and thrills of discovery and provides insights into the scientists who changed the way the nucleus was regarded. Illustrated.

Arthur L. Alt

1961

Physics
Robert Hofstadter, United States
Rudolf Ludwig Mössbauer, West Germany

Chemistry
Melvin Calvin, United States

Physiology or Medicine
Georg von Békésy, United States

Literature
Ivo Andrić, Yugoslavia

Peace
Dag Hammarskjöld, Sweden

RUDOLF LUDWIG MÖSSBAUER
1961

Born: Munich, Germany; January 31, 1929

Nationality: West German
Area of concentration: Gamma radiation

Mössbauer observed the resonance emission and absorption of nuclear gamma radiation (known as the Mössbauer effect), provided a theoretical explanation for his discovery, and devised an apparatus which allowed study of these extremely narrow gamma resonances. The very sharp resonances of the Mössbauer effect have allowed many observations in physics, including studies of the properties of solids and a laboratory test of the theory of relativity

The Award

Presentation

On December 10, 1961, King Gustav VI of Sweden presented the Nobel Prize in Physics to Rudolf Ludwig Mössbauer and Robert Hofstadter on behalf of the Royal Swedish Academy of Sciences. The prizewinners were introduced to the king by Professor Ivar Waller, a member of the Academy. Waller identified the work of both men as a continuation of the chain of discoveries about the nature of the atomic nucleus that had begun with the work of Ernest Rutherford (1871-1937) and had continued with that of Hideki Yukawa (1907-1981). He described Mössbauer's work on the resonance emittance and absorption of gamma radiation by using an analogy to a radio receiver: To absorb a signal from a radio station, a radio receiver must be tuned to the correct frequency; similarly, a nucleus of the same kind as that which emitted the gamma radiation can act as a tuned receiver for the gamma radiation. Gamma radiation is far more energetic than radio waves, although they are both examples of electromagnetic radiation. Gamma rays carry more momentum than radio waves. When the nucleus emits or absorbs gamma radiation, it must recoil to conserve momentum. This recoil takes energy away from the gamma radiation. Because nuclear energy levels are very narrow, this loss of energy to the recoil "detunes" the gamma radiation and the absorbing nucleus so that the gamma radiation cannot be resonantly absorbed.

Mössbauer showed that if the nucleus is bound in a solid material, the recoil can be absorbed by the solid, leaving the amount of energy in the gamma radiation that is necessary for resonance absorption. He also used the Doppler shift of the gamma radiation obtained by moving the source or the absorber nucleus to decrease and finally obliterate the resonance. Since the nuclear resonance is very narrow, the necessary velocities, which depend on the details of the nuclear transition, may be as small as a few millimeters per hour. The study of these very narrow resonances permitted the measurement of very small changes in the energy of the gamma radiation, measurements that could be made with no other technique. Topics studied using the Mössbauer effect have included the properties of solids and the experimental consequences of the theory of relativity.

Nobel lecture

In his Nobel lecture, entitled "Recoilless Nuclear Resonance Absorption of Gamma Radiation," Mössbauer presented the story of his unexpected discovery of the Mössbauer effect, an explanation of recoilless emission and absorption of gamma radiation, and a brief summary of the areas where study of the Mössbauer effect was producing exciting results. He provided a clear explanation of the Mössbauer effect and an intriguing glimpse of his reactions when, as a graduate student, he had first observed resonance emission and absorption of gamma radiation.

Mössbauer opened his lecture with a brief outline of the history of the study of nuclear resonance, which began in 1929 when the possibility of the phenomenon's existence was first proposed. Quantum energy levels are not precisely located at a single energy; they have a small but finite width in energy space that is determined by the Heisenberg uncertainty principle, which states that the product of the half-life of the state and its width in energy must be at least equal to Planck's constant divided by 2π. When a nucleus emits or absorbs a photon, or a particle of gamma radiation, the nucleus must recoil to conserve momentum and take energy for the recoil from the gamma transition. The high energies of nuclear states mean that a nucleus cannot absorb a photon which has lost enough energy to allow for nuclear recoil. In 1951, scientists observed nuclear resonance absorption by using very high velocities to increase the energy of the emitted gamma by means of the Doppler effect, thereby compensating for the nuclear recoil during emission and absorption. The experiments were complex and not easily repeated. Other methods developed after the initial observations all used large Doppler shifts, the production of which required high velocities of the source or absorber, to compensate for the nuclear recoil.

Mössbauer credited his professor at the Max Planck Institute in Heidelberg, Heinz Maier-Leibnitz (born 1911), with directing his attention to the field of nuclear resonance in 1953, and he thanked his teacher for supporting his experiments during the next five years. Mössbauer had attempted to use resonance absorption to measure the lifetime of an excited state in the isotope iridium 191. When he cooled his source and absorber, Mössbauer expected to see a marked decrease in resonant absorption. To his surprise, resonant absorption increased dramatically and ruined his initial attempts to measure the half-life of the nuclear state. In attempting to explain these strange results, Mössbauer first checked extensively to make certain that the unexpected increase was not a fluke. He then recalled the work of Willis Eugene Lamb (born 1913) on the resonance absorption of slow neutrons. Mössbauer realized that Lamb's theory could be adapted to explain the resonant absorption of gamma radiation by nuclei bound in crystals. Essentially, this theory says that crystals can absorb vibrational energy only in finite quantities. Thus, if the energy of a nuclear recoil is smaller than that quantum of vibrational energy, there is a finite, calculable probability that the nucleus can absorb or emit a gamma photon without recoil, since a recoil effectively adds energy to the crystal lattice.

Mössbauer successfully completed his theoretical studies of resonant absorption and emission and turned his attention to constructing a device which took advantage of the very narrow energy width of the nuclear resonances to measure the changes in nuclear energy levels produced by the fields of electrons surrounding the nucleus. The device varied the energy of nuclear gamma radiation by using the Doppler shift created by moving the source or absorber. Because the nuclear resonances were so narrow, the velocities required were extremely slow and were easily produced in the laboratory.

Mössbauer concluded his lecture by pointing out that precise measurements of the magnetic fields and electrical field gradients at the site of nuclei in solids were already yielding exciting new information about the structure of nuclei and the nature of crystal structure; they were even providing laboratory confirmation of the change in photon energy in Earth's gravitational field predicted by the theory of relativity.

Critical reception

In 1961, when he won the Nobel Prize, Mössbauer was a Senior Research Fellow at the California Institute of Technology (Caltech) in Pasadena. He had previously held a post as a scientific assistant at the Technische Hochschule München, the Munich Technical University. His low academic rank was easily explained by the fact that he was only thirty-two at the time and had completed his doctorate a mere three years earlier. Mössbauer was undoubtedly less known than the corecipient of the Nobel Prize, Robert Hofstadter, who was both an older man and an established leader in the scientific community. The popular press was delighted to adopt Mössbauer as a Californian, and he was hailed along with Hofstadter, of Stanford, and Melvin Calvin, of the University of California, who had won the Nobel Prize in Chemistry. *The Christian Science Monitor* of November 3 ran a story headlined "Research Brings 'Nobelity' to California."

Despite Mössbauer's youth, the scientific press and indeed the scientific community agreed that his discovery had permitted the making of so many critical measurements in both physics and chemistry that the work was clearly worthy of the Nobel Prize. *Physics Today*, the journal of the American Physical Society, remarked, "By the end of 1959 . . . the precision in measurement made possible by Mössbauer's discovery had stimulated so much interest that meeting programs and journal pages were on the verge of being flooded with reports of new applications of the effect." *Science* magazine said, "This effect, which now bears his name, is of fundamental importance in atomic research." On the day the prizes were announced, Hofstadter himself wired Mössbauer to say that he was "delighted to share this award with you." Perhaps most significantly, both the Technische Hochschule München and Caltech announced Mössbauer's promotion to professor of physics shortly after the announcement.

The popular press was delighted with Mössbauer's youth and good looks. *Current Biography 1962* noted that he looked more like a student than a teacher on the Caltech campus. *The Christian Science Monitor* described his "handsome plumes of jet black hair and his penetrating black eyes." Unfortunately, the press was also frustrated by the complexity of the Mössbauer effect. *Time* magazine said that Mössbauer had published "a sensational paper reporting that gamma rays given off by certain radioactive isotopes can be used for infinitely delicate measurements." Almost all articles cited the experimental use of the Mössbauer effect to measure the effect of Earth's gravitational field on the energy of a photon, which had provided laboratory proof of the general theory of relativity. This experiment was only one of many important uses of the Mössbauer effect, but it was clearly perceived as the most glamorous, and many announcements devoted as much space to this work as to Mössbauer's own discoveries. *The New York Times* was careful to point out that the Mössbauer effect could also be used to study "the magnetic fields surrounding the nucleus of the atom." Frustrated with trying to describe the Mössbauer effect, *The Christian Science Monitor* quoted Mössbauer himself as saying, "It's always a little tricky to say. . . . We still have fights among the scientists to describe it." His wife, "attractive Mrs. Elizabeth Moessbauer," had said, "My husband can make his work very plain and exciting, but sometimes even physicists don't understand."

Mössbauer himself seems to have accepted the burst of publicity following the announcement with calm dignity; he did not seek press coverage. Most accounts describe him as quiet and scholarly. After winning the Nobel Prize, Mössbauer received little continuing publicity, although he certainly continued to be active as a physicist.

Biography

Rudolf Ludwig Mössbauer was born in Munich, Germany, on January 31, 1929. He was the only son of Ludwig Mössbauer, a phototechnician, and his wife, Erna Ernst. He had one sister, Eva-Maria Mössbauer Rheinfelder. He grew up in Munich and was educated at the *Oberschule*, the nonclassical secondary school, in Munich-Pasing. After leaving the *Oberschule* in 1948, he worked for several months as a laboratory assistant for the Rodenstock Optics Factory in Munich. He then enrolled in the Technische Hochschule München, where he read physics and was awarded a preliminary degree in 1952 and a diploma in 1955. During 1953 and 1954, he conducted research for his thesis and served as an assistant mathematics lecturer at the school. It was in this period of his life that he began to study gamma absorption. He continued his research at the Max Planck Institute of Medical Research in Heidelberg under the sponsorship of Heinz Maier-Leibnitz and received his doctoral degree in January, 1958. He continued his work in Heidelberg through 1958 and then taught as a scientific assistant at the Technische Hochschule München in 1959. His findings on resonant gamma absorption were published in *Zeitschrift für Physik* early in 1958.

In March, 1960, Mössbauer accepted an appointment as a Research Fellow at Caltech, where he continued his studies of the resonant absorption of gamma rays, exploiting the technique he had discovered to measure internal fields at the sites of nuclei in solids. He was later appointed a Senior Research Fellow, and he held this position at the time he won the Nobel Prize. After the announcement of the prize, he was appointed professor of physics at both Caltech and the Technische Hochschule München. He returned to Germany in 1964 as a professor of experimental physics at the Technische Universität München where he continued his studies of applications of the Mössbauer effect. In 1972, he accepted the directorship of the Institut Max von Laue-Paul Langevin in Grenoble. He held that post until 1977, when he returned to the Technische Universität München.

Mössbauer wed Elizabeth Pritz, who was a fashion designer; they have two daughters and a son. His hobbies include photography, music, and mountaineering.

Scientific Career

Rudolf Mössbauer discovered the effect that bears his name while he was a graduate student attempting to use resonance absorption to measure the half-life of the 129 kilo-electron volt state of the isotope iridium 191. The half-life of a nuclear state is the time it takes for half the nuclei in that state to decay. Because the half-life and the energy width of a quantum transition are inversely related, Mössbauer planned to use resonance absorption to study the energy width of the transition and then calculate the half-life of the state using the Heisenberg uncertainty principle. The uncertainty principle says that the product of the energy width and half-life of a nuclear state must be at least equal to Planck's constant divided by 2π. The experiment was suggested by Mössbauer's professor at Munich, Heinz Maier-Leibnitz, who also made it possible for his student to continue his research at the Max Planck Institute.

The energy width of a quantum decreases as it becomes more energetic. Nuclear energy states have narrow extents in energy, because they have energies of at least tens of thousands of electron volts; atomic energy states have energies of a few electron volts and broad extents in energy. Resonance absorption of photons by atomic states is comparatively easy to observe, since atomic states are broader in energy space than nuclear states. The momentum of a photon of electromagnetic energy is equal to its energy divided by the speed of light. The photons produced by atomic transitions have energies on the order of a few electron volts. Thus, they carry far less momentum than the gamma photons produced in nuclear transitions, which have energies on the order of tens of thousands of electron volts.

Mössbauer planned to vary the nuclear line width of the 129 kilo-electron volt state of iridium 191 by controlling the temperature of the lattice in which the absorbing nucleus was bound. If the temperature is increased, the absorbing nucleus moves faster and "sees" the incoming gamma radiation with a broader range of energies because of the increased Doppler shift brought about by its own more rapid motion both toward and away from the radiation. Cooling the absorber will decrease the energy width of the incoming gamma radiation from the point of view of the absorbing nucleus. Decreasing the temperature of the absorbing nucleus, and thus the width in energy of the incoming gamma radiation, should decrease the number of gamma photons that have energies matching the energy transitions of recoiling nuclei and can therefore be resonantly absorbed. By varying the temperature of the absorber or the source, Mössbauer hoped to measure the energy width of the gamma rays emitted, since he could calculate the expected Doppler broadening caused by the change in the average motion of the iridium nuclei. For the 129 kilo-electron volt transition in iridium 191, he expected to see some resonant absorption at room temperature, because the gamma radiation from the transition has low enough energy to carry a relatively small amount of momentum. He chose to cool his absorber because he believed that effects of chemical bonding would be more evident at low temperatures than at high temperatures.

Mössbauer constructed an apparatus in which he could control the temperatures of both the source and absorbing nuclei which were bound in crystal lattices, a fact which made his experiment very different from other experiments on nuclear reso-nant absorption. He initially cooled both the source and the absorber and was astounded to see a large increase in resonant absorption of gamma radiation. He initially assumed that this increase was a fluke, the result of a factor introduced into the experiment by the cooling of the absorber. He tried cooling only the source and finally managed to see the small decrease in absorption he expected and to make his measurement of the half-life of the nuclear state. He then earned his Nobel Prize by explaining the effects that had led to the initial increase in gamma absorption after he had cooled the absorber. His results proved that the increase was no accident, and the young student reconsidered the theory of resonant gamma absorption in the light of the quantum theory of crystal bonding and Willis Lamb's theory of the resonant absorption of neutrons by nuclei bound in crystals.

Consider a nucleus bound in a crystal where the quantum energies of excitation of the crystal's modes of oscillation are very much greater than the energy of recoil of the nucleus when it emits or absorbs a particular gamma photon. According to quantum mechanics, it is possible for the nucleus to absorb or emit a gamma photon without exciting the oscillation of the crystal so that the nucleus itself does not recoil. Thus, the full energy of the gamma transition is contained in the photon, and a very sharp resonance can be observed. The probability of recoilless emission or absorption depends on the characteristics of the nuclear transition and the chemical bonding of the crystal, and it increases sharply as the temperature of the crystal is reduced. Mössbauer worked out the theory of resonance emission and absorption of nuclei bound in crystal lattices and published it along with his experimental results on iridium in a paper, "Kernresonanzfluoreszenz von Gammastrahlung in Ir^{191}," which was received by *Zeitschrift für Physik* on January 9, 1958.

The young physicist received his degree and continued to work as a scientific assistant at the Technische Hochschule München while he developed a device to sweep through the very narrow nuclear absorption resonances. The Doppler shift is the effect whereby the energy of a wave increases as an observer moves toward its source and decreases as the observer moves away. Mössbauer varied the energy of the gamma radiation using a Doppler shift produced by velocities of a few centimeters per second. Such speeds are easy to obtain in the laboratory, and Mössbauer constructed a device that would allow him to make such measurements using a gear system borrowed from a mechanical toy. The energy width of the observed gamma absorption was on the order of the natural energy width of the nuclear energy state as determined by the Heisenberg uncertainty principle. In the case of the 129 kiloelectron volt transition in iridium 191, Mössbauer obtained a line width of 4.6×10^{-5} electron volts. This width is on the order of changes in the energies of nuclear energy levels brought about by the interaction of the nuclear electrical and magnetic dipole moments with the electrical field gradients and magnetic fields produced at the site of the nucleus by the atomic electrons. Thus, if one knows the atomic fields, one can directly measure the nuclear properties, and if one knows the properties of the nucleus, one can measure the strengths of the fields at the site of the nucleus as one changes the chemical state of the nucleus. Mössbauer realized that his discovery provided a new probe into the detailed structure of the solid state.

In early 1959, Mössbauer published a description of his apparatus in *Zeitschrift für Naturforschung*. He also published a shorter paper, which appeared in *Naturwissenschaften* in the latter part of 1958. Mössbauer was well aware that he had discovered an important new physical tool, and he seemed to be somewhat disappointed that his work was not recognized immediately. He later remarked, a little bitterly, that no one read the German scientific literature anymore.

The scientific community reacted to these early papers with great skepticism. At Los Alamos National Laboratory in the United States, research on the Mössbauer effect was begun because one physicist bet another a nickel that he could not repeat Mössbauer's work. As Mössbauer's results were extended, the importance of the Mössbauer effect as a probe both of nuclear structure and of the variation of internal fields in solids was widely recognized. The most dramatic use of the Mössbauer effect was to measure the very small difference in the energy of a gamma photon at the top of a tower on the Harvard campus and at the bottom of the tower, a difference caused by relativistic effects of Earth's gravitational field. Mössbauer himself was recognized as the discoverer of the effect, and he was invited to Caltech as a visiting researcher.

With the announcement that he had been awarded the Nobel Prize in Physics, Mössbauer's academic status increased dramatically, and Caltech made him a professor of physics. He returned to Munich in 1964 and assumed the rank of professor of experimental physics at the Technische Universität München. There, he continued his work on applications of the Mössbauer effect, extending it to the study of large biological molecules. He was also active in developing new instrumentation for use in the study of the Mössbauer effect. In 1972, he followed in the footsteps of his teacher Maier-Leibnitz and accepted the directorship of the Institut Laue-Langevin in Grenoble with responsibility for the French-German-British High-Flux Reactor.

Mössbauer began to take an interest in other aspects of basic nuclear physics, particularly neutrino physics.

After returning to Munich in 1977, Mössbauer published papers in major physics journals on the oscillation and decay of reactor neutrinos and on the effect of synchrotron radiation on the speedup of coherent decay measured in an antiferromagnet. Over the years since he received the Nobel Prize, his publication record has shown him to be a productive member of the physics community, although, perhaps not surprisingly, none of his subsequent work has had the impact of the discovery of the Mössbauer effect. He has received a variety of academic honors, including memberships in the national academies of science of both the United States and the Soviet Union, and a large number of honorary degrees. He was awarded the Research Corporation Award in 1960, the Röntgen Prize of the University of Giessen in 1961, the Elliot Cresson Medal of the Franklin Institute in 1961, and the Bavarian Order of Merit in 1962.

The impact of Mössbauer's discovery of recoilless emission and absorption of gamma radiation on physics, chemistry, geology, and biology has been monumental. Annual conferences are held on results achieved with the technique, which has been combined with such other techniques as Coulomb excitation to extend its utility and the isotopes to which it applies. The annual publication of the *Mössbauer Effect Data Index* lists thousands of papers published each year on studies using the effect. The Mössbauer effect has proved itself to be a valuable probe of the solid state and nuclear structure and a useful tool for a variety of high-precision measurements. In chemistry, it has been used to probe the geometry of chemical bonds in a variety of molecules. In biology, it has been used to study details of such interactions as that of oxygen with the iron in hemoglobin; the Mössbauer effect is sensitive only to conditions in the vicinity of the iron and "ignores" the rest of the gigantic protein molecule. In geology, Mössbauer techniques have been used to study samples of Moon rock and to look at the behavior of iron in such samples. The effect has been used to examine the techniques employed in ancient metallurgy and the glazes on prehistoric pottery. In sum, it has become a pervasive technique in the sciences.

Bibliography

Primary

PHYSICS: "Kernresonanzfluoreszenz von Gammastrahlung in Ir¹⁹¹," *Zeitschrift für Physik*, vol. 151, 1958; "Kernresonanzabsorption von Gammastrahlung in Ir¹⁹¹," *Naturwissenschaften*, vol. 45, 1958; "Kernresonanzabsorption von Gammastrahlung in Ir¹⁹¹," *Zeitschrift für Naturforschen*, vol. 14a, 1959; "Recoilless Nuclear Resonance Absorption," *Annual Reviews of Nuclear Science*, vol. 12, 1962; "General Aspects of Nuclear Hyperfine Interactions in Salts of the Rare Earth," in *Proceedings of the Third International Conference on the Mössbauer Effect, Ithaca, New York*, 1963; "Recoilless Nuclear Resonance Absorption and Its Applications," in *Alpha-, Beta-, and Gamma-Ray Spectroscopy*, 1965; "Gamma-

Resonance and X-Ray Investigations of Slow Motions in Macromolecular Systems," *Hyperfine Interactions*, vol. 33, 1987.

Secondary

Frauenfelder, Hans, ed. *The Mössbauer Effect*. New York: W. A. Benjamin, 1963. This collection of early reprints on applications of the Mössbauer effect includes English translations of Mössbauer's original papers and other early applications of the Mössbauer effect to problems in physics. It contains an introduction which presents both a simple, classical physics approach to the Mössbauer effect and a more complex, quantum interpretation.

Gonsor, U., ed. *Mössbauer Spectroscopy*. Vol. 2, *The Exotic Side of the Method*. Berlin: Springer-Verlag, 1981. This collection of articles deals with applications of the Mössbauer effect to the more glamorous aspects of physics, such as the laboratory proof of general relativity. Although the major importance of the Mössbauer effect has been its application to more mundane problems of chemistry, the exotic experiments described in this volume have lent the method much of its popular appeal.

Greenwood, N. N., and T. C. Gibb. *Mössbauer Spectroscopy*. London: Chapman and Hall, 1971. This comprehensive text discusses the major applications of the Mössbauer effect to problems in chemistry, physics, and biology. It demonstrates the range of applications that make the effect such an important tool in chemistry, physics, biology, and geology.

──────────. "Rudolf Ludwig Mössbauer." In *Modern Scientists and Engineers*, vol. 2. New York: McGraw-Hill, 1980. This article offers a brief biographical sketch which is as complete as any of the published material on this rather elusive Nobel laureate.

Weber, Robert L. "Rudolf Ludwig Mössbauer." In *Pioneers of Science: Nobel Prize Winners in Physics*, edited by J. M. A. Lenihan. Bristol, England: Adam Hilger, 1980. This volume also offers a very brief biography of Mössbauer, who seems to have successfully avoided biographers since winning the Nobel Prize.

Wertheim, Gunther K. *Mössbauer Effect: Principles and Applications*. New York: Academic Press, 1964. This source presents the simplest available introduction to the Mössbauer effect and the apparatus used to observe it. Although some physics background is needed to read it, the book offers the best available description of the Mössbauer effect for nonspecialists.

Ruth H. Howes

1962

Physics
Lev Davidovich Landau, Soviet Union

Chemistry
John C. Kendrew, Great Britain
Max F. Perutz, Great Britain

Physiology or Medicine
Francis H. C. Crick, Great Britain
James D. Watson, United States
Maurice Wilkins, Great Britain

Literature
John Steinbeck, United States

Peace
Linus Pauling, United States

LEV DAVIDOVICH LANDAU
1962

Born: Baku, Azerbaijan, Russian Empire; January 22, 1908
Died: Moscow, Soviet Union; April 1, 1968
Nationality: Soviet
Area of concentration: Quantum mechanics

Landau's development and application of quantum mechanical methods led him to a theory of large-scale quantum behavior and an understanding of the nature of phase transitions. This work led to the development of a theory of the properties of quantum liquids

The Award

Presentation

Lev Davidovich Landau was unable to travel to Stockholm to receive his Nobel Prize, as he was still in the hospital recovering from a near-fatal traffic accident in which he had been involved earlier in the year. Landau's award was the first peacetime award made outside Stockholm; the award and medal were presented to Landau by Rolf Sohlman, the Swedish ambassador to Moscow, in a conference room at the Academy of Sciences Hospital. At the ceremony were Mstislav Keldysh, Igor Tamm, Nikolai Semenov, Pyotr Kapitsa, Landau's wife, and some of the hospital staff. The ceremony took place on December 10, 1962. Ambassador Sohlman quoted from the presentation speech of Professor Ivar Waller of the Royal Swedish Academy of Sciences, which was delivered on the same day, in Stockholm.

Waller began his speech with an outline of Landau's life and went on to note his achievements in a wide variety of fields with special reference to his contributions to the understanding of liquid helium in the superfluid state. He noted that Landau's model represented an important step toward a complete understanding of the properties of liquids, one of the major goals of physics. Waller concluded his presentation by commenting on Landau's great originality of thought. He explained that Landau could not travel to Sweden because of his injuries and that the Nobel Prize was being awarded to him in Moscow by Ambassador Sohlman.

Nobel lecture

Landau was unable to present a lecture to the Swedish Academy. He said to those gathered at the hospital in Moscow, "I am deeply honored for this award."

Evgenii Lifshitz has noted of Landau, "To him fell the tragic fate of dying twice." On January 7, 1962, Landau was a passenger in a car being driven by the physicist Vladimir Sudakov on the ice-covered roads of Moscow. Sudakov swerved to avoid a child, and the car skidded to a halt on the wrong side of the Dimitrovsky Highway, where it was struck by a truck that was unable to stop because of the icy conditions. Sudakov and his wife were uninjured, but Landau's body appeared to be lifeless; his chest had been compressed, his skull fractured, and his legs broken. An examination performed on his arrival at a hospital revealed a long list of injuries, several of which could have proved fatal on their own. That Landau ever survived to be awarded the Nobel Prize was remarkable. He was still in the hospital a year after the presentation.

Critical reception

The awarding of the Nobel Prize in Physics to Landau was well received. Landau was known as one of the world's greatest theoretical physicists; he was a national hero in the Soviet Union, and in the Western world he was thought to be a major contributor to the Soviet nuclear weapons and space programs. Articles about Landau's award focused either on his supposed contributions to these programs or on the miracle of his still being alive after his accident. Landau's actual involvement in military and space activities, however, was not as large as was imagined in the West. He was interested in space physics and had done some astrophysical calculations, but he had made no direct contributions to the Soviet rocket program. Landau was associated with the institutes that were involved in the development of nuclear weapons, he had done some fundamental work on nuclear fusion reactions in stars, and he was associated with some of the committees working on the nuclear weapons, but his involvement in these programs was not major. Landau was in jail when the atom bomb program began, and the Soviet development of thermonuclear weapons was largely engineered by Andrei Sakharov. Thus, the reactions to Landau's award, though favorable, were based to some extent on incorrect information. In the physics community, however, Landau's work on quantum fluids was well-known and regarded as clearly worthy of the prize.

Time magazine covered the award in two articles, one announcing the award (November 9) and one devoted to his accident and inability to attend the awards ceremony (December 14). *Time* also speculated on whether the Soviet government would have allowed Landau to travel to Sweden to accept the award had he been able; it was thought that as the fourth Soviet Nobel laureate, he would have been allowed to make the trip. *Life* of December 7 devoted a two-page feature article to the award entitled "After Death a Nobel Prize." Again, the focus was on Landau's recovery rather than on the prize. A reporter for the magazine had talked to Landau in his hospital room and carried back the news that the laureate wished to credit Niels Bohr for influencing his worldview. *Newsweek* of November 12 also covered the announcement in a story emphasizing the medical miracle, and *Esquire* ran a similar feature article. Thus, Landau received wide attention, but little comment was made on the work for which he had been given the Nobel Prize.

Biography

Lev Davidovich Landau was born in Baku, Azerbaijan, on January 22, 1908, the son of David Llovich Landau and Lyubov Veniaminovna Garvaki-Landau. His father was a petroleum engineer and the chief engineer at an oil field in Baku. His mother was a physician and a teacher. Landau finished high school at the age of thirteen. He wanted to go to the University at Baku to study mathematics, but his father wanted him to have a career in finance or administration and thus sent him instead to the Baku Economics Technicum. After a year of reluctant study at the economics college, Landau refused to continue. His father relented and sent him to the University of Baku in 1922, where he studied chemistry, physics, and mathematics.

At the age of sixteen, Landau went to the University of Leningrad, where he studied physics. There he met George Gamow, with whom he would later collaborate scientifically. Landau published his first paper, on the spectra of diatomic molecules, when he was eighteen. While at Leningrad, he had a research scholarship at the Leningrad Röntgen Institute, where he worked on the developing science of quantum mechanics.

In 1929, Landau received a government traveling fellowship and a Rockefeller Fellowship. These awards enabled him to travel in Western Europe for eighteen months; in that time, he met and worked with many of the developers of quantum mechanics and became an outstanding theoretical physicist. This trip marked the beginning of his scientific career.

Scientific Career

Landau was already an active physicist when he became a graduate student at the Leningrad Physicotechnical Institute in 1927, having published his first paper the previous year. In the early part of his career, he was primarily interested in quantum mechanics, the area of physics that deals with the interactions of atomic and subatomic particles. He read papers on quantum mechanics as soon as they were published and was soon working independently in the field.

When Landau left the Soviet Union in 1929 for eighteen months, he visited Germany, Denmark, England, and Switzerland. On his journeys, he met many of the world's greatest physicists, among them Max Born, Werner Heisenberg, Niels Bohr, Paul Dirac, Pyotr Kapitsa, Ernest Rutherford, Wolfgang Pauli, and Rudolf Peierls. Several of these men were, or were to become, Nobel laureates. Landau spent some of his time at Niels Bohr's Copenhagen Institute, where much of the theory of quantum mechanics was developed; he came to admire Bohr and to regard him as his teacher.

Landau worked on a variety of problems at Bohr's institute. While there, he began to collaborate with Rudolf Peierls, and this work led to a joint paper that pointed out some problems in quantum electrodynamics. It was with this publication that Landau's international reputation began to grow. He was to collaborate with Peierls again in Zurich, where he had traveled to study with Wolfgang Pauli. When he arrived there, Peierls was working with Leon Rosenfeld and Felix Bloch on the problem of applying the methods of quantum mechanics to the electrons in metals. Landau became involved in this research, and after working on the topic for a week, he arrived at a solution to the problem. This solution was the Landau theory of diamagnetism, his first major contribution to theoretical physics. The presence of a magnetic field can cause materials to become magnetized. (In physics, fields are used to describe quantities that are defined throughout space.) Diamagnetic materials are materials that become magnetized in the presence of a magnetic field in such a way that they are repelled by the field that produces them. Landau was able to explain this behavior in terms of a quantum mechanical model. Landau and Peierls also collaborated on an extension of quantum mechanics to particles that travel at speeds close to the speed of light, the so-called relativistic quantum mechanics.

By the end of his fellowship period, in 1931, Landau had met, studied under, and worked with almost all the founders of quantum mechanics, and he had become one of the world's leading theoretical physicists. At this time, he decided to return to the Soviet Union. He went to Leningrad, which was then still the center of Soviet physics, and there he became a researcher and teacher at his old university. He did not remain there long; in 1932, he was appointed as head of the theoretical physics division of the Ukrainian Physicotechnical Institute, which had been set up by the University of Leningrad in Kharkov. He was awarded a doctorate by the University of Leningrad in 1935 and became a professor of general physics at the University of Kharkov the same year. The Kharkov years were a time of intense research for Landau. At the same time, he devised a program for the education of theoretical physicists known as the "theoretical minimum." This program eventually led to his writing, with Evgenii Lifshitz (a student of his at Kharkov), a multivolume textbook of theoretical physics. While at Kharkov, Landau performed research in low-temperature physics, in acoustics, and on semiconductors. He also met his future wife Concordia (Cora) Drobantseva, an engineer in a chocolate factory. They were married in 1937.

That year, Landau moved to the Institute of Theoretical Problems in Moscow. The Institute had been formed by Pyotr Kapitsa, who had been prevented from returning to the University of Cambridge in 1934. Landau remained there for the rest of his active career, except for when he was imprisoned by Joseph Stalin and when he was evacuated with the rest of the Institute during World War II. Kapitsa had resumed work on low-temperature physics and was investigating the properties of liquid helium. Liquid helium possesses some strange properties at temperatures that are close to absolute zero—that is, at temperatures close to 0 Kelvins or −273 degrees Celsius. At these low temperatures, liquid helium can flow out of sealed containers. (A solid form of helium does not exist.) Landau realized that the behavior of liquid helium at these temperatures had features in common with the onset of the superconducting state. At a temperature of 2.19 Kelvins, liquid helium undergoes a change of state, and the properties that it exhibits are the result of large-scale quantum behavior. In the course of this work, Landau began to develop his theory of phase transitions. He divided them into first and second order changes. First-order phase changes are those that materially change the material, such as when water freezes to become ice or vaporizes to become steam. Second-order phase changes do not produce such obvious differences; instead, a material which seems to be in the same state begins to have different physical properties. The superfluid and superconducting transitions are both examples of second-order phase changes, in that the superfluid or superconducting material looks the same but has quite different properties. The fundamental paper outlining this theory of phase transitions was published in 1937.

In 1938, Landau was arrested and given a ten-year prison sentence for espionage. He was alleged to be a German spy. That he was of Jewish descent rendered the charge ridiculous, but under Stalin's regime, charges were often illegitimate. Landau remained imprisoned for almost a year. He was released when Kapitsa interceded on his behalf, and he returned to work at the Institute. On his return he was, along with many of the world's scientists, involved with war work, and he later published several papers on the detonation of explosives.

At the end of the war, Landau was his country's leading theoretical physicist, and he began to receive many honors. In 1946 he became a full member of the U.S.S.R. Academy of Sciences. In 1951, he became a member of the Danish Royal Academy of Sciences; in 1956, a member of the Netherlands Royal Academy of Sciences; and in 1960, a foreign member of the Royal Society. In these years, he also received two Orders of Lenin and three State Prizes. In 1962, he was awarded the Lenin Prize as well as the Nobel Prize.

Landau kept himself abreast of developments in physics and worked out many of his ideas in seminars. At these seminars, his coworkers and students were required to present the latest theories. The discussions that followed these presentations led to the development of much new physics and also made it unnecessary for Landau to read any of the primary literature himself. The reconstruction of the work of other physicists with only a cursory knowledge of their methods and results is not uncommon among creative theoretical physicists. Another prominent physicist who found no great need to read the scientific literature was Enrico Fermi.

In these later years at the Moscow Institute, Landau worked on a wide variety of subjects. He made fundamental contributions to nuclear physics, quantum electrodynamics, and fluid dynamics, and he continued his work on liquid helium and other quantum liquids. Besides continuing his researches, he was actively writing textbooks to educate physicists at all levels. He began to collaborate with Evgenii Lifshitz, and in 1949 they started to write a six-volume textbook on theoretical physics. (Lifshitz, in collaboration with L. Pitaevskii, has kept this work up to date and in fact has expanded it since Landau's death.) Landau was also planning to write a book on mathematics for physicists, but his accident occurred before he could start on it, and his career as an active physicist was over. Landau did eventually leave the hospital, and although it was thought at one point that it would be necessary to perform brain surgery, he eventually recovered without it. His memory returned to him and he seemed to retain his complete mastery of theoretical physics, but he was never to work creatively again. He was constantly in pain and was unable to concentrate on scientific problems.

Landau was one of the greatest physicists of the century. His work is of enduring importance, he is known to advanced physics students throughout the world through his textbooks, and he was one of the major figures in the rise of Soviet physics. Landau is one of those few Nobel laureates who could have been awarded the prize for many different aspects of his work; in this respect, he ranks with Einstein, Bohr, and Dirac. He truly was one of the last generalists.

Bibliography

Primary

PHYSICS: Landau's writings are inaccessible to all but professional physicists and advanced students of physics. The simpler works, *Kurs obshchei fiziki* (1965; *General Physics*, 1967) and *Physics for Everyone* (1974), were largely written by the coauthors and do not reflect the full power of Landau's ability to communicate physical ideas. The early Russian works are the basis of his nine-volume course on theoretical physics. Selected publications are *Statisticheskaya fizica*, 1938 (with E. Lifshitz; *Statistical Physics*, 1938); *Teoria polya*, 1941 (with Lifshitz; *Theory of Fields*, 1951); *Mekhanica sploshnykh sred*, 1944 (with Lifshitz); *Kvantovaya mekhanika*, 1948 (with Lifshitz; *Quantum Mechanics*, 1965); *Lekstskii po teori atomnogo yadra*, 1955 (with Yakov A. Smorodinsky; *Lectures on Nuclear Theory*, 1958); *Elektrodynamika sploshnykh sred*, 1957 (with Lifshitz; *Electrodynamics of Continuous Media*, 1960); *Mekhanika*, 1958 (with Lifshitz; *Mechanics*, 1960); *Collected Papers of L. D. Landau*, 1965; *Kurs obshchei fiziki*, 1965 (with A. I. Akheizer and Lifshitz; *General Physics*, 1967); *Physics for Everyone*, 1974 (with A. Kitaigorodsky).

Secondary

Dorozynski, Alexander. *The Man They Wouldn't Let Die*. New York: Macmillan, 1965. The most complete available biography of Landau. The account of Landau's earlier life was compiled from secondary sources, since the author did not meet Landau until after his accident. A major part of the book is devoted to telling the story of Landau's almost fatal accident and his long recovery. The author of the book is American, and he gives a complete account of Landau's life that contrasts with the incomplete biographies and biographical sketches of Landau that originated in the Soviet Union. One of the chapters is devoted to the development of the Soviet nuclear weapons capability.

French, Anthony P., and P. J. Kennedy, eds. *Niels Bohr: A Centenary Volume*. Cambridge, Mass.: Harvard University Press, 1985. This volume is devoted chiefly to Niels Bohr, but it contains much other material. In particular, as much of quantum mechanics was developed at Bohr's institute, the development of quantum physics and its Copenhagen interpretation are discussed. The book contains some information about Landau's time at the institute. Landau regarded Bohr as his teacher, so this is a valuable reference for those who would like to gain insight into Landau's method of working.

Gamow, George. *My World Line: An Informal Biography.* New York: Viking Press, 1970. Although this autobiography is mainly devoted to Gamow's early life, it relates several incidents involving Landau. The book provides a view of the lives of scientists, such as Landau and Gamow, who were attending universities in the early postrevolutionary era. It also discusses the problems that physicists advocating modern physics suffered because of its basic conflict with Soviet political philosophy.

——————. *Thirty Years That Shook Physics: The Story of Quantum Theory.* Garden City, N.Y.: Anchor Books, 1966. An introduction to quantum mechanics written by a great expositor and one of Landau's early colleagues. A good starting point for someone completely unfamiliar with modern physics.

Lifshitz, Evgenii. "Lev Davidovich Landau." In *Mechanics.* 3d ed. Elmsford, N.Y.: Pergamon Press, 1976. Written by Lifshitz to accompany the publication of Landau's collected papers, this article provides a thorough introduction to Landau's life and work. It is probably the best source for the mathematically educated reader. The reader without a mathematical background will find Dorozynski's book more helpful.

Livanova, Anna. *Landau: A Great Physicist and Teacher.* Translated by J. B. Sykes. London: Pergamon Press, 1980. A biography in the Soviet tradition. Care should be taken when using Soviet sources, since embarrassing facts are usually omitted. Landau's imprisonment by Stalin, for example, is unmentioned. The book provides a readable account of Landau's scientific work. The period after Landau's accident is not covered.

Stephen R. Addison

1963

Physics
Eugene Paul Wigner, Hungary and United States
Maria Goeppert Mayer, Germany and United States
J. Hans D. Jensen, West Germany

Chemistry
Giulio Natta, Italy
Karl Ziegler, West Germany

Physiology or Medicine
Sir John Eccles, Australia
Alan Lloyd Hodgkin, Great Britain
Andrew Huxley, Great Britain

Literature
George Seferis, Greece

Peace
International Red Cross Committee
League of Red Cross Societies

EUGENE PAUL WIGNER
1963

Born: Budapest, Hungary; November 17, 1902

Nationality: Hungarian; after 1937, American
Area of concentration: Atomic theory

Wigner's pioneering application of group theory to the atomic nucleus established a method for discovering and applying the principles of symmetry to the behavior of physical phenomena

The Award

Presentation

On December 10, 1963, Professor Ivar Waller, a member of the Swedish Academy of Sciences, presented the Nobel Prize to Eugene Wigner, Maria Goeppert Mayer, and J. Hans D. Jensen for their discoveries concerning the theory of the atomic nucleus and elementary particles. These discoveries were based on atomic research that had been conducted during the first three decades of the twentieth century. In the 1930's, it was discovered that the atomic nucleus is composed of protons and neutrons and that its motions are explained by the laws of quantum mechanics.

In 1933, Wigner deduced that the force between two nucleons is the same whether the nucleon is a proton or neutron. The force is weak when the distance between them is small but very great when the distance is large. Wigner demonstrated that the essential properties of the nucleus follow the symmetries of the laws of motion. These laws are the same for any situation and its mirror image, and they are the same for forward and backward directions in time. Wigner laid the groundwork for the revision of concepts concerning right-left symmetry by Chen Ning Yang and Tsung-Dao Lee, who won the Nobel Prize in Physics in 1957. In addition to his discovery and his application of symmetry principles in nuclear and other branches of physics, Wigner offered a general theory of nuclear reactions and contributed substantially to the practical application of nuclear energy. He also worked independently to find models which visually suggest the motion of the nucleons.

Nobel lecture

On December 12, 1963, Eugene Wigner delivered his Nobel lecture on "Events, Laws of Nature, and Invariance Principles." In this lecture, he examined the general role of symmetry and invariance principles in both classical and modern physics. Wigner observed that physics does not explain nature; it restricts its objectives to explaining the regularities in the behavior of natural objects. These regularities are called the "laws of nature," and like legal precedents, they regulate actions and behavior under certain well-defined conditions. The elements of behavior not specified by the laws of nature are called the "initial conditions." Prior to quantum theory, classical physics assumed that the laws of nature and initial conditions, taken together, would determine the behavior of an object.

Wigner said that there was reason to hope that the regularities, or laws, of nature "form a sharply defined set, and are clearly separable from . . . initial conditions, in which there is a strong element of randomness." The principle of invariance, he said, should allow scientists to establish new laws and should serve as touchstones for the validity of all laws. The important categories for invariance transformations are Euclidean transformations (permissible when correlated events occur at different locations but in the same relation to each other), time displacements (permissible when events occur at different times but are separated by the same intervals), and uniform motion (permissible when events appear to be the same as other events from the viewpoint of a uniformly moving coordinate system). In other words, the laws of nature do not change from place to place, from time to time, or from observer to observer. The invariance principles are all geometric transformations; they change the events' location in space and time, and their state of motion, but they do not change the events. In many instances, a law may be deduced from the mathematical consequences of a theory and the postulate that the unknown law must conform with invariance principles.

Wigner concluded with a description of current research on principles of symmetry in relation to conservation, approximate invariance relations, and a wide-ranging contrast between the function of invariance in classical mechanics and quantum mechanics.

Wigner's Nobel lecture, like his own contributions to physics, was distinguished by his ability to use extremely complex mathematical logic to explain physical principles with great simplicity. In his acceptance speech, Wigner paid tribute to his high school mathematics teacher, L. Ratz; to his lifelong friend the mathematician John von Neumann; and to his graduate mentor, Michael Polanyi. The philosophical character of his thought may owe much to the influence of Polanyi, whom he credits with having taught him that science consists, first, in observing coherence and regularity in phenomena and, second, in creating concepts which express these regularities in a natural way. Wigner perceived this concern with regularities as the definitive principle of the scientific method. Viewed in this way, the scientific method has relevance to other branches of learning in a way that scientific concepts, such as matter or energy, may not.

Critical reception

No one was surprised when Wigner was awarded the Nobel Prize in 1963. He had already received the Presidential Medal for Merit, the Max Planck Medal of the German Physical Society, the Atoms for Peace Award, the Franklin Medal of the Franklin Institute, the Fermi Award, and honorary degrees from six colleges and universities. Wigner had also been a member of the National Academy of Sciences for eighteen years. When he finally received the Nobel Prize in 1963, Wigner was already internationally recognized for his contributions to physics. The Nobel award acknowledged his stature as a physicist and particularly his work in the 1930's.

Wigner's contributions to physics could not be questioned; his politics, however, were controversial. There is evidence in the Nobel ceremony itself that Wigner's conservative position on nuclear research for defense did not sit well with the committee. The American Linus Pauling, the 1954 laureate in chemistry, received the 1963 Nobel Peace Prize. The presenter lauded Pauling for his opposition to the development of the hydrogen bomb and for his crusade to ban nuclear tests. He also pointed out that Pauling was subjected to political pressure and labeled a Communist during the Cold War of the 1950's. The speech became political when two scientists were identified by name as Pauling's opposition: Edward Teller and W. F. Libby. They were also identified as members of the U.S. Atomic Energy Commission. Their position on nuclear testing was described as a calculated interest in weapons which contrasted with Pauling's respect for human life:

> Teller and Libby readily admit that radio-active fallout is harmful, but they consider that this is a relative matter, comparing this potential harm with the risk one runs by not being in a position to secure more and more effective armaments on the basis of nuclear tests.

Edward Teller is a close friend of Wigner. From 1952 to 1957, while research on the hydrogen bomb was under way, Wigner served as a member of the General Advisory Committee to the U.S. Atomic Energy Commission.

The Nobel presenter also praised Pauling for opposing bomb shelters on grounds that they are likely to give people the false impression that nuclear war is safe. This view contrasts with Wigner's strong support of civil defense, a commitment which was prompted in large part by his service on the Atomic Energy Commission. In the summer of 1963, just before receiving the award in physics, he became the director of the Harbor Project, a six-week study of civil defense commissioned by the National Academy of Sciences. He later spent time editing collections of essays urging a civil defense program. These collections, titled *Who Speaks for Civil Defense?* (1968) and *Survival and the Bomb: Methods of Civil Defense* (1969), appeared after the Nobel ceremony, but Wigner had made no secret of his support for civil defense before the 1963 ceremony. As he indicates in his preface to *Survival and the Bomb*, he hoped to initiate a pragmatic discussion of civil defense in light of the possibility of nuclear war.

In 1972, a full ten years after he was awarded the Nobel Prize, Wigner's work on group theory was described in *Physics Today* as so farsighted that it was not understood when it was first published and as so significant that it would come to be recognized as pioneering work in mathematical physics.

Biography
Eugene P. Wigner was born on November 17, 1902, in Budapest, Hungary. He attended Budapest Lutheran High School, where he met John von Neumann

(1903-1957), the lifelong friend to whom he paid tribute in his Nobel acceptance speech. Wigner studied chemical engineering at the Institute of Technology in Budapest and then at the Institute of Technology in Berlin, where in 1925 he received his doctorate in chemical engineering. Along with von Neumann, Leo Szilard (1898-1964), and Edward Teller (born 1908), Wigner belongs to the group of Hungarian scientists who left Europe in the 1930's and settled in the United States. Wigner first came to the United States in 1930 as a lecturer in mathematics at Princeton. He spent most of his career at Princeton, but from 1935 to 1937 served as a visiting professor at the University of Wisconsin. He credits his time in Wisconsin with showing him the texture of American life and inspiring his deep love of his adopted country. He worked on a series of projects during World War II, including the Manhattan Project. After the war, he visited the University of Leiden from 1957 to 1958.

He became a naturalized citizen of the United States on January 8, 1937. In 1938 he became Thomas D. Jones Professor of Mathematical Physics at Princeton University, a position from which he retired in 1971. His marriage to Mary Annette Wheeler in 1941 produced two children, David and Martha. His sister Margit married Paul Dirac, the brilliant Nobel laureate whose mathematical talents dazzled his contemporaries. Wigner always described Dirac as "my famous brother-in-law."

Scientific Career

By 1933, the political situation in Europe meant that Eugene Wigner could not continue to spend six months a year in Germany. In February, 1933, President Paul von Hindenburg of the Weimar Republic, after failing to establish a stable coalition, named Adolf Hitler as his chancellor. Wigner understood the political implications of the totalitarian movement within Germany, and he realized that he could not continue as a European. His scientific career, however, was thriving. He had already evolved the principles for applying group theory to quantum mechanics. During the mid-1930's, Wigner applied group theory to the classification of atomic spectra, working with John von Neumann to use group theory to develop a theory of energy levels in atoms. His 1931 book on group theory became a classic; it was reprinted and then translated into English.

Wigner's contributions were not limited to nuclear physics. He and Pascual Jordan (1902-1980) had published a basic paper in field theory. His definitive work with Victor Weisskopf on the relationships between line shape and transition was becoming an integral part of theoretical physics. With his student Frederick Seitz, he had also contributed substantially to solid-state physics.

Wigner's central European background and his intimate knowledge of the German scientific scene made him extremely sensitive to the political atmosphere in Germany. He understood that Europe was moving toward World War II. In 1939, Wigner, along with his Hungarian scientific colleagues Leo Szilard and Edward Teller, persuaded Albert Einstein to write to President Franklin D. Roosevelt concerning future research on nuclear energy. According to Wigner, Einstein needed little persuasion; he understood the potential threat of nuclear research conducted under a totalitarian regime. Einstein's letter to Roosevelt emphasized the need for the United States to secure a supply of uranium ore. The letter also pointed out the likelihood that nuclear power could be used to make bombs and emphasized that German scientists could and would produce bombs in support of their government's plan to achieve world dominance.

Important as this official overture to the government was, another even more impressive event occurred behind the scenes. Wigner, his Hungarian colleagues, and other scientists who understood the German scientific establishment succeeded in persuading the scientific community to classify voluntarily papers related to the atomic bomb project. Gregory Breit, who had worked closely with Wigner at the University of Wisconsin, became the chairman of a subcommittee on uranium research for the National Academy of Science. He managed to arrange for editors of scientific journals to allow his committee to screen articles relating to atomic research before publication. The receipt date of scientific articles was to be noted, but an article was not to be made public if it seemed likely that it could further research on nuclear weapons. It is noteworthy that the scientific community, a group intensely committed to academic freedom, voluntarily exerted pressure on itself to observe secrecy on issues relating to national security before the government imposed such measures. In 1979, Leona Marshall Libby, one of the youngest people to work on the Manhattan Project, was to say that the United States owes more than it has ever acknowledged to the farsightedness of Leo Szilard, Eugene Wigner, and Edward Teller. They promoted secrecy about nuclear research, publicized the advanced state of German science, and drew the U.S. government's attention to the nuclear threat.

On December 2, 1942, Enrico Fermi's research group at the University of Chicago succeeded in setting off the first nuclear chain reaction. After the visitors had departed, Eugene Wigner arrived with a bottle of wine and some paper cups. He offered no toast but wryly pointed out his forethought in the face of wartime shortages. He had obtained the imported Italian Chianti before he left Princeton and had produced it on this occasion in honor of Fermi's nationality.

Although Wigner was a theoretical physicist, his early training as an engineer made him especially valuable in applied projects. He worked on the Hanford project, which produced a plutonium-production reactor in eighteen months. He also anticipated a dangerous phenomenon later named after him, the Wigner disease. He predicted that fast neutrons striking carbon atoms in a crystalline graphite moderator between the fuel elements would knock carbon atoms out of the layers in the crystals into residual places, producing a distortion of the crystals. Neutron concentration would cause the entire pile to swell. Because Wigner had predicted that any crystalline material irradiated by high energy would contract this "disease," a solution was identified before casualties could occur. This principle was later developed into a useful means of dating old pottery and other baked materials.

Wigner supported the development of the hydrogen bomb, the "super," because he believed it an essential deterrent to Soviet aggression. He also remained strongly supportive of Edward Teller, who was labeled a "hawk" and a "warmonger" because of his interest in thermonuclear research. In the years after J. Robert Oppenheimer, the former director of research at Los Alamos, was deprived of his security clearance, Teller received very bad press. At a press conference, Wigner told reporters a story about Teller. He described himself as sitting by Teller near a swimming pool and talking about astrophysics. Teller had lost a foot in an accident, and he sat with his good foot propped up. Wigner noticed that a stream of ants was running across Teller's good foot. He asked if they were biting, and when Teller affirmed that they were, Wigner asked him why he did not kill them. Teller replied, "I don't know which ones did it."

As a teacher, Wigner's impact was immense. Chen Ning Yang, who, with Tsung-Dao Lee, was awarded the Nobel Prize in Physics for 1957, came to the United States to study with Fermi and Wigner. It says much about Wigner's contributions to physics that Yang, as a student looking for a mentor, coupled him with Fermi, who had received the Nobel Prize in 1938. Another of Wigner's students, John Bardeen, with Walter H. Brattain and William Shockley, was awarded his first Nobel Prize in 1956, several years before Wigner received his award; Bardeen received his second Nobel prize in 1972.

After World War II, as a scientist addressing the general public, Wigner chose the stance least likely to be applauded. He has been the principal spokesman for civil defense, an extremely unpopular notion. Those who believe that superior weapons are the only strategy for peace and those who believe that disarmament is the only answer unite in their contempt for the concept of civil defense. The issue, which Wigner spent much time and effort promoting, no longer receives much attention. In a 1973 interview in *Science*, Wigner reiterated his concern that none of the recommendations of his task force had been implemented.

Wigner's essays in *Symmetries and Reflections* (1967), especially "Remarks on the Mind-Body Question" and "The Growth of Science: Its Promises and Its Dangers," probe deeply into philosophical and ethical issues. In the former, he rejects the materialistic view that matter is everything. Acknowledging that it may be premature to assume that the philosophy of quantum mechanics will constitute a permanent feature of physical theory, he adds that it is remarkable that the study of the external world has only confirmed that human consciousness is a reality. In his essay on the future of science, he by no means assumes that science will confer only blessings on future generations.

Wigner's comments on his experiments as a scientist and on the future direction of science merit thoughtful attention. In 1972, he described theoretical physics, his choice of occupation, as monastic. To choose physics was to choose a realm in which influence and power were irrelevant. Many branches of modern physics require expensive equipment, and the need to acquire influence so as to pay for this costly equipment has changed physics as a profession; nevertheless, it has not necessarily changed the monastic code. Significantly, Wigner, who resists premature generalization, does not deplore "big science." The two extremes, he suggests, are for science to be taken over by administrators who would manage it as a business and for individual scientists to retreat into a vacuum to contemplate number theory for their personal satisfaction. As an alternative, he suggests competition between these two extremes, competition which may result in a golden mean. To the layman, such issues may seem technical, related only to the government's role in funding science and to the differing degrees of prestige awarded to professionals within a highly specialized community. These questions, however, have moral implications. Wigner's view of science assumes that no intellectual activity can be divorced from its human context. To extend his arguments in directions suggested by his own life, the individual—whether scientist, poet, philosopher, artist, or entrepreneur—must pursue satisfaction, but he must never lose sight of his responsibilities as a participant in the human community.

Bibliography

Primary

PHYSICS: For a list of articles by Wigner complete through 1962, see V. Bargman et al., "To Eugene Wigner on His Sixtieth Birthday," *Reviews of Modern Physics*, vol. 34, 1962. Some of his major works are *Gruppentheorie und ihre Anwendung auf die Quantunmechanik der Atomspektren*, 1931 (*Group Theory and Its Application to the Quantum Mechanics of Atom Spectra*, 1959); *Nuclear Structure*, 1958 (with Leonard Eisenbud); *The Physical Theory of Neutron Chain Reactors*, 1958 (with Alvin M. Weinberg); "An Appreciation on the Sixtieth Birthday of Edward Teller," in Hans Mark, ed., *Properties of Matter Under Unusual Conditions*, 1969; *Aspects of Quantum Theory*, 1972; *Reminiscences About a Great Physicist: Paul Adrien Maurice Dirac*, 1987.

OTHER NONFICTION: *Symmetries and Reflections: Scientific Essays of Eugene P. Wigner*, 1967.

EDITED TEXTS: *Physical Sciences and Human Values*, 1947; *Ladislaus Farkas Memorial Volume*, 1952; *Who Speaks for Civil Defense?*, 1968; *Survival and the Bomb: Methods of Civil Defense*, 1969.

Secondary

Davis, Nuel Pharr. *Lawrence and Oppenheimer*. New York: Simon & Schuster, 1968. The author contrasts Ernest Orlando Lawrence, the experimental physicist who invented the cyclotron, with J. Robert Oppenheimer, the theoretical physicist who directed the creation of the atomic bomb at Los Alamos. The study is biased against Lawrence.

Libby, Leona M. *The Uranium People*. New York: Crane, Russak, 1979. This account of the creation of the atomic bomb was written by a young scientist who participated in the project and knew Wigner, Teller, and other members of the team.

Seitz, Frederick. "Eugene Wigner: A Tribute on his Seventieth Birthday." *Physics*

Today 25 (1972): 40-43. This article, illustrated with pictures of Wigner, was adapted from a talk given by a former student on the occasion of Wigner's retirement in 1971. The article surveys Wigner's life, describes his impact on mathematical physics, and comments on Wigner's effectiveness as a teacher.

Snow, C. P. *The Physicists*. Boston: Little, Brown, 1981. This extremely readable book was completed just before Snow's death in 1980. A first draft of what was to have been a longer study, the book was largely written from memory. Snow offers an international perspective on the story of physics in the twentieth century. He also reprints his own editorial, dated September, 1939, anticipating the discovery of the atom bomb.

Walsh, J. "A Conversation with Eugene Wigner." *Science* 181 (1973): 527-33. This excellent article offers an objective and essential perspective on Wigner's conservative political stance on defense research and civil defense. Wigner is questioned on issues such as the delay in developing atomic power for civilian purposes and the future of science.

Jeanie R. Brink

1963

Physics
Eugene Paul Wigner, Hungary and United States
Maria Goeppert Mayer, Germany and United States
J. Hans D. Jensen, West Germany

Chemistry
Giulio Natta, Italy
Karl Ziegler, West Germany

Physiology or Medicine
Sir John Eccles, Australia
Alan Lloyd Hodgkin, Great Britain
Andrew Huxley, Great Britain

Literature
George Seferis, Greece

Peace
International Red Cross Committee
League of Red Cross Societies

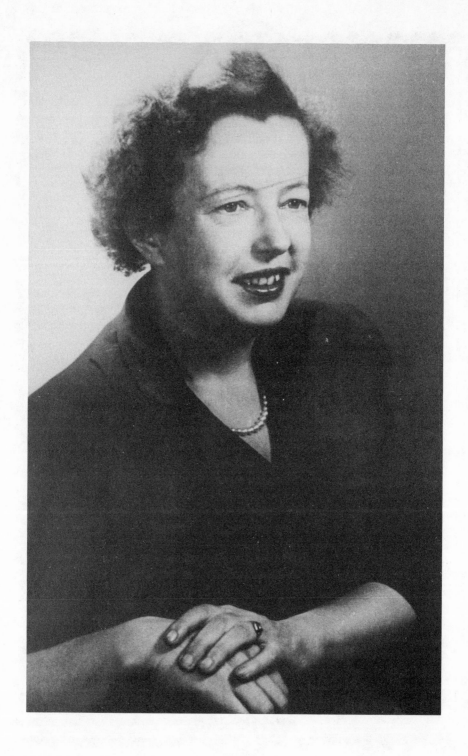

MARIA GOEPPERT MAYER
1963

Born: Kattowitz, Upper Silesia, Germany; June 28, 1906
Died: San Diego, California; February 20, 1972
Nationality: German; after 1933, American
Area of concentration: Nuclear physics

Goeppert Mayer's shell model of the atomic nucleus explained the periodic changes in nuclear properties characterized by the existence of certain very stable nuclei which contain "magic numbers" of protons or neutrons. The shell model, which was developed independently by J. Hans D. Jensen, has organized and stimulated research into the structure of the atomic nucleus

The Award

Presentation

On December 10, 1963, Maria Goeppert Mayer received the Nobel Prize in Physics from King Gustav VI of Sweden. Professor Ivar Waller, a member of the Swedish Academy of Sciences, introduced the winners of the 1963 award. Half of the prize was awarded to Eugene Paul Wigner (born 1902) and half to Goeppert Mayer and J. Hans D. Jensen (1907-1973). Waller summarized the history of research into the structure of atomic nuclei and recounted Wigner's use of symmetry properties to clarify both the structure of the nucleus and the behavior of elementary particles. He explained that nuclear behavior is characterized by unusual stability whenever the number of protons or the number of neutrons in a nucleus is one of the so-called magic numbers—2, 8, 20, 28, 50, 82, and 126—and recognized Goeppert Mayer's work in systematically interpreting experimental data showing the effects of the magic numbers on a variety of nuclear properties.

Regular changes in the behavior of nuclei suggest that nucleons (protons and neutrons) move, under the influence of a central force, in allowed orbits that fall into groups separated by energy gaps, just as electrons fall into shells around the nucleus. Goeppert Mayer and Jensen independently realized that the magic numbers represented closed shells of nucleons. Their model, the shell model of the nucleus, brought order to existing data on the ground and low-excited states of the nucleus and predicted new properties, thereby stimulating experimental and theoretical work, including the use of Wigner's symmetry principles in applications of the shell model.

Nobel lecture

Goeppert Mayer delivered her Nobel lecture, entitled "The Shell Model," in English. Her outline of the development of the model, its implications for the field of nuclear physics, and its shortcomings was presented with unusual clarity and illustrated why she was considered an excellent teacher. She began with a summary of the experimental data on nuclei which had led to the recognition that when a nucleus had one of the "magic" numbers (2, 8, 20, 28, 50, 82, or 126) of either protons or neutrons, it was unusually tightly bound. The fact that the magic numbers emerge when nuclear data are plotted against either proton number or neutron number but not when they are plotted against nucleon number provided important evidence that the nuclear force is the same for protons and neutrons. Data supporting the existence of magic numbers include the abundance of isotopes for nuclei with magic numbers of protons and the abundance of isobars for nuclei with magic numbers of neutrons. There also are discontinuities in beta decay energies for nuclei with magic numbers of either protons or neutrons. The binding energy for the first proton or neutron beyond a magic number is much less than for the previous nucleon, which completed a magic number.

The behavior of nuclei at magic numbers strongly suggests an analogy with the behavior of electrons at the point where atomic shells are closed. Goeppert Mayer briefly described the well-studied shell theory of atoms and the evidence that supports it, stressing that the basic assumption of atomic shell theory is that electrons move in spherically symmetrical, essentially independent orbits. Where there are energy gaps between orbits, the electron in the lower-energy orbit is said to complete a shell. Like nucleons near magic numbers, these electrons exhibit high binding energies compared to the next electron bound in the atom.

Reasoning in analogy to the atomic case, physicists sought a central force that would predict the magic number behavior of nuclei. Goeppert Mayer, following a suggestion made by Enrico Fermi (1901-1954), had noted that a model using a simple harmonic oscillator potential along with a very strong coupling between the angular momentum caused by the spin of a nucleon and the angular momentum caused by its orbital motion (spin-orbit coupling) produced an energy-level pattern for nucleons with large energy gaps corresponding to the filled shells at the magic numbers. When the repulsion of the charged protons was added to the model, this shell model of the nucleus reproduced much of the existing data on the properties of nuclei. Furthermore, the model predicted new properties of nuclei. For example, the angular moments, or spins, or nuclei with neutron or proton numbers up to fifty could be predicted on the basis of the shell model. The shell model predicted many of the properties of certain low-lying excited states of nuclei, such as their unusually long lifetimes, which result from the difference in spin between the excited nuclear state and the ground state.

With typical modesty, Goeppert Mayer closed her Nobel lecture with a discussion of the failures of the shell model, including the fact that it presented too simple a picture of nuclear behavior to allow for very accurate calculation or to predict the magnetic moments of nuclei. She even mentioned that the model's basic assumption of strong spin-orbit coupling might be open to question for light nuclei. In closing, she stressed once again that the shell model had played a major role in stimulating nuclear research, both experimental and theoretic.

Critical reception

The scientific community accepted the Royal Swedish Academy's choice of the 1963 Nobel laureates in physics with typically moderate enthusiasm. The contributions of the shell model to the development of nuclear physics were not questioned, nor was there any doubt that Goeppert Mayer deserved credit for its development. *Scientific American* announced that the Nobel Prizes in science were awarded to "reflect currently active themes of investigation." *Physics Today* split its announcement of the award as the prize itself was divided, devoting half its story to Wigner and the other half to Goeppert Mayer and Jensen together. Clark Kerr, the president of the University of California, telephoned to congratulate Goeppert Mayer on "the high honor she has brought to herself and to her university" and was quoted as saying, "Mrs. Mayer becomes the 12th member of the U.C. faculty to receive the Nobel Prize and the sixth faculty member to be given this award in the last four years."

The popular press found the fact that Goeppert Mayer was the first American woman to win the Nobel Prize in Physics and only the second woman to receive it far more exciting. *The New York Times* ran a sidebar story headlined "Woman Laureate to Get Her Wish: Always Wanted to Meet a King—Wigner Baffled." The story took its headline from a chance comment made by Goeppert Mayer after she had been told that she was to receive the Nobel Prize and Wigner's modest disclaimer of his own fame. *Newsweek* led its story on the prizes with a discussion of Wigner's work, but the headline was "Just Ask Mrs. Mayer." Reporters made much of the fact that in her youth Goeppert Mayer had been known as "the Beauty of Göttingen" and was still an attractive woman, although a stroke she had suffered had left her handicapped. Her distinguished husband and supportive children were all interviewed.

McCall's responded to the popular interest in the Nobel laureate with a story by Mary Harrington Hall titled "An American Mother and the Nobel Prize: A Cinderella Story in Science." The story barely mentioned Goeppert Mayer's work on the structure of the nucleus, concentrating instead on her family life and personal characteristics. She was described by a friend as a woman "who makes people happy in her home." The author concentrated on Mayer's childhood in Germany and the poverty that forced the family to live on turnip soup in order to share food with the children in the clinic which her father ran. The laureate was described as a superwoman of the sixties who did brilliant work in nuclear physics while maintaining a perfect marriage with well-adjusted children. She was portrayed functioning as a perfect hostess at a seated dinner for twenty-six which she had cooked herself in honor of her husband's birthday. Goeppert Mayer herself is repeatedly quoted as denying any feeling of having experienced discrimination because she was a woman.

By the time of her death, nine years later, Goeppert Mayer had become a symbol of the married professional woman who pursues a brilliant career against all odds while maintaining a happy marriage and rearing successful children. An obituary in

Physics Today ends, "She overcame quite subtle obstacles in the course of her life—she was a woman, a foreigner, she started her career in the days of the depression. How many of us could have achieved half the success that she did?" Goeppert Mayer's stress on hard work, ignoring obstacles and keeping an eye firmly on the physics problem at hand, made her a role model for many women physicists. From her own comments, one suspects that she would not have been greatly interested in the women's movement but would have been passionately concerned with the latest modifications to the shell model of the nucleus.

Biography

Maria Goeppert Mayer was born on June 28, 1906, in the town of Kattowitz, which was then a part of Germany; she moved in 1910 to Göttingen, where she grew up and received her education. She was the only child of Friedrich Goeppert, a professor of pediatrics at the University of Göttingen, and his wife, Maria Wolff Goeppert, a former schoolteacher and a proficient musician. Professor Goeppert was the sixth generation of his family to be a university professor, and he reared his only daughter to maintain the family tradition and urged her not to be "just a woman." During World War I and the runaway inflation that followed, he insisted that his own family go without food so that the children in the clinic he ran might eat, and Maria Goeppert remembered with loathing the turnip soup that formed the staple of the Goeppert diet in those hard days. The family and the children of the clinic were saved from malnutrition by care packages sent from the United States when *The New York Times* printed a story describing their plight.

After the hard times, Maria Goeppert managed to enter the University at Göttingen in 1924 to study mathematics, despite the fact that even the Frauenstudium, a private school which prepared the few women who wished to take the examinations to enter the university, closed before she had completed her studies there. In 1928, she won a fellowship to study for a term at Girton College in Cambridge, England; on her return to Göttingen, she met and wed an American chemist, Joseph Edward Mayer (born 1904). In 1930, Goeppert completed her dissertation and left Germany for Baltimore, Maryland, where she was given office space at The Johns Hopkins University to continue her work. She bore two children, Maria Anne, born in 1933, and Peter Conrad, born in 1938. Joseph Mayer accepted a position as an associate professor at Columbia University in 1939, and Maria was provided with office space until she accepted a half-time teaching job at Sarah Lawrence College in 1941. In 1942, she went to work full time on isotope separation problems for the Manhattan Project. In 1946, the Mayers moved to Chicago, where Maria held a half-time position as a staff physicist at the Argonne National Laboratory and as an associate professor without pay at the University of Chicago, where she performed the research for which she was awarded the Nobel Prize. In 1959, both Mayers accepted full professorships at the University of California at San Diego. Goeppert Mayer suffered a crippling stroke soon after that, and her health declined steadily until her death from heart failure on February 20, 1972.

Scientific Career

In 1924, when Maria Goeppert entered the University of Göttingen, the university had attracted two of the brightest and most active quantum physicists of the day. Max Born (1882-1970) was appointed to the chair of theoretical physics in 1921, and Born appointed James Franck (1882-1964) to the chair of experimental physics. Born approached theoretical physics mathematically; Franck preferred an intuitive approach with less reliance on mathematics. Between them, Born and Franck were in the process of shifting research at Göttingen from its traditional emphasis on mathematics to a focus on quantum physics. Along with Copenhagen, Göttingen became the major center of theoretical physics in Europe, and most of the physicists who developed quantum theory spent long periods of time there. For example, J. Robert Oppenheimer (1904-1967) traveled to Göttingen in 1927 to study theoretical physics.

Maria Goeppert intended to study mathematics, but Born recognized her talents and in 1927 invited her to join his seminar on quantum physics, where her strong background in mathematics matched Born's own strength. She had originally intended to become a high school teacher, but the required courses in psychology and philosophy proved so boring that she followed her inclination and her father's urging and began work for a doctoral degree. She was awarded a fellowship to study physics at Girton College in Cambridge in 1928; she attended lectures by the English physicists there but claimed that the main value of her stay in Cambridge was the improvement of her English. In 1930, she completed a theoretical thesis in which she calculated the probability that an electron would emit not one but two photons, or quantum units of light, as it decayed to a lower allowed orbit. The thesis was purely speculative at the time it was written, but with the advent of lasers, the double-photon process has become the object of experimental interest and Goeppert Mayer's thesis has received more attention than it did at the time of its completion.

Also in 1930, Goeppert was married to an American chemist, Joseph Edward Mayer, who had received a Rockefeller fellowship to study chemical physics after completing his doctorate in experimental chemistry at the University of California at Berkeley. Mayer sought lodgings with Frau Goeppert, who had been compelled to take in boarders since her husband's death in 1927; he met her daughter and, to the surprise of the Göttingen community, persuaded her to marry him. On completing his fellowship, Mayer accepted a position as an associate in chemistry at The Johns Hopkins University in Baltimore, Maryland.

In 1930, when Maria Goeppert Mayer arrived in Baltimore, there was no question of offering her a position at the university, both because of nepotism rules and because the depression made a second job in one family a luxury. The physics department managed to offer her a very modest assistantship which allowed her an office and access to the facilities of the university and eventually permitted her to offer lectures in graduate courses. Quantum physics was just beginning to reach the United States, and Goeppert Mayer applied her skills to teaching her husband and his colleagues. Not surprisingly, she began to work on problems in chemical physics and published several papers in that field on topics such as the entropy of polyatomic molecules and the behavior of hydrogen dissolved in palladium. She also spent the summers of 1931, 1932, and 1933 in Göttingen working with Born and published a long article in the *Handbuch der Physik* with him on the dynamic lattice theory of crystals. In 1935, she extended her work on the double-photon process to nuclear physics and published a paper on double beta decay, the process by which a nucleus decays by emitting two beta particles simultaneously, just as the atoms in her thesis had emitted two photons simultaneously. In 1935, James Franck came to Johns Hopkins, having been forced to leave Göttingen by the rise of the Nazis. Goeppert Mayer was able to renew her association with him as well as with the stream of atomic physicists who came to visit him there. In particular, she began to work with Edward Teller (born 1908), who was then at George Washington University and whose ideas she found exciting. Finally, in 1938, she and her husband began work on a textbook on statistical mechanics; it was published in 1940 and became a classic in the field. Joseph Mayer published a second edition in 1977 which is still on library shelves. By this time, she was advising graduate students and giving lectures in graduate chemistry and physics seminars; she was also the mother of two young children.

Denied tenure at Johns Hopkins, Joseph Mayer accepted an associate professorship at Columbia University in New York in 1939, and the physics department there also offered to arrange office space for his wife. At Columbia, Goeppert Mayer worked with Enrico Fermi, who suggested she study the valence-shell structures of man-made elements heavier than uranium—elements that had been predicted but not yet discovered. Her prediction that they would form a new, rare series proved surprisingly accurate. She also continued to study theoretical problems in chemical physics. In December, 1941, she was offered a half-time teaching position at Sarah Lawrence College. She earned a salary for the teaching which she continued to do off and on during the war. In 1942, she joined the isotope separation project that was Columbia's contribution to the Manhattan Project. She worked on the thermodynamic properties of uranium hexafluoride (the gaseous compound of uranium used in isotope separation by diffusion) and on the possibilities of using photochemical reactions for isotope separation.

In 1946, Joseph Mayer moved to the University of Chicago as a professor of chemistry, and Goeppert Mayer took a position as a voluntary associate professor of physics without salary in the newly formed Institute for Nuclear Studies. The University of Chicago at this time was one of the most exciting centers of physics, particularly nuclear physics, in the world. The Manhattan Project had completed its mission. The war with Germany and Japan had ended, and the physicists who had devoted their energies to the production of the atom bomb and other war efforts, such as the development of radar, underwater detection of submarines, and the design of specialized explosives, were at last free to pursue basic physics. Fermi moved from Los Alamos to the University of Chicago and brought his research group with him. With the help of Teller, who interested her in studying properties of radiation and matter at very high temperatures, Goeppert Mayer became a consultant at the Metallurgical Laboratory, where she supervised several graduate students. When the Metallurgical Laboratory became the Argonne National Laboratory, she received a position as senior physicist which carried a half-time salary. Argonne's mission was to promote the peaceful use of nuclear power, and Goeppert Mayer learned to use the newly developed electronic computer ENIAC to model liquid-metal breeder reactors.

In addition to this work at Argonne, she worked on publishing some earlier work she had done on isotopic exchange reactions and began a project with Teller on the cosmologic origin of the chemical elements. While compiling data to test their models, she noted, as others had before her, the existence of periodic properties for nuclear isotopes which became clear when one plotted proton or neutron number against such nuclear properties as numbers of stable isotopes, beta-decay energy, quadrupole moments, and binding energy. These periodic properties resembled properties of the electron shells in atoms, and they seemed to be evidence for nuclear shells which "closed" at the so-called magic numbers of protons or neutrons. In 1948, Goeppert Mayer published a paper in *Physical Review* in which she suggested a shell theory of the nucleus and presented a review of the new and compelling experimental evidence for its existence. She also recognized that there were several higher magic numbers than had been known to previous theorists.

In 1949, during an offhand discussion of Goeppert Mayer's data, Fermi asked her about the effects of spin-orbit coupling, the interaction between a nucleon's angular momentum and its orbit. Goeppert Mayer immediately recognized that including a large spin-orbit interaction with a model of the central nuclear force as a simple harmonic oscillator would predict the magic number behavior of nuclei. She prepared her results for publication as a letter to *Physical Review* in 1949 and then learned of a paper done independently by Jensen and his collaborators in Germany. She asked the editor of the *Physical Review* to delay publication of her letter announcing her discovery until the two papers could appear in the same issue. Two longer papers published in 1950 in *Physical Review* set out the complete shell model of the nucleus and the data that supported it. Also in 1950, Goeppert Mayer finally met Jensen, with whom she had been in correspondence. Their collaboration produced new insight into the shell model of the nucleus, and they collaborated on a book, *Elementary Theory of Nuclear Shell Structure* (1955), which extended their original shell model of the nucleus and is still the clearest presentation of the nuclear shell model. This work won for them the Nobel Prize in 1963.

Goeppert Mayer worked not only on the shell model of the nucleus but also on such divergent topics as beta decay, neutrino theory, and the theory of nuclear fission. Teller left Chicago in 1952, and Fermi died in 1954, so the excitement at the University cooled; Goeppert Mayer was willing to accept her first real academic appointment as a professor of physics at the University of California at San Diego in 1960, particularly as her husband was also offered a position as a professor of chemistry. Unfortunately, she suffered a severe stroke shortly after the move to San Diego. Her work began to be hampered by ill health, although she continued to work on problems using the shell model. Her last publication, written with Jensen, appeared in 1965 and was a review of the shell model.

The shell model of the nucleus proved to be the organizing principle behind a mass of nuclear data. It not only organized the experimental results of the previous twenty years but also stimulated experimental and theoretical studies in nuclear physics for the next thirty years. When combined with the collective model of the nucleus, which treated the nucleus as a plastic solid, the shell model explained most of the phenomena of nuclear physics then known. The shell model was primarily a phenomenological model, as Goeppert Mayer was careful to point out in her Nobel lecture. It was based on observation of regularities in nuclear data and not on a profound understanding of the nuclear binding force. In later years, fundamental particle physics led to a more profound understanding of the nuclear force based on the fact that the proton and neutron are composed of quarks. Nuclear theory today is working out the implications of this theory for the structure of the nucleus, and the shell model is seen as a useful tool for gaining deeper knowledge. Modern texts in nuclear physics treat the shell model in chapters that can be skipped if the instructor desires, although it is still an essential starting point in discussing nuclear data. The Nobel Prize was richly deserved because of the critical role the shell model played in the development of nuclear physics.

It is not possible to assess completely Maria Goeppert Mayer's scientific work without mentioning the personal difficulties under which she accomplished it. Supported by her husband, who appreciated both the high quality of her work and her need to do it, she managed to produce work judged worthy of a Nobel Prize without ever holding a full-time position in physics. In addition, she accomplished this feat before it was socially acceptable for a married woman to hold a job outside the home and while rearing two children, to whom she was devoted. Her solid achievements as a physicist are enhanced by the obstacles she had to overcome.

Bibliography

Primary

PHYSICS: *Statistical Mechanics*, 1940 (with Joesph E. Mayer); *Elementary Theory of Nuclear Shell Structure*, 1955 (with J. H. D. Jensen).

Secondary

Cohen, Bernard L. *Concepts of Nuclear Physics*. New York: McGraw-Hill, 1971. This standard and respected introductory text in nuclear physics presents a basic picture of the shell model in its heyday. Chapters 4-6 of the text provide an introduction to the shell model of the nucleus which demonstrates how it can be used to perform calculations of nuclear properties.

Dash, Joan. *A Life of One's Own: Three Gifted Women and the Men They Married*. New York: Harper & Row, 1973. This book is the best biography of Maria

Goeppert Mayer yet published. It concentrates on her personal life and particularly on her relationship with Joseph Mayer, her father, and her teacher Max Born. It also stresses social rather than professional interactions with the major scientific figures of the period. Although it tends to neglect the important scientific themes of Goeppert Mayer's life, it provides a comprehensive portrait of the woman who was the scientist.

Frauenfelder, Hans, and Ernest M. Henley. *Subatomic Physics*. Englewood Cliffs, N.J.: Prentice Hall, 1974. This introduction of nuclear physics incorporates theories in particle physics into its discussion of the shell model. It is useful reading for those interested in the modifications introduced by developments in physics. Chapter 15 presents a more modern view of the shell model. Written for undergraduate physics majors.

Krane, Kenneth S. *Introductory Nuclear Physics*. New York: John Wiley & Sons, 1987. This modern introduction to nuclear physics, written for undergraduate physics majors, relegates the shell model to a chapter which can be skipped at the instructor's discretion and describes the position of the shell model in the study of nuclear physics.

Sachs, Robert G. "Maria Goeppert Mayer." *Biographical Memoirs of the National Academy of Sciences* 50 (1979): 310-328. This portrait of Maria Goeppert Mayer was written by a physicist who was a graduate student under her supervision at Johns Hopkins and who knew her well as a scientist. Sachs traces Goeppert Mayer's scientific career and the development of her theoretical model of the nucleus. The article contains a complete list of her publications.

Stuewer, Roger H., ed. *Nuclear Physics in Retrospect: Proceedings of a Symposium on the 1930's*. Minneapolis: University of Minnesota Press, 1979. This collection contains comments on the development of nuclear physics in the 1930's by physicists who were an active part of the physics community then, as was Goeppert Mayer. The symposium provides insights into the time during which she did the work that culminated in the nuclear shell model in 1949. She emerges from the memoirs as both a theoretical physicist and a homemaker, although she is not the central figure of any of the essays published here.

Ruth H. Howes

1963

Physics
Eugene Paul Wigner, Hungary and United States
Maria Goeppert Mayer, Germany and United States
J. Hans D. Jensen, West Germany

Chemistry
Giulio Natta, Italy
Karl Ziegler, West Germany

Physiology or Medicine
Sir John Eccles, Australia
Alan Lloyd Hodgkin, Great Britain
Andrew Huxley, Great Britain

Literature
George Seferis, Greece

Peace
International Red Cross Committee
League of Red Cross Societies

J. HANS D. JENSEN
1963

Born: Hamburg, Germany; June 25, 1907
Died: Heidelberg, West Germany; February 11, 1973
Nationality: German
Area of concentration: Nuclear physics

Jensen's investigations of the so-called magic numbers of neutrons and protons for certain highly stable elements and their several isotopes led to the abandonment of the theoretical "liquid drop" picture of the atomic nucleus. Jensen independently developed the shell model of the atomic nucleus at virtually the same time as Maria Goeppert Mayer

The Award

Presentation

Professor Ivar Waller awarded the Nobel Prize in Physics to Eugene Wigner, Maria Goeppert Mayer, and J. Hans D. Jensen jointly on December 10, 1963, on behalf of the Royal Swedish Academy of Sciences and King Gustav VI. The prizes were presented by the king, as is customary. In his presentation, Waller briefly described the development, during the first three decades of the twentieth century, of a coherent theoretical model of the atom as governed by the laws of quantum mechanics. The proposed "nucleons," or moving components of the nucleus (protons and neutrons), did not come to be more fully described in their interrelations, however, until 1933, when Wigner's experimental results pointed to certain determinable characteristics of nuclear forces, such as the extreme strength of the short-range attractive force between nucleons in comparison with the forces between electrons orbiting the nucleus. Wigner also helped to create a fundamental theory of the necessarily symmetrical behavior of elementary particles.

Yet real visualization of the motion of nucleons could not be undertaken until Goeppert Mayer and Jensen (with O. Haxel and H. E. Suess) independently devised the shell model of the nucleus to account for the high stability of elements whose numbers of either kind of nucleons amount to 2, 8, 20, 28, 50, 82, or 126. According to Waller, these "magic numbers" could not be satisfactorily explained within the framework of the atomic theory of Niels Bohr (1885-1962), but Goeppert Mayer and Jensen had solved the problem by elaborating on their primary insight that nucleons should have different energies according to the direction in which they "spin" around the center of the nucleus.

Goeppert Mayer and Jensen subsequently collaborated on a book on the shell model which was published in 1955. Their success in predicting new atomic phenomena led to the general acceptance of shell theory, and the application of the model has been further advanced by its amenability to proven methods developed by Wigner.

Nobel lecture

Jensen delivered his Nobel Prize lecture in German (it was later translated as "Glimpses at the History of the Nuclear Structure Theory") on December 12, 1963. The lecture, which Jensen dedicated in his opening remarks to his great teacher Niels Bohr, was both a summary of scientific research and a contemplative essay on the history of modern ideas about the ultimate nature of matter.

Jensen began his "Glimpses" by describing the infancy of nuclear physics and sketching the rough image of the atom, with its positively and negatively charged building blocks (protons and electrons), that was inherited from nineteenth century physics. A conceptual impasse had been reached, however, which was first overcome with the confirmation of the existence of an uncharged counterpart to the proton. The discovery of the neutron by Sir James Chadwick (1891-1974) in 1932 allowed for tremendous advances in describing nuclear structure and predicting natural phenomena at the atomic level. Much of the credit for theoretical advances Jensen gave to Wigner and to Werner Heisenberg (1901-1976), whose contributions he discussed in detail. Their study of nucleon-nucleon forces (forces governing the behavior of particles within the nucleus) led to conclusions about the orbit and spin of nucleons that are fundamental to the shell model of the nucleus.

Jensen proceeded to a discussion of the rapid growth of experimental nuclear physics that followed the discovery and subsequent manipulation of the neutron. Enrico Fermi (1901-1954), for example, provided further impetus for nuclear research by drawing "radical consequences from the idea that the proton and the neutron are two quantum states of one single fundamental particle, the nucleon." Transitions between these two states are indeed possible; they result in the creation of not only electrons but also neutrally charged electrical particles called "neutrinos."

Interspersed among Jensen's historical assessments of individual theoretical contributions were autobiographical remarks about influences in his own professional development (such as his many trips to consult with Bohr in Copenhagen) and his early work on what Wigner had termed "magic numbers." He credited his colleagues and elders Haxel and Suess with sensing that some profound significance lay in the interpretation of these numbers; their insistence had spurred his work. Jensen remembered reading some of Mayer's early ruminations on the subject before submitting his own theoretical study to the journal *Physical Review* in 1948.

In closing, Jensen analyzed in some detail the shortcomings of the shell model and subsequent modifications made by several groups of colleagues at work in theoretical physics. He briefly identified the most propitious directions for further research and concluded with lines from a poem by the great Austrian poet Rainer Maria Rilke (1875-1926) in which is described the feeling of promise that accompanies the slow revelation of new knowledge.

Critical reception

The selection of a woman as a Nobel Prize winner in physics—the first woman to be so honored since Marie Curie had received the award sixty years earlier—

tended to overshadow the choice of Jensen and Wigner as corecipients of the award in 1963. Moreover, Maria Goeppert Mayer's achievement held much interest for the popular press (see, for instance, *McCall's* for July, 1964) precisely because she had brought about, through years of determined and largely unrewarded efforts, a major scientific breakthrough in spite of the blatant sexual discrimination of the American academic establishment at the time.

Similarly, *Scientific American* made primary reference to Goeppert Mayer. In its December, 1963, issue the magazine also pointed out that one half of the prize money had been allotted to Wigner alone for his work on "quantum mechanics, the theory of solids and the theory of nuclear chain reactions." *Newsweek* had reported this fact as well on November 18 of the same year, and it also focused primarily on Mayer's life and work in an article called "Just Ask Mrs. Mayer," in which Jensen is identified initially as "another scientist in another country [who] had independently come upon an identical theory." *The New York Times* of November 6, 1963, carried a somewhat more balanced treatment of the recipients of the Nobel Prize in Physics, including biographical descriptions and photographs of all three winners. The article gave credit to Mayer and Jensen for creating a theoretical explanation for the previously observed fact "that the number of particles on the various levels of the multi-shell nucleus increased abruptly from two in the inner one to eight in the second, 20 in the third and so on up to 126 in the sixth."

The choice of Jensen as a Nobel Prize recipient met with a more attentive and laudatory reception in his homeland. The professional physics journal *Physikalische Blätter* published a three-page discussion of Jensen's contribution in its first issue of 1964. The article pointed to unanimous acclaim for Jensen's work among colleagues in the physics institutes of West Germany. In addition, the authors offered a historical analysis of developments leading up to the revolutionary scientific paper first published by Jensen, who had at the time been acting as primary researcher in collaboration with Haxel and Suess. It is interesting to note that the original paper was rejected as "nothing but number games" by the editor of the first journal to which it was sent.

Biography

Johannes Hans Daniel Jensen was born in Hamburg, Germany, on June 25, 1907. He was not a child of the middle or upper classes, but the son of a gardener, Karl Jensen, and his wife, Helene Jensen (née Ohm). Hans Jensen's entry into a professional career was the result of the efforts of a teacher who recognized his abilities early and obtained for him a scholarship at the Oberrealschule (a science-oriented secondary school), from which he was graduated in 1926. He studied for a time at the University of Freiburg and was awarded a doctorate in physics at the University of Hamburg in 1932. He remained there as a faculty member until 1941, when he accepted a position as professor ordinarius at the Institute of Technology at Hannover. In 1949 he became a professor at the University of Heidelberg.

Jensen lived the busy, if quiet, life of a German academic, and he gardened in his spare time. The war years had been a time of relative isolation for him. In the two decades after World War II, however, he made several trips to the United States as a guest professor, lecturing at the Universities of Wisconsin, California at Berkeley, and Indiana and at the Institute for Advanced Study in Princeton, New Jersey. He died in Heidelberg on February 11, 1973.

Scientific Career

It is indisputable that the shell model of the nucleus already existed in one form or another in the minds of many physicists prior to the work of Goeppert Mayer and Jensen; these two scientists simply took the final bold steps in defining and devising the theory so as to make it convincing and acceptable to a majority of experts. The idea was being discussed as early as 1934 in papers by V. M. Elsasser and K. Guggenheimer in *Le Journal de physique et le radium*, although James H. Bartlett had in fact introduced a very rudimentary version of the shell concept in 1932.

The extent to which shell theory is taken for granted as a natural outgrowth of quantum mechanics and Niels Bohr's atomic model is indicated by the blithe inclusion of Mayer's and Jensen's principles of shell theory in physics textbooks, often with no reference to the names of the originators. Even monographs devoted exclusively to shell theory routinely honor the groundbreaking work of Mayer and Jensen only with a single footnote.

Yet, this limited recognition is also surely a reflection of the relative youth of the field of shell theory. A great unifying vision has yet to be achieved. Mayer and Jensen were themselves well aware of that. As they wrote in the preface to their collaborative *Elementary Theory of Nuclear Shell Structure* in 1955, "The state of nuclear physics today is somewhat analogous to that of the concepts of the structure of matter *before* quantum mechanics." They were convinced that science had not yet reached the point where it would again undergo conceptual upheavals on the scale of those of the first three decades of the twentieth century, when Max Planck (1858-1947), Albert Einstein (1879-1955), Niels Bohr, and others were reshaping the very foundations of physics. Accordingly, the work of Mayer and Jensen has entered the apparatus of conventional physics, and that—in addition to the honor of receiving the Nobel Prize—constitutes ample recognition.

Jensen's career was marked by a distinctly unflamboyant devotion to detailed theoretical research coupled with admiration for the verve of the more meteoric figures on the scientific horizon, such as Erwin Schrödinger (1887-1961). Jensen was short of stature, solid of physique, and quick-witted. He possessed a good sense of humor, as *The New York Times* reported on the occasion of the announcement of the Nobel Prize in 1963, and enjoyed, for example, "word games such as taking English idiom and translating it literally into German." In his later years at Heidelberg he was known for tending the garden at the Physics Institute there and for his special fondness for pet turtles.

In 1936, four years after completing his doctorate at Hamburg, Jensen defended his inaugural dissertation there and was promoted from assistant lecturer to docent.

In the same year, Hans A. Bethe published his work on nucleon-nucleon forces and particle spin in an article in *Reviews of Modern Physics*; as Jensen pointed out in his Nobel lecture, the paper was seen as a major breakthrough and soon came to be known as "Bethe's Bible." Yet, Jensen readily admitted that some of his later discoveries about the orbits, spins, and interactions of nucleons were made possible by the fact that he was not as well versed in Bethe's bible as many of his colleagues. He was therefore more willing to accept the idea of "strong" rather than "weak" interaction in the coupling of nucleon spin and orbit. He was also undogmatic about the general structure of Bohr's model of the nucleus, envisioned as a compact entity characterized by surface tension, like a "liquid drop."

Jensen insisted on acting as a kind of conceptual free agent in approaching theoretical difficulties, and he refused, for the most part, to maintain partisan attachments to any one particular school of thought, even though he developed a close association with Bohr at Copenhagen over the years. Another factor that contributed to a certain independence of mind in Jensen's early work was the interdisciplinary nature of his collaboration. Hans E. Suess, with whom he worked at Hamburg for the greater part of the 1930's, was not a physicist but a geochemist whose interest was element and isotope abundances. The more broad-minded approach of Suess's cosmo-chemical studies, as Jensen called them, most likely contributed to the comprehensive nature of the insights behind the shell model. Suess himself, speaking in 1977 at a conference on the history of nuclear physics in the 1930's, recalled that Jensen had taken on the methods of a chemist, "who derives conclusions from many facts, while a physicist studies one problem or experiment exhaustively." This openness would stand Jensen in good stead as he contemplated certain external clues to the hidden secrets of the internal structure of the nucleus.

The key to the stability or lability of nuclei seemed to lie in the shape of "shells" in which a given number of protons and neutrons orbited the center of the nucleus. How were these various shells organized? What role was played by the "spin" of nucleons occupying them to varying degrees of fulfillment? The existence of spin in moving subatomic particles had been known for some time, and important experimental research had been done at Jensen's own university in the 1920's. Scientists had identified spin, which could occur either parallel or antiparallel to orbital motion, as a fundamental property of elementary particles and had measured its magnetic effects. The relationship of nucleon spin and nuclear stability, however, had just begun to be explored by Jensen, Goeppert Mayer, John A. Wheeler, and others. It was unclear whether the secret lay in the as yet unexplained pattern of "magic numbers."

Jensen's earliest work had been on ionic lattices and on the effects of extreme pressure on matter; the magic numbers captured his attention by a circuitous route. Suess, at Hamburg, had shared with the experimental physicist Otto Haxel, then at Berlin, his bemusement at the stability of elements and isotopes having very specific even numbers of protons (2, 8, 20, 28, 50, 82, and 126). Both then discussed the matter with Jensen and convinced him of the probable significance of these numbers. Subsequently, Jensen examined V. M. Goldschmidt's paper on these numbers published in 1938 in the *Proceedings of the Norwegian Academy*. He began to try to interpret these numbers in terms of a correlation between "the magic nucleon numbers and the sequence of nuclear spins and their multiplicities," as he recounted in his Nobel Prize acceptance speech.

When it became clear to him that the "old framework" of the single-particle model would not be sufficient, Jensen eventually made use of some of the newer theoretical techniques to describe nucleon behavior, including Schrödinger's wave mechanics. In 1948, ten years after beginning his research, Jensen had come upon the key principles of shell theory. In articles in 1949 in *Die Naturwissenschaften* and in the *Physical Review* (the same journal in which Goeppert Mayer, at the encouragement of Enrico Fermi, published her results), Jensen introduced his ideas about the strong link, or "coupling," that exists between spin and the orbital momentum of the individual nucleon. Spin and orbit tend to share parallel directions, but it is possible for a nucleon to spin in the direction opposed to its motion of revolution around the center of the nucleus; in this case, the nucleon will have a different energy from that of a nucleon spinning in the same direction as its orbital motion. These and other notions have important theoretical implications for the modern image of shell structure within the nucleus. Moreover, Jensen's construct of the various levels for nucleons provides an explanation of the magic numbers of nucleons in the most stable elements and their isotopes.

Within two years after the publication of his theory, Jensen accepted guest professorships at universities and institutes in the United States, including the University of Wisconsin, the University of California at Berkeley, and the Institute for Advanced Study, in Princeton. The Heidelberg Academy of Sciences had already inducted him into its ranks in 1949, and the venerable Max Planck Gesellschaft honored him with membership in 1960. In 1963 he received perhaps the ultimate honor for scientific achievement, the Nobel Prize. All the while he continued to extend and refine his model for nuclear structure, and subsequent work by others has tended to verify his ideas. He collaborated in the 1950's with Goeppert Mayer on an influential manual of shell theory, *Elementary Theory of Nuclear Shell Structure* (1955). The book was acclaimed not only for its excellent physicomathematical illustrations but also for the appropriateness of its suggested experimental applications. Amos de Shalit and Igal Talmi wrote an updated textbook of shell theory in 1963, *Nuclear Shell Theory*, which was followed in 1980 by R. D. Lawson's ambitious *Theory of the Nuclear Shell Model*.

Jensen was active until virtually the end of his life. He joined Otto Haxel as coeditor of the long-established German-language journal of physics *Zeitschrift für Physik* in 1955, continuing in that role until his death in 1973 at the age of sixty-six. He pursued science for its own sake and was not known for public moral stances or ideological positions, either in regard to the Nazi regime under which he had worked in the 1930's and 1940's or in regard to the use and development of atomic weaponry in the Cold War years.

Bibliography

Primary

PHYSICS: *Elementary Theory of Nuclear Shell Structure*, 1955 (with Maria Goeppert Mayer); "The Nuclear Shell Model," in Kai Siegbahn, ed., *Beta- and Gamma-Ray Spectroscopy*, 1955; *Lectures in Theoretical Physics*, 1960.

Secondary

Lawson, R. D. *Theory of the Nuclear Shell Model*. Oxford: Clarendon Press, 1980. This lengthy textbook will be useful to the advanced student of physics only. Its purpose is to strike a balance between the experimental orientation of Mayer and Jensen's 1955 book and the almost purely mathematical approach of Shalit and Talmi (1963). Contains extensive footnotes and bibliography.

Stech, B., and H. A. Weidenmüller. "Der Nobelpreis 1963 für das Schalenmodell." *Physikalische Blätter* 20 (1964): 7-10. Since the American press generally emphasized Marie Goeppert Mayer's attainment of the Nobel Prize (she was not only a naturalized American citizen but also the first woman to win the physics prize since Marie Curie in 1903), this German-language article is listed here to compensate for the paucity of secondary references to Jensen. It is a good source of information on Jensen's status as a scientist in Germany and on the line of thinking that led to his formulation of shell theory.

Stuewer, Roger H., ed. *Nuclear Physics in Retrospect: Proceedings of a Symposium on the 1930's*. Minneapolis: University of Minnesota Press, 1979. One of the most compelling features of this fine collection of reflections on the history of science in the rich period of the 1930's is its inclusion of the informative discussions that ensued after each paper was delivered. Many of the actors in the development of modern nuclear physics were present, and their passionate interest in their subject and its history comes through very clearly. Considerable attention is devoted to shell theory, and the student of Jensen's work will be particularly interested in Hans E. Suess's anecdotal remarks on page 27.

Weber, Robert L. *Pioneers of Science: Nobel Prize Winners in Physics*. Bristol, England: Adam Hilger, 1980. This well-written book, designed primarily for the layman, contains biographical information on Maria Goeppert Mayer and a two-page analysis of Jensen's career and scientific contributions.

Mark R. McCulloh

1964

Physics
Charles Hard Townes, United States
Nikolay Gennadiyevich Basov, Soviet Union
Aleksandr Mikhailovich Prokhorov, Soviet Union

Chemistry
Dorothy M. C. Hodgkin, Great Britain

Physiology or Medicine
Konrad Bloch, United States
Feodor Lynen, West Germany

Literature
Jean-Paul Sartre, France

Peace
Martin Luther King, Jr., United States

CHARLES HARD TOWNES
1964

Born: Greenville, South Carolina; July 28, 1915

Nationality: American
Area of concentration: Quantum electronics

Townes's invention of the maser was a result of his investigations into the means of using the stimulated emissions of atoms for the amplification of microwaves. An essential ingredient in Townes's discovery was the creation of an inverted population of atoms

The Award

Presentation

On December 10, 1964, Professor B. Edlén, a member of the Royal Swedish Academy of Sciences, presented the Nobel Prize in Physics to Charles Townes, Nikolay Gennadiyevich Basov, and Aleksandr Mikhailovich Prokhorov on behalf of the Academy and King Gustav VI. Edlén discussed the design and development of the maser in the years following its invention by Townes. He described the type most widely used at the time of the award, which involved ions of certain metals embedded in a suitable crystal. These masers worked as extremely sensitive receivers for short radio waves. They were of great importance in radio astronomy and were being used in space research programs to record radio signals from satellites.

The optical maser (the word stands for "microwave amplification by stimulated emission of radiation") dates from 1958. The step from microwaves to visible light demanded a 100,000-fold increase in frequency. In the case of the laser, the radiating matter is enclosed between two mirrors that force the light to traverse the matter many times. By this process, the high radiation density required for the stimulated emission to become dominant is achieved. The laser emits coherent light; it is therefore different from ordinary light sources, in which the atoms radiate independently of one another. The first and most frequently used type of laser consisted of a ruby rod whose polished and silvered end faces served as mirrors. Another type of laser, in which the light was emitted from a gas excited by an electric discharge, produced continuously a radiation that could be used to measure lengths and velocities with a previously unattainable precision.

The invention of the laser, said Edlén, had provided a powerful new tool for research in many fields. The extreme power concentration obtainable with a laser was limited to short time intervals and very small volumes; therefore, the device was most useful for microscale operations.

Nobel lecture

Townes opened his lecture, which was delivered on December 11, 1964, and entitled "Production of Coherent Radiation by Atoms and Molecules," with brief general and historical comments describing the differences between light which comes primarily from spontaneous emission—such as incandescent light and infrared, ultraviolet, or gamma rays—and radio waves. He acknowledged the work of Max Planck, who expounded the radiation formula called the "black body law," which determines the maximum intensities for radiation from hot objects. This law meant that radio waves were so weak that their emission from hot objects could not, for a long time, be detected. Hence, their discovery by Heinrich Hertz and the eventual widespread use of radio waves depended on the availability of oscillators (devices for producing alternating electromagnetic currents) and amplifiers (devices that amplify such currents), for which the idea of temperature and black body radiation is not relevant.

Radio electronics and optics, said Townes, had come together in the field of quantum electronics. The development of radar had stimulated many important applications of electronics to scientific problems, and in the late 1940's, Townes had become particularly occupied with microwave spectroscopy, the study of interactions between microwaves and molecules. From this research, he hoped to obtain considerable information about molecular, atomic, and nuclear structure. The basic problem with electronic amplifiers and oscillators seemed to be that inevitably, some part of the device which required careful and controlled construction had to be about as small as the wavelength generated; this necessity set a limit on the construction of operable devices.

Townes was led to ponder the use of atomic and molecular oscillators already "built" by nature. This theme had been repeatedly rejected because of thermodynamic arguments which show that the interaction between electromagnetic waves and matter at any temperature cannot produce amplification. Yet, a review of Albert Einstein's conclusions concerning the nature of interactions between electromagnetic waves and a quantum-mechanical system immediately suggested to Townes a way in which atoms or molecules could, in fact, amplify. He realized that probably only through the use of molecular or atomic resonances could coherent oscillators for very short waves be made, and in 1951, he discovered a particular scheme which seemed to offer the possibility of a substantial generation of short waves by molecular amplification.

In his concluding remarks, Townes predicted rapid improvement in the field of quantum electronics. He said that the time had come for masers and lasers to become everyday tools of science. "It is this stage of quantum electronics," he said, "which should yield the real benefits made available by the new methods of dealing with radiation."

Critical reception

Most of the attention devoted to the 1964 Nobel Prizes went to Martin Luther King, Jr., the winner of the Peace Prize, and Jean-Paul Sartre, the winner in literature. Sartre refused the award, generating a controversy that overshadowed any objections that might have arisen over the Nobel Committee's choice of physics laureates. Townes did receive more notice in the Western press than his two cowinners, Prokhorov and Basov, but no one suggested that all three physicists did not deserve the honor. Townes himself was quoted in *Time* magazine (November 6, 1964) as saying, "They are fine scientists. They . . . quite properly share in the award."

The scientific periodicals briefly described the nature of the laureates' research and noted that masers and lasers represented an important breakthrough in quantum electronics. *Nature* (December 5) reported that the maser was novel in two respects: its low level of "noise" when used as an amplifier and its high-frequency stability when used as an oscillator. An editorial by J. P. Gordon which appeared in *Science* (November) was similarly straightforward; it outlined the physics of lasers, first describing Townes's work and then, more succinctly, explaining how the two Soviets had achieved the same results.

The American public had failed to take much interest in lasers after it had become apparent that weapons of mass destruction were not going to be an immediate result of the new technology. The popular press, therefore, did not run lengthy articles on the laureates. Attempts were made, however, to explain the prizewinning work in terms simple enough for the layman and to emphasize the practical possibilities for Townes's research. *Time* magazine mentioned an atomic clock, based on a laser, that would gain or lose only one second every thirty thousand years. It reported that lasers were also being used for welding and surgery. *Newsweek* (November 9) said that lasers were at work carrying messages, tracking satellites, and helping scientists to understand the nature of light itself. Masers, it was added, were being used in the antennae that monitored signals from the Telstar satellites, and they could amplify what they "heard" by a factor of ten thousand.

Both *Time* and *Newsweek* repeated Townes's story of how he had been sitting on a park bench, admiring some azalea bushes, when it had "occurred to him that molecules and atoms are nature's original broadcasters." Both magazines also remarked on the coincidence that two sets of physicists, half a world apart, had learned almost simultaneously how to stimulate atoms so that they would emit energy at microwave frequencies. Townes had summarized his work's significance by saying only, "Masers give us one more control over electromagnetic waves," but *Newsweek* had stronger praise for the laureate's work: It had "revolutionized radio astronomy and communications."

Biography

Charles Hard Townes was born in Greenville, South Carolina, on July 28, 1915, the son of Henry Keith and Ellen Hard Townes. In Greenville, he skipped the seventh grade and was graduated from high school at age fifteen. In 1935, at age nineteen, he was graduated summa cum laude from Furman University with a bachelor of science degree in physics and a bachelor of arts degree in modern languages. Physics had fascinated him since his college days because of its "beautifully logical structure," and he received a master's degree at Duke University in

1936. His work at the California Institute of Technology (Caltech) on isotope separation and nuclear spins earned for him a doctoral degree in 1939. In 1941, he wed Frances H. Brown. They would have four daughters. In 1948, Townes was appointed to the faculty of Columbia University, where he did research in microwave physics. From 1958 to 1961, he was a member of the Scientific Advisory Board of the U.S. Air Force; in 1959, he became a consultant to the President's Scientific Advisory Committee. He accepted the position of provost and physics professor at the Massachusetts Institute of Technology (MIT) in 1961, and in 1967, he moved to the University of California at Berkeley to become a university professor of physics.

His honors and awards include the Comstock Award of the National Academy of Sciences (1959), the Stuart Ballantine Medal of the Franklin Institute (1959 and 1962), the Thomas Young Medal and Prize (1963), the Niels Bohr International Gold Medal (1979), and the National Science Medal (1983). He was named to the National Inventors Hall of Fame in 1976 and to the Science Hall of Fame in 1983.

Townes has received honorary degrees from Furman University, Clemson College, Wesleyan University, Columbia University, Swarthmore College, and the Polytechnic Institute of Milan. He has published widely in scientific journals on such subjects as microwave spectroscopy, molecular and nuclear structure, and masers. His book *Microwave Spectroscopy*, written with A. L. Schawlow, was published in 1955. He is a member of numerous science and technology societies, including the American Physical Society, the Institute of Electrical and Electronics Engineers, the Société Française de Physique, the National Academy of Sciences, the American Philosophical Society, and the Physical Society of Japan.

Scientific Career

Townes is internationally known for his invention of the maser and for his research in the field of microwave physics. From 1941 to 1947, he was employed at the Bell Telephone Laboratories, where he worked extensively in designing radar bombing systems. This project was followed by a period of radar research, which turned Townes's attention to the field of microwave spectroscopy. From 1948 to 1961, he was a professor at Columbia University, where he continued his work in microwave physics and served as the executive director of the Columbia Radiation Laboratory and the chairman of the physics department. He also became interested in astronomy, conducting research in both the infrared and the radio portions of the electromagnetic spectrum. In 1951, Townes conceived the idea for the maser. Seeking to produce shorter microwaves, he pondered the possibility of using controlled molecular or atomic activity. His idea proved correct, and the word "maser" was coined. Townes's first maser used ammonia gas as the active material. In 1958, Townes and Arthur L. Schawlow showed theoretically that masers could be made to operate in the optical and infrared region. The optical laser which resulted from this work allowed some of the most exciting uses of the fundamental maser idea. Both masers and lasers became important tools in basic science and communications research.

Townes employed the maser as an atomic clock to verify precisely the famous Michelson-Morley experiment, which demonstrated that the speed of light is constant. He also did extensive research with masers in radio astronomy. From 1961 to 1967, he was provost and a physics professor at MIT; in 1967 he became a member of the faculty at the University of California at Berkeley. Later he was given the title of Professor Emeritus.

Masers and lasers have brought about a revolution in radio technology and physics, and scientists believe that these developments may lead to many more discoveries and inventions. Townes has been involved in developing ground-based interferometric instrumentation to study the characteristics of electromagnetic objects. This research may lead to the detection of a planet revolving around some distant star.

Bibliography

Primary

PHYSICS: *Microwave Spectroscopy*, 1955 (with A. L. Schawlow); "Production of Coherent Radiation by Atoms and Molecules: Nobel Foundation Lecture," *Science*, vol. 149, 1965; "The Centre of the Galaxy," *Nature*, vol. 301, 1983; "Ideas and Stumbling Blocks in Quantum Electronics," *IEEE Journal of Quantum Electronics*, vol. 20, 1984; "Spatial Interferometry in the Mid-Infrared Region," *Journal of Astrophysics and Astronomy*, vol. 5, 1984.

Secondary

Bertolotti, M. *Masers and Lasers: An Historical Approach*. Bristol, England: Adam Hilger, 1983. This book offers a detailed account of the development of the maser and laser. It is rather technical and may be difficult for the reader without a background in physics. Townes's work is discussed and compared with the research that was being done simultaneously in the Soviet Union. The contributions of minor figures in the field are also outlined.

Hecht, Jeff, and Dick Teresi. *Laser: Supertool of the Eighties*. New York: Ticknor & Fields, 1982. Most of this book is devoted to descriptions of the various applications of lasers. It covers their uses in medicine, manufacturing, the arts, energy production, defense, and communications. Explanations suitable for the layman are provided of the principles of laser action and the design of various types of lasers and masers. Townes's contributions to laser development and the conflicts that arose among American scientists over patent rights are also discussed.

Weber, Robert L. *Pioneers of Science: Nobel Prize Winners in Physics*. Edited by J. M. A. Lenihan. Bristol, England: Adam Hilger, 1980. Consisting of brief biographies of all the Nobel physics laureates to 1980, this source is useful for charting Townes's career.

N. A. Renzetti

1964

Physics
Charles Hard Townes, United States
Nikolay Gennadiyevich Basov, Soviet Union
Aleksandr Mikhailovich Prokhorov, Soviet Union

Chemistry
Dorothy M. C. Hodgkin, Great Britain

Physiology or Medicine
Konrad Bloch, United States
Feodor Lynen, West Germany

Literature
Jean-Paul Sartre, France

Peace
Martin Luther King, Jr., United States

NIKOLAY GENNADIYEVICH BASOV
1964

Born: Usman, near Voronezh, Soviet Union; December 14, 1922

Nationality: Soviet
Area of concentration: Quantum electronics

Basov played an essential role in the invention of quantum microwave amplifica-tion devices (masers) and light amplifiers (lasers), which operate on the principle of stimulated emission of radiation. He collaborated with Aleksandr Prokhorov, with whom he shared the Nobel Prize, to produce the first Soviet maser and did pioneer-ing work on the use of semiconductors in lasers

The Award

Presentation

Professor B. Edlén, a member of the Royal Swedish Academy of Sciences, pre-sented the Nobel Prize in Physics to Nikolay Gennadiyevich Basov and Aleksandr Mikhailovich Prokhorov of the Soviet Union and Charles Townes of the United States on December 10, 1964. Edlén began his presentation, which he delivered in English, by noting that the principle of stimulated emission had been predicted by Albert Einstein but that it had long been regarded as a purely theoretical concept, because net stimulated emission can only occur in an "inverted population," in which more atoms are in a high-energy state than in a ground state, and it was not known how to create such conditions. He noted that the Soviet researchers and Townes, working independently, had produced practical designs for quantum ampli-fiers in the microwave region in 1954 and that crystal-based masers were currently widely used.

Although it has the same theoretical basis, the laser (or "optical maser") was so radically different in design that it constituted a new invention. In a ruby laser, a simple example, the laser effect is based on excited energy states of chromium atoms in the crystal lattice, which also give the ruby its red color. An inverted population is created in the crystal by the light from a xenon flash lamp. Some of the inverted chromium atoms revert to the ground state spontaneously; the photons they emit initiate a cascade of induced emission. Parallel mirrors force radiation to traverse the crystal many times. What eventually emerges is a powerful beam of monochromatic light which is coherent—that is, all the wave crests coincide. This quality of coherence accounts for many of the special properties of laser light.

Laser light can be stored and emitted in bursts of exceedingly short duration and high intensity. The high energies produced and the extreme precision with which they can be delivered opened tremendous possibilities for research instrumentation. Edlén concluded by emphasizing that large-scale destructive applications of lasers were very unlikely to be realized.

Nobel lecture

Basov began his Nobel lecture, "Semiconductor Lasers," with a discussion of styles of research in physics which restated, in personal terms and without political jargon, the Marxist view of an appropriate approach to scientific research. In his view, one group of physicists sets out to create a theory and supporting mathematical models; new physical devices may be produced as a by-product of the research, but the theory is regarded as the end product. The second group seeks primarily to create physical devices based on new physical principles, and this group considers hypotheses and theories to be a by-product. Both groups generate theories and both generate inventions; the difference is one of approach and focus rather than a strict dichotomy between theorist and inventor. By placing himself in the second group, Basov was not merely stating a fact but also affirming his loyalty to Soviet science policy.

Semiconductors are crystalline substances which are incapable of conducting electricity in the ground state but become conductors when some of the electrons in the crystal lattice are excited to a higher energy level. As in isolated atoms and molecules, the electrons in a crystal can occupy a number of discrete energy levels, of which there are an enormous number, since the whole crystal functions as a sort of giant molecule sharing all the outer-orbit electrons. These energy levels are grouped in narrow bands: the valence band, analogous to the unexcited state of an isolated molecule, and the conductance band, analogous to the excited state of an isolated molecule. Between the two is a band of forbidden energy. In semiconductors, the energy difference between the valence and conductance bands corresponds to wavelengths in the infrared and optical range.

Semiconductors act as insulators when all the electrons are in a ground state; in this state, all possible positions for electrons are occupied, and they are unable to move under the influence of an electric field. Semiconductors become conductors when "holes" are created. Moving an electron to a higher energy level creates a hole. It is also possible to create holes by incorporating impurities into a crystal. There are two types of impurities: donor (n) impurities, which have more electrons in their outer shell than the semiconductor itself and contribute electrons to the conduction band, and acceptor (p) impurities, which have fewer electrons and create holes in the valence band. Crystals with a sharp demarcation between areas with p impurities and areas with n impurities possess a p/n junction, which has important functions in semiconductor lasers and other semiconductor devices.

For a semiconductor to act as a laser, it is necessary to create an inverted population in which there are more electrons in the conduction band and corresponding holes in the valence band than there are electrons in the ground state. Otherwise, absorption will predominate over stimulated emission, and the device will function as a photoelectric cell. A useful property of semiconductors is the relatively long lifetime of electrons and holes.

Basov outlined a number of methods for obtaining an inverted population in a semiconductor. As with the ruby laser, it is possible to do so by optical pumping.

Electrons in a crystal can also be excited by a beam of fast electrons. A method specific to semiconductors themselves utilizes the properties of a p/n junction. In the absence of a current, the p side of the junction has an excess of holes without corresponding electrons; the n side has electrons without corresponding holes. An electrical potential difference between the two prevents the movement of either across the junction. If one applies an external voltage sufficient to overcome the potential difference, current will flow and electron hole pairs will be created. A high concentration of impurities is necessary to create an inverted population under these circumstances.

Semiconductor lasers have useful properties distinguishing them from other types of lasers. Since the surface of a semiconductor crystal is highly reflective, the crystal itself can serve as the cavity. That makes it possible to construct extremely small lasers. By varying the type and concentration of impurities, one can make semiconductor lasers with a wide range of emission wavelengths. Lasers utilizing p/n junctions are highly efficient at converting electrical energy to light. Disadvantages of semiconductor lasers include small power, large spatial divergence, and low monochromaticity relative to other types of lasers.

Critical reception

Unlike some of their countrymen who have received the Nobel Prize in areas other than science, Basov and his colleague Prokhorov were being honored for an achievement for which they had already been officially recognized in their own country; their award was well publicized in the Soviet press at the time, and they were allowed to travel to Stockholm in person to receive it. Despite a tremendous emphasis on science, especially the physical sciences, the Soviet Union has produced relatively few Nobel laureates in this area, and those who do hold this honor are held in great esteem.

Reaction to the 1964 Nobel Prizes in the physical sciences was muted in the Western press. Any controversy which might have attended the prizes in physics and chemistry in that year was overshadowed by the attention given the Peace Prize, which went to Martin Luther King, Jr., and the prize in literature, which went to Jean-Paul Sartre, who refused the honor.

The account in the October 30, 1964, issue of *The New York Times* understandably emphasized the role of Townes, the American who shared the physics prize with Basov and Prokhorov, and provided more detailed information on him and his discoveries; nevertheless, it was careful to credit the two Soviets. An editorial in the same issue commented that the laureates' work was a classic case of near-simultaneous discovery of a principle by independent groups of researchers. This phenomenon of parallel development and the muddy question of priority—of who had really discovered masers and lasers—is one of the most intriguing aspects of the history of quantum electronics. A careful examination of chronology of publications, such as that presented in the *American Journal of Physics* (1966), supports the statement that the discovery of the maser principle was nearly simultaneous and resulted from completely independent research.

It is important to realize that the development of the maser took place when communication between American and Soviet scientists was at an all-time low. Joseph Stalin was in power in the Soviet Union, and Senator Joseph McCarthy was at the height of his influence in the United States. In the Soviet Union at a time when even routine biological assays using radioisotopes were regarded as classified and could not be published openly in scientific journals, maser research, which was expected to have military applications, was a carefully guarded secret. Even in America, Gordon Gould, a controversial figure in the early history of laser development, found himself unable to obtain a security clearance to work in his own research laboratory because of communist connections that he had formed in the 1930's. Informal discussions at scientific meetings, an important medium for the exchange of ideas, did not take place, because Soviet scientists did not travel abroad. By the time that the maser research results were formally published, both groups had independently unraveled the fundamental principles involved.

A degree of insularity was still evident twenty years later; the pages of *Science Citation Index* made it evident that, in the 1980's, Soviets cited Soviet research and Americans Western research to a much greater extent than either cited the other, despite vastly improved communication. This phenomenon was by no means limited to quantum electronics.

Biography

Nikolay Gennadiyevich Basov was born on December 14, 1922, in Usman, near Voronezh, in the Soviet Union, the son of Professor Gennadiy Fedorovich Basov and Zinaida Andreevna Basova. He was graduated from the Voronezh secondary school in the early days of World War II; thereafter, he enlisted in the army, enrolled in the Kiev school of military medicine, and later served at the front as a lieutenant in the military corps. After the war, he entered the Moscow Institute of Mechanics, from which he was graduated in 1950. In 1948 he joined the staff of the oscillation laboratory of the Lebedev Physics Institute, first as a laboratory technician and later as a senior scientist. There began the fruitful collaboration with Aleksandr Prokhorov that led to their receiving the Nobel Prize for laser research in 1964.

Basov's rise through the ranks of the Soviet science hierarchy was exceptionally rapid. In 1956, at the age of thirty-three, he was awarded the degree of doctor of science for work which included the construction of the first Soviet maser. The Soviet degree of doctor of science has no exact American equivalent; it involves the defense of a thesis by a senior scientist who already has the equivalent of a doctorate and considerable subsequent research experience, and it is rarely attained by persons under forty. From 1958 to 1973, Basov was deputy director of the Lebedev Institute; he became its director in 1973. In 1966 he was elected as a member of the Soviet Academy of Sciences, the most prestigious and influential scientific body in the Soviet Union; since 1967, he has been a member of its presidium, or governing body. In 1959, together with Prokhorov, he was awarded the

Lenin Prize, his nation's most prestigious award, for their joint work on stimulated emission.

Basov has also been active politically. A member of the Communist Party since 1951, he was a deputy to the USSR Supreme Soviet in 1974 and has served on the Soviet Committee for the Defense of Peace. He wed Kseniya Tikhonova Nazarova in 1950; the couple has two sons, Gennadiy and Dmitriy.

Scientific Career

In 1948, when Basov joined the staff of the Lebedev Institute, science in the Soviet Union was just beginning a period of rapid expansion which was shortly to give the Soviets the atom bomb and which would culminate in the successes of the Soviet space program a little more than a decade later. The disastrous science policies of the 1930's, followed by war, had left a vacuum. In many ways, there was an ideal climate for a brilliant young scientist to make his mark, despite continuing paranoia and ideological interference. The work for which Basov became noted, and which has been the focus of nearly all of his scientific endeavors, is the discovery of systems in which stimulated emission of radiation can be demonstrated, controlled, and harnessed for a wide variety of scientific and industrial purposes.

Research on stimulated emission began, paradoxically, with investigation of the opposite phenomenon, resonance absorption. Basov and Prokhorov were studying the microwave absorption spectra of molecules for clues to molecular structure. When a substance (a gas, for example) is irradiated with broad spectrum electromagnetic radiation, certain wavelengths are selectively absorbed; those wavelengths are specific to the substance being irradiated and correspond to energy states of bonds between atoms in a molecule, to rotational, vibrational, and magnetic states of the molecule, and to energy levels of electrons.

Three processes can be distinguished in the interaction of matter and electromagnetic radiation: absorption, which is responsible for the absorption spectra that were being investigated and which occurs when a photon interacts with a molecule in the ground state; spontaneous emission, which occurs when an excited molecule reverts to the ground state, emitting a photon; and stimulated emission, which occurs when a photon interacts with an excited molecule, causing the excited molecule to emit a photon, with a resulting net amplification of the signal. Because of the law of conservation of momentum, the emitted photon coincides with the stimulating photon in phase and direction. This quality of coherence accounts for many of the important properties of the signal from a quantum amplifier.

The proportion of molecules in a stimulated energy state is inversely related to the energy input needed to excite the molecule; the wavelength of the radiation absorbed or emitted is also inversely proportional to energy level. In other words, the longer the wavelength, the greater the probability of stimulated emission. In the microwave region, the stimulated emission is significant enough to interfere with the observation of faint absorption lines.

In 1954, Basov and Prokhorov published a detailed theoretical paper in the *Zhurnal eksperimentalnogo i teoreticheskogo fiziki* (journal of experimental and theoretical physics) outlining parameters for constructing a system for creating separate beams of excited and unexcited molecules and for using the beam of excited molecules as a quantum amplifier. Basov's background in physics engineering was evident in the fact that although both men worked on the theoretical considerations, it was Basov who, in 1955, produced the first working maser in the Soviet Union.

Basov then turned his attention to designing systems based on stimulated emission in the visible and infrared region of the spectrum—that is, toward the development of a laser. He focused on the possible use of semiconductors to produce coherent light, a logical choice based on the energy transitions available in semiconductors but one which presented serious technical difficulties, since semiconductor technology at the time fell short of what was needed and knowledge of the optical properties of semiconductors was limited. Basov's persistence, however, was rewarded; semiconductor lasers have proved to be one of the most valuable and versatile classes of quantum amplifiers. Later, Basov conducted investigations into the use of lasers in controlled thermonuclear reactions, the design of chemical lasers, the use of lasers to study chemical reactions, and the use of lasers in optical information transfer and processing.

Because he is an academician and the head of the Lebedev Institute, Basov's scientific role has become increasingly advisory; nevertheless, he continues to play an active role in laser research. A survey of issues of *Physics Abstracts* shows a total of twenty-one articles in major journals authored or coauthored by Basov in 1985, forty in 1986, and thirty in 1987. These papers covered such diverse topics as eximer lasers, mechanisms in laser welding, the optics of laser light, polyphosphonitrate synthesis in the plasma of an electron beam initiated discharge, and the development of an intense neutrino source. An emphasis on engineering and design problems is evident in the spectrum of topics. Although most of these papers represent collaborative efforts in which the main impetus came from other members of the research team, Basov's contributions were not negligible.

Basov occupies a position of high respect in the Soviet scientific community. He is editor in chief of the popular science magazine *Priroda* (nature) and a Soviet journal of quantum mechanics. Although he passed the usual Soviet retirement age of sixty in 1982, he continues to be a leading researcher in his field, an active force in science policy and science administration, and a mentor to younger physicists.

Bibliography

Primary

Physics: The following are among the most frequently cited of Basov's articles. English-language editions of Soviet physics journals cited are available in major academic libraries. The dates of publication given are for the original Russian-language versions. "Applications of Molecular Beams to the Radio Spectroscopic Study of the Rotation Spectra of Molecules," *Zhurnal eksperimentalnogo i teoreticheskogo fiziki*, vol. 27, 1954 (with A. M. Prokhorov); "Possible Methods of Obtaining Active Molecules for a Molecular Oscillator," *Zhurnal eksperimentalnogo i teoreticheskogo fiziki*, vol. 28, 1955 (with Prokhorov, O. N. Krokhin, and Y. M. Popov); "Theory of the Molecular Generator and the Molecular Power Amplifier," *Zhurnal eksperimentalnogo i teoreticheskogo fiziki*, vol. 30, 1956 (with Prokhorov); "Generation, Amplification, and Detection of Infrared and Optical Radiation by Quantum Mechanical Systems," *Soviet Physics-Uspekhi*, vol. 3, 1961 (with Krokhin and Popov).

Secondary

Bertolotti, M. *Masers and Lasers: An Historical Approach*. Bristol: Adam Hilger, 1983. The aim of Bertolotti's book is to provide the reader who has a considerable background in the physical sciences with a technical account of the development of the maser and laser. Since the narrative depends heavily on mathematical equations, it is likely to be too complex for the average nonspecialist. The contributions made by Prokhorov and Basov are discussed in some detail and placed in the context of research being done at the same time in the United States. The author's attention to chronology, the specifics of each discovery, and the contributions of minor figures to the laser's development makes this book a particularly valuable reference.

Brophy, James J. *Semiconductor Devices*. New York: McGraw-Hill, 1964. A useful background reference for understanding how semiconductor lasers function. Terminology is defined and explained in nonmathematical terms; the book is aimed at the nonspecialist using semiconductor devices who wants a basic knowledge of how they work. There is a brief discussion of semiconductor lasers themselves. Although there has been an enormous amount of semiconductor research since 1964, the book accurately describes the state of the art at the time that Basov delivered his Nobel lecture, and it is still accurate in its essential details.

Hecht, Jeff, and Dick Teresi. *Laser: Supertool of the Eighties*. New York: Ticknor & Fields, 1982. The bulk of this book (nine of fourteen chapters) is devoted to the uses and potential uses of lasers in medicine, communications, warfare, manufacturing, energy production, publishing, holography, and the arts. There are good, nontechnical descriptions of the general principle of laser action and the design and function of various masers and lasers. The section devoted to the history of the laser concentrates on the American contribution and the conflicts that arose between American workers over patent rights, but it does include some information on Basov and Prokhorov.

Isakov, A. I., O. N. Krokhin, D. V. Sobeltsyn, and I. I. Sobelman. "Nikolai Gennadievich Basov, on His Fiftieth Birthday." *Soviet Physics-Uspekhi* 16, no. 1 (1973): 165-166. This testimonial, written by a number of Basov's fellow physicists, gives a chronological account of Basov's life and research. It is characteristic of brief testimonial biographies that they present a one-sided view of the person portrayed; this one provides a good outline of Basov's scientific career but contains little personal data. The Soviet view of individual effort as a part of a master plan is also evident.

Medvedev, Zhores. *Soviet Science*. New York: W. W. Norton, 1978. Although this source is a standard reference on science in the Soviet Union, it is principally a critique of the Soviet scientific establishment and makes no direct mention of Basov and Prokhorov, lasers, or the Lebedev Institute. It is a useful reference for understanding the scientific hierarchy in the Soviet Union, the significance of awards and titles, and issues of ideology and censorship.

Weber, Robert L. *Pioneers of Science: Nobel Prize Winners in Physics*. Edited by J. M. A. Lenihan. Bristol, England: Adam Hilger, 1980. This book consists of brief sketches of the lives of Nobel Prize-winning physicists to 1980. Its chief use is as a source of biographical data, and it includes personal data on Soviet scientists which Soviet sources do not include. Since it is complete to 1980, it is helpful for charting the careers of living physicists.

Martha Sherwood-Pike

1964

Physics
Charles Hard Townes, United States
Nikolay Gennadiyevich Basov, Soviet Union
Aleksandr Mikhailovich Prokhorov, Soviet Union

Chemistry
Dorothy M. C. Hodgkin, Great Britain

Physiology or Medicine
Konrad Bloch, United States
Feodor Lynen, West Germany

Literature
Jean-Paul Sartre, France

Peace
Martin Luther King, Jr., United States

ALEKSANDR MIKHAILOVICH PROKHOROV
1964

Born: Atherton, Queensland, Australia; July 11, 1916

Nationality: Soviet
Areas of concentration: Quantum radiophysics and quantum electronics

The independent research of Prokhorov and Nikolay Basov in the Soviet Union and Charles Townes in the United States on stimulated emission of radiation in the microwave and optical regions of the spectrum led to the development of masers and lasers

The Award
Presentation

Professor B. Edlén, a member of the Royal Swedish Academy of Sciences, presented the Nobel Prize in Physics to Charles Hard Townes of the United States and Aleksandr Mikhailovich Prokhorov and Nikolay Gennadiyevich Basov of the Soviet Union on December 10, 1964, on behalf of the Academy and King Gustav V, from whom Prokhorov accepted the prize. Edlén's presentation consisted of a brief chronology of the research on the stimulated emission of radiation, a nontechnical description of laser action, and comments on current and potential uses of lasers. He noted that the principle of stimulated emission had been introduced as a theoretical concept by Albert Einstein. In addition to the selective absorption of electromagnetic radiation at frequencies corresponding to the energy levels of molecules and atoms, and spontaneous emission by excited molecules and atoms, Einstein had postulated a third process, stimulated emission, in which radiation interacting with a substance in an excited state triggers an emission of energy, amplifying the incident radiation. It was long doubted that this effect could be used or even observed, since more atoms must be in an excited state than in a ground state for amplification to occur. In 1954, Townes and his coworkers at Columbia University and Basov and Prokhorov of the Lebedev Institute simultaneously and independently announced that they had developed microwave amplifiers (masers) based on the principle of stimulated emissions. Both laboratories then turned their efforts toward applying the maser principle to the optical part of the spectrum and made critical contributions to the development of the laser, although credit for the first working laser belongs to yet another researcher.

Lasers are notable for the amount of power that they can deliver in a concentrated area and the precision in measurement afforded by the sharply defined wavelength. Edlén noted the research and technical potential of lasers and stressed that actual and foreseeable applications of lasers were far removed from the "death ray" of fiction.

Nobel lecture

In his Nobel lecture, delivered on December 11, 1964, and entitled "Quantum Electronics," Prokhorov took a historical approach to explaining the development of masers and lasers. Prokhorov acknowledged the contributions made by a number of workers, explained the principles behind masers and lasers and the conditions necessary for constructing them successfully, and concluded with a discussion of the potential of multiquantum transitions in laser research.

Absorption and emission of radiation by molecules are complementary processes. When incident radiation strikes a molecule in its ground (low-energy) state, the radiation is absorbed and stored in the form of altered (excited) states of molecular bonds and electron energy levels. Under normal conditions, excited molecules rapidly and spontaneously revert to their ground state, emitting radiation at the same wavelength as the absorbed radiation or, in the case of multiquantum transitions, at defined wavelengths which are mathematically related to it. It is the specific energy levels associated with electron orbits and molecular bonds that account for the quantum aspect of quantum electronics. On the molecular level, a unit of electromagnetic energy, or photon, will be absorbed only if its energy (which is proportional to its wavelength) is equal to an energy transition level in the molecule with which it is interacting, and an excited molecule will emit photons only at sharply defined wavelengths corresponding to the energy level of the excited bonds.

In addition to absorption and spontaneous emission, there is a third process, stimulated emission, which occurs when a photon of the appropriate frequency strikes a molecule which is already in an excited state. In this case, the molecule emits a second photon, and a net amplification occurs. Both quanta coincide not only in frequency but also in phase and direction; this quality of coherence accounts for many of the important distinctions between laser light and ordinary light, which is the product of spontaneous emission. The principle of stimulated emission was first elucidated by Einstein in 1916. Thus, the theory on which lasers and masers are founded was in existence for nearly forty years before the first masers were actually constructed, in 1954. Although it was clear from the theory that radiation could be amplified by a substance in which most of the atoms were in an excited state, such amplification was long regarded as a practical impossibility.

The development of masers and lasers began as an approach to a problem in high-resolution radiospectroscopy. Induced emission, a negligible factor in optical systems at thermal equilibrium, is a significant phenomenon in the radio range, and scientists in the United States and the Soviet Union were initially searching for a means of reducing induced emission in order to improve the resolution of instruments detecting absorption spectra in the radio range. One approach was to pass the beam of a molecular-beam generator through an inhomogeneous magnetic or electric field, which is capable of separating excited and unexcited molecules in the microwave region. Thus, one condition for the construction of a maser—a medium with a negative absorption, or with more molecules in an excited state than in an unexcited state, so that net stimulated emission is possible—was satisfied. For such a system to operate, induced emission must take place in a cavity. A cavity, in this sense, must have two important properties: It must be able to contain and reflect electromagnetic radiation, and its dimensions must be such that waves propagated within the cavity oscillate in phase. A radio tube is an example of a cavity oscillator; the cavity in a ruby laser consists of a pair of parallel mirrors. The characteristics of cavities in the microwave region had already been worked out by radio engineers; it remained to combine the two into a device capable of amplifying microwaves by stimulated emission.

Once amplification by stimulated emission had been demonstrated in the microwave region, it was logical to attempt to produce quantum amplifying systems in other parts of the electromagnetic spectrum—in the infrared, optical, and X-ray ranges. With decreasing wavelength, additional difficulties manifest themselves. The lifetime of particles in the excited state decreases, and the density of the particles needed to produce the proper action increases. Moreover, cavity resonators derived from radio engineering are unsuitable. Practical problems in producing an "optical maser," or laser, were not resolved until 1960, and even then, problems with the X-ray region were yet to be resolved.

Prokhorov concluded his lecture with speculation about the use of multiquantum transitions to produce a tunable laser, suggesting that such a laser could be used to excite specific bonds within a molecule and thereby influence the direction of chemical reactions.

Critical reception

Any controversy which might have attended the 1964 Nobel Prize in Physics was overshadowed in the Western press by two highly controversial prizes awarded in that year: the Peace Prize, which went to Martin Luther King, Jr., and the Prize in Literature, which went to Jean-Paul Sartre, who refused the honor. Unlike some Soviet recipients of Nobel Prizes, Prokhorov and his colleague Basov held important posts in the Soviet scientific hierarchy and had already been honored by their own government for the work. Their achievement was widely publicized in the Soviet press at the time and continues to be recognized. In the Soviet Union, where scientific accomplishment is more consistently honored than in the West and brings with it significant monetary and social rewards, the position of the relatively few Soviet Nobel laureates in the sciences is high indeed.

Reaction in the Western press was colored by the usual focus of interest on American winners in the United States, but no one questioned that all three physicists were entitled to the honor. The combined account of the chemistry and physics prizes in *The New York Times* (October 30, 1964) included a description of masers and lasers, a chronology of their development, and biographical data on the recipients. An editorial in the same issue commented that the laureates' work had been a classic case of the near-simultaneous discovery of a principle by independent groups of researchers. Although the newspaper's reporters understandably emphasized the role of Townes, the American prizewinner, and were able to provide a more detailed picture of him and his work, they were careful to credit the work of the two Soviets. An editorial by J. P. Gordon, a graduate student of Townes and another pioneer in laser research, in the November issue of *Science* adopted the same approach, describing the American research in a detailed narrative and then indicating how the two Soviet physicists and their research fitted into the general picture.

The concluding comment of Gordon's editorial, "but much work needs to be done before all of the uses of these fascinating devices will be discovered, and before it is known which of its many uses are important," summarized the attitude of the educated American public toward laser research in 1964 and accounted for the lukewarm response to the Nobel award. Unquestionably, the discovery of lasers constituted an important scientific breakthrough; unquestionably, they were valuable research tools. Popular interest had waned, however, as it became clear that whatever direction laser research was likely to take, spectacular weaponry was not an expected result. If the editorial writer could have foreseen how ubiquitous lasers would become in the short span of twenty years, he might have waxed more enthusiastic.

Biography

Aleksandr Mikhailovich Prokhorov was born on July 11, 1916, in Atherton, Queensland, Australia, the son of Mikhail Ivanovich Prokhorov and Mariia Mikhailovna Prokhorova. His father was an opponent of the czarist regime who had escaped to Australia from Siberian exile in 1911; the family returned to the Soviet Union in 1923. After receiving his degree in physics, with honors, from Leningrad State University in 1939, Prokhorov enrolled as a graduate student at the Institute of Physics of the Soviet Academy of Sciences. World War II interrupted his graduate career. In 1941 he joined the Soviet Army, in which he served from 1941 to 1943. After having been wounded twice, he was released and returned to the Institute of Physics, where he began working on the frequency stabilization of vacuum-tube oscillators under the direction of S. M. Rhytov; he defended his first dissertation (the equivalent of an American doctoral dissertation) on this subject in 1948. His second doctoral dissertation, a major piece of research that was concerned with coherent radiation in synchrotrons, was defended in 1951. Thus, despite the interruptions of military service and the generally difficult conditions in the immediate postwar period, Prokhorov had surmounted this last important hurdle (for which there is no exact American equivalent) at the exceptionally young age of thirty-five. In keeping with his research career, which has been characterized by the quick accomplishment of goals and extraordinary productivity, his progress in the Soviet scientific hierarchy was rapid. He was appointed as the head of a laboratory of the Lebedev Institute of Physics in 1954 and as deputy director of the entire institute in 1968. In 1959 he was appointed as a professor at the University of Moscow, where he organized the Radio Spectroscopy Laboratory of the Nuclear Physics Research Institute. In 1960 he was elected a corresponding member; in 1966 he became a full member and a member of the Presidium of the Soviet Academy of Sciences, an elite organization of approximately four hundred senior scientists and the most influential scientific body in the Soviet Union. He also became an honorary member of the American Academy of Sciences.

In 1959, Prokhorov shared with Basov the Lenin Prize, the Soviet government's highest honor, for his work on quantum electronics; he was honored as a Hero of Socialist Labor in 1970. In 1941 he wed Galina Shelepina; they have one son, Kirill.

Scientific Career

Prokhorov's long and productive scientific career falls, roughly, into three phases: an initial phase, corresponding to his graduate and early postgraduate years, involving the exploration of a variety of aspects of the generation, propagation, and measurement of electromagnetic radiation and increasingly focusing on quantum processes; a second phase dominated by pioneering research in quantum electronics and culminating in the development of the laser; and a third phase, when, as a senior scientist and the deputy director of the Lebedev Institute, he has overseen and directed numerous projects involving quantum electronic theory, the expansion and refinement of laser design and capabilities, and applications of lasers in a wide variety of research fields and has taken an active role in training a new generation of physicists.

The three areas of radiophysics in which Prokhorov worked during the early years of his scientific career—the propagation of radio waves on Earth's surface, the frequency stabilization of vacuum-tube oscillators, and the coherent radiation of synchrotrons—are quite distinct, and his researches in these areas represented distinct, "from scratch" approaches to scientific problems rather than a single evolving train of thought. Although none of them led directly to maser and laser research, threads from each can be discerned in his subsequent work.

While he was still in the process of finishing his dissertation on synchrotron radiation, Prokhorov, at the suggestion of Soviet Academician D. V. Sobeltsyn, began working in the field of radiospectroscopy. Specifically, he was investigating the use of radiospectroscopy to study the rotational and vibrational states of molecules.

The absorption spectrum of a substance can be likened to its electronic fingerprint. Broad spectrum electromagnetic radiation does not pass uniformly through a substance; some wavelengths are selectively absorbed. It is selective absorption in the optical region that gives transparent objects their color. Microwave absorption spectra were of particular interest to Prokhorov because they correspond to energy states of bonds within molecules and provide a powerful tool for studying the structure of molecules. A related problem, which Prokhorov was also pursuing, was the use of microwave absorption spectra to produce frequency and time standards. (The now-familiar quartz clock operates on a similar principle.) To improve the accuracy of the standards, which were dependent on the observed width of absorption lines, Prokhorov and his coworkers used spectroscopes operating with a molecular beam; however, the capabilities of the spectroscopes were limited by the faintness of the observed lines. This faintness was caused by the small difference between populations in the ground state (which were absorbing radiation) and those in the excited state (which were stimulated to emit additional radiation at the same frequency) in the molecular beam. Prokhorov's team concluded that line intensity could be improved by creating a beam of molecules in the ground state, which can be accomplished by applying an asymmetrical electrical or magnetic field. Such a system can also produce a beam of excited molecules which amplify incident radiation at a specific wavelength. Thus, the microwave amplifier that works on the principle of stimulated emission, or maser (called a "molecular generator" by Prokhorov), was born. Prokhorov and Basov published a detailed theoretical description of masers in 1954, after Townes and his coworkers had produced the first working maser, in late 1953, and had reported briefly on their discovery in *Physical Review*. A working maser was not produced by the Soviets until 1955.

Masers are important research tools, but they have limited applications; they are used, for example, in radioastronomy to amplify weak signals with great precision. Success with the first prototype maser, however, stimulated the search for other systems which would amplify radiation through stimulated emission. Prokhorov, Basov, and their colleagues spearheaded this research in the Soviet Union. Between 1955 and 1960, they studied a large group of crystals which they believed might be used in quantum paramagnetic amplifiers and proposed the use of two-quantum and multiquantum transitions for producing the inverted population necessary for stimulated emission.

Multiquantum transitions are important to laser action in the optical portion of the spectrum, and virtually all laser systems employ them. The production of an inverted population at submillimeter (infrared, visible light, and ultraviolet) wavelengths requires the introduction of energy, or pumping. In a single-quantum transition, the pumping energy and the energy required to stimulate emission are equivalent, creating practical difficulties. In a two-quantum transition, of which the classical ruby laser is an example, reversion of an excited molecule to the ground state is a two-step process, and the energy of a photon needed to stimulate emission at either of these transitions is not equivalent to the pumping energy.

Ironically, none of the men who shared the 1964 Nobel Prize for developing the laser was the first to produce a laser; that honor belongs to the American Theodore Maiman of Hughes Research Laboratories, who demonstrated a working ruby laser in 1960. At the same time, the Soviets were pursuing the production of optical wavelengths by means of maser-type molecular beam generators and were experimenting with the use of semiconductors in quantum electronics.

In their popular account of lasers and their development, Jeff Hecht and Dick Teresi comment that Prokhorov and Basov were the only important figures involved in laser research who were still active in the field in the early 1980's. After his early successes, which culminated with his winning the Nobel Prize in 1964, Prokhorov continued his researches into the theory, design, and applications of quantum electronic devices. It is characteristic of his approach to science that his research efforts ranged from the highly theoretical and general to specific problems of applied research and encompassed not only quantum electronics but also anything which impinged on it. A 1986 issue of *Physics Abstracts*, for example, lists Prokhorov as the author or coauthor of papers on the design of an eximer laser, a mechanism for investigating laser plasmas, processes in ruby crystal formation, the structure and formation of germanium crystals, the destruction of biological tissues by carbon dioxide lasers, and the design of mirrors made from porous materials. Although he passed the normal Soviet retirement age of sixty in 1976, he continues to be an active scientist, administrator, and mentor to junior colleagues. His name appeared on sixty-two papers in major journals in 1985, sixty-five papers in 1986, and forty-six papers in 1987, and although most of these works were collaborative efforts, his role in them was not negligible. Since 1969, he has served as editor in chief of the *Great Soviet Encyclopedia*, a measure of the status and respect he enjoys in the Soviet academic community.

Scientists do not work in a vacuum but are part of a social and governmental framework. Although in theory, science in the Soviet Union has the full support of the government, many branches of science have been hampered by ideological considerations; that was particularly true during the Stalin era, which was when Prokhorov was doing his pioneering maser research. At that time, ideology dictated a sharp distinction between purely theoretical, "bourgeois" research and "Communist" science, which needed to be justified in practical grounds of service to the state and Communism. Building on bourgeois roots was also discouraged; those in power believed that the results would be better if scientists with proper proletarian credentials "reinvented the wheel." Fortunately for Prokhorov, he was working in a relatively new branch of science, radiophysics, which lacked excessive bourgeois roots, and he had the vision to begin with a practical problem and pursue it to its theoretical conclusions. The fellow physicists who eulogized Prokhorov on the occasion of his fiftieth birthday could honestly point to him as a model of Soviet citizenry: politically orthodox and politically involved, dedicated to collective effort, brilliant and industrious, and nationally and internationally known for the development of a principle with far-reaching practical implications.

The discovery of practical means for magnifying electromagnetic signals through stimulated emission was important to the progress of physics and science as a whole not so much because it had revolutionary theoretical implications as because it provided a powerful new tool capable of unprecedented precision and concentration of power. Lasers were first used as tools in research laboratories, where they continue to be indispensable.

The impact of these devices in the marketplace has been impressive; few fundamental inventions in the history of technology have become so commonplace so rapidly. The optical scanner at the supermarket checkout stand and the office laser printer are ubiquitous in the United States. Lasers are extensively used in printing, precision machining, and other industrial processes. The communications industry makes extensive use of them, and they have important medical applications. Although publicity about the "Star Wars" strategic defense network has again called attention to the concept of giant, killer lasers in military contexts, actual military uses remain limited.

Bibliography

Primary

PHYSICS: The following are among the most widely cited of Prokhorov's articles. English-language editions of the Soviet physics journals cited are available in major academic libraries. The dates of publication given are for the original Russian-language versions. "Application of Molecular Beams to the Radio Spectroscopic Study of the Rotation Spectra of Molecules," *Zhurnal eksperimentalnogo i teoreticheskogo fiziki*, vol. 27, 1954 (with N. G. Basov); "Possible Methods of Obtaining Active Molecules for a Molecular Oscillator," *Zhurnal eksperimentalnogo i teoreticheskogo fiziki*, vol. 28, 1955 (with Basov, O. N. Krokhin, and Y. M. Popov); "Quantum Electronics," *Science*, vol. 149, 1966; "Propagation of Laser Radiation in Randomly Nonuniform Media, *Uspekhi fizicheskii nauk*, vol. 114, 1974 (with F. V. Bunkin, K. S. Gochelashvily, and V. I. Shishov); "Laser Irradiance Propagation in Turbulent Media," *Proceedings of the IEEE*, vol. 63, 1975 (with Bunkin, Gochelashvily, and Shishov); "Laser Thermonuclear Fusion," *Uspekhi fizicheskii nauk*, vol. 19, 1976 (with S. I. Anisimov and P. P. Pashinin).

Secondary

Barchukov, A. I., N. G. Basov, F. V. Bunkin, V. G. Veselago, N. A. Irisova, N. V. Karlov, and A. A. Manenkov. "Personalia: Aleksandr Mikhailovich Prokhorov, on His Fiftieth Birthday." *Soviet Physics-Uspekhi* 9, no. 4 (1966): 637-640. An account of Prokhorov's life and research through 1966, written as a testimonial by his colleagues, including fellow Nobel laureate Nikolay Basov. All aspects of Prokhorov's research are discussed, and the account is relatively nontechnical. Besides the personal data and the conventional tally of scientific discoveries, degrees, and honors, the article offers commentary on how well Prokhorov fills the role of a scientist in a Communist state.

Bertolotti, M. *Masers and Lasers: An Historical Approach*. Bristol, England: Adam Hilger, 1983. In this technical account intended for a reader with considerable background in the physical sciences, Bertolotti traces the many threads of research that led to the development of masers and lasers. The specific contributions made by Prokhorov and Basov are discussed in some detail and placed in the context of research that was concurrently being done in the United States. The author's attention to chronology, the specifics of each discovery, and the contributions of minor figures make this book a particularly valuable reference.

Hecht, Jeff, and Dick Teresi. *Laser: Supertool of the Eighties*. New York: Ticknor & Fields, 1982. Written for the layperson, this book includes nontechnical descriptions of how various types of laser operate. It provides a history of the development of the laser which concentrates on the conflicts between American laser researchers over patent rights but also includes information on the Soviet contributions. Nine of fourteen chapters are devoted to the uses of lasers in medicine, communications, warfare, manufacturing, energy production, publishing, holography, and the arts.

Medvedev, Zhores. *Soviet Science.* New York: W. W. Norton, 1978. Medvedev, a biologist who emigrated from the Soviet Union, concentrates his attention on the failures of Soviet science and conditions in the Soviet system which discourage scientific innovation. Although the book makes no mention of lasers, their creators, or the Lebedev Institute, it is a useful reference for understanding the hierarchy of Soviet science and the climate of research that existed in the Soviet Union during the late 1940's and early 1950's, especially with respect to issues of censorship and conformity to ideology.

Weber, Robert L. *Pioneers of Science: Nobel Prize Winners in Physics.* Edited by J. M. A. Lenihan. Bristol, England: Adam Hilger, 1980. This book consists of brief sketches of the lives of all the Nobel laureates in physics to 1980. Its chief use is as a source of biographical data, and it is helpful in charting the careers of living physicists. The sketch of Prokhorov includes a description of a ruby laser, although that was not Prokhorov's specific contribution.

Martha Sherwood-Pike

1965

Physics
Shin'ichirō Tomonaga, Japan
Julian Seymour Schwinger, United States
Richard P. Feynman, United States

Chemistry
Robert B. Woodward, United States

Physiology or Medicine
François Jacob, France
André Lwoff, France
Jacques Monod, France

Literature
Mikhail Sholokhov, Soviet Union

Peace
United Nations Children's Fund

SHIN'ICHIRŌ TOMONAGA
1965

Born: Tokyo, Japan; March 31, 1906
Died: Tokyo, Japan; July 8, 1979
Nationality: Japanese
Area of concentration: Quantum electrodynamics

Tomonaga's theoretical work in developing a completely relativistic quantum field theory led to the first successful form of quantum electrodynamics, other forms of which were later developed independently by Julian Schwinger and Richard Feynman

The Award
Presentation

Professor Ivar Waller, a member of the Royal Swedish Academy of Sciences, presented the Nobel Prize in Physics to Shin'ichirō Tomonaga, Julian Seymour Schwinger (born 1918), and Richard P. Feynman (1918-1988) on December 10, 1965, on behalf of the Royal Swedish Academy of Sciences and King Gustav VI. Unfortunately, Tomonaga was prevented by an accident from receiving his prize in Stockholm, so it was presented to him by the Swedish ambassador to Japan on May 6, 1966.

Waller's presentation reviewed the application of quantum mechanics to the hydrogen atom. In 1947, Willis Eugene Lamb, Jr. (born 1913), and Robert C. Retherford (born 1912) had measured small discrepancies in some energy levels of the hydrogen atom. The work of Tomonaga, Schwinger, and Feynman had explained this "Lambshift" and predicted several other important phenomena. Their work was a continuation of earlier work by Paul Adrien Maurice Dirac (1902-1984), Werner Heisenberg (1901- 1976), and Wolfgang Pauli (1900-1958), who had applied quantum mechanics to the interaction of electrons and the electromagnetic field. This earlier form of quantum field theory had led to calculations indicating that electron mass and charge were equal to infinity, a useless result.

In 1943, Tomonaga developed a completely relativistic form of quantum electrodynamics. When he heard about the Lamb experiment in 1947, he recognized that the experimentally observed electron mass and charge could be substituted into his equations in such a way as to cancel the undesirable infinities. This process of renormalization led to a correct formula for the Lambshift. Similar work was done independently and published in 1948 in the United States by Schwinger and Feynman, who found several other important applications of quantum electrodynamics. These results agreed with experiments to about one part in a million, making the theory one of the most accurate in physics. The new formalism was important in the further development of several areas of physics, especially elementary particle physics.

Nobel lecture

Tomonaga's Nobel lecture, titled "Development of Quantum Electrodynamics: Personal Recollections," was delivered at the Tokyo University of Education on May 6, 1966. He clearly explained his contribution to the development of quantum electrodynamics, acknowledging his debt to the work of others and reviewing the similar work done by Schwinger and Feynman. He described the quantum field theory of Heisenberg and Pauli and its modification by Dirac in 1932. Under the guidance of Yoshio Nishina (1890-1951), Tomonaga had shown that Dirac's theory was consistent with the Klein-Nishina scattering formula for radiation.

Following a suggestion by Hideki Yukawa (1907-1981) in 1942, Tomonaga was able to develop a relativistically covariant form (one completely consistent with relativity theory) of Dirac's theory in 1943. Both theories, however, contained infinite quantities associated with field reactions in various processes. Earlier calculations by Sidney Dancoff had revealed several of these infinities when Dirac's theory was applied to scattering processes. After finding a mistake in Dancoff's work, Tomonaga was able to show that his covariant field theory eliminated most infinities in the scattering process, leaving only infinite mass and charge. Finally, following a suggestion by Shoichi Sakata (1911-1970), he was able to show how the experimentally observed mass and charge could be substituted in such a way as to cancel all infinities. This renormalization procedure made it possible to obtain finite results from his covariant field theory.

In 1947, word reached Japan of the discovery of the Lambshift in the energy levels of hydrogen and of the idea suggested by Hans Albrecht Bethe (born 1906) that this might be a result of the field reaction. Tomonaga was able to confirm this hypothesis using his covariant field theory. Similar work by Schwinger and Feynman was later shown to be mathematically equivalent to Tomonaga's by Freeman Dyson (born 1923).

Critical reception

No controversy attended the announcement of the 1965 Nobel physics prize, perhaps because of the esoteric nature of the work that was recognized. *The New York Times* gave a brief description of the work in its October 22, 1965, issue, together with brief biographies of the three recipients. It was noted that the award honored research performed more than twenty years earlier, when Japan and the United States had been at war. It was also observed that the research was based on work done in the early 1930's that had led to the discovery of the positron (a form of antimatter) and of the processes of creation and annihilation associated with matter and antimatter. The report pointed out the enormous difficulties associated with calculations of the interplay between charged particles and said that the methods developed independently by the three recipients had led to highly accurate results in the description of atomic systems and elementary particles.

The biographical summary of Tomonaga in the same issue of *The New York Times* suggested that he had seemed unsure about which of his achievements was being honored when he was told of the prize. It mentioned the difficulty of conducting research under wartime conditions and noted that Tomonaga was only the second Japanese citizen to win a physics Nobel Prize. The 1949 prize had gone to Hideki Yukawa, with whom Tomonaga had once shared a research laboratory at Kyoto University.

In an editorial on October 23, *The New York Times* described the laureates as "advancing fundamental understanding of the nature of matter, though the highly mathematical nature of their work makes most of it inaccessible to lay understanding." It acknowledged that Tomonaga was relatively unknown in the United States but went on to note that both Feynman and Schwinger were products of New York City public schools. The October 29, 1965, issue of *Science* carried a tribute to Tomonaga, Schwinger, and Feynman by Freeman Dyson, who had been the first to show the equivalence of their work. He expressed his opinion that quantum electrodynamics could be considered the most nearly perfect and the most highly developed part of physics. He also mentioned that Tomonaga's work involved the most basic physical principles and that his papers were the clearest and most straightforward.

The December, 1965, issue of the professional journal *Physics Today* gave a more detailed discussion of the development of quantum electrodynamics. It mentioned the successes of the earlier quantum field theories initiated by Dirac in accounting for many atomic processes but noted the difficulties caused by the emergence of infinite divergences. It also mentioned experimental discoveries in the 1940's that could not be explained by the earlier theories and the successful resolution of these problems by the new theory. Tomonaga was credited with the first theoretical breakthrough, even though it had had no influence on physicists outside Japan because it was published during the war in Japanese. The similarity of Schwinger's later work and the equivalence of Feynman's work were also noted.

Biography

Shin'ichirō Tomonaga was born in Tokyo, Japan, on March 31, 1906. He was the eldest son of Sanjuro and Hide Tomonaga. His family moved to Kyoto in 1913 when his father was appointed as a professor of philosophy at the Imperial University of Kyoto. Tomonaga attended the Third High School in Kyoto with Hideki Yukawa. He was graduated in 1924 and studied physics with Yukawa at Kyoto University from 1926 to 1929. Both Tomonaga and Yukawa remained at Kyoto University as unpaid assistants for three years, sharing the same office and studying quantum mechanics together with little instructional assistance. They were, however, able to attend a series of lectures on quantum mechanics by Yoshio Nishina, from Tokyo, and lectures by visiting professors Paul Dirac and Werner Heisenberg.

In 1932, Tomonaga was appointed to the position of research associate by Nishina at the Institute of Physical and Chemical Research (Riken) in Tokyo, where he began to work with Nishina on quantum field theory. In 1937 he joined Heisenberg's theoretical group in Leipzig, Germany. There, he did the work on nuclear physics that was to be the basis for his doctor of science thesis, completed at Tokyo Imperial University in December, 1939. In 1940, he wed Ryoko Tomonaga, daughter of K. Sekiguchi, who had been the director of the Tokyo Metropolitan Observatory. In 1941, Tomonaga became a professor of physics at Tokyo Bunrika University (reorganized as Tokyo University of Education in 1949), although he retained his connection with Riken.

During the war, Tomonaga did research for the Japanese Navy on microwave theory while continuing his academic research in quantum theory. Afterward, he established a research program with several young assistants. During this period, his most productive, he worked under difficult conditions, living in one ruined room with his wife, who was ill, and three small children. His work soon began to attract attention in the United States, and he was invited for a one-year stay at the Institute for Advanced Study, Princeton, New Jersey, in 1949.

When Nishina died in 1951, Tomonaga assumed his administrative duties and also established interuniversity research institutes at Kyoto and Tokyo universities. In 1956 he became president of the Tokyo University of Education, a post he held for six years. He served as president of the Science Council of Japan from 1963 to 1969. After retiring in 1970, he turned his efforts to writing several books.

Scientific Career

Tomonaga's scientific career began with his appointment in 1932 as a research associate at the Institute of Physical and Chemical Research (Riken) in Tokyo. There, he collaborated with Yoshio Nishina on the problem of nuclear forces, which was later solved by Hideki Yukawa, and also worked on neutron and positron theory. This joint effort with Nishina produced several papers on aspects of pair creation and mutual annihilation of electrons and positrons, marking the beginning of Tomonaga's work on quantum electrodynamics.

After Yukawa published his meson theory of nuclear forces in 1935, Tomonaga resumed his work in nuclear physics. During two years at Werner Heisenberg's institute in Leipzig from 1937 to 1939, he worked on nuclear and meson theories. Using the liquid-drop model of the nucleus devised by Niels Bohr (1885-1962), he studied the way in which impinging neutrons heat the nucleus. This work was published in 1938 and became the basis of his doctoral thesis in 1939. In the meantime, he also tried to relate Yukawa's meson (a particle that transmits the force that holds the nucleus together) to the cosmic-ray mesons (later called muons), which were first observed in 1936. After a period of frustration, he was led by Heisenberg to consider the field reaction in meson-nucleon scattering. On returning to Japan, he published a paper on the absorption and decay of slow mesons which showed that when cosmic-ray mesons are stopped in matter, repulsion by the nucleus should prevent positive mesons from being absorbed, while negative mesons would be absorbed before decaying. This paper led to further work on the development of an intermediate-coupling approximation for mesons that is now known as the "Tamm-Dancoff approximation." During this time, it became increasingly clear that the cosmic-ray meson interacted weakly with matter and thus was not the Yukawa meson, as was finally suggested by Shoichi Sakata's group in 1943.

In 1942, Yukawa suggested that quantum field theory needed a relativistically invariant formulation and a solution to the problem of infinite divergences. Tomonaga took up the first part of this suggestion and by the next year had achieved the first successful solution to the problem. In 1943 he published his work, but because the paper appeared in Japanese during World War II, it did not become known outside Japan until later. In the fall of 1946, it was published in English. Tomonaga had followed Dirac's idea that in a relatively moving reference frame, two points should be assigned different times. Applying Dirac's many-time concept to a field theory required a time coordinate for each volume element of space in the generalized Schrödinger quantum equation, leading to a "super-many-time" covariant theory of quantum electrodynamics.

After 1943, Tomonaga did research in ultra-high-frequency electronics for the Japanese Navy. His work on the production of microwaves and associated waveguide circuits by magnetron oscillators utilized many of the theoretical methods of quantum mechanics. He developed a general theory of magnetron oscillations by applying electromagnetic theory to the motion of an electron cloud. He also applied Heisenberg's matrix formulation of scattering theory to waveguide circuits. He was awarded the Japan Academy of Sciences Prize for his theory of magnetrons. Similar work on the electromagnetic problems of microwaves and waveguides was done by Schwinger during World War II.

After the war, Tomonaga and his young associates began a research program to extend and apply covariant quantum field theory. Their work led to the discovery of renormalization theory, which eliminated infinite divergences in quantum electrodynamics. Further development of a new method of calculation involving unitary transformations of the covariant field equations resulted in successful renormalization results. When word reached Japan of the Lambshift measurements, which were first reported at Shelter Island, New York, in 1947, Tomonaga made calculations from his theory that agreed beautifully with the reported results. Willis Lamb and Robert Retherford had measured the fine-structure separation of the first two energy levels of the hydrogen atom caused by the self-energy of its bound electron. They had applied microwave techniques developed during the war to the resonance absorption of a beam of atoms. The experiment had yielded a value of 1,057.862 megahertz as compared to the theoretical value of 1,057.864 megahertz, a difference of only two parts in a million.

In his book *Disturbing the Universe* (1979), Freeman Dyson tells of his experience at Columbia University in the spring of 1948, when Hans Bethe received the first issues of the new English-language journal *Progress in Theoretical Physics* that had been published in Kyoto in 1946. He described their astonishment at finding Tomonaga's article, which had been translated from the original Japanese paper of 1943. He expressed his amazement at Tomonaga's ability to conduct groundbreaking research in theoretical physics amid the ruin and turmoil of war and completely isolated from the rest of the world. When Dyson met Tomonaga the next year, he wrote, "He is more able than either Schwinger or Feynman to talk about ideas other than his own. And he has enough of his own. He is an exceptionally unselfish person."

Tomonaga's interest in cosmic-ray research continued during his studies of quantum electrodynamics. By this time, the distinction between cosmic-ray mesons (muons) and Yukawa's nuclear force meson had been recognized. In 1949, Tomonaga published the result of an investigation with Satio Hayakawa (born 1923) of the effects of deep-penetrating muons. In the same year, he published the first volume of his book *Ryoshi-rikigaku* (1949-1953; *Quantum Mechanics*, 1962-1968) and accepted J. Robert Oppenheimer's invitation to visit the Institute for Advanced Study, in Princeton, New Jersey. There, he did pioneering work on the quantum many-body problem using a method developed by Felix Bloch (1905-1983) for analyzing sound waves. This work was generalized five years later into a study of quantum collective motion.

After Nishina's death in 1951, Tomonaga accepted his administrative responsibilities and began to improve the research conditions available to younger Japanese scientists. In 1955 he established the Institute for Nuclear Studies at the University of Tokyo. His scientific work stopped in 1956, when he became the president of the Tokyo University of Education. From 1963 to 1969, he was president of the Science Council of Japan. During this period, he also served as the director of the Institute for Optical Research at the Tokyo University of Education and published a second volume of his book on quantum mechanics. These books proved to be very popular; several hundred thousand copies have been sold.

After his retirement in 1970, Tomonaga began a third volume on quantum mechanics which was to discuss field theory but which was never finished. He also wrote books directed to the general public on nuclear disarmament, with Yukawa as a coauthor, and on the history of science, such as *Butsurigaku to wa Nandaro ka* (1982; what would be physics), which describes concepts of mechanics and thermodynamics in layman's terms. Other books, published after his death, cover such topics as science and the humanities and the social responsibilities of scientists. Tomonaga's honors and awards included the Japan Academy Prize (1948), the Order of Culture (1952), and the Lomonosov Medal, from the Soviet Union (1964).

Bibliography

Primary
PHYSICS: *Ryoshi-rikigaku*, 1949-1953 (*Quantum Mechanics*, 1962-1968); *Scientific Papers of Tomonaga*, 1971-1976; *Soryushi no Sekai*, 1978; *Butsurigaku to wa Nandaro ka*, 1982; *Ryoshi Rikigakuteki Sekaizo*, 1982; *Ryoski Denki Rikigaku no Hatten*, 1983; *Makuro no Sekai kara Mikuro no Sekai*, 1983; *Butsurigaku no Shuhen*, 1983.
OTHER NONFICTION: *Kaku Gunshuku e no Atarashikoso*, 1977; *Kagaku to Ningen*,

1982; *Kagakusha no Shakaiteki Sekinin*, 1982; *Nikki, Shokan*, 1985; *Gakumon o Suru Shisei*, 1985.

Secondary

Brown, Laurie M., and Lillian Hoddeson, eds. *The Birth of Particle Physics: Proceedings of the International Symposium on the History of Particle Physics, May, 1980*. Cambridge, England: Cambridge University Press, 1983. Two chapters in this book discuss Tomonaga's work. In chapter 18, "Some Characteristic Aspects of Early Elementary Particle Theory in Japan," Takehiko Takabayasi compares Tomonaga's approaches with those of Yukawa and other Japanese scientists. In chapter 22, "Two Shakers of Physics: Memorial Lecture for Sin-Itiro Tomonaga," Julian Schwinger describes Tomonaga's work in relation to similar work done by him.

Brown, Laurie M., M. Konuma, and Z. Maki, eds. *Particle Physics in Japan 1930-1950*. Kyoto: University of Kyoto, 1981. This volume was sponsored by the Research Institute for Fundamental Physics at the University of Kyoto. It contains an extensive discussion with Tomonaga and translations from Tomonaga's Japanese writings by Funiko Tanihara and Noriko Eguchi.

Hayakawa, Satio. "Sin-Itiro Tomonaga: Obituary," *Physics Today* 32 (December, 1979): 66-68. A clear summary of Tomonaga's life and scientific career. Includes good descriptions of his most important scientific contributions and his administrative responsibilities by one of his former students.

Heitler, Walter. *The Quantum Theory of Radiation*. 3d ed. Oxford, England: Clarendon Press, 1954. A highly technical review of quantum field theory, from its classical origins to the successful culmination of quantum electrodynamics. The methods developed by Tomonaga and his contemporaries are discussed.

Schwinger, Julian, ed. *Selected Papers on Quantum Electrodynamics*. New York: Dover, 1958. A collection of the most important scientific articles on the topic of electrodynamics. Contains two by Tomonaga and a paper by Dyson, titled "Radiation Theories of Tomonaga, Schwinger, and Feynman," that shows the mathematical equivalence of the three laureates' work.

Weinberg, Steven. "The Search for Unity: Notes for a History of Quantum Field Theory." *Daedalus* 106 (Fall, 1977): 17-35. This clearly written article traces the history of quantum field theory. The perfecting of quantum electrodynamics by Tomonaga and his contemporaries is described. Includes a discussion of the influence of the Shelter Island conference at which the Lambshift was first reported.

Joseph L. Spradley

1965

Physics
Shin'ichirō Tomonaga, Japan
Julian Seymour Schwinger, United States
Richard P. Feynman, United States

Chemistry
Robert B. Woodward, United States

Physiology or Medicine
François Jacob, France
André Lwoff, France
Jacques Monod, France

Literature
Mikhail Sholokhov, Soviet Union

Peace
United Nations Children's Fund

JULIAN SEYMOUR SCHWINGER
1965

Born: New York, New York; February 12, 1918

Nationality: American
Area of concentration: Quantum electrodynamics

Schwinger developed a theory of quantum electrodynamics which precisely described how photons, electrons, and positrons interact within the atom. The theory is fully in agreement with Albert Einstein's theory of relativity and has been described as one of the most accurate of all theories within the physical sciences

The Award

Presentation

At the Nobel ceremonies held on December 10, 1965, Professor Ivar Waller of the Royal Swedish Academy of Sciences presented the Nobel Prize in Physics to Julian Schwinger and his cowinners, Richard P. Feynman of the United States and Shin'ichirō Tomonaga of Japan. The three physicists shared the award for the simultaneous development of the theory of quantum electrodynamics. In his speech, Waller reviewed the events that had led to the award.

In 1947, the American physicist Willis Eugene Lamb, Jr. (born 1913), had discovered an experimental discrepancy in the predicted subatomic energy levels of hydrogen. This effect, called the "Lambshift," greatly puzzled physicists who were attempting to pin down mathematical models of exactly how subatomic particles behave. The Lambshift demonstrated that experimental verification of the current theories was impossible and that the mathematical theories that explained the workings at the core of the atom were somehow in error.

Early in the 1920's, work was under way in the community of experimental and theoretical physics to derive the general quantum mechanical laws that would define exactly how electrons interact with the mechanical and electrodynamic environment of the atom. These laws would also define how energy is liberated from the atom in the form of electromagnetic emissions (as light and photons). At about this time, the work of Albert Einstein (1879-1955) on the theories of relativity was being accepted and applied to the new science that described the actions of charged subatomic particles—specifically, electrons and the electromagnetic field. The science was called quantum electrodynamics, or QED. It had its problems, however, among them inherent errors which led to predictions that the electron or its electromagnetic field would have infinite values.

Julian Schwinger developed a method called "mathematical renormalization" to calculate the proper masses and charges. Waller described the method as "the formalism of the new quantum electrodynamics." Schwinger had made it useful for practical calculations. The three laureates' work had yielded one of the most accurate concepts in theoretical physics. Waller concluded his remarks by noting that their ideas had enabled advances to be made in solid-state physics, nuclear physics, and statistical mechanics.

Nobel lecture

Schwinger opened his lecture, "Relativistic Quantum Field Theory," by briefly mentioning the originators of quantum electrodynamics, Paul Adrien Maurice Dirac (1902-1984), Werner Heisenberg (1901-1976), and Wolfgang Pauli (1900-1958). Yet, notably, Schwinger first referred to his topic not as "quantum electrodynamics" but as "the relativistic quantum theory of fields," anticipating the direction of his lecture. He asserted that relativistic quantum field theory is "the union of the complementarity principle of [Niels] Bohr with the relativity principle of Einstein." He then noted that mathematics was an irreplaceable tool in describing his theory and begged his listeners' indulgence for its inevitable introduction. Schwinger also said that his approach was different from Feynman's. Feynman used his own unique "integral" approach; Schwinger and Tomonaga used a "differential" approach.

Schwinger immediately identified the variables for his mathematical foray into the theory, noting how "the differential version transcends the correspondence principle." One of the significant variables he defined was time, in order to "represent an abstraction of the dynamical role of the measurement apparatus." After this rigid definition of time, he went on to describe the system.

Schwinger noted that classical mechanics is a determinate theory (that is, knowledge of a system's state enables the prediction of a measurement of a given systemic property) but that quantum mechanics is only statistically determinate (knowledge of a system's state yields results based on probability). He then went on to define a relativistic quantum system in terms of "an infinite number of degrees of freedom." Since "before" and "after" have no meaning in a quantum system, spacelike regions are causally independent (cause and effect between the regions is irrelevant), and since there is no limit to the number of such disjointed regions, they can be considered infinite. Yet, Schwinger assigned his system an "extravagantly large" number of degrees of freedom in order to define it conceptually.

Schwinger continued painstakingly to define his system. He then entered into a discussion of field theory as it is related to quantum electrodynamics. He tied the introductory concepts of systems and fields together by noting that particles and fields can be one and the same in the quantum world. He approached the foundations of his theory via a discussion of weakly interacting and strongly interacting systems. He noted that a phenomenon called "vacuum polarization" is one of the most important interaction aspects of quantum electrodynamics. Vacuum polarization, as a field theory concept, defines the creation of charges and countercharges at the subatomic level. Schwinger said that the understanding of how these charges interact "is the basis for charge renormalization" and the essence of the mathematical solutions of quantum electrodynamics.

Schwinger then reviewed the state of relativistic field theory and speculated about discoveries to follow. He said, "Surely, one must hope that this bewildering complexity [of an ever-growing number of particles] is the dynamical manifestation of a conceptually simpler substratum." He expressed his belief that relativistic field theory was leading toward "a new conception of matter."

At the heart of Schwinger's discussion was the implication that the interactions of fields and particles could be simplified at a deeper level. This idea he would ultimately convey to a graduate student, Sheldon Lee Glashow, who would mathematically unify the electromagnetic force and the weak nuclear force. Glashow's model would become the first of the "grand unification" schemes, whose goal is the unification of all the forces of nature.

Critical reception

The world of theoretical physics was quick to voice high praise for the Nobel Committee's choices. The selection of Schwinger, Feynman, and Tomonaga as the recipients of the 1965 Nobel Prize in Physics was met not with dissension but with acclaim. *Science* (November, 1965) reported that the theories had distilled "the vast middle ground of physics . . . into a small number of principles of great quality and elegance." That characterization was written by physicist Freeman J. Dyson. It was Dyson who had demonstrated the identical mathematical relationships of the theories of Schwinger, Feynman, and Tomonaga. He proved their interchangeable numerical identities by integrating the differential equations to find the commonalities.

Science applauded the winners' independent approaches, saying that "the theory gained in breadth and richness." It described Schwinger as "the first to hack his way through the math . . . and arrive at a definite numerical value . . . . His papers were monuments of formal ingenuity." The theories were iconoclastic, however, only in that they used innovative approaches; they did not violate any basic tenets of physical law. Said *Science*, the victory was, in the end, "a victory for conservatism."

Physics Today (December, 1965) also took special care to note the differences among the approaches of Schwinger, Feynman, and Tomonaga. It said that Schwinger's idea had originated in field theory, where the "fundamental physical qualities are magnetic fields." The article went on to report that the three physicists had developed the theory by ridding the electron of its intrinsic mass, which had been the source of error in the original application of the Dirac equations. It was also mentioned that the laureates questioned their formulations at "extreme relativistic energies," a curious disclaimer for one of the most accurate physical theories of modern times. *Newsweek* (November 1, 1965) quoted Feynman in that regard. "As far as I'm concerned," he said, "the math isn't solved completely yet." *Newsweek* also quoted Schwinger as stating that quantum electrodynamics "gives a kind of reality to the field that we are creating inside particle accelerators."

The Science Newsletter (October 30, 1965) pointed out that the theory of quantum electrodynamics was considered "brilliant by other scientists," adding that the theory represented the first major contribution to quantum mechanics since its development in 1920. The periodical also noted that the work of Schwinger, Feynman, and Tomonaga had "refined the complicated mathematical equations that govern the [atomic processes] on which all life depends."

Biography

Julian Seymour Schwinger was born in New York City on February 12, 1918, the son of Benjamin and Belle Rosenfeld Schwinger. As a boy, Schwinger was by all accounts a single-minded scientific and mathematical prodigy who ignored virtually all else. He was graduated from New York's Townsend Harris High School at fourteen, three grades ahead of his peers, and he entered the College of the City of New York.

Already, Schwinger was going from library to library reading every available book on physics. He was also ignoring all of his other subjects at City College and not doing well as a result. At this point, he caught the attention of Isidor Isaac Rabi (born 1898) at Columbia University, who immediately recognized Schwinger's unusual scientific potential. In 1935 Schwinger was accepted at Columbia, with a lecture on the importance of attending classes, under Rabi's sponsorship. His mentor frequently introduced Schwinger to visiting dignitaries. After a visit with Hans Albrecht Bethe (born 1906), discoverer of the nuclear processes of stars, Rabi suggested that Schwinger already knew 90 percent of physics and that the rest would "only take a few days."

The authors of *The Second Creation* (1986) were told that at Columbia University, Schwinger still had the annoying habit of not attending classes but was nevertheless able to pass his examinations. One professor said that Schwinger never came to a single class in statistical mechanics; in the final examination at the end of the semester, however, he worked some of the derivations more simply than the other students, who used the method taught in class. Lloyd Motz told the authors that "Schwinger was to physics what Mozart was to music."

Schwinger received his bachelor of arts degree from Columbia in 1936. Under the auspices of a Tyndall Traveling Fellowship, he attended graduate classes at Columbia, Purdue, and the University of Wisconsin. He received his doctorate from Columbia in 1939. He then accepted a National Research Council Fellowship and worked with J. Robert Oppenheimer as a research associate at the University of California at Berkeley. From Berkeley, he moved to Purdue University as a professor of physics in 1941, then to the University of Chicago's Metallurgical Laboratory two years later. At the University of Chicago, Schwinger worked on reactor designs. Still involved in the war effort, he consciously avoided the atom bomb project at Los Alamos, New Mexico, and went to the Massachusetts Institute of Technology in the fall of 1943. There, he worked to develop an improved radar system and began to "think in the language of electrical engineering." It was these thought processes, he said, that eventually led to his formulating the solutions on the theory of quantum electrodynamics.

Schwinger became a professor at Harvard University in 1945; he was elevated to the status of full professor at age twenty-nine, becoming one of the youngest in the history of the university. He retired from full-time teaching in the summer of 1988 from the University of California at Los Angeles, accepting the position of professor emeritus.

Scientific Career

World War II had demanded the attention of nearly every scientist in the world, and even those who did not work directly with the war effort were thwarted in their full-time study of pure theoretical physics. Having been employed on war projects virtually since his graduation from Columbia, Schwinger did not fully return to theoretical physics until he was appointed to his Harvard professorship in 1947, the year of the first Shelter Island Conference.

At Shelter Island, New York, on June 2, 3, and 4, 1947, the leading research physicists of the time met to discuss the state of experimental physics. It was to be a kind of postwar academic regrouping. The Shelter Island Conference headlined physicist Willis Lamb and Schwinger's Columbia mentor, Isaac Rabi. Most interesting and alarming was the work of the former scientist, who had discovered the Lambshift and placed the science of quantum electrodynamics — and even quantum field theory as a whole — in serious question. As Schwinger noted in his Nobel autobiographical sketch, the year of Shelter Island was also the year of his marriage to Clarice Carrol of Boston. On a tour of the country with his new bride in the fall of 1947, Schwinger thought furiously about the problem. Thanks to his gift for mathematics, he had the solution in hand by January of 1948.

Schwinger did not stop there. Fascinated by his discovery, he continued to develop and refine the concept and build what became known as "the formalism of the new quantum electrodynamics." That was no empty depiction: Schwinger had constructed a massive mathematical edifice of formal quantum electrodynamics. Said one critic of the finished work, which can be described as a mathematical symphony, "Other people publish to show how to do it, but Julian Schwinger publishes to show you that only he can do it."

Schwinger formally presented his theory at the second Shelter Island Conference, on March 30, 1948. This gathering was actually held in the Pocono Mountains of Pennsylvania. Among the attendees were Niels Bohr (1885-1962) and J. Robert Oppenheimer (1904-1967). It was Oppenheimer who, on leaving the conference, made the connection between the work of Schwinger and Tomonaga.

From the time of his discovery, Schwinger took a rather solitary approach to physics. Even as he was awarded the Nobel Prize in 1965, he was describing himself as working in a "pattern of concentration on general theoretical questions rather than the problems of immediate experimental concern." He also said he was "disgusted in over-speculative ventures in physics," referring to the purely theoretical aspects of physics that are impossible to support by experiment. He maintained two passions: teaching, and the belief that a unified theory of the electromagnetic and weak forces (called the "electroweak theory") was achievable.

There are four natural forces of nature. The two best known are the electromagnetic force and the gravitational force, which act over very large distances and are readily recognizable. The other two forces act over distances on the order of atomic diameters. They are the strong force, which holds the nucleus together, and the weak force, which is responsible for aspects of nuclear decay. The unification of all these forces into a single, unified mathematical theory has been a dream of physicists. It can be accomplished in several steps: the unification of two of the forces into one theory, then the combining of this unified theory with a third, and so forth. These theories are called "grand unification schemes."

If there is another legacy that Schwinger will leave with the physics community, it will be his steadfast belief in the unification of the electromagnetic force and the weak force and the work he did to foster that expectation. In 1956 he published a paper in which he claimed that evidence was mounting that an electroweak solution was possible. One of his students, Sheldon Lee Glashow, pursued that goal and wrote his graduate thesis on the theme of electroweak unification. By 1960, Glashow had published the paper on the mathematical structure of the electroweak theory that would be utilized some seven years later by Steven Weinberg and Abdus Salam. A paper published in 1971 by Dutch physicist Gerard 't Hooft brought all three efforts together, and Glashow, Weinberg, and Salam won the 1979 Nobel Prize in Physics for their electroweak theory. Said Glashow of Schwinger's influence and belief in the project's ultimate success, "I accepted this faith." Schwinger's range of involvement in the field of theoretical physics was wide. He contributed his extraordinary mathematical capabilities not only to the electroweak theory but also to such quantum enigmas as gravitons and photons, inelastic scattering, electron-positron annihilation, photon propagation, the new statistical atom, and a whole series of investigations into the nature of electrons.

As for his view of the evolution of quantum electrodynamics, Schwinger contends that it came about in four distinct phases. According to him, the preparation phase (1934-1936) consisted of collating relevant data and theories into a critical mass of information. The noncovariant relativistic theory phase (1947) was the year in which the collective solutions to quantum electrodynamics came to light. The third phase (1947-1948) saw the development of the first covariant relativistic theory, and the final phase (1949-1950) gave birth to the second.

Schwinger had been a crucial link in the unification of the electromagnetic and weak forces. Yet, he believes it may be too early to arrive at the final theory that will unify all natural forces. He says, "I believe in unification, but I do not believe the time is ripe for its discovery." Schwinger's conviction is that each generation of physicists seeks to uncover all there is to know, and he describes this campaign as a kind of hubris.

In 1986, Schwinger published *Einstein's Legacy*, a book written for a lay audience about the impact of Albert Einstein's work on the physics community and the world in general. It negates criticism that Schwinger's work is intelligible to Schwinger alone. *Einstein's Legacy* was written as an addition to the publisher W. H. Freeman's Scientific American Library, and it is a superior work that clearly describes to the general reader some of the most complex theories in physics.

Schwinger retired from active teaching at the University of California, Los Angeles, in the summer of 1988 and began pursuing various writing and research endeavors.

Bibliography

Primary
PHYSICS: *Particles and Sources*, 1969; *Quantum Kinematics and Dynamics*, 1970; *Particles Sources and Fields*, 1970-1973; *Einstein's Legacy*, 1986.
EDITED TEXT: *Quantum Electrodynamics*, 1958.

Secondary
Crease, Robert P., and Charles C. Mann. *The Second Creation: Makers of the Revolution in Twentieth Century Physics*. New York: Macmillan, 1985. This book reveals the personal saga of discovery in modern physics, from the Einsteinian revolution to modern "atom smashers." It tells the story of the individuals who made the discoveries, including Schwinger, and how they changed history. It is written for the individual with some knowledge of science and physics, or for those who like a good adventure story and who do not mind skipping the technical aspects of the work. Heavily illustrated. Index and glossary.

Ferris, Timothy. *Coming of Age in the Milky Way*. New York: William Morrow, 1988. This book tells the story of astronomy and cosmology from the days of the ancient Egyptians to the quest to unlock the atom's innermost secrets. It is written for the general reader, and it places Schwinger among his peers, clearly fixing him against the backdrop of history. It is fully illustrated and contains a detailed glossary and bibliography.

Feynman, Richard P., with Ralph Leighton. *Surely You Must Be Joking, Mr. Feynman: Adventures of a Curious Character*. New York: Norton, 1984. Feynman's autobiography is a series of personal recollections from his childhood days to his work in solving the problems of quantum electrodynamics. It is a text filled with humor, and it offers fascinating insights into the life of a famous physicist and the ways in which he solved some of physics' most complex problems. Includes recollections of Schwinger and tells how Feynman's and Schwinger's approaches to quantum electrodynamics were so different.

Pagels, Heinz R. *The Cosmic Code: Quantum Physics as the Law of Nature*. New York: Bantam Books, 1984. Physicist Heinz Pagels begins his discussion of physics with Einstein, the true father of what has been called "modern physics." He then explores what is not so well-known or understood: the meaning and importance of quantum physics. It is all accomplished without mathematics and in language easily understood by readers with some grounding in the sciences. Pagels lends historical relevance to the work, making it at once interesting and meaningful. Complete with illustrations, index, and bibliography.

_____. *Perfect Symmetry: The Search for the Beginning of Time*. New York: Bantam Books, 1986. This work relates the history of modern physics, beginning with the viewpoint of the nineteenth century astronomer William Herschel. It continues with a discussion of the revolution in physics that occurred at the turn of the twentieth century by discussing Einstein and his inheritors, among them Schwinger. Pagels tells how physics moved from its first simple knowledge of the existence of the atom to the processes that disassembled the atom's most elementary parts. Written for the general reader. Bibliography, illustrations, and index.

Zee, Anthony. *Fearful Symmetry*. New York: Macmillan, 1986. This highly acclaimed book defines the role of symmetry in modern physics. It is written specifically for the lay reader and is developed in such a way that even those with little background in physics can grasp the history of high-energy particle physics. It profiles the discoveries that led to today's knowledge, including Schwinger's contributions. Illustrated and indexed.

Dennis Chamberland

1965

Physics
Shin'ichirō Tomonaga, Japan
Julian Seymour Schwinger, United States
Richard P. Feynman, United States

Chemistry
Robert B. Woodward, United States

Physiology or Medicine
François Jacob, France
André Lwoff, France
Jacques Monod, France

Literature
Mikhail Sholokhov, Soviet Union

Peace
United Nations Children's Fund

RICHARD P. FEYNMAN
1965

Born: New York, New York; May 11, 1918
Died: Los Angeles, California; February 15, 1988
Nationality: American
Area of concentration: Quantum electrodynamics

Feynman developed a theory of quantum electrodynamics that described the interaction of electrons, positrons, and photons. He reconstructed quantum mechanics and electrodynamics in his own terms, formulating a matrix of measurable quantities visually represented by a series of graphs known as the Feynman diagrams

The Award

Presentation

Professor Ivar Waller, member of the Royal Swedish Academy of Sciences, presented the Nobel Prize in Physics to Richard P. Feynman on December 10, 1965. Waller's presentation was directed to Feynman and his cowinners, Japanese physicists Shin'ichirō Tomonaga and U.S. physicist Julian Schwinger; the three men shared the prize for their simultaneous discoveries.

Waller noted that their work explained an experimental discrepancy in the predicted subatomic energy level of hydrogen, which was discovered in 1947 by American physicist Willis Eugene Lamb, Jr. (born 1913), an effect called the Lambshift. Waller reviewed the work of the 1920's in general quantum mechanical laws, work which defined how electrons interact with the mechanical/electromagnetic environment of the atom and how they emit electromagnetic energy. This work then led to a theory that such interactions could exist between matter and electromagnetic fields, taking into account Albert Einstein's theory of relativity. The new theory become known as quantum electrodynamics. The early formulations had inherent errors, however, which predicted an infinite mass for the electron or its electromagnetic field or both.

Feynman, Waller noted, had departed radically from conventional methods by developing a graphic interpretation of quantum electrodynamics, which became known as the Feynman diagrams. These diagrams enabled an interpretation of the interaction of electrons and emitted light by a graphic, physical means. The work of Feynman, Tomonaga, and Schwinger enabled the anomalous part of the Lambshift calculations to be resolved, and their concurrent theories resulted in the most accurate of all theories in theoretical physics. Feynman's method, particularly, enabled precise calculation of multiple subatomic particles, especially valuable in elementary particle physics research. Waller also noted that their work led to valuable insights into solid-state physics, nuclear physics, and statistical mechanics.

Nobel lecture

Ivar Waller introduced Feynman's approach to quantum electrodynamics as radical. Feynman's lecture "The Development of the Space-Time View of Quantum Electrodynamics," was probably equally radical when compared to the characteristic, formal presentation style of traditional Nobel lectures.

Feynman opened his lecture by asking the Academy's indulgence in his attempt to make his lecture entertaining. Feynman introduced his lecture as an anecdotal account of the story of his discovery from the beginning, and he said that he was going to leave the scientific paper to journal articles. Such a purely narrative approach was unusual, given that most Nobel lectures presented to the Academy are typically more rigorously scientific.

Feynman said his quest to solve the problems of quantum electrodynamic theory began while he was reading the work of English physicist Paul Adrien Maurice Dirac (1902-1984) as an undergraduate student at the Massachusetts Institute of Technology. He was inspired not by the solution offered but by what was presented as still unknown.

The problem with quantum electrodynamic theory was that the mass and charge of an electron, under the old theory, were incalculable. The theory was incapable of expressing all the conditions of the atomic state, including that of the electron. As one approached the theory from a classical or mechanical sense, one could not make the data converge (align) with quantum theory. In order for the theory of quantum electrodynamics to have practical use in predicting the results of particle physics, this convergence was essential.

Feynman began working on the classical problem first. He described his fascination with quantum electrodynamics as similar to falling in love with a woman: ". . . it is only possible if you do not know much about her, so you cannot see her faults." Eventually, with the help of Professor John H. Wheeler, at Princeton University, Feynman concluded that "positrons could simply be represented as electrons going from the future to the past."

With the classic theory solved to his satisfaction, he set out to reconcile classical concepts with quantum theory. As Feynman stated, however, "there is no unique way to make a quantum theory from classical mechanics, although all the textbooks make believe there is." Later, while Feynman was at a beer party, a faculty member introduced Feynman to a recently published Dirac equation. He began to modify it on the spot and carried it forward to make the differential calculations of classical quantum electrodynamics equal to a singular case of the quantum description.

What Feynman had done was to represent the actions of the electron in terms of the amplitude for its path. Although formulated by a completely different pathway, Feynman's solution equaled the expressions discovered by Erwin Schrödinger (1887-1961) and Werner Karl Heisenberg (1901-1976). Thus, having arrived at his own unique and elegant solution, Feynman published his thesis, titled "The Principle of Least Action in Quantum Mechanics," and earned his Ph.D.; but he felt that all was not yet right with his analysis.

At about the same time, Professor Hans Albrecht Bethe (born 1906) used conventional quantum electrodynamic calculations to pin down the Lambshift based on relativistic assumptions and thus made what Feynman described as "the most important discovery in the history of quantum electrodynamics." Working further with Bethe, Feynman refined his quantum electrodynamic calculations and devised a set of diagrams which made it easier to track variables and work the quantum integrals. These have become known as the Feynman diagrams. Eventually the quantum electrodynamic problems refined themselves to a set of problems that Feynman described as a question of the interaction of an electron with a neutron using "pseudo scalar theory with pseudo vector coupling and pseudo scalar theory with pseudo scalar coupling." (These are mathematical representations for evaluating subatomic interactions and products.)

Said Feynman, "So, I went home, and during the evening I worked out the electron neutron scattering for the pseudo scalar and pseudo vector coupling, saw they were not equal and subtracted them, and worked out the difference in detail." This summary of his final thrust to solve the problems of quantum electrodynamics, this final push to the summit, was the best description he could muster. This single evening's work by Feynman had solved the remaining unknown in quantum electrodynamics. At the urging of his peers, he published the work, although he felt that there were still loose ends. It would be this work that would culminate in his award of the Nobel Prize, although he could not shake the feeling that it was still unfinished.

Feynman ended his Nobel lecture by reviewing the methods which had led to the discoveries in quantum electrodynamics over the years, describing the process of discovery as extremely inefficient. He attributed that inefficiency to the reality that a given scientific observation can have many equivalent approaches and solutions, each offering totally unrelated processes but ultimately leading to identical conclusions. Thus, he felt it essential that physicists have the widest range of methods available to them so that the range of solutions to a given problem is maximized.

Critical reception

The academic and world community expressed no dissenting opinion to the selection of Feynman, Schwinger, and Tomonaga as winners of the 1965 Nobel Prize in Physics. Indeed, the scientific community was quick to mount praise for the elegant theories of all three.

Science (November 1965), in an article written by Freeman J. Dyson, stated that the new theoretical approach to quantum electrodynamics "brought order and harmony to the vast middle ground of physics . . . into a small number of principles of great quality and elegance. It is in a certain sense the most perfect and the most highly developed part of physics." No stranger to quantum electrodynamics, it was Dyson himself who had demonstrated the identical mathematical relationships of each of the theories by integrating the differential equations to find a common starting place among them all. As a result of the independent development of the theories, *Science* applauded the result as "a different viewpoint . . . so the theory gained in breadth and richness." It described the approach of Feynman as the most original of the three, noting that Feynman had reconstructed the whole of quantum mechanics and electrodynamics from his own point of view. Without radical innovation, *Science* noted the victory was, in the end, "a victory for conservatism."

Physics Today (December, 1965) retraced the detailed path to the discoveries, detailing the differences, notably the use of Feynman's "S" matrices and diagrams. The periodical took special care to note the specific reasons the three were able to develop theories: by disposing of the electron's intrinsic mass, which had been a major point of contention (and error product) in the original application of the Dirac equations. *Physics Today* also made note of the limitations of the work, a fact curiously noted as a major part of a *Newsweek* (November 1, 1965) article, which quoted Feynman as stating, " . . . but as far as I'm concerned, the math isn't solved completely yet." Apparently, without recognizing this statement as an artifact of a careful scientist's approach and most notably one of Feynman's own personality, *Newsweek* failed to mention that the scientific community itself regarded the theories as being very close to perfect, and hence quantum electrodynamics is perhaps the most reliable of all the scientific disciplines.

Time (October 29, 1965) made the barest mention of the award, merely noting the recipients' names and that the work had occurred two decades earlier. *The Science Newsletter* (October 30, 1965) mentioned that the work "refined the complicated mathematical equations that govern the (atomic processes) . . . on which all life depends." The publication also noted, accurately, that the work was considered "brilliant by other scientists," adding that the theories represented the first major contribution to quantum mechanics since its development in 1920.

Biography

Richard Phillips Feynman was born in New York City on May 11, 1918, the son of Melville Arthur Feynman and Lucille Phillips Feynman. His father predicted before he was born that he would become a scientist. He set out to ensure this aspiration for his son by encouraging young Feynman to work in an improvised home laboratory, teaching Richard math as a toddler. Richard, in turn, continued this interest and taught himself calculus. Feynman's love for puzzles spilled into giving magic shows based on chemical effects. He also fixed radios and small appliances for friends and neighbors. He described his precociousness as a reflection of his father, who "didn't know anything exactly . . . but he understood everything."

Feynman was graduated from Far Rockaway High School in 1935, with his peers, at age seventeen. He entered the Massachusetts Institute of Technology in Cambridge, where, in 1939, he received his B.S. degree with honors. While there, as Feynman noted in his Nobel lecture, he discovered the "fundamental problem of the day" in quantum electrodynamics and began his search for the answers to the dilemma.

Feynman entered Princeton University in 1939 under physicist John Wheeler. During this period, the United States was preparing for what many feared would be entry into World War II. Feynman accepted a position at the Frankfort Arsenal in

Philadelphia to assist in the development of an automated artillery aiming device. While at Princeton, Feynman used his ability to visualize broad aspects of problem-solving to refine his understanding of quantum mechanics, which would later prove invaluable in the final assault on the problem of quantum electrodynamics.

From 1942 to 1945, Feynman joined a group of scientists at Los Alamos, New Mexico, in the development of the first atom bomb. Working with J. Robert Oppenheimer (1904-1967), Niels Bohr (1885-1962), and Enrico Fermi (1901-1954) at Los Alamos, Feynman became a group leader. It was at Los Alamos that Feynman earned his reputation as a "curious character" by routinely neutralizing security precautions, picking locks, and cracking safe codes for amusement. He witnessed the world's first atomic blast at Alamogordo. This event and his participation in creating the bomb later depressed him to the point that he believed that the destruction of society was inevitable. Years later, he tempered this stance: "Perhaps it's like the man who had fallen off the 100 story building and, as he passes the 50th floor says, 'It doesn't feel bad yet.'" Compounding his difficulties at this point in his life, Feynman's first wife, Arlene, was terminally ill, and Feynman spent all of his free time from Los Alamos visiting her in the hospital.

After Princeton and Los Alamos, Feynman went to Cornell University from 1945 to 1950, as Professor of Theoretical Physics. He then went on to the California Institute of Technology (Caltech), in Pasadena, becoming the Richard Chance Tolman Professor of Theoretical Physics in 1959. He stayed at Caltech for the rest of his academic career. In 1986, President Ronald Reagan named Feynman to the presidential commission established to investigate the space shuttle *Challenger* disaster. Not too long after his intensive work for the commission, Feynman died of abdominal cancer in Los Angeles, on February 15, 1988.

Scientific Career

Following the war, Feynman became an associate professor of physics at Cornell University at Ithaca, New York. Still reeling from the ethical implications of his work at Los Alamos and attempting to adjust to his new position at Cornell, Feynman lost the joy he had always associated with being a physicist.

One afternoon, while enjoying the antics of a student tossing a plate in a Cornell cafeteria, it occurred to Feynman that the spin of the plate in the air and the relationship of the spin to the wobble had an intriguing connection to his neglected concepts of quantum electrodynamics. As Feynman began to work out the calculations of the plate's motion he decided to start doing physics "for the fun of it" again. He renewed his work on the problems of quantum electrodynamics, which he had all but abandoned with the war. Later, he admitted, "The [Feynman] diagrams and the whole business that I got the Nobel Prize for came from that piddling around with the wobbling plate."

As mentioned in his Nobel lecture, what Feynman was attempting to do was unite and quantify the interaction of light and matter and, except for gravitation, provide quantifiable rules for predicting what other subatomic research was providing in the form of raw, only partially undifferentiated data. As he constructed his diagrams, Feynman was laying out a roadmap to the subatomic world that would be defined by quantum electrodynamics. He prepared his map in the form of a diagram, completed with vector-graphic arrows, describing the three basic rules of his science: the movement of electrons, the movement of photons, and the interaction of the two within the confines of the atom itself.

Under this diagrammed regime of logic, Feynman supported what Professor John Wheeler had expressed to him years earlier at Princeton: Electrons could apparently move "backward" in time. This apparent paradox occurred when the electron appeared to emit a photon, rush backward in time and absorb another photon, then continue forward again. These concepts were published in 1949. For these ideas, Feynman won the Nobel Prize in Physics sixteen years later. Feynman left Cornell in 1950 and taught in Brazil for one year prior to accepting a position as a theoretical physicist at Caltech.

During the mid-1950's, Feynman became fascinated with a quantum effect relating to the unusual properties of liquid helium. At temperatures near absolute zero, liquid helium loses heat rather than gaining it when flowing; the substance flows with no apparent friction through very small-diameter tubes and appears to flow up the walls of containers in apparent defiance of gravity. These are a set of properties called "superfluidity." Russian physicist Lev Landau (1908-1968) had postulated twenty years earlier that this behavior was the result of a quantum action he ascribed to "phonons" and "rotons" (collections of helium molecules in the shape of a torus). Feynman expanded on Landau's explanation by deriving the rotons mathematically, using Bose-Einstein statistics of quantum mechanics. Feynman began to concern himself with the theory of the "weak force," a fundamental force that—along with gravity electromagnetism, and the strong force—comprises all the unifying forces of nature.

Together with his colleague Murray Gell-Mann (born 1929), Feynman used his own diagrams to demonstrate pictorially that beta decay (the phenomenon that demonstrated the weak force by ejection of an electron from an atomic nucleus) was in fact a feature of the weak interaction itself. This discovery was named the "conserved vector current theory" by Feynman and Gell-Man and was published in 1958.

From 1960 to 1968, Feynman turned his attention to the quantum theory of gravity, whose ultimate prize is the Grand Unified Theory of the forces of nature. He was not successful at finding this link. By the late 1960's, Feynman had returned to the world of particle physics, bringing with him the knowledge of the strong force: the force that binds the nucleus and its subatomic particles together. During this time, there was some evidence that protons consisted of smaller, even more elementary particles. Feynman called them "partons." Concurrently, Gell-Mann had deduced these particles in a similar theory and called them "quarks." These theories ultimately opened a new branch of theoretical physics called quantum chromodynamics.

When the space shuttle *Challenger* exploded in January, 1986, President Reagan named Feynman to the presidential commission that was to investigate the tragedy. Feynman accepted the task with characteristic enthusiasm, stating to his wife Gweneth, "I'm going to commit suicide for six months. I won't be able to do any work with this physics problem I've been having fun with; I'm going to do nothing but work on the shuttle—for six months." Feynman, however, said he could not find corresponding enthusiasm among other board members, and so he conducted his own investigation of the accident, even issuing his own thirteen-page report, criticizing the space agency and the commission's own final conclusions. Shortly thereafter, hardly having time to reenter the academic world and to continue with the problem with which he was having so much fun, Feynman died.

Richard Feynman left behind him the self-appointed description of a "curious character," and, as distinguished by one periodical in 1988, the legacy of "a curious genius with an impish grin." He also left a healthy irreverence for the tendency toward pompousness of organized science and a childlike fascination for learning, which he chronicled in the classic series "The Feynman Lectures in Physics."

Yet Feynman's most notable legacy will probably be his uniquely creative approach to viewing the esoteric reality of a relativistic universe. It is a universe, he instructed, where time can move simultaneously forward and backward.

Bibliography

Primary
PHYSICS: *Forces in Molecules*, 1939; *Quantum Electrodynamics*, 1961; *The Feynman Lectures in Physics*, 1963-1965; *The Character of Physical Law*, 1965; *Photon-Hadron Interactions*, 1972; *Statistical Mechanics: A Set of Lectures*, 1972; "An Outsider's Inside View of the Challenger Inquiry," *Physics Today*, 1988.
OTHER NONFICTION: *Surely You're Joking, Mr. Feynman! Adventures of a Curious Character*, 1984 (with Ralph Leighton); *What Do You Care What Other People Think? Further Adventures of a Curious Character*, 1988 (with Leighton).

Secondary
Crease, Robert P., and Charles C. Mann. *The Second Creation: Makers of the Revolution in Twentieth Century Physics*. New York: Macmillan, 1985. This book reveals the personal sagas of discovery in modern physics from the Einsteinian revolution to the super atom smashers. It tells the story of the individuals who have made the discoveries, including Richard Feynman, and how they have changed history. Written for the individual with some knowledge of science and physics, or for those who like a good adventure story, the volume is heavily illustrated, indexed, and contains a complete glossary.
Ferris, Timothy. *Coming of Age in the Milky Way*. New York: William Morrow, 1988. This book tells the whole story of astronomy and cosmology from the days of the ancient Egyptians to the quest to unlock the atom's innermost secrets. It is written unambiguously for the general reader and relates the place of Feynman

among his peers, clearly fixing him against the backdrop of history. Fully illustrated, with a detailed glossary and bibliography.

Feynman, Richard P., with Ralph Leighton. *Surely You're Joking, Mr. Feynman! Adventures of a Curious Character*. New York: W. W. Norton, 1984. Feynman's autobiography, a collection of personal recollections from his childhood days to his work in solving the vague problems of quantum electrodynamics. The text is filled with humor and history and gives fascinating insights into the life of a famous physicist and how he solved some of the most complex problems in physics. Provides Feynman's recollections of other famous physicists as well. Feynman's open and consistent wit leaves few questions unanswered.

_____. *What Do You Care What Other People Think? Further Adventures of a Curious Character*. New York: W. W. Norton, 1988. This continuation of Feynman's first autobiographical sketch deals in considerable depth with the shuttle investigation and his difficulties with the National Aeronautics and Space Administration and the Rogers Commission, which investigated the shuttle's accident. It also details his early years, his love for his father, and his first wife, who died suddenly. Probably less humorous than the first autobiography volume, but reveals Feynman's depth of emotion and caring.

Hawking, Stephen W. *A Brief History of Time*. New York: Bantam Books, 1988. Written by one of the great physicists of the twentieth century, this book enumerates for the average reader the details of space and time in terms of a physical reality that is easy to grasp. Hawking discusses Feynman's contribution to this concept of the modern universe and how ideas are unfolding as the data from quantum and subatomic investigations are evaluated.

Dennis Chamberland

1966

Physics
Alfred Kastler, France

Chemistry
Robert S. Mulliken, United States

Physiology or Medicine
Charles B. Huggins, United States
Francis Peyton Rous, United States

Literature
Shmuel Yosef Agnon, Israel
Nelly Sachs, Sweden

Peace
no award

ALFRED KASTLER
1966

Born: Guebwiller, Alsace, Germany; May 3, 1902
Died: Bandol, France; January 7, 1984
Nationality: French
Areas of concentration: Optical spectroscopy and Hertzian resonances

Kastler's discovery in 1950 of double resonance and his combining of this method in 1952 with the technique of optical pumping resulted in new knowledge of atomic structure and led to the development of masers and lasers between 1952 and 1958 by Townes in the United States and Prokhorov and Basov in the Soviet Union

The Award

Presentation

The Nobel Prize in Physics for 1966 was awarded to Alfred Kastler of France. It was presented to him on the evening of December 10, 1966, in Stockholm by King Gustav VI. The presentation speech was made by Ivar Waller, a member of the Nobel Committee for Physics.

Waller reviewed Kastler's scientific career from its beginning to the period that had produced the prizewinning work. Kastler had begun by studying the Hertzian resonances produced when atoms interact with radio waves or microwaves. Such electromagnetic radiation permits the study of fine details in spectra. Kastler was following the path of the Austrian-American physicist Isidor Isaac Rabi, who was the first to use Hertzian resonances for this purpose. In 1938, Rabi had been able to measure with close precision the splitting of atomic energy levels into several sublevels, including hyperfine structures associated with the magnetic moments of nuclei.

Kastler, however (with the help of Jean Brossel), was the first to propose a successful optical method to investigate Hertzian resonances. He believed that selected magnetic sublevels could be excited from excited states by polarized light having the same resonance frequency. He showed that if a high-frequency oscillating magnetic field is applied to radio waves or microwaves, Hertzian resonance is induced when the ratio of this frequency to the magnetic field is appropriately selected. He held that the Hertzian resonances would tend to equalize the magnetic sublevel system and in this way would influence the observed polarization of the fluorescence. New disclosures about the atomic process connected with the scattering of resonance radiation prompted Kastler to consider the method of optical pumping. In this method, atoms are illuminated by resonance radiation (generally circularly polarized). These atoms return to the ground state to concentrate themselves at certain sublevels and assume preferential orientations in space. According to Kastler, the use of this method would permit the orientation of both atoms and atomic nuclei. In 1952, Kastler performed an experiment that confirmed the practicality of his recommendation and the validity of his theory.

Kastler's use of "double resonance" (optical and Hertzian) and his development of a practical optical pumping apparatus gave him a sensitive way of detecting Hertzian resonances, whose effects are optical and easily observed. Kastler's method proved fertile. At first, optical pumping was done with atomic beams (streams of neutral atoms), and this method led to a study of the interactions between quanta in an oscillating magnetic field and atoms. An improvement in the method of pumping came about when these experiments were successfully conducted on the vapor in the resonance chamber. Other experiments investigated the relaxation of atoms back to the disordered state after pumping, providing information on the nature of the mechanism whereby interatomic collisions and collisions between atoms and chamber walls take place. Other important experiments and developments followed as the result of Kastler's work, including the laser, sensitive magnetometers, and atomic clocks.

Nobel lecture

In his Nobel lecture, titled "Optical Methods for Studying Hertzian Resonances," Kastler recalled his first year as a student at the École Normale Supérieure in Paris, when he was introduced to quantum physics by his teacher, Eugène Bloch. Bloch advised him to read Arnold Sommerfeld's treatise *Atombau und Spektrallinien* (1922; atomic structure and spectral lines). In perusing it, Kastler discovered the special interest he would pursue in physics research: He wished to study the application of the conservation law of angular momentum to the basic interactions between electromagnetic radiation and the fundamental particles of the atom.

Kastler then spoke of the 1931 work of W. Hanle and R. Bär, who had studied the polarization of Raman spectra (the characteristic spectra that are observed when a fixed, single frequency of light is scattered by a pure substance) at right angles to the incident beam, lighting the medium with circularly polarized light. They observed that the Raman lines that scattered longitudinally had the same circular polarization as the incident light for totally symmetrical lines, whereas the direction of circular polarization was reversed for lines not totally symmetrical. Hanle and Bär were able to classify Raman spectra into two types: depolarized and polarized. C. V. Raman and S. Bhagavantam saw in Hanle and Bär's experimental result proof of the existence of photon spin. Kastler himself published a note pointing out that their result was a consequence of the effect of the conservation of angular momentum law as it applied to light scattering.

Kastler devoted himself to the investigation of that conservation law. Having concluded that the optical excitation of atoms in steps was a very promising area of research, he applied this method to the mercury atom. As a result, he was the first to obtain through polarization selective excitation of specific magnetic sublevels. Kastler and his former student Jean Brossel began to discuss ways of extending the techniques of radio-frequency spectroscopy to the excited states of atoms. They concluded that a simple technique that they had conceived together should produce the results they were seeking. This technique involved the optical method of Hertzian resonance. Their idea was to combine magnetic with optical resonance (double resonance) in conjunction with optical pumping. They would optically excite atoms with circularly polarized light so as to transfer the angular momentum carried by the light to the atoms, a procedure that would eventually concentrate them in the ground state. It should be possible, they believed, by this optical pumping to effect an atomic orientation and also an orientation of the nuclei. These conditions should permit the study of the system's return to the original state, either by the natural relaxation process or by the influence of a resonant field. When tested, their theory proved correct.

In 1951, Brossel completed his studies in the United States and returned to Paris. He and Kastler formed a team of student researchers at the École Normale Supérieure to develop the optical methods of Hertzian resonance in a systematic fashion. These young people, in about a dozen theses, added significant contributions to the work begun by Kastler and Brossel, especially in their studies of the excited and ground states of atoms. Additional data were obtained on relaxation processes, and precise measurements were made of the intervals of fine and hyperfine structures. These techniques allowed the figuring of very precise values for the nuclear magnetic moments and led to the discovery of numerous phenomena connected to high-order irregularities among the atomic and nuclear particles.

In the course of their careers, Kastler and Brossel had the satisfaction of seeing their own work confirmed by the experiments of others. For example, in resuming Brossel's experiments on the excited state of mercury and adding an electric field to the magnetic field, J. E. Blamont studied the Stark effect (the splitting, shifting, and broadening of spectral lines in the presence of an electric field) for the even and odd isotopes. He discovered a narrowing of the magnetic resonance curves relative to the increase in density of the mercury vapor. The study of this width permitted the measurement of the lifetime of this excited state. Another member of Kastler's team, N. Rollet, showed that the increasing depolarization of resonance light is a function of the density of the mercury vapor and that this feature is a result of the multiple scattering of photons and not of collisions. M. A. Guiochon showed that only the atoms of the same isotope in the mixture of the resonance cell produce the narrowing. Jean-Pierre Barrat developed a theory of coherent scattering and verified all the predictions of this theory. He was the first to study an effect of Hertzian coherence between atomic states and to show that this effect can be described formally by the density matrix. J. C. Pebay-Peyroula proved the fruitfulness of the technique of atomic excitation by electron impact. Later, J. P. Descoubes combined this technique with the level-crossing method, which permitted the analysis of the fine and hyperfine structure of many levels of helium 3 and helium 4 atoms.

Critical reception

The awarding of the 1966 Nobel Prizes was reported in *The New York Times* of December 11. The reporter noted that "to Prof. Alfred Kastler, 64, of Paris, went the physics prize . . . for his work on the structure of energy levels inside the atom." He pointed out that the value of the prizes amounted "to the equivalent of nearly $60,000 in each category," and he further remarked: "Although lavish praise was heaped on all six [recipients] for their achievements, it was undoubtedly Mr. Agnon and Miss Sachs [the winners of the literature prize] who won the hearts of the distinguished guests."

When controversy has arisen over the justice of the Nobel awards, it has generally been in regard either to the literature prize or to the peace prize; seldom have the science awards been criticized. In the case of Kastler's prize, however, there seemed to be a general feeling of guilt mixed with elation that an injustice committed in the past had been rectified. This mixed feeling could be traced to the controversy that had erupted in France after the award of the 1964 Nobel Prize in Physics to the American Charles Hard Townes and the Soviet physicists Aleksandr Mikhailovich Prokhorov and Nikolay Gennadiyevich Basov for their discovery of the maser-laser principle. According to Isaac Asimov, when Townes and the Soviet scientists were awarded the Nobel Prize in 1964, "there was some dissatisfaction in France over the ignoring of Kastler. This was made up for when Kastler was awarded the 1966 Nobel Prize for physics."

The French dissatisfaction was increased by Jacques Monod's 1965 attack on the French "establishment," which consisted of the Ministry of Education and the prestigious universities. He castigated the indifference of this establishment to the real merit of scientists outside its fold, such as Pierre Curie, who was never able to obtain a decent laboratory for his scientific investigations. Monod was a French biochemist who, together with his colleagues at the Pasteur Institute, won the 1965 Nobel Prize in Physiology or Medicine. In a startling interview granted to the left-wing journal of opinion *Le Nouvel Observateur* (October 20, 1965), Monod spoke openly of the difficulties he and his colleagues had encountered in attempting to gain recognition and support from their government and the prestigious educational institutions. He concluded by sharply criticizing the scientific complacency that he believed had characterized France since the time of Napoleon. This criticism may have helped Kastler win the recognition he deserved.

Biography

Alfred Kastler was born at Guebwiller, Alsace, Germany, on May 3, 1902. He was the son of Frederick and Anna Frey Kastler. Having attended elementary school in Guebwiller, Kastler moved to the secondary level at the Oberrealschule of Colmar (which became the Lycée Bartholdi when Alsace was returned to France in 1918), where he had the opportunity to study modern languages, mathematics, and physical science. At the *lycée*, his mathematics teachers whetted his interest in science. Impressed by the rigor of his thinking, they recommended him for admission to the very prestigious school of education in Paris, the École Normale Supérieure, whose object was to supply teachers for the *lycées* and the *collèges* of France. Kastler entered the École Normale in 1921.

While still a student there, he wed in 1924 a former student, Elsie Cosset. They would have three children: Daniel (born 1926), Mirelle (born 1928), and Claude-Yves (born 1936). In 1926, Kastler obtained his teaching degree. He then taught at the *lycées* in Mulhouse, Colmar, and Bordeaux. In 1931 he was appointed the assistant to Pierre Daure, a professor in the faculty of science at the Université de Bordeaux, a state institution. His teaching duties were light, and his wife worked as a teacher of history in the secondary schools so that her husband might devote all of his free time to scientific research. In 1936 he received his doctorate in physical science. From 1936 to 1938, he was a lecturer attached to the faculty of science at the Université de Clermont-Ferrand, located in the industrial city of that name in the Auvergne region of central France. In 1938 he was made a professor at the Université de Bordeaux, where he remained until 1941, when he assumed a professorship at his alma mater, the École Normale.

There, Kastler worked assiduously in his laboratory, but it was not until 1945 that he was able to send any students to other Western countries so that they could learn the latest developments in physics. In 1945 he sent Jean Brossel to the Massachusetts Institute of Technology, where he studied under Francis Bitter. After completing his studies at MIT in 1951, Brossel returned to the École Normale, where he and Kastler collaborated, forming a team of students to assist them in their research work. As the leader of this collective effort, which proved unusually successful, Kastler was honored by being awarded the Nobel Prize in Physics in 1966.

Kastler continued in his professorial post at the École Normale until 1968. In the meantime, he had spent the year 1953-1954 at the Université Catholique de Louvain in Belgium. In 1958 he became a member of the management board of the Centre National de la Recherche Scientifique (CNRS) and director of the Atomic Clock Laboratory. He was director of research of CNRS from 1968 to 1972. Kastler received honorary degrees from many renowned universities, and in 1954 he was awarded the Howeck Medal and Prize by the Physical Society of the United Kingdom. He was a *grand officier* of the French Légion d'Honneur and a *grand officier* of the Ordre National du Mérite.

After World War II, Kastler became active in peace movements, opposing the French presence in Algeria and the development of France's nuclear arsenal. His position on these matters caused his apartment in Paris to be bombed by right-wing extremists. Apart from scientific investigation and his family, he loved especially two things: nature and German poetry. Kastler died in Bandol, France, on the French Riviera, on January 7, 1984. He was eighty-one years old. *The New York Times* noted his death in its issue of Sunday, January 8.

Scientific Career

Kastler was introduced to quantum physics (as opposed to classical physics) by his teacher, Eugène Bloch, in Kastler's first year at the École Normale Supérieure. Bloch advised him to study German physicist Arnold Sommerfeld's *Atombau und*

Spektrallinien. A professor at the University of Munich, Sommerfeld was an important figure in the development of modern physics. He had modified Niels Bohr's model of the atom to allow for elliptical orbits for electrons, the result of applying Albert Einstein's theory of relativity and Max Planck's quantum theory to atomic structures. Kastler was fortunate to obtain the progressive Bloch for his teacher, because in France at that time Einstein's relativity theory was virtually ignored and Planck's quantum theory was rarely taught. In reading Sommerfeld, Kastler became especially interested in the principle of conservation of angular momentum when photons interacted with atoms. ("Angular momentum" refers either to a particle orbiting a nucleus or to a particle spinning around its axis.)

Kastler's scientific career might be said to have begun when he was appointed graduate assistant to Pierre Daure at the Université de Bordeaux in 1931. By this time, he had become interested in fluorescence and combination scattering in vapors or gases and in crystals. This interest continued until 1949. He had hardly arrived at Bordeaux when he began to publish notes and papers. His first publication was a note, written in 1931, explaining the cause of some curious behavior that W. Hanle and R. Bär had observed in their study of Raman spectra. Kastler attributed the phenomenon to the principle of conservation of angular momentum as it applied to light scattering. His doctoral thesis was published in 1936. Titled *Recherches sur la fluorescence visible de la vapeur de mercure* (investigations into the visible fluorescence of mercury vapor), it is a study—resulting from closer examination of the consequences of the principle of angular momentum in light scattering and fluorescence—of the degrees of intensity to be observed in the process of optical fluorescence with respect to mercury vapor. In 1949, Brossel and Kastler published an important paper in which they proposed that radio-frequency resonances of optically excited states of atoms could be detected by the double resonance method, a procedure whereby atoms are excited by polarized light in a magnetic field.

Meanwhile, having been granted his doctorate by the Université de Paris, Kastler had become a lecturer at the Université de Clermont-Ferrand. In 1938 he returned to Bordeaux to assume a professorship. In 1941, following the fall of Paris and the formation of the Vichy government under Philippe Pétain, he had accepted a professorship at his old school, the École Normale, where he was to enjoy one of the largest and best-equipped academic physics laboratories in France. There he was to remain until 1968.

The second stage of Kastler's scientific career embraced the years from 1950 to 1966. He was to be awarded the Nobel Prize in 1966 and after that, his active researches into the mysteries of atomic structure seem to have been curtailed. In 1950, Kastler turned his attention to the possibilities of investigating atomic structure through the use of double resonance, or the combining of optical with magnetic resonance, in conjunction with the technique of optical pumping, or the use of a light beam to induce excitement in atoms by electron collision and thus produce a population of a particular set of energy levels. In this year, he showed in an article what might be done in the way of production and detection of inequalities in the population of spatially quantized levels of atoms. In his Nobel lecture, which discussed optical methods for studying Hertzian, or radio-frequency, resonances, he explained that "the optical excitation of atoms with circularly polarized light made it possible to transfer the angular momentum carried by the light to the atoms and thus to concentrate them in the ground state," and that it was possible, by this optical pumping, to create both atomic and nuclear orientations. He believed it possible "to obtain distributions very different from the Boltzmann distributions and thus to create conditions permitting the study of the return to equilibrium" of the excited states of the atoms. At this time, Kastler's former pupil Jean Brossel was applying the double resonance method to the study of the excited state of the mercury atom at MIT. Brossel was studying under Francis Bitter, who had first suggested that optical pumping might prove fruitful in the study of atomic structure. The method Bitter had proposed, however, had proved inexact.

In 1951, Brossel returned from MIT to the laboratory of the École Normale. Through correspondence between them, Brossel and Kastler had already devised a simple technique that they thought would produce the desired results, and they decided to form a team of students who would pursue research in the manner their teachers proposed on the excited and ground states of atoms. In 1952, Brossel, Kastler, and J. M. Winter produced the first successful optical pumping experiment. This new approach to the investigation of the excited and ground states of atoms was the primary occupation of Brossel and Kastler and their team of young researchers from 1952 well into the 1960's. They went on simplifying and refining their experimental technique, especially by working with vapors in a sealed container. Other fruitful results followed: a wealth of data on relaxation processes; precise measurements of Landé splitting factors and of intervals of fine and hyperfine structure, from which nuclear magnetic moments could be deduced; and the discovery of numerous phenomena related to high-order perturbations of atomic particles. Furthermore, foreign experimenters, by adopting the Brossel-Kastler technique, made numerous contributions to knowledge of the behavior and structure of atoms, eventually producing the maser and the laser. Kastler continued to participate in experimental research until 1966, the year he was awarded the Nobel Prize.

The third stage of Kastler's career extended from 1967 to the year of his retirement in 1972. During this period, he appears to have devoted his time almost exclusively to administrative duties, especially after retiring from the École Normale faculty in 1968.

Bibliography

Primary

PHYSICS: Kastler's published works amount to more than thirty notes and articles in various reports, journals, and conference proceedings. Those in French appeared mostly in *Comptes rendus hebdomadaires des séances de l'Académie des sciences* and in the *Journal de physique et de radium*. Those in English appeared usually in the *Journal of the Optical Society of America*. A few of his works are in German. The following selections typify his publications: "Sur la polarisation de la lumière de fluorescence de la vapeur de mercure pure," *Comptes rendus*, vol. 197, 1933; "Le Taux de polarisation de la fluorescence de la vapeur pure," *Comptes rendus*, vol. 198, 1934; "Le Taux de polarisation de la fluorescence de la vapeur de mercure en présence d'azote," *Comptes rendus*, vol. 198, 1934; "Recherches sur la fluorescence visible de la vapeur de mercure," *Annales de physique*, vol. 6, 1936 (with Jean Brossel); "La Détection de la résonance magnétique des niveaux excités: L'Effet de polarisation des radiations de résonance optique," *Comptes rendus*, vol. 229, 1949; "Quelques suggestions concernant la production optique et la détection optique d'une inégalité de population des niveaux de quantification spatiale des atomes: Application à l'expérience de Stern et Gerlach et à la résonance magnétique," *Journal de physique*, vol. 11, 1950 (with Brossel and J. M. Winter); "Création optique d'une inégalité de population entre les sous-niveaux Zeeman de l'état fondamental des atomes," *Journal de physique*, vol. 13, 1952 (with Jean-Pierre Barrat and Brossel); *La Diffusion de la lumière par les milieux troubles*, 1952; "Production optique d'une orientation atomique dans la vapeur saturante de sodium," *Comptes rendus*, vol. 239, 1954; "Optical Methods of Atomic Orientation and Their Applications," *Proceedings of the Physical Society of London A*, vol. 67, 1954 (with N. Rollet and Brossel); "Polarisation de la résonance optique de l'isotope 198 de mercure," *Comptes rendus*, vol. 242, 1956; "Optical Methods of Atomic Orientation and of Magnetic Resonance," *Journal of the Optical Society of America*, vol. 47, 1957 (with C. Cohen-Tannoudji and Brossel); "La Conservation de la phase lors de la collision d'un atome sodium orienté et d'un atome d'hélium," *Comtes rendus*, vol. 245, 1957 (with J. C. Pebay-Peyroula and Brossel); "Sur la résonance magnétique des niveaux atomiques du mercure excités par bombardement électronique," *Comptes rendus*, vol. 244, 1957 (with Pebay-Peyroula and Brossel); "Résonance magnétique nucléaire du mercure ^{201}Hg, aligné par pompage optique," *Comptes rendus*, vol. 246, 1958; *Cette Étrange Matière*, 1976.

Secondary

Bernheim, Robert. *Optical Pumping: An Introduction*. New York: Benjamin, 1965. A general survey organized into two parts: a description of optical pumping, the phenomena involved in an experiment, and pumping as it applies to the investigation of the energy levels of atoms and molecules and of the intermolecular interactions that take place. Includes reprints of an article by Brossel and Kastler (in French) and of two articles by Kastler (one in French and the other in English). Also provides a useful bibliography, with the foreign-language titles translated into English.

Hagelberg, M. Paul. *Physics: An Introduction for Students of Science and Engineering*. Englewood Cliffs, N.J.: Prentice-Hall, 1973. An excellent, clear introduction to physics which includes an introduction to quantum physics and relativity. A special feature of the text is that electromagnetism is not discussed until after quantum physics and relativity have been treated. Assumes a basic knowledge of differential and integral calculus.

Kittel, Charles. *Introduction to Solid State Physics*. 3d ed. New York: John Wiley & Sons, 1966. On the whole, this book is an elementary account of the physics of solids—that is, of the properties displayed by atoms and molecules in arrangements of crystals. Chapter 16 is a discussion of magnetic resonance, or the dynamics of the magnetic effects associated with the angular momentum of electrons and the nuclei of atoms.

Mitchell, Allan Charles Gray, and Mark W. Zemansky. *Resonance Radiation and Excited Atoms*. New York: Macmillan, 1934. This book presents an analysis of the polarization of resonance radiation of atoms and was often cited by Kastler in his publications. It is a scientific classic of historical interest that has been reprinted twice since its original appearance in 1934.

Oldenberg, Otto, and Wendell G. Holladay. *Introduction to Atomic and Nuclear Physics*. 4th ed. New York: McGraw-Hill, 1967. This book is intended for the student who has had an introductory course in physics and has an elementary knowledge of chemistry, but it requires no understanding of calculus. It deals with the atomic structure of matter, first from the standpoint of chemistry and then from the standpoint of physics, and with the discrete structure of electricity and light.

Sears, G. W. "Thirty Years of Optical Pumping." *Contemporary Physics* 22 (1981): 487-509. A retrospective view of the work of Kastler and of Brossel and Bitter. The author describes double resonance and optical pumping. He also treats such topics as the magnetization of gases and vapors, the angular momentum of particles, metastability exchange, orientation by collision, and laser spectroscopy.

Richard P. Benton

1967

Physics
Hans Albrecht Bethe, United States

Chemistry
Manfred Eigen, West Germany
Ronald G. W. Norrish, Great Britain
George Porter, Great Britain

Physiology or Medicine
Halden Keffer Hartline, United States
George Wald, United States
Ragnar A. Granit, Sweden

Literature
Miguel Ángel Asturias, Guatemala

Peace
no award

HANS ALBRECHT BETHE
1967

Born: Strassburg, Germany; July 2, 1906

Nationality: American
Areas of concentration: Nuclear physics and astrophysics

Bethe's extensive investigation of nuclear reactions included his discovery of the carbon cycle, a repetitive series of reactions in which carbon acts as a catalyst for the production of helium from hydrogen. He also discovered how temperature determines whether the carbon cycle or the proton-proton cycle is primarily responsible for the production of energy in the Sun and other stars

The Award

Presentation

Professor O. Klein, a member of the Royal Swedish Academy of Sciences, presented the Nobel Prize in Physics to Hans Albrecht Bethe on December 10, 1967. Klein began his presentation by describing the context in which Bethe had carried out his prizewinning research in the 1930's. Speculation about the Sun's source of energy had taken a new and fruitful direction following the discovery of radioactivity at the end of the nineteenth century. Three subsequent decades of research resulted in a model of the atom composed of negatively charged electrons orbiting a nucleus made up of much more massive positively charged protons and electrically neutral neutrons. Indeed, the discovery of the neutron in 1932 marked the true beginning of the new field of nuclear physics. Bethe quickly moved to the forefront. In 1936 and 1937, he published three long articles in which he so thoroughly and brilliantly presented the current state of nuclear physics that they soon became known as "Bethe's bible." In 1938 he applied this knowledge to the problem of energy production in stars.

As early as 1926, Arthur Eddington had convinced astrophysicists that hydrogen and helium are the primary elements in the interior of the Sun; Bethe set out to determine how nuclear reactions might transform hydrogen into helium and release enormous amounts of energy in the process. In spite of the limited experimental data available, Bethe showed that two series of reactions are particularly important. The first of these, discovered and discussed in a preliminary fashion by Carl von Weizsäcker and R. Atkinson, involves the capture of protons by hydrogen nuclei. The second process is a more complicated set of reactions in which carbon acts as a catalyst. The significance of Bethe's accomplishment is evident from the fact that his research not only broke new ground in the 1930's but also became the basis for all subsequent understanding of stellar energy production and the evolution of stars.

Nobel lecture

Bethe's prizewinning research originally was published in a 1939 article titled "Energy Production in Stars"; he appropriately commemorated this work by using the same title for his Nobel lecture. He began by quickly summarizing the historical context for his work. By 1933, the new particle accelerators had begun generating valuable data on nuclear reactions. In 1938, George Gamow and Edward Teller made important improvements in the equations describing the rate of the "thermonuclear" reactions that take place at the high temperatures inside stars. Bethe recalled that he had begun seriously studying stellar energy in April, 1938, when Gamow had helped to organize a cross-disciplinary conference for astrophysicists and physicists. In the first substantive section of his lecture, Bethe reviewed the calculations required to estimate the central temperature of the Sun and the implications the temperature has for the nuclear reactions that take place there. He pointed out that when the equations for gravitational stability and energy flow were solved using computers in 1964, the temperature of the center of the Sun was calculated to be slightly less than 16 million degrees Celsius. In 1938, Bethe had relied on the prevailing estimate of about 19 million degrees. Since the probability of various nuclear reactions varies with temperature, the inaccurate 1938 estimate influenced Bethe's original conclusions about the relevant reactions for the Sun. Nevertheless, he was the first to identify the reactions concerned and determine how their probabilities and energy outputs depend on temperature. Some of the most important of these reactions involve the temporary production of isotopes, nuclei which do not contain the usual number of neutrons for a particular element.

The first important series of reactions starts with a proton which is transformed into an isotope of helium after capturing two other protons; two isotopic helium nuclei then fuse to produce ordinary helium nuclei accompanied by a large release of energy and protons which become available to continue the cycle. In 1938, Bethe laboriously studied the possibility of similar cycles involving other elements. He concluded that only a cycle involving carbon, nitrogen, and oxygen was possible at the approximate temperature of the Sun. In this cycle, a carbon nucleus captures a proton, producing an unstable nitrogen isotope. This nucleus spontaneously decays into a carbon isotope, which is transformed successively into nitrogen and then oxygen through two more proton captures. The unstable oxygen nucleus then decays into another nitrogen isotope, which captures a final proton to produce helium and carbon and allow the cycle to repeat. Carbon, therefore, is not consumed and acts as a catalyst for the vast production of energy during three of the reactions in the cycle. It later was shown that the carbon cycle requires higher temperatures than the temperature of the Sun and thus contributes primarily to stellar energy production by hotter, more massive stars.

Bethe concluded his lecture with a lengthy description of how his analysis had been experimentally confirmed and how it had become the basis for an understanding of how stars evolve through different stages of energy production as their temperatures change.

Critical reception

The choice of Hans Bethe as the 1967 recipient of the Nobel Prize in Physics did not receive extensive fanfare in either the scientific or the popular press. Indeed, the physics community's only reaction was surprise that the award had come so late to a man of such long-standing merit. Bethe's original research on stellar energy production had been carried out thirty years earlier; the majority of his results had stood the test of time and were too familiar to generate controversy or extensive publicity at this stage of his career.

Scientific publications such as *Physics Today* and *Science News* quoted the Swedish Academy of Sciences' citation honoring Bethe for his "contributions to the theory of nuclear reactions, especially his discoveries concerning the energy production of stars." Both journals summarized Bethe's analysis of the hydrogen and carbon cycles he had identified as the primary source of energy in main sequence stars. Other highlights of Bethe's career were mentioned briefly: the initial theory of electron-positron pair production and developments in the theory of light nuclei such as the deuteron. His research on the interaction of fast, charged particles with materials was cited as being of major importance for the design of shielding for nuclear reactors and space vehicles, the study of cosmic rays, and the design of experiments in high-energy physics.

In addition to listing Bethe's scientific accomplishments, *Science News* also summarized his efforts to influence the military and industrial applications of physics. During World War II, Bethe headed the Theoretical Physics Division while the first atom bombs were being produced at Los Alamos, New Mexico. It was there that he began a long career as an advocate for the civilian control and development of atomic energy. After the war, he became an important spokesman for the negotiated banning of nuclear weapons testing and the limited test-ban treaty of 1963.

In a short article on Bethe and the 1967 Nobel Prize winners in chemistry, *Newsweek* gave approximately equal attention to Bethe's scientific and political efforts. His well-informed status as a consultant for Avco Corporation was cited as the basis for his consistent opposition to the development of an antiballistic missile system; he was quoted as stating, "We can conclude that any system we build will be obsolete in a very few years, even as a defense against Chinese missiles." For Bethe, the importance of this issue demanded that he address it immediately on his return from the Nobel ceremonies in Sweden. He presented his argument against deployment at the December, 1967, meeting of the American Association for the Advancement of Science in New York. Writing in *The New York Times Magazine* in March, 1968, Lee Edson used this event as the focus for his characterization of Bethe as a "scientific man for all seasons." Although he provided a brief description of Bethe's Nobel Prize-winning research, Edson concentrated on Bethe's role as "American's most outstanding and influential advocate of nuclear disarmament."

Aside from a few biographical details, *Physics Today* strictly confined itself to Bethe's scientific achievements. In the same issue in which Bethe's prize was announced, the editors responded to recent correspondence from their readers by arguing that *Physics Today*, as the official publication of the American Institute of

Physics, was not the appropriate medium for scientists to express their views about political issues.

Biography

Hans Albrecht Bethe was born on July 2, 1906, in Strassburg, Alsace-Lorraine, which was then part of Germany. His father, Albrecht Theodore Julius Bethe, was a physiologist; his mother was Anna Kuhn, the daughter of a professor of medicine at the University of Strassburg. Bethe attended the Goethe Gymnasium in Frankfurt am Main between 1915 and 1924 and developed an interest in mathematics and physics. He studied at the University of Frankfurt for two years, and in 1928 he completed his doctorate in theoretical physics under the guidance of Arnold Sommerfeld at the University of Munich. After brief periods of teaching physics at the Universities of Frankfurt and Stuttgart, Bethe became a *Privatdozent* in physics at the University of Munich in May, 1930. Although he held this position until 1933, an International Education Board travel fellowship allowed him to study with Ernest Rutherford at Cambridge, England, in the fall of 1930 and with Enrico Fermi in Rome during the spring semesters of 1931 and 1932. He became an assistant professor at the University of Tübingen during the winter semester of 1932-1933. Bethe's mother was Jewish, and his position was taken from him as the Nazi Party came to power in 1933. He emigrated to England and held a temporary position as a lecturer at the University of Manchester, which was followed by a one-year fellowship at the University of Bristol beginning in the fall of 1934. He went to the United States to become an assistant professor of physics at Cornell University in February, 1935, and he became a full professor in the summer of 1937.

In 1939, Bethe wed Rose Ewald, the daughter of Paul Ewald, under whom he had studied X-ray scattering at Stuttgart. He became a United States citizen in March, 1941. During World War II, he worked for the Radiation Laboratory at the Massachusetts Institute of Technology and then became head of the Theoretical Physics Division at Los Alamos Scientific Laboratory, where the first atom bombs were produced. After the war he returned to Cornell, where he took up permanent residence except for sabbaticals and a brief return to Los Alamos in 1952. Bethe served on President Dwight D. Eisenhower's Science Advisory Committee from 1956 to 1959.

Scientific Career

Two general characteristics consistently set the tone for Bethe's scientific career. Stemming from his early interests in mathematics, Bethe delighted in the mathematical representation of complex phenomena and the invention of new mathematical techniques to demonstrate linkages between theory and experiment. He thus falls under the general category of "theoretical" rather than "experimental" physicist. Second, Bethe was unusual in the breadth of knowledge he managed to maintain during a period of increasing specialization in physics. His Nobel Prize-winning research is only one of many cases in which his knowledge of more than one field resulted in important innovations.

Bethe was fortunate in that the decade following the completion of his doctorate was one of extraordinary excitement and creativity in physics. During the preceding two decades, the revolutionary development of quantum mechanics had been the center of attention. The earlier classical electrodynamics, with its emphasis on the continuous propagation of electromagnetic radiation, was confronted by a multitude of new phenomena in which the energy emitted by atoms and the interaction of radiation with matter took place discontinuously, at a limited set of "quantized" magnitudes. The creation of a new quantum electrodynamics thus was intimately tied to the exploration of the internal structure of the atom and particularly its nucleus. Sir James Chadwick's discovery of the neutron in 1932 gave this research such a new orientation that it is justifiably taken to mark the beginning of nuclear physics. Throughout the 1930's, Bethe was one of a select few in the vanguard of the new field.

During the first half of the decade, Bethe's extension of his doctoral research placed him in a pivotal position. Under the direction of Arnold Sommerfeld, Bethe had explored the diffraction of electrons by crystals. In particular, he studied how the interaction of electrons with matter resembles the interaction of electromagnetic radiation, such as X rays. In 1930 he published one of his most influential papers on the energy radiated when charged particles pass near the electrons and nuclei of atoms, a subject relevant to what was becoming an increasingly recalcitrant problem: the identification and analysis of the atmospheric radiation that Robert Millikan had christened "cosmic rays." Assuming that either electrons or protons were responsible, physicists tried to determine whether experimental data could be reconciled with calculations based on quantum electrodynamics. Bethe was brought up to date on the experimental data during a visit to Cambridge in the fall of 1930; in 1931, while studying with Enrico Fermi in Rome, he extended the radiation theory by including the results of the special theory of relativity. Then, in 1933, he began a fruitful collaboration with Walter Heitler at Manchester; the result was their 1934 publication of what quickly became the famous Bethe-Heitler radiation formula. At an important cosmic-ray conference in London in October, 1934, Bethe concluded that for high energies it was impossible to reconcile the experimental evidence with the theoretical predictions of quantum electrodynamics.

This state of crisis continued until 1938, when the impressive cloud chamber photographs taken by Jabez Street and Edward Stevenson convinced Bethe that a new particle other than the electron or proton was responsible. The exact mass of this negatively charged "muon" (from "mu-meson") was not determined until after World War II, and Bethe again would play a crucial role. He thus became a central figure in the origins of the new field of high-energy particle physics. Acute interest in the new particle was a result of hopes that it might be the particle postulated by Hideki Yukawa, the 1949 Nobel laureate, in his 1935 theory of nuclear forces. Yukawa had argued that the force that holds neutrons and protons together inside the nucleus might be caused by these particles "exchanging" another particle, a "meson" with about two hundred times the mass of an electron. Bethe's early contributions to the discovery of how muons are related to Yukawa's meson, the "pion" (from "pi-meson"), initiated a lifelong interest that in 1955 culminated in his impressive two-volume study *Mesons and Fields*, written with the collaboration of Silvan S. Schweber and Frédéric de Hoffmann.

The analysis of cosmic rays, however, was by no means the full extent of Bethe's accomplishments in nuclear physics during the 1930's. At Manchester during 1934 and 1935, he worked with Rudolf Peierls to develop an early model for the structure of the deuteron, the simple nucleus composed of one proton and one neutron. Their study of how protons deflect bombarding neutrons helped to highlight the properties that eventually would have to be incorporated into an accurate representation of nuclear forces. It also became the basis for the "effective range" scattering calculation techniques that Bethe invented in 1949.

Early in 1935, Bethe joined the physics department at Cornell University. This congenial setting would become his permanent base of operations for the remainder of his career. Finding himself repeatedly besieged by questions about nuclear physics, he decided to present the state of the new field in three lengthy articles for *Reviews of Modern Physics*. Two of his new colleagues, Robert F. Bacher and M. S. Livingston, collaborated on the first and third of these articles respectively. They were part of a department that quickly made Bethe feel at home. His three articles immediately became known as "Bethe's bible" and were the primary source for the education of a generation of nuclear physicists. Because of the worn condition of most of the original copies, it is appropriate that in 1986 they were republished in a single volume.

The completion of these review articles was an ideal preparation for the problem of stellar energy production, which Bethe tackled in 1938. In April of that year, George Gamow and Edward Teller organized a conference for physicists and astrophysicists in Washington, D.C. There Bethe learned that an interesting problem was ripe for solution: What nuclear reactions are responsible for the production of the energy radiated by the Sun and other stars? It took Bethe six weeks to eliminate all possibilities except the proton cycle that von Weizsäcker already had investigated and the carbon cycle that Bethe had discovered. Although the 1938 estimate for the central temperature of the Sun was too high and thus led Bethe to an incorrect expectation that the carbon cycle was the primary process responsible for the Sun's energy production, his calculations of the temperature dependence of nuclear reactions were of lasting importance. These calculations became the basis for all future understanding of the transformation of hydrogen into helium within the Sun and of the evolution of stars as their temperature varies.

World War II was a turning point in Bethe's career. After receiving American citizenship in March, 1941, he received a security clearance and in April, 1943, joined the Manhattan Project as director of the Theoretical Physics Division at Los Alamos Scientific Laboratory. As was the case with many other physicists, the threat posed by the possibility that German scientists might provide Adolf Hitler with nuclear weapons was enough to motivate Bethe to work on the American project. He disagreed with Teller, however, arguing that it was inappropriate to begin work on more destructive weapons, such as Teller's "super," the hydrogen fusion bomb.

Bethe carried out his duties as director of the Theoretical Division with a systematic approach that soon earned for him a nickname, "the Battleship." He was responsible for the solution of innumerable technical problems that arose in the course of the project. In particular, he and Richard Feynman developed the formula for the calculation of the destructive power of a nuclear weapon.

After the war, Bethe returned to Cornell and resumed the research that had been interrupted. Throughout the remainder of his career, however, he would devote a significant proportion of his time to issues related to the social implications of nuclear energy and nuclear weapons. His concern for the civilian control of nuclear energy and the prevention of a nuclear arms race began at organizational meetings at Los Alamos and continued thereafter through his active participation in both the Federation of Atomic Scientists and the Federation of American Scientists. He wrote extensively on these subjects, beginning in 1946 with his contribution to the famous anthology *One World or None*, in which he argued that excessive worry about guarding nuclear "secrets" was misguided, since the development of a nuclear weapon without such information would not take a country such as the Soviet Union more than five years, anyway.

When the first Soviet bomb was exploded in 1949, Bethe refused to join Teller's crash program to produce H bombs. Escalation into a new dimension of nuclear destruction struck Bethe as madness. Nevertheless, in 1951, after the outbreak of the Korean war, Bethe did decide to contribute to the project for several months, a decision he later regretted. His reason for joining Teller's team was that since the work would get done in any case, it was important for him to be close to the project in order to have firsthand information when disarmament or arms limitation negotiations called for expert testimony.

This emphasis on well-researched technical information as a basis for decisions became a trademark of Bethe's contributions to public policy. During his service on President Eisenhower's Science Advisory Committee between 1956 and 1959, Bethe developed a seismic method for the detection of nuclear tests and used it as part of his arguments in favor of a nuclear test-ban treaty. Although in 1961, Bethe failed to convince President John F. Kennedy to refrain from atmospheric testing, he was instrumental in the acceptance of a limited test-ban treaty in 1963.

Later in the 1960's, Bethe became a chief spokesman against the deployment of an antiballistic missile (ABM) system. Indeed, immediately on his return from the Nobel ceremonies in 1967, he appeared before the American Association for the Advancement of Science to argue that the deployment of an ABM system would be technically ineffective, unnecessarily expensive, and seriously destabilizing because of its contribution to a false sense of superiority. On March 4, 1969, during the height of the Vietnam War, the Union of Concerned Scientists sponsored a series of speeches and panel discussions at the Massachusetts Institute of Technology on the relation of science to government and society. Bethe delivered a stirring technical argument against deployment of the ABM system and concluded by emphasizing that "it is the responsibility of a scientist and an engineer not to be satisfied by something that appears on the surface as saving lives."

During the 1980's, Bethe took a similar stand against President Ronald Reagan's Strategic Defense Initiative, commonly known as "Star Wars." His argument was based on the same types of technical analysis he had used against deployment of an ABM system, and he cogently presented it in a short pamphlet, *Reducing the Risk of Nuclear War*. Ironically, Bethe's coauthor was Robert S. McNamara, the same man who, as Secretary of Defense under President Lyndon B. Johnson, had failed to consult Bethe before announcing the decision to deploy the ABM system in 1967.

Besides making efforts to reduce the risk of nuclear war, Bethe became an outspoken advocate for the peaceful use of nuclear power. While acknowledging the risks of accidents such as the one that took place at the Three Mile Island nuclear power station in March, 1979, Bethe concentrated on eliminating unnecessary hysteria and highlighting the safety lessons that could be drawn from an accurate analysis of such accidents. During the 1970's, Bethe was particularly optimistic about the energy capacity of the Canadian deuterium uranium reactors.

Throughout all these important postwar activities, Bethe continued to play a prominent role in theoretical physics. In June, 1947, he was a valuable participant in an important conference held at Shelter Island, New York. Two results of the conference depended particularly on Bethe's insights. He performed the calculations required for a quantum electrodynamic explanation for slight shifts in the energy states of electrons of hydrogen atoms observed by Willis Lamb. Second, he coauthored a paper with Robert Marshak to support the "two meson" hypothesis Marshak had presented to the conference. Bethe and Marshak argued that the muon was a decay product of another meson, the meson required by Yukawa's 1935 theory of nuclear forces and subsequently called the "pion."

Among the many other topics in which Bethe made major contributions to nuclear physics, his work on nuclear models was particularly influential; he was a central figure in the application of the "shell model" of the nucleus and the "compound nucleus" that temporarily forms during some nuclear reactions. His textbooks provide a lasting testimonial to his influence on his discipline.

Bibliography

Primary

PHYSICS: *Elementary Nuclear Theory*, 1947; *Mesons and Fields*, 1955 (with Silvan S. Schweber and Frédéric de Hoffmann); *Quantum Mechanics of One- and Two-Electron Atoms*, 1957 (with Edward E. Salpeter); *Intermediate Quantum Mechanics*, 1964 (with Roman W. Jackiw); *Basic Bethe: Seminal Articles on Nuclear Physics, 1936-1937*, 1986.

OTHER NONFICTION: *The H-Bomb and World Order*, 1950 (with Peter Kihss and William W. Kaufmann); *The Future of Nuclear Tests*, 1961 (with Edward Teller); *Reducing the Risk of Nuclear War*, 1985 (with Robert McNamara).

Secondary

Bernstein, Jeremy. *Hans Bethe: Prophet of Energy*. New York: Basic Books, 1980. This biographical sketch is drawn from articles Bernstein wrote for *The New Yorker*; it relies heavily on long excerpts from a series of interviews with Bethe between 1977 and 1979. Although this is the best existing single source of biographical material on Bethe, it by no means provides a complete picture of either his scientific accomplishments or his political and personal life. Bernstein concentrates on Bethe's prizewinning research on stellar energy, his work at Los Alamos, and his advocacy of nuclear power.

Brown, Laurie M., and Lillian Hoddeson, eds. *The Birth of Particle Physics*. Cambridge, England: Cambridge University Press, 1983. Supplemented by a valuable introduction by the editors, this collection is based on lectures and panel discussions that took place at the International Symposium on the History of Particle Physics held at Fermilab in May, 1980. It is primarily concerned with the emergence of particle physics, a result of issues raised by cosmic-ray physics and nuclear physics between 1930 and 1950, the most exciting period in Bethe's career. Bethe did not participate, but many of his colleagues did. Of particular interest are essays by Willis Lamb on the fine structure of hydrogen and Robert Marshak on the period 1947-1952.

Galison, Peter. *How Experiments End*. Chicago: University of Chicago Press, 1987. In chapter 3 of this collection of interesting case studies, Galison provides a valuable analysis of the cosmic-ray studies that culminated in the identification of a new particle, the muon. He gives considerable attention to Bethe's participation in the 1930's crisis in quantum electrodynamics when the Bethe-Heitler radiation formula was unsuccessfully compared with the cosmic-ray data.

Marshak, Robert E., ed. *Perspectives in Modern Physics: Essays in Honor of Hans Bethe on the Occasion of His 60th Birthday, July 1966*. New York: Interscience, 1966. Published just prior to Bethe's Nobel Prize, this collection consists primarily of original research papers. It also includes a sketch of Bethe's career by Robert Bacher and Victor Weisskopf and a bibliograpy of Bethe's publications through 1964.

Schweber, Silvan S. "Shelter Island, Pocono, and Oldstone: The Emergence of American Quantum Electrodynamics after World War II." *OSIRIS* 2 (1986): 265-302. Schweber provides a valuable discussion of the context in which Bethe made his important contributions to the 1947 Shelter Island Conference.

Stuewer, Roger H., ed. *Nuclear Physics in Retrospect: Proceedings of a Symposium on the 1930's*. Minneapolis: University of Minnesota Press, 1979. Bethe was one of eight distinguished nuclear physicists who gave the retrospective lectures recorded in this volume. Bethe commented in detail about his memories of the

reception of Werner Heisenberg's first use of neutrons and about the early developments of the shell model and the compound nucleus.

James R. Hofmann